Mrs. W. H. Wait.

A present from
her husband

Oct. 4," '89

A General View of the Fine Arts.

MANUAL

OF

THE FINE ARTS

CRITICAL AND HISTORICAL.

WITH AN INTRODUCTION

BY

D. HUNTINGTON, M. A.

A. S. BARNES & COMPANY,
NEW YORK AND CHICAGO.

1875.

PREFACE TO SECOND EDITION.

THE preparation of the following work was suggested by the interested inquiries of a group of young people, concerning the productions and styles of the great masters of art, whose names only were familiar to them. The aim has been, to avoid on the one hand the dryness of the mere dictionary, and on the other, the anecdote and detail of biography; in a word, to present a brief account of the most eminent artists merely as artists, giving, at the same time, a view of the rise and progress of art in different countries. The principle of selection from the desultory fields of art literature, kept constantly in view, has been to admit little that has not a critical bearing, and thus a tendency to develope the taste. Many a volume has been rifled of every tangible and informing idea, while its details of mere narrative have necessarily, from the limits of the work designed, been almost wholly rejected. This element of the volume fits it especially for a text-book in schools, where it might advantageously precede the critical works of Kaimes, Alison and Burke, now in vogue; here theory is superseded by the analysis of artistic principles actually developed. The study of the book has been found to produce a decided improvement in the written compositions of the classes that have used it. Without cramping the mind with specific rules, it has served to awaken an insight into the primary laws of construction, which are the same in literature and art.

Contents.

PAINTING.

PAGE

SCULPTURE.

ARCHITECTURE.

MUSIC.

Introduction.

THE man who is a true lover of the fine arts, is generally benevolent and cheerful, not seldom also is he a passionate admirer of nature, and often a devout worshipper of the great Author of all that is beautiful and good. The man who is a sensualist, who chooses his companions among dissolute and profligate men, whose chief care is that his table should be well furnished with delicious viands, whose eye lights up only when bottles and glasses begin to rattle, whose cheeks are streaked with the unnatural redness of high living, is rarely a lover of art—unless it be the art of cooking, or making punch. Neither does the miser care for sculpture or for painting. Your true money-lover despises the fine arts; he likes well enough to pass his grasping and shrivelled fingers over the stamped guinea, but the clearness of its relief, and the music of its ring, charm him only because they speak of full weight in the gold. And so it is with the treacherous, the cruel, the sly, and the crafty; their selfish and corrupt passions unfit them for the tranquil enjoyment of the arts, which are in their nature social, kindly, and purifying, inclining those who are much engaged in them to refined studies, to a generous frankness, a free imparting to others of the pleasures enjoyed.

The study of the fine arts having then an elevating and softening influence, a tendency to render man less sensual, more benevolent, more alive to the beauties of nature and truth, should be as generally cultivated as possible.

The following work is intended to diffuse a taste for such studies, by gathering into a small compass, and making accessible to all, that information which before was scattered through many voluminous and expensive publications. It is a comprehensive glance at the whole history of art, especially as exhibited in the lives of its most eminent professors, in all ages, and in every department. While it embraces so wide a field, it is at the same time clear, concise, and richly attractive in its details. By its simple and natural arrangement, its completeness in all its parts, and by the ease with which any class of art, era, or individual artist, may be referred to, the work is rendered admirable for popular use. For the same reason it might be introduced, with great advantage, as a text-book, into the higher schools and academies.

At the present time, and in our own country, almost every one has some acquaintance with art; and numbers will be glad to possess a book which presents such an amount of information on the subject which interests them; so well arranged, so varied, lively, and picturesque, in the matter, and couched in a style which evinces an earnest enthusiasm for the arts, and an extended knowledge of their masterpieces. It is the fruit of the leisure hours of a lady, who, while employed upon it, was practically engaged with the palette and colours. It needs no argument to persuade us, that one who is actually conversant with the progress of an artist's studies, should be the best able to describe them; that one who has passed through the lessons of the studio, traced the careful outline, touched in the first faint shades, and then the deep and powerful relief, and brought out the living character and expression, by colours vivid and truthful—who is, in a word, an artist, should be able to spread before us with the greatest charm and force, the incidents of artistic life, and the varied effects their works have produced on the mind.

The work makes no pretension to entire originality; much of the labour has been that of careful compilation, and the patient investigation, and delicate, discriminating taste, by means of which so great an amount of confused material has been adapted and arranged into one complete whole, without marring its interest, but rather heightening it, is worthy of all praise.

D. H.

A General View of the Fine Arts.

ORIGIN OF THE FINE ARTS.

THE word art, derived from the Latin *artes*, skill with the hand, used in its higher acceptation, is applied to the creations of the imagination, by which nature is reproduced in new forms and combinations, and refers rather to the emanations of the mind and heart, than to the mechanical dexterity of the hand.

Ornamental Architecture, Sculpture, Painting, Poetry, and Music, in distinction from the merely useful arts, are called fine, or beautiful arts. Their prime object is the creation and development of beauty in all its subtle forms and evanescent hues. The vast cathedral, the pencilling of a rose-leaf, the peal of the organ, and the spirit harmonies of verse, alike come within their scope. They are addressed through the eye and the ear to that fine inner sense, which can seize the meaning of the artist from his inanimate handiwork, and sympathize with the offspring of his imagination as if they were living realities,

> "Giving Virtue a new birth,
> And a life that ne'er grows old."

The idea of their enduringness, also binds us by an indefinite sympathy with all who ever have, or who ever will, ponder with delight the same visions of beauty, and gratifies

"That instinct of our kind,
To link in common with our own
The universal mind."

Although the sources of the fine arts are to be traced to primal faculties of the mind, as certainly as mathematical and logical sciences, it may not be uninteresting to endeavour to trace their first developments, and to glance at the myths of the ancients, in regard to their origin. "Opinions have differed, as to what people first practised the fine arts; but it is an unnecessary inquiry, as the love of the beautiful is innate with all. Love, celebrated by the mythologists as the governor of nature, was the parent of the arts; and music after their system was his first-born. According to a Grecian apologue, a young girl was the first artist, who, perceiving the profile of her lover cast on the wall by the strong light of a lamp, drew the first recorded outline from this cherished object of her affections. From such a slight beginning, according to the fable, arose those arts whose softening and humanizing qualities have moderated the barbarism of man, and alleviated the disastrous effects of vice; those arts by which an inspired musician appeased, with the tones of his harp, the ragings of a barbarous prince; by which a poet, by an ingenious apologue, recalled a mob to truth and reason; by which the sculptor and the painter, under the veil of pathetic allegory, presented to the depraved the forgotten traits of virtue."

There is a simple story which ascribes the origin of the Corinthian capital to Callimachus. A votive basket of flowers was left on the grave of a young Corinthian girl, around which the graceful leaves of the acanthus grew, and suggested to her lover the idea of the capital of the most superb of the Grecian orders.

In the Grecian mythology, the sacred Nine of Pieria, who presided over the liberal arts, were the offspring of Heaven and Earth, and infused into the productions of mortals, who drank from their consecrated fountains, the influence of their celestial origin, until their works often partook more of heaven than earth. And the Promethean fire that aroused the souls of men in the infancy of time, failed not to awaken the jealousy of Olympus

Hermes, or Mercury, may be regarded as, in some degree, a personification of the Egyptian priesthood. He was designated by the name Thot, which signifies in the Egyptian language, an assembly; and more particularly one composed of sages and educated persons, the sacerdotal college of city or temple. Thus the collective priesthood of Egypt, personified and considered as unity, was represented by an imaginary being, to whom was ascribed the invention of language and writing, which he had brought from the skies and imparted to man, as well as the origin of geometry, arithmetic, astronomy, medicine, music, rhythm, the institution of religion, sacred processions, the introduction of gymnastic exercises, and, finally, the less indispensable, though not less valuable, arts of architecture, sculpture, and painting. So many volumes were attributed to him, that no human being could possibly have composed them. All the successive improvements in astronomy, and, generally speaking, the labours of every age, became his peculiar property, and added to his glory. In this way, the names of individuals were lost in the numerous order of priests, and the merit which each one had acquired by his observations and labours turned to the advantage of the whole sacerdotal association, in being ascribed to its tutelary genius. Mercury was the inventor of the lyre. "The Nile," says Apollodorus, "after its overflow, left on the shore a tortoise, the flesh of which being dried and wasted by the sun, nothing was left within the shell but nerves and cartilages, and these being contracted, were rendered sonorous. Mercury, happening to strike his foot against the shell, was so pleased with the sound it produced, that it suggested to him the idea of a lyre, which he afterwards constructed in the form of a tortoise."

As soon as the physical necessities of man were supplied, the no less importunate cravings of his intellectual nature called for gratification. However long, Adam and Eve may have dwelt in the garden of delights, before the fall, we can hardly suppose that they turned their attention in any way to art. Their souls in perfect harmony with the faultless nature around them, they could have no further wants to be supplied by human invention. And art, in its highest exercise, seems to be an effort to realize and develop a vision of beauty, that haunts the soul as some relic of a pristine state of greater glory and perfection. The struggle is indeed often a fruitless one, the paradisiacal memories, if I may be allowed the expression, float in mystic grace through the brain of the artist, but the material vehicle stubbornly refuses to embody them in all their ideal loveliness.

Soon after man had fallen from a state of innocence, we read of his practising the arts. Cain, we are told, built a city; and Jubal, in the seventh generation from Adam, was the father of all such as handle the harp and organ; his brother, Tubal Cain, was an instructor of every artificer in brass and iron. The vast fabric which Noah framed, with first, second, and third stories, proves that the mechanical arts, at least, had in his day reached a high degree of perfection. Immediately after the deluge, the bold and stupendous attempt to rear the tower on the plains of

Shinar, which was in its failure called the Tower of Babel, shows that the vigorous mind of the youthful world could grasp great ideas, and feared no difficulties. And among their cunning workmen, there is, from the experience of all ages, every reason to suppose that there were some in whom the creative energies of the imagination stirred, until they were prompted to use the skill acquired with tools and instruments, in the production of mere ornament and objects which could minister only to the gratification of the fancy.

It was, doubtless, the effort to erect a fit dwelling-place for Deity, or for gods many, that first called forth the ingenuity of man to any extraordinary display of architectural skill. This attempt was not only a natural consequence of the desire to pay honour to superior beings, but it had a foundation in the philosophy of our moral nature. For the effect of fine architecture is to give an elevated tone to the feelings, raising them above the ordinary things of life. The exhibition of beautiful proportions, of strength, firmness, durability, and loftiness, calls forth corresponding emotions, and tends to develop the latent powers of the soul by association and sympathy. It makes man forget the presence of his fellow, and prompts him to seek communion with a higher power.

The Egyptian style of architecture seems to have derived its characteristics from the caves and excavations in which their forefathers dwelt; the Grecian, from the wooden cabin, the trunks of trees forming the models for the columns which always adorn their finest edifices; while the Gothic style has for its type the overarching glades of dense forests.

That the distinctive architecture of a nation takes its rise, in a great measure, from the intellectual character of its people may be seen by the various styles that have prevailed in different countries and ages. The ponderous colossal architecture of the Egyptians, excluding the light of day, gloomy and grand, but never soaring from the earth, except in the pyramids, the extent of whose ground-plan takes away the idea of extraordinary height, might almost suggest to us the nature of their government—despotic and iron-handed; and of their religion—grovelling and mysterious.

Indian architecture is slight, tapering, and grotesque; and we find that their government is unstable, and their religion wild and fanciful.

The architecture of the Greeks, chaste and stately, speaks of their intellectual refinement, and the political independence of the people. The architecture of Rome was, like its warlike people, rude and unpolished, until, on the conquest of more refined nations, it adopted their arts. During the reign of luxurious and unmanly indulgence, which preceded the fall of the state, it loaded the borrowed orders of the Greeks with extravagant ornaments,

In the Gothic style, we see typified the lofty aspirations and soaring hopes of Christianity, and still, amid much that is grand, we discover in some of its Protean forms evidences of the wild and romantic superstitions of the middle ages. In the baronial castles of this period, we see exemplified the spirit of feudalism. Modern nations can scarcely claim any distinctive style as their own.

A close observation of children will show the universality of the principle that seeks for gratification in the beautiful. Shakespeare says,

> "The poet, the lunatic, and the lover,
> Are of imagination all compact."

He should have also added, the little child. Children have powers of perception, and a keen sense of delight in whatever is beautiful and true, little dreamed of by the undiscerning observer. With what unwearied ecstasy will they pluck flower after flower, never satiated with sweets; how do they joy in the "fringed margin of the brook," or in the still forest, where the twinkling sunshine spreads a shifting carpet for their feet. No fiats of criticism, no comparisons of merits or demerits, disturb their pure enjoyment; they quench their thirst for beauty as from an inexhaustible well-spring, and only feel that which maturer minds reflect and reason upon.

> "Trailing clouds of beauty do we come
> From God, who is our home:
> Heaven lies about us in our infancy!
> Shades of the prison-house begin to close
> Upon the growing boy,
> But he beholds the light, and whence it flows,
> He sees it in his joy;
> The youth, who daily from the East
> Must travel, still is Nature's priest,
> And by the vision splendid
> Is on his way attended;
> At length the man perceives it die away,
> And fade into the light of common day."

The beneficent Creator has garnished all nature with beauty: the sky with stars and the ever-changing loveliness of clouds; the earth with the agreeable variety of hill and valley, rock and forest, rapid stream and quiet lake—yes, and finished the picture with minute touches, the delicate flower and glowing fruit, the soft-plumed bird and brilliant insect; but how soon is the sense of delight in all these, swallowed up in the pleasures and cares of what is called life. The imaginative faculties, which should be fostered by the study of the higher arts, are suffered too generally to lie uncultivated, or rather, in the words of a brilliant essayist, "Education, as we commonly practise it, amounts simply to the rooting out of God's predilections, and the planting of our own in their stead. Every indigenous germ is carefully weeded away, and the soil exhausted in producing a scanty alien crop. The safe instincts of nature are displaced by conventional sciolisms."

ADVANTAGES OF A CULTIVATION OF THE FINE ARTS.

The fine arts are not mere idle vanities, which may with impunity be cherished or cast aside at the dictation of caprice or convenience, they are intimately connected with the framework of man's nature, and no mind can be completely developed without the power of appreciating their excellence. The propriety of cultivating a taste for these sources of refined pleasure, is founded both in nature and reason. Man is endowed with an imagination, and it cannot be admitted that the All-wise Creator, who formed nothing without a design, could have bestowed the gift that it might lie dormant, or rather, that its continual outgushings should be repressed, or become the means of tormenting apprehensions. This, as well as every other mental faculty, should have its appropriate sphere of action, for, if left untrained, it either pines away and leaves the mind without its fairest ornament, or chokes it with a sickly luxuriance of weeds.

The cultivation of art is a source of innocent pleasure, a recreation from the sterner duties of life. There is an intimate connexion between the physical and mental states, and perhaps half the cases of prolonged ill-health arise from want of proper intellectual stimulus or cheerful recreation, or from slavish devotion to business or labor—often, from the petty vexations and rivalries of society. A cultivation of the taste, by a proper degree of attention to literature and the fine arts, elevates the mind above trivial cares and conventional jealousies, giving it a vigorous independence, and a fund of inexhaustible resources within itself. They present a means of quiet enjoyment, that gently exhilarates the spirits, and produces a cheerful state of mind highly conducive to health. 'Delightful scenes," says Addison, "whether in nature, painting, or poetry, have a kindly influence on the body, as well as the mind; and not only serve to clear and brighten the imagination, but are able to disperse grief and melancholy, and to set the animal spirits in pleasing and agreeable motions. For this reason, Sir Francis Bacon, in his Essay on Health, has not thought it improper to prescribe to his readers a poem or a prospect, where he particularly dissuades him from knotty and subtle disquisitions, and advises him to pursue studies that fill the mind with splendid and illustrious objects, histories, fables, and the contemplation of nature."

The daily realities of earth, the seeking after gain, and often no less toilsome seeking after pleasure, are not sufficient to fill the desires of the human soul. Neither, indeed, can earth, with all its stores of nature and art, give it a safe resting-place; its goal is beyond the confines of mortality, where perfect beauty is the emblem of perfect holiness. By infusing a love of the beautiful, the fine arts have a tendency to disgust the mind with the deformity of vice; and though not always leading to the practice of virtue, they at least tend to the admiration of it. "Perfect virtue," says Madame De Staël, "is the ideal beautiful of the moral world: and there is some similitude and affinity between the impression which virtue makes upon us, and that sentiment which is inspired by whatever is sublime either among the productions of the fine arts, or in the aspect of the physical world. The regular and graceful proportions of antique statues, the calm and pure expression of certain paintings, the harmony of music, the view of a beautiful prospect over a fruitful country, transport us with an enthusiasm by no means uncongenial to that admiration to which we are raised by the contemplation of generous and heroic actions."

"The master-pieces of literature, independent of the fine examples which they furnish, produce a kind of moral and physical emotion, an agitating transport of admiration, which excites us to the performance of generous deeds. The legislators of Greece attached no mean importance to the effect that might be produced by music of a martial or voluptuous character. The sentiment of the intellectual beautiful, while it is employed upon literary objects, must inspire a repugnance for every thing mean or ferocious" Though the cultivation of the taste will not create moral principles in the mind where they do not exist, it is maintained that there is an affinity between the refinements of taste and the virtues of the soul; between the beautiful and the good. Heaven, the peculiar abode of holiness, is represented as a place of transcendant beauty and glory. And granting that the fine arts are utterly powerless to implant pure principles, still, if not abused, they will foster and expand them, and imbue them with a fine sensibility.

Truth and virtue may be inculcated by emblems, or rather embodiments of themselves. The philosophical Wordsworth represents natural objects as training into beauty, not only the mind, but the body. He represents Nature as thus promising to mould her favoured child,

"She shall be sportive as the fawn
That, wild with glee, across the lawn
Or up the mountain springs;
And hers shall be the breathing balm,
And hers the silence and the calm
Of mute insensate things.

"The floating clouds their state shall lend
To her; for her the willow bend.
Nor shall she fail to see,
E'en in the motions of the storm,
Grace that shall mould the maiden's form,
By silent sympathy.

"The stars of midnight shall be dear
To her; and she shall lean her ear,
In many a secret place,
Where rivulets dance their wayward round,
And Beauty, born of murmuring sound,
Shall pass into her face."

And, in the same manner, the statue of a great and good man fills the beholder with aspirations after a like exalted place in the hearts of men, or, at least, inspires him with a higher trust in human nature, and in his own powers. The influence of the painter is still wider, he speaks in parables that are of an easy interpretation; and who can express the fine impulses that have been given to society by the poet and the musician?

The successful artist is always an enthusiast: without an ardent love, a passion for his art, effort will be fruitless. Indeed, a "fine phrensy" is requisite to the production of superior excellence. Southey tells us, that the happiest period of his life was that in which he wrote most poetry. With the artist, labour brings its own recompense, though for a time, his productions, undervalued by the world, may scarcely obtain for him a subsistence; princes might envy him the enjoyment he experiences in embodying the visions of beauty that rise before his spiritual sight, and expand into full-blown beauty as he ponders over them.

The love of fame which the artist feels, is surely different from that of the warrior or the statesman; it is more a desire for sympathy, a desire that that which has delighted himself should delight others. "By a law of our nature," says Coleridge, "he who labours under a strong feeling is impelled to seek for sympathy, and a poet's feelings are all strong." Akenside, therefore, speaks with philosophical accuracy, when he classes love and poetry as having the same effects:

> "Love, and the wish of poets, when their tongues
> Would teach to others' bosoms what so charms
> Their own."

Again, Coleridge writes, "I expect neither profit nor general fame from my writings, and I consider myself as having been amply repaid without either. Poetry has been to me its own exceeding great reward; it has soothed my afflictions, it has multiplied and refined my enjoyments; it has endeared solitude, and it has given me the habit of wishing to discover the good and the beautiful in all that meets and surrounds me."

Nature is replete with lessons of faith, and hope, and love, but the uncultivated mind, unless of rare and peculiar organization, seldom finds

> "Sermons in stones, books in the running brooks,
> And good in every thing."

Office of Artist.

It is the office of the artist to give a moral to nature, to trace the analogies between the spiritual world and the natural. By the rude and ignorant, the loveliest and most magnificent works of nature are disregarded. Though they may produce an unconscious effect, he sees not the soul of things.

> "A primrose by the river's brim,
> A yellow primrose is to him,
> And it is nothing more."

While to him who has wandered the earth in company with the poet, it will bring up sweet thoughts of spring; bright memories of vernal seasons past, and brighter hopes of an eternal awakening from wintry torpor. Hear with what the poet, who is wont

> "To play with similies,
> Loose types of things through all degrees,"

can invest this little flower, giving it a voice which will not be hushed, but shall echo on from year to year, and find a response in many a heart:

> "I sang, let myriads of bright flowers,
> Like thee in field and grove,
> Revive, unenvied—mightier far
> Than tremblings that reprove
> Our vernal tendencies to hope
> In God's redeeming love.
>
> "Sin-blighted though we are, we, too,
> The reasoning sons of men,
> From our oblivious winter called,
> Shall rise and breathe again,
> And in eternal summer lose
> Our threescore years and ten."

Poetry, addressed to both the eye and the ear, has by far the widest range in the dominion of the Muses. Her flights are only limited by the power of the imagination. From its capability of being indefinitely multiplied, it is more universally diffused than any of the other arts. It can be carried into the depths of the forest, and be borne to and fro on the bosom of the deep, while the other fine arts, in any thing like perfection, are confined to populous cities. The creation of the poet, while it adorns the library of the palace, and is enjoyed by the prince, at the same time may enrich the scanty bookshelf of the cottage, and rejoice the hearts of its humble inhabitants. The names of other artists, however celebrated, are known and cherished but by the few, while the names of our eminent poets are watchwords that call up an echo in almost every heart. The highest office of poetry is to delineate the emotions and passions of the human soul; and here she has the advantage of the other arts, for she can trace them from their cause to their effects, while they can only seize and portray some fleeting moment. So, in description, poetry can soar from morn to dewy eve, and from torrid to frigid climes, without a pause in her flight, at the same time giving the storied associations connected with each scene. To the cultivated mind, what subtle beauty, what far-soaring thought, may a single line of the poet convey. Take a line or two of Milton:

> "Listening to what unshorn Apollo sings,
> To the touch of golden wires."

The break of the metre in the first line is half its beauty. It brings the ear attent to hear—what? The touch of golden wires. *Unshorn* Apollo—what an humble epithet! yet, who would attempt to substitute a better? We behold the brightrayed orb of day careering through the skies, rejoicing in his might, and yet this is but the background of the imagery. We see afar off, half veiled in the showery radiance, the human-like god, with floating locks, touching the celestial golden lyre, and hear the united harmony of all that high bards have sung. And all this, too, in a moment of time, even as the eye glances over the lines. Such is the winged power of art, it can transport us to the heavens; such its mysterious potency, it can make ages pass in review before us in a moment.

The contemplation of the works of the painter cultivates a minute observation of natural objects. The lover of the beauties of nature is best prepared to appreciate the excellencies of art, and the devotee of art, traces in nature many beauties which by the uncultivated eye are unnoticed. And, in the delineation of the human face, what sweetness, what nobleness, what gentleness, and what strength of soul may the artist teach! Silently, but surely, will his lessons take effect. "As in water face answereth to face, so the heart of man to man;" and does not genius give a heart and a soul to the painting, the statue, and even to the architectural pile? The cultivation of the fine arts has, then, not only intellectual but moral advantages. And should they not be used in the work of education? The imagination will be active, then surely it is expedient to direct it into proper paths, and to provide it with nutritious food.

Among savage tribes, where even the useful arts are almost unknown, there is still found a rude appreciation of beauty, shown in the ornaments and trinkets with which they seek to adorn themselves and the uncouth objects of their worship. But in proportion as civilization and elegance of manners advance, the fine arts rise in excellence, and in their zenith of splendor mark the highest point of a nation's refinement.

Art is a universal language, limited to no age and no country. It speaks to us from the past in a well-known voice, and binds us to the generations of the departed with feelings of sympathy which it is well to cherish. But for her poets, her painters, her sculptors, her architects, how would Greece,

"Immortal Greece, dear land of glorious lays,"

address us from the olden time? But in the harsh and discordant voice of anarchy and war, and far from being a watchword to call up thoughts of chaste and exalted beauty, and lofty heroic glory, she would scarcely appear elevated above the barbarous tribes of the north.

To Italy, the present sanctuary of the arts, the eye turns with peculiar fondness, as to the trysting-place of the world; a neutral ground, where all become fellow-denizens with the great souls of the past, who still live in their works. Nature, in its sublimest scenes, awes and subdues the soul, while art excites the mind, and challenges it to activity. It is the achievement of man, and conveys the idea of human power and energy; and by that action and reaction that passes from mind to mind, till, like the restless waves of ocean, commingling and separating, each forms a part of each; by that pervading sympathy that forms, and moulds, and develops, as, with increasing power, it passes from age to age, does it call aloud on the soul of man to awake and act.

A FEW GENERAL RULES OF CRITICISM.

The rules of criticism are not arbitrary, they are drawn necessarily from the constitution of our intellectual nature

There is in the mind of man an innate power of appreciating the beautiful. True, the wayward prejudices of fashion may, for a time, esteem deformity an excellence; it may even find delight in distorting that most perfect work of nature, the human form. Still the standard of beauty is unchanged and unchangeable, however custom may sanction that which is ungraceful and inelegant. Both the eye and the ear may become the slave of habit, and receive most pleasure from the peculiarities of manner to which they have been accustomed; hence enlightened criticism will seek for beauty independently of differing styles.

Art is not satisfied with merely copying nature; it seeks to refine it, or rather to seize its hidden soul, and embody it anew. It rejects all that is common-place, and even succeeds in enduing matter with an air expressive of intellect or sentiment, A column of fine proportions seems to tower up in conscious majesty, and the poet may impart a peculiar expression to the delicate flower, or the beetling cliff. Art, then, in its highest development, is not only an imitation of nature, but an ideal, an etherealized representation both of natural objects and of human nature. Who cannot recall some scene, that, without particular interest when beheld in broad sunshine, became invested with exceeding beauty when the sun threw his gorgeous cloudy mantle to the breeze, and suffused earth and air in a flood of soft radiance; when the deepening shadows of twilight brought out more fully each feature of the landscape, and beautified it as much by what it hid as by what it revealed. Thus, exalted art casts an ideal light, a sunset glow over the object imitated. The artist aims not only at copies of nature, but at re-creations of it. In this consists the nature of artistic genius; talent can copy, or cement together scattered fragments, but genius alone can, out of various elements, bring organized life and beauty.

Whatever is lovely or grand in the natural world, the mysterious stars, the gloomy storm, the sunset sky, the frail flower, the soaring mountain, the glittering dew-drop, all serve to open the artist's mind and interest his heart. And in that other world, the world of illimitable spirit, he is continually searching and wondering. The knowledge of mankind, as learned from observation and the developments of art, is enlightened by a self-consciousness which can sympathize with, and understand the workings of the human heart, revealing, in all their depth, the passions and aspirations of man. This gathered fund of natural beauty and knowledge of humanity, forms, so to speak, the chaos of the artist, whence his creations are produced. And not exactly by combining a selection from these objects; for as the forest leaves, and the flowers that grew in their shade, are decomposed, and wither into dust but to spring afresh into organized beauty, so outward things enrich the artist's mind and heart. And while thousands can appreciate the beauties of nature and art, many with as pure a love as that of the artist himself, yet it is but here and there that one is found who can reproduce these materials into order and beauty. The power to do this constitutes genius; a relish for the beautiful is denominated taste.

Art is the natural language of the higher faculties of the mind, and is comprehended by every cultivated intellect. Whatever calls into exercise the powers of the mind, delights us; and whatever is agreeable to all well developed minds must be the standard of the rules of art. What would be agreeable to a perfect mind, if such could exist in our fallen world, might be called the standard of the *laws* of art. Taste is the result of the harmony of many faculties. They need exercise in order to development, but they are inherent in the mind.

Oneness may be called the first requisite in a production

of art. In literary works of genius there is ever a right onwardness, a rushing to the end, which keeps the mind awake and alert. So in all works of art there should be nothing superfluous, nothing to break the unity or confuse the identity; there should be one focus of attraction, or rather one radiating point, whence the interest should flow. Every episode and concomitant circumstance should be subordinate, and should bear a definite and explanatory relation to the whole. A beautiful work of art is often ruined by having some foreign circumstance grafted upon it, while the two subjects, separately executed, would both have been excellent. Again, nothing should be omitted that is necessary to *completeness.* Every production of art should, as it were, live of itself, and be endowed with a voice to speak its own intention. The "Ancient Mariner," is a poem that entirely fails in this respect. It was even expedient to place along the margin an explanation that "telleth what the text meaneth." And yet the wizard genius has touched it with his wand, and it gleams with enchanting beauty. Written probably without design and without aim, its undersong of kindly all-pervading love has, I doubt not, sunk into many an unconscious heart. Rules do not create genius, but genius creates rules, and may also dispense with them.

In the next place, *truthfulness,* or consistency is essential. The mind is disgusted with falsehood in any shape. Though the poet lay his scenes in fairy-land, or the painter place upon his canvass the imaginary beings of the supernatural world, there must be no inconsistency of circumstances, nothing impossible in the nature of things as represented; every thing must seem to be produced by an adequate cause. That a fairy should engage in actual conflict with a furious beast, or that a Titan should dally with tiny flowers, would be alike ridiculous; while the fairy might tame the animal by a magic syllable, or reduce to weakness the sinewy giant by anointing him with the juice of charmed flowers, without violating probability, for no limit can be placed upon supernatural power.

Again, *symmetrical proportions* are necessary. Every part should have its due relation to all the others, and to the whole, and should be made prominent and conspicuous in proportion to its importance. Heavy columns to support a light architrave, or a large portico to a small building, is invariably displeasing. With regard to the form of single objects, when viewed without respect to utility or their relation to other things, we seem to judge by innate perception; certain shapes are intrinsically beautiful. Two vases may be of nearly the same dimensions, and equally adapted to hold the precious perfume or the floral treasure, and yet the form of one be really unpleasing to the eye, while that of the other may excite strong feelings of delight. Gently curving and undulating outlines are most beautiful, and thence are generally employed by Nature in her smaller and more delicate productions, while bold angular outlines characterize her larger and sublimer works; each is agreeable in its place.

The advantages of *contrast* to heighten effect are so well understood, that it is constantly employed by the artist. But if the design be obvious, the effect will most probably be lost. The mind refuses to believe that one object is large because another is small, or that one is beautiful because another is not. When properly used we are unconscious of its employment, while we feel its power. "False and groundless comparisons," says Sir Joshua Reynolds, "never strike us as such, if they answer the end designed." And as the eye is pleased with contrast, so also is it gratified with exact uniformity. We delight to compare two similar objects, and discover that they exactly resemble each other. But if the resemblance is not perfect, and yet too slight to admit of contrast, we are disappointed and displeased. The windows of a building should be all perfectly alike, or so different that the various kinds would strongly contrast with each other. In the corresponding parts of a regular body, we can be satisfied only with exact conformity, and in their mere similarity dwells a species of beauty.

Variety is another means of giving interest. That is most pleasing which calls into activity the greatest number of faculties, provided there be no confusion. Nothing could be more tiresome than a long poem that presented none but heroes to our notice, or if they were the principal actors, if they were not variously discriminated. In architecture, curved and straight lines opposed to each other, give an agreeable variety to a building. And the skilful musician knows how to delight, and is himself delighted, by the inexhaustible variety of combinations that "unbind the hidden soul of harmony."

To be a faultless critic, it were necessary that all the faculties of the mind should be fully developed. It was an axiom of Coleridge, that a work of art should be judged by its intrinsic merits, not by its faults. And while the vulgar eye may perceive the defects of even the sublimest works of imagination, it takes a high degree of cultivation really to appreciate and sympathize with their excellencies.

Painting.

PAINTING, in a technical sense, is the art which represents the appearance of natural objects on a plane surface, by means of colour and the management of light and shade, so as to produce the appearance of relief. As a fine art, its highest object is the beautiful, exhibited in visible forms by colours. "The ideas thus conveyed to us, have this advantage," says Richardson, an enthusiastic old writer on his art, "they come not by a slow progression of words, or in a language peculiar to one nation only; but with such a velocity, and in a manner so universally understood, that it resembles inspiration or intuition—as the art by which it is effected resembles creation; things so considerable and of so great price being produced out of materials so inconsiderable, and of a value next to nothing. What a tedious thing would it be to describe by words the view of a country, and how imperfect an idea would, after all, be afforded! Painting does it effectually, with the addition of so much of its character as can be known from thence; and, moreover, in an instant recalls to your memory at least the most considerable particulars of what you have heard concerning it, or occasions that to be told which you have never heard.

"Agostino Caracci, discoursing one day on the excellency of the ancient sculptures, was profuse in his praises of the Laocoon, and observing that his brother Annibale never spoke, nor seemed to take any notice of what he said, reproached him as not enough esteeming so masterly a work. He then went on describing every particular of that noble relic of antiquity. Annibale turned himself to the wall, and with a piece of charcoal drew the statue as exactly as if it had been before him. The rest of the company were surprised, and Agostino, silenced, confessed that his brother had taken a more effectual way than himself to demonstrate the beauties of that wonderful piece of sculpture. '*Li poeti dipingono con le parole, li pittori parlano con l'opere*'—(The poet paints with words, the painter speaks with works,) said Annibale.

"The business of painting is, to perform much of the effect of discourse and books, and, in many instances, more speedily and with more reality. To consider a picture aright, is to read it; but taking into account the beauty with which the eye is all the time entertained, (whether of colour or composition,) it is not only to read a book, and that finely printed and well bound, but as if a concert of music were heard at the same time. You have at once an intellectual and a sensual pleasure.

"By an admirable effort of human genius, painting offers to our eyes every thing which is most valuable in the universe. It presents to us the heroic deeds of ancient times as well as the facts with which we are more conversant, and distant objects as well as those we daily see. In this respect, it may be considered as a supplement to nature, which gives us a view of present objects only."

The noblest field of the painter is that in which he vies with the poet, embodying ideas and representing them to the spectator; but as there are innumerable gradations in poetry, from the most elevated epic or drama to the shortest lyric, the excellence of which may consist merely in giving effect to a single sentiment or situation, comic, touching, &c., so pictures may present all varieties, from the elevated productions of a Michael Angelo to the image of a single dew-drop, a leaf, or a feather.

Objects which attract no attention and are of little interest in themselves, when imitated by the artist are often interesting and even beautiful. In the still life of the Flemish painters, turnips and cabbages are translated into a higher sphere, and as evidence of the skill of the painter become invested with interest and a humorous sort of beauty. And as things indifferent may thus be made worthy of notice, so may beautiful and elevated objects be idealized, appearing as if in being transfused through the mind of the artist they had undergone some etherealizing process, or been imbued with a kind of intellectuality. A landscape on canvass, though a copy of nature rigidly correct, fails to give high satisfaction, unless there is a poetic spirit breathing through the scene, even as we see portraits unquestionably like the body of the original, yet without a spark of the soul. And how valuable the art that can arrest the smile of joy on the lip of beauty, and fix it for ages; that can perpetuate and hand down to posterity the features of the great and good, with their virtues inscribed on their countenances.

"To know an art thoroughly," says Opie, "we must know its object, which, in regard to painting, is not quite so easy as it appears at first; for though all agree that its purpose is to imitate nature, yet the vast superiority of many works of art over others equally challenging to be considered as true and faithful representations of nature, shows that some limitation and explanation of this very extensive and complicated term, is necessary to our forming a correct idea of its meaning in respect to art; without which it will be vain to hold it up as a standard.

"In taking a general view, and comparing the productions of art, they will be found easily divisible into three distinct classes, formed upon three distinct principles or modes of seeing nature, and indicative of three distinct ages or stages of refinement in the progress of painting. First, those of which the authors, agreeing with Dryden, that "God never made his works for man to mend," and understanding nature as strictly meaning the visible appearances of things, (any alteration of which would be at least unnecessary and impertinent, if not profane,) have, in consequence, confined themselves to the giving, as far as in them lay, an exact copy of their originals, as they happened to present themselves, without choice or selection of any kind as to the manner of their being. Secondly, those in which the artists, departing a little from this bigotry in taste, have ventured to reject what they considered as mean and uninteresting in nature, and endeavoured to choose the most perfect models, and render them in the best point of view. The third class would consist of the works of those who, advanced another step in theory, have looked upon nature as meaning the general principles of things, rather than the things themselves; who have made the imitation of real objects, give way to the imitation of an idea of them in their utmost perfection; and by whom we find them represented, not as they actually are, but as they ought to be.

"This last stage of refinement, has been called the ideal, the beautiful, or the sublime style of art. It founds its pretensions to superiority on the very superior powers required to excel in it, and on the infinitely greater effect, both as to pleasure and improvement, which it is calculated to produce on the mind of the spectator; and hence the pure, simple, energetic, and consistent principle on which it rests, is, indubitably, to be considered as the true and real interpretation of the term nature, always to be kept in view, not only by those who would excel in painting, but by all who wish to attain the highest style in any of the imitative arts.

"Many painters and critics, from observing the difficulty of settling the proper meaning of the term nature, have thought fit to substitute beauty in its stead, as the immediate object of the great style of art. But beauty being a word to the full as indefinite, if not as complex, as the word nature, we shall not be surprised to find that many painters, of no mean abilities, have been led into very fatal mistakes from erroneous and inadequate conceptions of its meaning; we shall not be surprised at the namby-pamby style of many of the works of Albani; we can hence account for the manner and affectation of Guido, who, understanding the term in too confined a sense, thought he was of course to paint, on every occasion, the most beautiful women; and taking, accordingly, in his opinion, the most beautiful antique statue for his model, he constantly repeated in his works the same face, without variation of expression or character, whatever was the subject, situation, or action represented: whether a Venus or a Milkmaid, the Assumption of the Virgin, the Death of Cleopatra, or Judith cutting off the Head of Holofernes. This principle has also evidently been the great stumbling-block of the whole French school, to which it owes the larger share of its absurdity and insipidity, its consumptive languor, and its coquettish affectation.

"I will not undertake the perilous task of defining the word beauty; but I have no hesitation in asserting, that when beauty is said to be the proper end of art, it must not be understood as confining the choice to one set of objects, or as breaking down the boundaries and destroying the natural classes, orders, and divisions of things, (which cannot be too carefully kept entire and distinct;) but as meaning the perfection of each subject in its kind, in regard to form, colour, and all its other associated and consistent attributes. In this qualified and, I will venture to say, proper acceptation of the word in regard to art, it may be applied to nearly all things most excellent in their different ways. Thus we have various modes of beauty in the statues of the Venus, the Juno, the Niobe, the Antinous, and the Apollo; and thus we may speak without exciting a confusion of ideas, of a beautiful peasant as well as of a beautiful princess; of a beautiful child or a beautiful old man; of a beautiful cottage, a beautiful church, a beautiful palace, or even a beautiful ruin.

"The discovery or conception of this great and perfect idea of things, of nature in its purest and most essential form, unimpaired by disease, unmutilated by accident, and unsophisticated by local habits and temporary fashions, and the exemplification of it in practice, by getting above individual imitation, rising from the species to the genus, and uniting, in every subject, all the perfection of which it is capable in its kind, is the highest and ultimate exertion of human genius. Hitherto shalt thou go, and no farther—every step in every direction from this pole of truth, is alike retrograde—for, to generalize beyond the boundaries of character, to compose figures of no specific age, sex, or destination, with no predominant quality or particular end to be answered in their construction, is to violate propriety, destroy interest, and lose the very essence of beauty in contemptible nothingness and insipidity.

"Let it, therefore, be always understood that the end of painting, in its highest style, is twofold: first, the giving effect, or the true appearance of objects to the eye; and secondly, the combination of this with the ideal, or the conception of them in their greatest perfection, and under such an arrangement as is calculated to make the greatest possible impression on the spectator.

"With such purposes in view, consisting of such a multiplicity of parts, and requiring such an uncommon assemblage of powers, mechanical and mental; of hand, of eye, of knowledge, of judgment, of imagination, and of indefatigable perseverance in study and practice, to enable a man to perform any one part with tolerable success, it can be no wonder that the art has not as yet, in modern times at least, reached the desired perfection; nor ought we to be surprised to find even the most celebrated masters materially defective in some one or more of its branches—those who possessed invention having been frequently deficient in execution; those who studied colouring having often neglected drawing; and those who attended to form and character having been too apt to disregard composition, and the proper management of light and shadow. The whole together, indeed, seems almost too great for the grasp of human powers, unless excited, expanded, and invigorated by such enthusiastic and continued encouragement as that which exclusively marks the bright era of Grecian taste."

The art of painting may be divided, according to its subjects, into three grand divisions: History, Landscape, and Still-Life. Under the general head of Historical, are classed all those designs which represent man in any of his relations—allegorical and mythological subjects, battle-pieces and portraits, as well as scenes drawn from history and common life. The representation of sea-views and other natural scenery, forms the second division. The term Still-Life refers to the imitations of all inanimate objects, as fruit, dead game, household furniture, &c.

Historical painting is the noblest and most comprehensive branch of the art, as it embraces man, the head of the visible creation. The historical painter, therefore, must study man, from the anatomy of his figure, to the most rapid and slightest gesture expressive of feeling, or the display of deep and subtle passions

He must have technical skill, a practised eye and hand, and must understand so to group his skilfully executed parts as to produce a beautiful whole. And all this is insufficient without a poetic spirit, which can form a striking conception of historical events, or create imaginary scenes of beauty. Long and patient cultivation both of the taste and the mechanical means of execution, are indispensable; for though a lively imagination may easily invent interesting scenes, how difficult is it for the inexperienced artist to present in visible forms that which he had thought perfectly distinct in his own mind. To obtain this skill, requires long practice, both in designing and colouring; the artist must have executed numerous studies, be familiar with the best models of art, and above all with the Protean forms of Nature.

THE FLORENTINE SCHOOL.

For many ages, the city of Florence has been one of the principal seats of the fine arts; and has produced, in all their various branches, a number of justly eminent professors. In the thirteenth century its senate introduced several artists from Greece, by whom the style and taste of the students were formed; and hence arose the elder Florentine school, at the head of which is Cimabue, the first Italian painter whose name is on record. With Leonardo da Vinci commenced the modern Florentine school. He was followed by Michael Angelo, and a host of other great masters. The leading principles of this school of painting may be denominated grandeur, dignity, and force. The gallery of the *Academia delle Belli Arti*, of Florence, presents a perfect epitome of the history of modern painting, from the first faint glimmer of the thirteenth century to the height of its glory

THE ROMAN SCHOOL.

It was the intense study of the inestimable relics of antiquity that formed the groundwork of the Roman school of painting, although in its progress it was mixed with both the Florentine and Venetian schools. To this school, however, we may justly attribute the truest principles and the finest examples of drawing, as well as of that scrupulous correctness which, nevertheless, was quite consistent with vigour and with beauty. Its followers were also eminent for their knowledge in the department of drapery, which knowledge they generally displayed in adopting ample and flowing robes and vestments, as may be observed in the matchless cartoons which form the chief ornament of Hampton Court. On the other hand, one must not seek in this school for any very superior exhibition of colouring; indeed, its artists seem to have been too intent on other branches of art, such as we have mentioned—on majesty, composition, and striking effects—to regard with any close attention the varieties and splendours of colour.

THE VENETIAN SCHOOL.

The Venetian artists applied themselves evidently to the contemplation of nature, and seized upon a source of fascination which had been in a great measure disregarded by their predecessors; namely, colour. Here start up to our view the most exquisite and brilliant arrangements of tints; and the delighted fancy of the connoisseur revels among the productions of the great prince of this department of art, Titian. Tintoret, Paul

Veronese, Giorgione, Sebastian del Piombo, &c., adorn with their illustrious names *the Venetian school* of painting; and the performances of all are more or less imbued with its peculiar characteristics, which are, vivacity and truth of colour, perfect distribution of light and shade, boldness of touch, and correct eye for nature. They sought out those scenes in landscape, as well as other subjects, wherein the contrasts and assimilations or combinations of colour presented the opportunity of exhibiting their greatest fascination. It should be remarked, however, that one explanation of this predominating excellence in the Venetian school, may be afforded by the circumstance of the Florentine and Roman artists painting chiefly in fresco and water-colours, while Titian and his celebrated brethren preferred the use of oils.

THE LOMBARD SCHOOL,

Sometimes denominated the Bolognese or Eclectic, was established by the Caracci. It was an attempt to combine and harmonize all the beauties of the different styles which had preceded it. But although the idea was comprehensive and fine, and manifested uncommon grasp and power in the minds of its suggestors, its unfixed, heterogeneous nature prevented it from holding together, and its avowed followers soon separated, each taking that particular path to which his individual genius appeared to impel him. It is common to rank among the Bolognese artists, Coreggio, Dominichino, Guido, Lanfranco, Caravaggio, &c.

THE FLEMISH SCHOOL

Is ordinarily considered to comprise all the celebrated painters and sculptors of the low countries, including Spaniards and Austrians. We may say, speaking generally, that this school carried to the highest point of perfection, that imitation of nature which is content with drawing from her most ordinary and uninviting moods, and takes no pains whatever to select or improve. The Flemish artists were also gifted with an abundant taste for character of the lower and more familiar description, and with great apprehension of the humorous. The name of Teniers is at the head of a long list of names eminent in a similar walk. The Flemish school is likewise extremely famous for its skill in colouring, and authorities have varied as to the palm of excellence, in that particular, between it and the Venetian school.

THE DUTCH SCHOOL.

The Dutch painters seem to have carried to a still greater extent than the Flemish the principle of taking Nature as they found her, without any regard to selection or embellishment. They made choice of the lowest subjects; and hence we so frequently find the scenes of their pictures laid in taverns, workshops, or watch-houses. They were much given to representing the noisy and drunken revels of villagers; and their success in this walk is unquestionably surprising. Their paintings are crowded with figures, just as they happen to come. Their heads are unintellectual, ugly, and vulgar; but, at the same time, characteristic and various, and often grotesque. These artists almost all challenge the praise of extreme neatness of execution and beautiful finish.

THE FRENCH SCHOOL

Is not very easily characterized, taking it *en masse*, since its elements are various, and it comprises within itself several wholly different styles. Of those artists who may be ranked among its ornaments, some have cultivated the Florentine, some the Roman, some the Venetian manner; while others, with a becoming ambition, have trusted to nature and their own genius.

With regard to distinguishing an original painting from a copy, the following directions of Richardson may be useful: "There are some pictures and drawings which are seen to be originals—though the hand and manner of thinking are neither of them known—and that by the spirit and freedom of them: which sometimes appears to such a degree as to assure us it is impossible they should be copies. But we cannot say, on the contrary, when we see a tame, heavy handling, that it is not original merely upon that account, because there have been many bad originals, and some good masters have fallen into a feebleness of hand, especially in their old age. The best counterfeiter of hands can rarely do it so well as to deceive a good connoisseur; the handling, the colouring, the drawing, the airs of heads—some, nay, all of these, discover the author; more or less distinctly, however, as the manner of the master happens to be: what is highly finished, for example, is more easily imitated than what is loose and free. Copies made by a master after his own work, are discoverable by being well acquainted with what that master did when he followed nature; these shall have a spirit, a freedom, a naturalness, which even he cannot put into what he copies from his own work."

THE DIFFERENT BRANCHES OF PAINTING.

The principal modes of painting are Water-Colour, Crayon, Miniature, Oil Painting, Fresco, Encaustic, Elydoric, and Painting on Glass.

Water-Colour—sometimes called limning, in which style the colours are prepared with gum or size, and applied with water. The characteristics are clearness and transparency of tint.

Crayon—in which the colours are ground in gum and water, and formed into small cylinders. When skilfully used, they give a peculiarly soft and pleasing effect.

Miniature.—Small portraits on ivory or vellum. Water-colours are used in this style. The colours are applied in minute dots, which gives great softness to the gradations of tint.

Oil Painting.—Colours ground in oils are not only more enduring, but more forcible in their effects.

Fresco.—The colours in this method are laid on a wall newly plastered, with which they become incorporated.

Encaustic is performed with colours mixed with wax and varnish or water; the word implies executed by fire, and heat is employed in the application of the colours, which are clear and brilliant.

Enamel.—A mode of painting with vitrified colours on gold, copper, silver, &c. The operation is performed by fire. The cases of Egyptian mummies are sometimes found ornamented with enamel, which proves the antiquity of this style.

Elydoric painting is that in which water and oil are both used in applying the colours. Its principal advantages are, that the artist is able to add the freshness of water-colours, and the high finishing of miniature, to the mellowness of oil painting, in such a manner, that the work appears like a large picture, when seen through a concave lens.

Mosaic, or Musaic, as it is sometimes called, is a kind of painting executed with small pieces of glass, or wood, pebbles, enamel, &c., fixed upon any substance with mastic. When an artist commences a work in Mosaic, he cuts on a stone plate a certain space, which he encircles with bands of iron. This space is covered with thick mastic, on which are laid, conformably to the particular design, the various substances intended to be used. Fifteen thousand different shades of colour are employed. The origin of Mosaic work must, apparently, be sought in the East, the rich carpets of which were imitated in hard stone. It is probable that the art was known to the Phœnicians, but to the Greeks its perfection and glory are to be attributed.

Glass.—In painting on this material, the paints are mixed with water or turpentine, and being laid on the glass are allowed to dry; the outline is then corrected with a sharp instrument. The glass is then placed in a heated furnace, and the colours are fused into it. The earliest notice of its existence is in the age of Pope Leo III., about the year 800. It did not, however, come into general use till the lapse of some centuries. The earliest specimens differ entirely from those of later date, being composed of small pieces stained with colour during the process of manufacture, and thus forming a species of patchwork or rude Mosaic, joined together with lead after being cut into the proper shapes. Venice, at an early period, was celebrated for her stained glass. During the thirteenth and fourteenth centuries, the era of the Gothic architecture, it was very generally applied to ecclesiastical structures. At the same period it had reached considerable excellence in England: of this, the windows of York Minster, the chapel of King's College, Cambridge, and the collegiate chapels and halls of Oxford, executed by native artists, afford sufficient proof. During the fifteenth century it made great progress under Albert Durer, Lucas Van Leyden, and other eminent artists of that era. Among the celebrated works of this period, are the beautifully painted windows of the church of Gonda, by Dirk and Wonter Crabeth. It declined in the sixteenth century, owing to the taste for fresco and oil-colours. But it was much used as a decoration for town-halls, the castles of the nobility, and heraldic emblazonry, &c. It was almost lost in the seventeenth, revived in a degree in the eighteenth, while about the beginning of the present century it was restored, with much of its pristine lustre, in Germany and France. Within a few years it has been cultivated in Great Britain and the United States.

Ancient Painting.

EGYPTIAN AND ORIENTAL PAINTING.

We find the earliest traces of this art in Egypt. Egyptian painting seldom, if ever, attempts more than an outline of the object as seen in profile, such as would be obtained by its shadow. To this rude draught, colours are applied, simply, and without mixture, or blending, or the slightest indication of light and shade. The process seems to have been; first, the preparation of the ground in white ; next, the outline was firmly traced in black ; and lastly, the flat colours were applied. The Egyptian artists employed six pigments, mixed with a gummy liquid—namely : white, black, red, blue, yellow, and green ; the first always earthy, the remaining vegetable, or, at least, frequently transparent. The specimens from which we derive these facts, are the painted shrouds and cases of mummies, and the still more frequent examples on the walls of the tombs. It can furnish no evidence of extraordinary experience or practice, that these paintings still retain their colour, clear and fresh ; the circumstance merely shows the aridity of the climate, and that the colouring matters were applied without admixture.

In Hindoostan, Persia, and other oriental countries, the brilliancy and variety of the colours are the only recommendation of their specimens of this art.

GRECIAN PAINTING.

We find the oldest Greek school of painting on the coast of Asia Minor and the islands. Fortunate circumstances here gave an early impulse to the art, the rudiments of which we find, even in the Homeric times, in the coloured carpets and weavings. Homer speaks of painting as being part of the employment of the beauteous Helen, at the time of the siege of Troy, as well as the art of embroidery :

> "Meantime, to beauteous Helen, from the skies,
> The various goddess of the rainbow flies.
> Her in the palace at her loom she found :
> The golden web her own sad story crown'd,
> The Trojan wars she weaved, (herself the prize,)
> And the dire triumphs of her fatal eyes."

If Helen could draw the representation of a battle, it is probable she knew how to fill up the outline with colours, and the existence of the rich tints of Tyre and Sidon proves, that they not only had a splendid variety of colours, but were also acquainted with their preparations.

Single pieces of painting were usually executed by the ancients upon wood, and therefore called tabular. The wood of the larch-tree was preferred, on account of its durability, and its not being liable to warp. They painted more rarely upon linen, as in the colossal picture of Nero, mentioned by Pliny. The most common kind of painting was that upon plaster, which is now called Fresco painting. Drawing or painting on ivory or marble, was less common. Fresco painting was executed upon a moist, as well as a dry ground. In this last mode of painting, the colours were laid on with a peculiar sort of glue or size, since, in many pieces of this kind, they are so well fixed that a wet sponge may be passed over them without injury.

The necessities of that idolatrous religion by which the Greeks were controlled, might, indeed, have alone required the exertion of all the talents the country could produce. In no other way is that immense advance to be explained which sculpture achieved before the art of painting, which was greatly influenced by this circumstance. Form predominated over the accuracy of colouring, and the expression which it conveys. The contour, and the local colours, seem to have been perfected in a great degree ; the perspective, much less. Some, indeed, have doubted whether the ancients had any knowledge of perspective ; but, as it is not to be dispensed with in any representation on a plane surface, and as the ancients were well acquainted with geometry and optics, we must suppose them to have possessed, in some limited degree, the use of perspective. It is more certain that they were ignorant of chiaroscuro, at least, until the time of Apollodorus. Landscape painting remained comparatively uncultivated. This branch depends, more than the others, on the rules of perspective, the perfection of colouring, and the charm of chiaroscuro. Pliny allows the ancients the use of but four colours, and yet, at other times, makes allusions which imply that their means were far more extensive. Their colours were, at least, both vivid and enduring. They employed a sort of varnish, called atramentum, to secure their paintings from the influence of the atmosphere. Their paintings were either moveable, or on the ceilings or compartments of buildings. Among the antiquities of Herculaneum, are four paintings on white marble.

The history of painting, among the Greeks, may be divided into four periods. The first terminated with Bularchus, the second period extends to Apollodorus, about 400 B. C. The third epoch ends with Apelles, who reached the acme of the art. The fourth period is dated from his time, and witnessed the decline of the art.

FIRST PERIOD.

In Pliny, we find an allusion to an artist, of the name of Saurius, who practised the earliest stage of the art. Cleanthes of Corinth, is, however, said to have been the inventor of drawing in outline. Ardices of the same city, and Telephon of Sicyon, the first who presented something more than the outline, and indicated light and shade. Charmades, the first who made a distinction in painting between light and shade. Subsequently came Eumanus, the Athenian, and Cymon of Cleonea, who advanced the art by giving a variety of attitude, attending to the folds of drapery, and marking the veins, joints, &c.

A representation of the defeat of the Magnesians, (790 B. C.,) by Bularchus, is the first considerable picture of which there is any record, yet the accounts which we have of it are, probably, exaggerated It was purchased by Candaules, king of Lydia, for its weight in gold. Bularchus appears to have been the first who employed various colours in his pictures.

SECOND PERIOD.

There seems to have been a great gap or chasm in the history of painting after the time of Bularchus, and the next allusion to the art seems to have been made by Anacreon, who, to express the abilities of any successful painter, said, "He is sovereign in the art which they cultivate at Rhodes." Hence we learn that the art must have flourished at Rhodes, in that era—about five hundred years before Christ. Phidias, the celebrated sculptor, is also cited by Pliny as eminent in the sister art of painting, and he flourished 445 years before our era. The brother of this illustrious ancient, Panænus, (or, according to others, Pannænsis,) acquired great reputation as a painter. He represented, in the temple of Jupiter Olympus, the subject of Atlas supporting the heaven and the earth, and Hercules offering to relieve him of his burden ; and another of Greece and Salamis (an island in the neighbourhood of Athens) personified ; together with many other pictures, the most famous of which was the Battle of Marathon, wherein, according to Pliny, the portraits of several generals, such as Miltiades, Callimachus, &c., might be recognized. We may observe that, even at this early period, prizes were contended for among the painters, Panænus having disputed, both at Corinth and at Delphos, with Timagorus of Chalsis.

Polygnotus was a native of Thasos, but obtained the right of citizenship at Athens. He flourished about 469 B. C. This distinguished painter seems to have contributed more largely to the advancement of his art than any who had preceded him. Before his time, the countenance was represented as destitute of animation and fire, and a kind of leaden dulness pervaded its features. His triumph was to kindle up expression in the face, and to throw feeling and intellect into the whole frame. He was the Prometheus of painting. He also first represented the mouth open, so that the teeth were displayed, and occasion was given to use that part of the visage in the expression of peculiar emotions. He first clothed his figures in light, airy, and transparent draperies, which he elegantly threw about the forms of his women. He was, in short, the author of both delicacy and expression in the paintings of Greece ; but his style is said to have been hard, and his colouring not equal to his designs. One of his pictures was preserved at Rome, representing a man on a scaling-ladder, with a target in his hand, so contrived that it was impossible to tell whether he was going upward or descending. Mycon was his cotemporary, and partner in the works which adorned the Pœcile at Athens. After Mycon, we proceed to mention Dyonysius of Colophon, in whose works, according to Ælianus, were to be found many of the excellencies of Polygnotus, such as choice of attitudes, flow of draperies, &c., but less grandeur of imagination. In the nineteenth Olympiad, we find mention made of Aglaophon, Cephissodorus, Phryllus, &c.

But it was not until the ninety-fourth Olympiad, 400 B. C., that the art of painting among the ancients appears to have reached its blaze of perfection. Hitherto objects had been represented on the canvass as flat, being almost without the magical effects of chiaroscuro, which gives relief and an appearance of projection to some portions of the picture, while others are made apparently to recede from the eye. To Apollodorus we owe this great discovery, and with him painting first rises into the regions of ideality

THIRD PERIOD.—APOLLODORUS.

Apollodorus was an Athenian, and flourished about 400 B. C He first discovered the art of softening and degrading, as it is technically called, the colours of a painting, and of imitating the exact effect of lights and shades. Pliny speaks of him with enthusiasm. Two chefs-d'œuvres still existed in his time at Pergamus. One was a priest at the altar, the other, Ajax struck by a thunderbolt.

ZEUXIS.

Zeuxis, a cotemporary of Apollodorus, was born at Heraclea. He seems to have rapidly risen to the highest distinction in Greece, and acquired, by the exercise of his art, not only renown, but riches. He appeared at the Olympic games attired in a mantle, on which his name was embroidered in letters of gold: a piece of unnecessary display in one whose name was deeply impressed on the hearts of the people by whom he was surrounded.

Very little is known respecting the life of this celebrated painter. He was not only successful in securing wealth, and the applause of the multitude, but was honoured with the friendship of Archelaüs, king of Macedon. For the palace of this monarch, he executed numerous pictures. Cicero informs us, that the inhabitants of Cretona prevailed on Zeuxis to come to their city, and to paint there a number of pieces, which were intended to adorn the temple of Juno, for which he was to receive a large and stipulated sum. On his arrival, he informed them that he intended only to paint the picture of Helen, with which they were satisfied, because he was regarded as peculiarly excellent in the delineation of woman. He accordingly desired to see the most beautiful maidens in the city, and having selected five of the fairest, copied all that was most beautiful and perfect in the form of each, and thus completed his Helen. Pliny, in his relation of the same circumstance, omits to give the particular subject of the painting, or the terms of the original contract, and states that the whole occurred not among the people of Crotona, but those of Agrigentum, for whom he says the piece was executed to fulfil a vow made by them to the goddess. The most celebrated of the pictures of Zeuxis, besides the Helen and the Alcmena, were a Penelope, in which Pliny assures us that not only form, but character was vividly expressed; a representation of Jupiter, seated on his throne, with all the gods around, doing him homage; a Marsyas bound to a tree, which was preserved at Rome; and a Wrestler, beneath which was inscribed a verse, to the effect that it was easier to envy than to imitate excellence. Lucian has left us an admirable description of another painting of his, representing the Centaurs, in which he particularly applauds the delicacy of the drawing, the harmony of the colouring, the softness of the blending shades, and the excellence of the proportions. He left many draughts in a single colour on white. The story respecting the contest between Zeuxis and Parrhasius, has been frequently related. It is said the former painted a cluster of grapes with such perfect skill, that the birds came and pecked at them. Elated with such unequivocal testimony of his excellence, he called on his rival to draw back the curtain which he supposed concealed his work, anticipating a certain triumph. Now, however, he found himself entrapped, for what he took for a curtain, was only a painting of one by Parrhasius; upon which he ingenuously confessed himself defeated, since he had only deceived birds, but his antagonist had beguiled the senses of an experienced artist. Another story is related of a similar kind, in which he overcame himself, or, rather, one part of his work was shown to have excelled, at the expense of the other. He painted a boy with a basket of grapes, to which the birds as before resorted; on which he acknowledged that the boy could not be well painted, since, had the similitude been in both cases equal, the birds would have been deterred from approaching. From these stories, if they may be credited, it would appear that Zeuxis excelled more in depicting fruit than in painting the human form. If this were the case, it is strange that all his greater efforts, of which any accounts have reached us, were portraits, or groups of men, or deities.

Zeuxis is said to have taken a long time to finish his chief productions, observing, when reproached for his slowness, that he was painting for eternity. Festus relates, that Zeuxis died of laughter at the picture of an old woman which he himself had painted. So extraordinary a circumstance, however, would surely have been alluded to by some other writer, had it been true.

PARRHASIUS.

Parrhasius, a native of Ephesus, but who eventually became a citizen of Athens, flourished about the ninety-fifth Olympiad; consequently, he was cotemporaneous with the two foregoing painters, though younger than either. He raised the art of painting to perfection in all that is exalted and essential. He compared his predecessors with one another, rejected what was exceptionable, and adopted what was admirable in each. The classic invention of Polygnotus, the magic tone of Apollodorus, and the exquisite design of Zeuxis, were all united in the works of Parrhasius. What they had produced in practice, he reduced to theory. He so circumscribed and defined, says Quintilian, all the powers and objects of art, that he was termed the legislator, and all cotemporary and subsequent artists adopted his standard of divine and heroic proportions. One of the most celebrated works of Parrhasius, was his allegorical figure of the Athenian people, or Demos. Pliny says, that it represented and expressed, in an equal degree, all the good and bad qualities of the Athenians at the same time. One might trace the changeable, the irritable, the kind, the unjust, the forgiving, the vain-glorious, the proud, the humble, the fierce, and the timid. How all these contrasting and counteracting qualities could have been represented at the same time, it is difficult to conceive. If we are to suppose it to have been a single figure, it is very certain that it could not have been such as Pliny has described it; for, except by symbols, it is totally incompatible with the means of art. The personification of the Athenian Demos was an object of sculpture, and its images by Lyson and Leochares were publicly set up; but there is no clew to decide whether they preceded or followed the conceit of Parrhasius.

TIMANTHES.

Timanthes, a native of Sicyon, was a cotemporary of Zeuxis and Parrhasius. He seems to have thrown a large share of intellect and thought into his productions. He appears to have been unequalled both in ingenuity and feeling, of which we have some remarkable examples. One of these was displayed in the picture on the noble subject of the sacrifice of Iphigenia, in which he represented the tender and beautiful virgin, standing before the altar, awaiting her doom, and surrounded by her afflicted relatives. These he depicted as moved by various degrees of sorrow, and grief seemed to have reached its utmost expression in the face of Menelaus ; but that of Agamemnon was left ; and the painter, heightening the interest of the piece by a forbearance of judgment, often erroneously regarded as a confession of the inadequacy of his art, covered the head of the father with his mantle, and left his agony to the imagination of the spectator. In Fuseli's Lecture on Ancient Art, this painting of Timanthes is made the subject of a full and very able criticism, in the course of which he dissents expressly from the opinion of Sir Joshua Reynolds, who agreed with M. Falconet in regarding the circumstance of the mantle enveloping the face of Agamemnon, as little better than a trick of the artist. The remarks of Fuseli, in answer to this, and similar animadversions, are worthy of much attention : "Neither the French, nor the English critic, appears to me to have comprehended the real motive of Timanthes. They ascribe to impotence, what was the forbearance of judgment. Timanthes felt like a father. He did not hide the face of Agamemnon because it was beyond the power of his art, nor because it was beyond the possibility, but because it was beyond the dignity of expression ; because the inspiring feature of paternal affection at this moment, and the action which, of necessity, must have accompanied it, would either have destroyed the grandeur of the character, and the solemnity of the scene, or subjected the painter, with the majority of his judges, to the imputation of insensibility. He must either have represented him in tears, or convulsed at the flash of the uplifted steel, forgetting the chief in the father, or in that state of stupefaction which levels all features and deadens expression. He might, indeed, have chosen a fourth mode; he might have exhibited him fainting and palsied in the arms of his attendants, and, by this confusion of male and female character, merited the applause of every theatre in Paris. But Timanthes had too true a sense of nature to expose a father's feelings, or to tear a passion to rags; nor had the Greeks yet learned of Rome to steel the face. If he made Agamemnon bear his calamity as a man, he made him also feel it as a man. It became the leader of Greece to sanction the ceremony with his presence; it did not become the father to see the daughter beneath the dagger's point. The same nature that threw a real mantle over the face of Timoleon, when he assisted at the punishment of his brother, taught Timanthes to throw an imaginary one over the face of Agamemnon. Neither height, nor depth, but propriety of expression, was his aim."

This celebrated piece was painted in contest with Colotes of Teos, a painter and sculptor from the school of Phidias, and it was crowned with victory at the rival exhibition. On another occasion, having painted a sleeping Cyclops in an exceedingly small compass, yet, wishing to convey the idea of his gigantic size, he introduced a group of Satyrs, measuring his thumb with a thyrsus. A deep meaning was to be discovered in every work of his pencil, yet the tendency to expression and significant delineation did not detract from the beauty of the forms which he created; for his figure of a prince was so perfect in its proportion, and so majestic in its air, that it appears to have reached the utmost height of the ideal. This picture was preserved in the Temple of Peace at Rome.

EUPOMPUS AND PAMPHYLUS.

Eupompus founded the first school of painting at Sicyon. The characteristics of this academy were, a stricter attention to dramatic truth of composition, and a finer and more systematic style of design. Pamphylus taught the principles of this school to Apelles. Such was his authority, says Pliny, that through his influence, first in Sicyon, and then throughout all Greece, noble youths were taught the art of drawing before all others; it was deemed of the highest importance. It was considered among the first of liberal arts, and was practised exclusively among the freeborn, for there was a law prohibiting all slaves the use of the cestrum. In this school of Pamphylus, the most famous of all the ancient schools of painting, the progressive courses of study occupied the long period of ten years, and the fee of admission was not less than a talent. Pamphylus, like his master, Eupompus, seems to have been occupied principally with the theory of his art, and with teaching, since we have few notices of his works. He left writings upon the arts, but they have unfortunately suffered the common fate of the writings of every other ancient artist. He wrote on painting and famous painters.

ARISTIDES.

Passing, with a bare mention of their names, Nicias, Eupheana, Perseus, Melanthius, and Antidotus, all distinguished painters of this period, we pause on Aristides, a native of Thebes. The refinements of the art were applied by him to the mind. He caught the passions as they rose from the lips, or escaped from Nature herself. His volume was man; his scene, society. He drew the subtle discriminations of mind, in every stage of life; the whispers, the simple cry of passion, and its complex accents. Such, as history informs us, was the suppliant whose voice you seemed to hear, such the sick man's half-extinguished eye and labouring breast; and, above all, the half-slain mother, shuddering lest the eager babe should suck the blood from her palsied breast. This picture was probably at Thebes when Alexander sacked that town; what his feelings were when he saw it, we may guess from his sending it to Pella. Its expression, poised between the anguish of maternal affection and the pangs of death, gives to commiseration an image, which neither the infant, piteously caressing his slain mother, in the group of Epigonus, nor the absorbed features of the Niobe, nor the struggle of the Laocoon, excites. Timanthes had marked the limits that discriminate terror from the excess of horror; Aristides drew the line that separates it from disgust. His subject is one of those that touch the ambiguous line of a squeamish sense. Taste and smell, as sources of tragic emotion, and, in consequence of their power, commanding gesture, seem scarcely admissible in art, or on the theatre, because their extremes are nearer allied to disgust, and loathsome or risible ideas, than to terror. The prophetic trance of Cassandra, who scents the prepared murder of Agamemnon at the threshold of the ominous hall; the desperate moan of Macbeth's queen, on seeing the visionary spot still uneffaced, infect her hand, are images snatched from the lap of terror, but soon would cease to be so, were the artist or the actress to enforce the dreadful hint with indiscreet expression or gesture. This, completely understood by Aristides, was as completely missed by his imitators: Raphael, in the Morbetto, and Poussin, in his Plague of the Philistines. In the group of Aristides, our sympathy is immediately interested by the mother, still alive, though mortally wounded, helpless, beautiful, and forgetting herself in the anguish for her child, whose situation still suffers hope to mingle with our fears; he is only approaching the breast of the mother. In the group of Raphael, the mother dead of the plague, herself an object of apathy, becomes one of disgust, by the action of the man, who, bending over her, at his utmost reach of arm, with one hand removes the child from the breast, while the other, applied to his nostrils, bars the effluvia of death. Our feelings, alienated from the mother, come too late even for the child, who, by his languor, already betrays the mortal symptoms of the poison he imbibed at the parent corpse. It is curious to observe the permutation of ideas which takes place, as imitation is removed from the sources of nature. Poussin, not content with adopting the group of Raphael, once more repeats the loathsome attitude in the same scene. He forgot, in his eagerness to render the idea of contagion still more intuitive, that he was averting our feelings with ideas of disgust. Attalus is said to have given a hundred talents ($105,559) for a painting by this artist. Some of the ancients ascribe to him the invention of painting on wax.

PAUSIAS.

Pausias was a painter of Sicyon, and cotemporary with Apelles. He was the first painter who acquired a great name for encaustic with the cestrum He excelled particularly in the management of the shadows; his favourite subjects were small pictures, generally of boys, but he also painted large compositions. He was the first who introduced the custom of painting the ceilings and walls of private apartments with historical and dramatic subjects. The practice, however, of decorating ceilings with stars and arabesque figures, (particularly those of temples,) was of very old date. The most famous work of his was the sacrifice of an ox, which in the time of Pliny was in the hall of Pompey. In this picture the ox is foreshortened; but, to show the animal to full advantage, the painter judiciously threw his shadow upon a part of the crowd, and he added to the effect by painting a dark ox on a light ground. Pausias in his youth loved a native of his own city named Glycera, who earned her living by making garlands of flowers, which led him into competition with her, and he eventually acquired great skill in flower painting. A portrait of Glycera, with a garland of flowers, was reckoned among his master-pieces. A copy of it was purchased by Lucullus, at Athens, at the great price of two talents, (nearly $2200.)

Pausias was reproached by his rivals for being a slow painter, but he silenced the censure by completing a picture in a single day, which on that account was called Hemeresius, (the work of one day.)

PROTOGENES.

Protogenes, a very eminent painter and statuary. was a cotemporary of Apelles. He appears, however, to have survived the latter artist, inasmuch as he was still living Olymp. 119, when Rhodes was besieged by Demetrius. Meyer conjectures, with considerable probability, that he was born about Olymp. 104. His early efforts were made amid the pressure of very contracted means. Who his master was, is unknown; and necessity for a long time compelled him to employ his abilities on subjects altogether unworthy of them. Compelled to paint ornaments on vessels, in order to secure a livelihood, he passed fifty years of his life without the gifts of fortune, and without any marked reputation. His talents and perseverance at length triumphed over every obstacle; and possibly the generous aid of Apelles may have contributed to hasten this result. Protogenes had painted a picture of Ialysus, which so delighted Apelles that he sailed to Rhodes on purpose to visit his accomplished cotemporary. There, finding him in poverty and obscurity, he is reported to have bought several of the performances of Protogenes, with the avowed intention of selling them as his own, and thus succeeded in exciting the notice of the people of Rhodes towards the abilities of their fellow-citizen, who thence rose from his hitherto humble situation, to fame and fortune.

Pliny tells a very pleasing story of Apelles and Protogenes. The former having come to Rhodes, where Protogenes was residing, paid a visit to the artist, but not finding him at home, obtained permission, from a domestic in waiting, to enter the atelier of the painter. Finding here a piece of canvass ready on the frame for the artist's pencil, he drew upon it a line (according to some, a figure in outline) with wonderful precision, and then retired, without disclosing his name. Protogenes, on returning home, and discovering what had been done, exclaimed that Apelles alone could have executed it. Still, however, he drew another himself, a line more perfect than that of Apelles, and left directions with his domestic, that when the stranger should call again, he should be shown what had been done by him. Apelles came accordingly, and perceiving that his line had been excelled by Protogenes, drew a third one, still more perfect than the other two, and cutting both. Protogenes now confessed himself vanquished; he ran to the harbour, sought for Apelles, and the two artists became the warmest friends. The canvass containing this famous trial of skill, became highly prized, and at a later day was placed in the palace of the Cæsars at Rome. It was destroyed by a conflagration, together with the edifice itself. Protogenes was employed seven years in finishing the picture of Ialysus, a celebrated huntsman, supposed to have been the son of Apollo, and the founder of Rhodes. During all this time the painter lived only upon lupines and water, thinking such elements would leave him greater flights of fancy; but all this did not seem to make him more successful in perfecting his picture. He was to represent in the piece a dog panting, and with froth at his mouth, but this he never could do with satisfaction to himself; and, when his labours seemed to be without success, he threw his sponge upon the piece in a fit of anger. Chance alone brought to perfection what the labours of the artist could not accomplish; the fall of the sponge upon the picture represented the froth at the mouth of the dog in the most perfect manner, and the piece was universally admired. The talents of Protogenes were not so fertile as those of many other artists, a circumstance to be ascribed to his minute and scrupulous care. This is the quality which Quintilian mentions as his great characteristic; and Petronius likewise observes that his outlines vied in accuracy with the works of Nature themselves.

APELLES.

Apelles, the most celebrated of ancient painters, is generally admitted to have been a native of the Island of Cos. His instructors were Euphorus, Pamphyius, and Melanthius. He flourished in the time of Alexander the Great, which monarch, would suffer his portrait to be taken by no other artist. It is related that Alexander having one day expressed himself, while in the painting-room of Apelles, rather ignorantly on the subject of the principles of art, the painter counselled him that it would be wiser in him to be silent, and not give the lads who ground his colours, occasion to laugh at the great Alexander. It is added, much to the credit of the king, that he bore the rebuke paitently. This remarkable person, the wonder of his age, was, if we may credit the tradition respecting him, gifted with such a combination of natural and acquired talents, as never perhaps either before or since fell to the lot of another individual. In addition, he had the happiness to live at that period wherein the genius of his country had reached its highest point of elevation. The name of Apelles, in Pliny, is the synonyme of unrivalled and unattainable excellence, but in our estimate of his talents we must candidly consider what modifications may be requisite on an enumeration of his actual works. His great prerogative consisted, perhaps, more in the unison than in the extent of his powers: he knew better what his capabilities could achieve, and what lay beyond them, than any other artist. Grace of conception and refinement of taste were his elements, and went hand in hand with grace of execution and completeness in finish, irresistible when found united; and when we reflect on the splendid achievements of architecture and sculpture in his era, we shall know how to appreciate the admiration the ancients expressed of these qualities. That he built both on the firm basis of the former system, not on its subversion, his well-known contest of lines with Protogenes irrefragably proves. What those lines were, drawn with nearly miraculous subtlety, in different colours one upon the other, or rather, within each other, it would be equally unavailing and useless to inquire; but the corollaries we may deduce from the contest are obviously these: that the schools of Greece recognized all one elemental principle; that acuteness and fidelity of eye, and obedience of hand, form precision; precision, proportion; proportion, beauty: that it is the "little more or less," imperceptible to vulgar eyes, which constitutes grace, and establishes the superiority of one artist over another; that the knowledge of the degrees of things or taste presupposes a perfect knowledge of the things themselves; that colour, grace, and taste are ornaments, not substitutes of form, expression, and character, and, when they usurp that title, degenerate into splendid faults. Such were the principles on which Apelles formed his Venus, or, rather, the personification of Female Grace, the wonder of art, the despair of artists; whose outline baffled every attempt at emendation, while imitation shrunk from the purity, the force, the brilliancy, the evanescent gradations of the tints. It was esteemed the most faultless creation of the Grecian pencil, the most perfect example of that simple but unapproachable grace of expression, of symmetry of form, and exquisite finish, in which may be summed up the distinctive excellencies of his genius. Apelles used to say of his cotemporaries, that they possessed, as artists, all the requisite qualities but one, namely, grace, and that this was his alone. On one occasion, when contemplating a picture by Protogenes, a work of immense labour, and in which exactness of detail had been carried to excess, he remarked, "Protogenes equals or excels me in all things but one, the knowing when to remove his hand from a painting." Apelles was also, as is supposed, the inventor of what artists call glazing. The modesty of Apelles, says Pliny, equalled his talents. He acknowledged the superiority of Melanthius in the art of grouping, and that of Asclepiodorus in adjusting on canvass the relative distances of objects. Apelles never suffered a day to pass, however much he might be occupied by other matters, without drawing one line at least in the exercise of his art, and from this circumstance arose the proverb, "*Nulla dies sine linea.*" He was accustomed also, when he had completed any one of his pieces, to expose it to the view of passengers, and to hide himself behind it, in order to hear the remarks of the spectators. On one of these occasions, a shoemaker censured the painter for having given one of the slippers of a figure a less number of ties, by one, than it ought to have had. The next day the shoemaker, emboldened by the success of his previous criticism, began to find fault with a leg, when Apelles indignantly put forth his head, and desired him to confine his decisions to the slipper.

The pictures produced by this consummate artist, appear to have been numerous, and the reader will find in Pliny an extensive list. A brief enumeration of some of them will serve to convey a just idea of the class of subjects generally chosen by him.

The portraits painted by him, both of Alexander the Great and his father, Philip, were numerous; some of them single, some accompanied by other figures. Alexander launching thunder, in the temple of Diana, at Ephesus, has been greatly extolled for its effect and the boldness of its relief, the hand which was raised appearing to come forward, and the lightning to be out of the picture. In another portrait of the same prince, he was represented in a triumphal chariot, and near him the figure of War, with his hands tied behind his back. This, and another Alexander, accompanied by Castor and Pollux, and a figure of Victory, were preserved by Augustus in the forum.

Many other portraits are alluded to: namely, Antiochus, king of Syria; Antigonus; Archelaus, with his wife and daughter; Abron, an effeminate debauchee; Clotus, on horseback, armed except his head, with an attendant delivering his helmet to him. In fanciful subjects we find, Diana attending a sacrifice, surrounded by her nymphs; Neoptolemus, son of Achilles, on horseback, contending with Persians; Hercules with his back towards the observer, and his head turned round so as to show his face.

ROMAN PAINTING.

The Roman artists make but a poor show after this brilliant enumeration of Greek artists. The most ancient paintings known in Rome were, indeed, executed by Etruscan artists, and in later times they seem rather to have been ambitious of removing *chefs-d'œuvres* of art from conquered Grecian provinces, than of cultivating it among themselves. The Greeks loved and cherished the arts, because they conferred honour and dignity on their country; the Romans suffered them, because they embellished their empire. In Greece, no man was disgraced by following the profession of an artist; in Rome, it was the business of slaves: with one, the arts were objects of love and desire; with the other, of convenient decorative necessity. This ignorance of the beauties of the fine arts, among this warlike people, lasted for several centuries—in short, till, having no more countries to conquer in the interior of Italy, they began to explore the seas and penetrate into the fertile regions of Sicily, where they were struck with amazement at the pomp and grandeur of the cities, and the beauties of the works of art in these highly cultivated regions. With such customs, laws, and dispositions, the Roman people were not very likely to make the fine arts flourish rapidly.

As a proof of the rarity of the practice of painting among the Romans during the consulate, may be adduced the fact, that

Fabius, who having spent some time among the Etruscans and acquired some knowledge of the fine arts, on painting the temple of Salus, was thenceforward denominated Pictor, (the painter;) this cognomen descending to his offspring. A few other names follow this artist's, but none of much notoriety. Turpilius had some fame in his day, and Pliny says of him, that he painted with his left hand. Arellius flourished at Rome a short time before the reign of Augustus. In the reign of this monarch, we find Marcus Ludius, a landscape and marine painter. The mania of Nero to be considered a painter, infected, as might be supposed, several members of his court; but the muse seems to have been inexorable to their addresses. Under Vespasian, Cornelius Pinus and Accius Priscus painted the temples of Virtue and of Honour. According to Pliny, the latter approached nearest to the manner of the Grecian artists.

Early Christian Painting.

CHRISTIAN painting may be first traced to the catacombs. It was on the walls of these subterraneous chapels and tombs that the first Christian artists drew their primitive sketches, which must ever be interesting, as the expression and symbol of adherence to their religious faith, in defiance of the most cruel oppression and persecution.

The conversion of the emperor Constantine, opened up a new career to religious painting. No longer imprisoned within the narrow walls of the catacombs, she had for her theatre the whole Roman empire. Vast basilicæ at Rome and Constantinople, and the principal cities of Europe and Asia, offered unlimited scope for the extension and improvement of the art. The application of a new process in mosaic, discovered in the reign of Claudius, promised to secure an indefinite duration to works in that style. Painting on a great scale was practised in the temples and basilicæ appropriated to Christian worship; and it is there, M. Rio remarks, we must seek its character during the second period of its development. The favourite composition of the Christians of Rome was the figure of Christ, between the apostles St. Peter and St. Paul; and though such works partake more or less of the general degradation of taste, they are distinguished from the cotemporary productions of profane art, by an indefinable dignity in the character and attributes of the personages—a dignity the more striking, that it does not interfere with the charm of execution, or the accessory details. The fundamental idea is there, in all its grandeur and simplicity. It is the embryo of the same pure and solemn style that was destined to characterize Christian art in later times. After contemplating the ancient mosaics of Rome, Ghirlandajo exclaimed, "That is the true painting for eternity!"

The Romano-Christian school, of which there are still extant many remains in Italy, survived, amid many vicissitudes, to the invasion of the barbarians, and even to a later period. It must, however, be admitted, as regards the technical department, that such works become more and more degraded, in proportion as they recede from the age of Constantine. The lines of the figures are coarsely marked; the shadows and middle tints disappear; the contours are deficient in boldness and fulness.

The Romano-Christian school, though interrupted and borne down by the successive invasions of the barbarians still continued to exist; in proof of which may be mentioned the new mosaics with which so many churches were decorated, besides numerous paintings in the catacombs, which had become the ordinary place of sepulture of the pontiffs. Pope John I., Felix IV., and John III., are cited as having restored and embellished the catacombs of St. Marcellino and St. Priscilla after the conquest of Italy by the Goths; to which may be ıdded the mosaics of Ravenna, under the superintendence of the bishop of the city. This school, after having answered the purpose of an intermediate link between the primitive types of the catacombs and the sublime inspirations of the new schools, was now destined to fall into a long slumber, showing but few signs of vitality. Before the reign of Charlemagne, the practice of painting the interiors of churches was general in Gaul, insomuch that there was a rivalship between the ultramontane artists and those ꜀f barbaric origin. The accession of Charlemagne gave a new impulse to art throughout the whole extent of his empire. The emperor directed special envoys to inspect the churches and works of art thoughout the provinces, stimulated the zeal of the artists and bishops, and even became the patron of art in other kingdoms. All the principal works of art of this reign, have perished; those that were not buried under the ruins of the edifices themselves, having been destroyed by time and the elements. To compensate this loss, there exist many interesting missals and manuscripts of this period, adorned with miniatures, bearing signs that they were undertaken by the order of Charlemagne. Numerous illuminated works of the same kind, show that this branch of art was making progress under the Carlovingian dynasty, without any reference to classical imitation, of which they exhibit no trace, either as regards style, character, or costume. Among these, the most noted are the Psalter, of the library of Vienna, the work of a German painter named Dagulf; the Evangiliaine of Charles the Bold, preserved in the library of Munich, with other treasures of art of the same epoch; the Hours of Queen Emma, a *chef-d'œuvre* for the time in which it was executed; and particularly the Benedictional of the English monk, Godemann, which, in elegance and delicacy of pencil, far surpasses all the most eminent painters of miniature of the tenth century. A central school was about the same time established at the celebrated convent of St. Gall, where two caligraphic painters, Sintramne and Modestus, had become already famous in the ninth century.

The traditions left by them were collected by the monk Notken, who cultivated, with equal success, painting and poetry; by Tutilon, who was painter, poet, musician, carver, and statuary; and by the monk Jean, whom the Emperor Otho III. invited to Aix-la-Chapelle to paint an oratory. The alliance of high ecclesiastical dignity with pre-eminence in the fine arts, was still more frequent in the eleventh century. many instances of which might be mentioned.

All these facts sufficiently demonstrate that original Scriptural art had taken deep root in the German nation, and that it was not, as has been alleged, a servile imitation of Byzantine and Italian art. The subjects of their missals and paintings, in churches as well as palaces, were chiefly from the Old Testament. The Synod of Arras was the means of consecrating this practice, already congenial to the national taste, by declaring painting to be the book of the ignorant, who could not read. About the same period, the arts of embroidery, tapestry, and painting on glass, began to be introduced.

Modern Italian Painting.

In spite of the numerous testimonies brought forward by Vasari and other Tuscan writers, that art first revived in Florence, it is certain that the school of Pisa, and even that of Sienna, had prior claims. That the revival of classical sculpture and design by the Pisan school extended its influence far and wide, and was the means of effecting a similar revival in painting, cannot be doubted. The school of Sienna, though more or less tinged with the Byzantine manner, produced many good painters. The great work of Duccio in the cathedral, on which he laboured three years with so much enthusiasm and perseverance, is happily preserved. Rumohr does not hesitate to place it above all the Byzantine Tuscan school, not excepting the Madonnas of Cimabue. The celebrated Ghiberti, the earliest historian of Italian art, gives the preference to Duccio. But, though Florence had no exclusive claim to be the cradle of art, and must share it with other schools, it must be admitted that Cimabue and his pupil Giotto, following the example of Nicolo Pisano and his school, made the first great and important step, and that, though she started later in the career, she soon outstripped all her competitors.

CIMABUE.

Giovanni Cimabue was born in the year 1240. He was a descendant of the ancient house of Gondi, one of the noblest of Florence. According to general opinion, several Greek artists being employed to adorn his native city, Cimabue, inspired by their productions, however imperfect, took up the pencil, and, soon excelling his masters, is said to have introduced a new style. He is generally considered as the reviver of painting in Italy; but he was preceded by Nicoli and Giovanni Pisani, and other Italian artists, little if it all inferior to himself.

The conquest of Constantinople, in 1204, had occasioned a freer intercourse between the Greeks and Italians, and doubtless greatly aided in promoting the rapid progress of the arts in the thirteenth century. In his twenty-sixth year, Cimabue painted the celebrated Madonna which is still to be seen in the church Santa Marie Novella. He believed himself inspired by the Virgin, whom he said sat to him in her own person. It was, when exhibited, pronounced a miracle, though miserably deficient in almost every mechanical detail. It has, however, an exalted expression, which stamps it as a work of genius. An idea of the rudeness of the productions of this age may be gathered from the fact, that it was often found necessary to issue a label from the mouth to signify the sentiment intended to be conveyed. Cimabue succeeded admirably in the heads of men of strong character, impressing them with a certain air of the lofty and sublime, which has hardly been surpassed in later times. Vast and comprehensive in his ideas, he gave the example of grand historical compositions executed in suitable proportions.

GIOTTO.

Giotto di Bondini was born at Vespignano, near Florence in 1276. He was a shepherd, and while he attended his flocks, he made rude sketches from nature. Cimabue is said to have discovered a figure drawn on a smooth stone by Giotto, and was so much struck with it, that he took him from the fields and instructed him in his art. His unlettered pupil made rapid advances in design; and, though he soon far surpassed his master, a strict friendship continued between them. To this artist the world is indebted for a portrait of the illustrious Dante.

The fame of Giotto was not confined to Florence. Pope Benedict sent for him, and employed his pencil in adorning the Vatican and St. Peter's church.

He was called, by his cotemporaries, the painter of nature; and it is related of him, that, when a boy, he painted a fly with such skill upon the nose of a portrait which Cimabue was engaged upon, that when his master was about to continue his work, he attempted to brush it away with his hand.

The pure taste of Giotto soon led him to discard the use of labels to express the sentiment intended to be conveyed by his figures. He died in 1336, in the sixtieth year of his age. The city of Florence erected a marble statue over his tomb. If Cimabue was the Michael Angelo, Giotto was the Raphael of that age. Giotto showed his contempt for the Byzantine traditions, by neglecting some that might have been retained, and paying no respect to long-established costumes.

MASACCIO.

Masaccio da San Giovanni Valdarno was born in 1402. He made great advances in his art, and was the first who introduced foreshortening; the first to conceive that parts are to constitute a whole; that composition ought to have a centre; expression, truth: and execution, unity. His line deserves attention, though his subjects led him not to the investigation of form ; and the shortness of his life forbade his extending those elements which Raphael, nearly a century afterwards, carried to perfection : it is sufficiently glorious for him to have been more than once copied by that great master of expression, and in some degree to have been the herald of his style. Masaccio lives more in the figure of Paul preaching on the Areopagus, and in the borrowed figure of Adam expelled from Paradise, in the loggia of the Vatican, than in his own mutilated or retouched remains.

Though his manner, says Reynolds, was dry and hard, his compositions formal and not enough diversified, according to the custom of painters in that early period, yet his works possess that grandeur and simplicity which accompany, and even sometimes proceed from regularity and hardness of manner. We must consider the barbarous state of the arts before his time, when drawing was so little understood that the best of the painters could not even foreshorten the foot, but every figure appeared to stand on his toes ; and what served for drapery, had, from the smallness of the folds, much the appearance of cords clinging round the body. He first introduced large folds, flowing in an easy and natural manner. Indeed, he appears to be the first who discovered the path that leads to every excellence to which the art afterwards arrived, and may therefore be justly considered as one of the great fathers of modern art.

He was as much distinguished, among his cotemporaries, for his diligence and industry, as he was for the natural faculties of his mind. We are told that his whole attention was absorbed in the pursuit of his art, and that he acquired the name of Masaccio, from his total disregard to his dress, his person, and all the common concerns of life. He is indeed a signal instance, of what well-directed diligence will do in a short time :

he lived but twenty-seven years, yet, in that short space, carried the art so far beyond what it had before reached, that he appears to stand alone as a model for his successors.

LEONARDO DA VINCI.

Leonardo da Vinci was born in the year 1452, at the Castello di Vinci in the Vald'arno. He was one of the most accomplished men of his age. "If it be true," says Opie, "'that one science only will one genius fit,' what shall we say to the man, who, master of all mental and all bodily perfections, equally excelled in painting, poetry, sculpture, architecture, chemistry, anatomy, mathematics, and philosophy; who renders credible all that has been related of the Admirable Crichton, who attempted every thing and succeeded in every attempt; who, sailing round the world of art and science, touched at every port, and brought home something of value from each?"

"This is the glory of Leonardo, and this was also his weakness; for, equally in love with grandeur and littleness, beauty and deformity, character and caricature, he bestowed his attention on them all by turns, and soared or dived, as the caprice of the moment directed. His genius, however, gave the death-blow to flatness and insipidity, by the invention of that deep tone of colour, strength of shadow, and bold relievo, which, afterwards carried to perfection, enchants us in the dreams of Coreggio, and electrifies us in the mysterious visions of Rembrandt.

"Leonardo's celebrated cartoon of the 'Horsemen contending for a Standard,' is one of the noblest inventions in the whole circle of modern art; it evinces a singular boldness and fertility of imagination, by the display of every attitude of the human body on horseback, in the various actions of striking, pulling, thrusting, warding and evading a blow, combined with a felicity and energy at once picturesque, interesting, and surprising; the whole is animated, every part is in motion, and we witness, by turns, the collected coolness of true courage, the devouring malevolence of rage, the contending emotions of hope and fear, the exultation of assured victory, and the despairing gasp of inevitable death. The horses, conceived with the fire of a true poet, and executed with the science of an anatomist, rear and plunge into the battle with a fury equal to that of their riders: in short, this composition was altogether unexampled at the time, and unrivalled for ages after, till it suggested to Rubens the first hint for those magnificent groups of horses and figures, in his battles of the Amazons, and of Constantine and Maxentius; and for those astonishing masses of men and animals in commotion, his huntings of the lion, the tiger, the crocodile, and the hippopotamus."

There is no possibility of calculating what such a man as Leonardo da Vinci may have lost by his versatility and want of perseverance. With such comprehension, and such invention, he might, doubtless, instead of furnishing hints and pointing out the promised land to others, have taken possession of it himself, and carried the principles of chiaroscuro and grouping to perfection.

To the discovery of central radiance the genius of Leonardo, with equal penetration, added its counterpart, purity of shade and the coalescence of both through imperceptible demi-tints. Whatever tone of light he chose, he never forgot that the shade intended to set it off was only its absence, and not a positive colour, and that both were to be harmonized by demi-tints composed of both; a principle of which no school anterior to him has left a trace.

His master-piece, the Last Supper, is thus eulogized by Fuseli: "Let us begin with the centre the seat of the principal figure, from which all the rest emanate like rays. Sublimely calm, the face of the Saviour broods over the immense revolution in the economy of mankind which throngs inwardly on his absorbed eye—as the Spirit creative in the beginning over the water's darksome wave—undisturbed and quiet; whilst every face and every limb around him, roused by his mysterious word, fluctuates in restless curiosity and sympathetic pangs. It has survived the hand of time in the study which Leonardo made in crayons, exhibited with most of the attendant heads in the British Gallery; and even in the feebler transcript of Pietro Testa.

"I am not afraid of being under the necessity of retracting what I am going to advance, that neither during the splendid period immediately subsequent to Leonardo, nor in those which succeeded to our time, has the face of the Redeemer been produced which, I will not say equalled, but approached the sublimity of Leonardo's conception, and in quiet and simple features of humanity, embodied divine, or, what is the same, incomprehensible and infinite powers. To him who could contrive and give this combination, the unlimited praise lavished on the inferior characters who surround the hero, whilst his success in that was doubted, appears to me not only no praise, but a gross injustice."

"The moment," says Lanzi, and says well, "is that in which the Saviour says to his disciples, 'One of you will betray me!' On every one of the innocent men, the word acts like lightning; he who is at a greater distance, distrusting his own ears, applies to his neighbour; others, according to their variety of character, betray raised emotions. One of them faints, one is fixed in astonishment; this wildly rises, the simple candour of another tells that he cannot be suspected: Judas, meanwhile, assumes a look of intrepidity, but though he counterfeits innocence, leaves no doubt of his being the traitor. Leonardo used to tell, that for a year he wandered about, perplexed with the thought, how to embody in one face the image of so black a soul; and frequenting a street which a variety of villains haunted, he met at last, by the help of some associated features, with his man. Nor was his success less conspicuous in furnishing the two Jameses with congenial and characteristic beauty; but being unable to find an ideal superior to theirs for Christ, he left the head, as Vasari affirms, imperfect; though Armenini ascribes the highest finish even to that.

"To the countenance and attitude of St. John, blooming with youth, innocent, resigned, partaking perhaps somewhat too much of the feminine, and those of the two Jameses invigorated by the strength of virility, energetic and bold, none will refuse a competent praise of varied beauty; but they neither are nor ought to be ideal, and had they been so, they could neither compete nor interfere with the sublimity that crowns the Saviour's brow, and stamps his countenance with the God.

"The felicity, novelty, and propriety of Leonardo's conception and invention, are powerfully seconded by every part of the execution: the tone which veils and wraps actors and scene into one harmonious whole, and gives it breadth; the style of design, grand without affectation, and if not delicate or ideal, characteristic of the actors; the draperies folded with equal simplicity and elegance, with all the propriety of presenting the highest finish, without anxiety of touch or thronging the eye.

"So artless is the assemblage of the figures, that the very name of composition seems to degrade what appears to be arranged by Nature's own hand. That the nearest by relation, characters, and age, should be placed nearest the master of the feast, and of course attract the eye soonest, was surely the most natural arrangement; but if they are conspicuous they are not so at the expense of the rest: distance is compensated by action; the centre leads to all, as all lead to the centre. That the great restorer of light and shade sacrificed the effects and charms of chiaroscuro at the shrine of character, raised him at once above his future competitors, changes admiration to sympathy, and makes us partners of the feast."

COREGGIO.

Antonio Allegri, commonly called Coreggio, from the place of his birth, was born, according to the most authentic accounts, in 1493. By some, says Opie, we are told that he was born, bred, and lived in poverty and wretchedness, and that he died at the age of forty, from the fatigue of carrying home a sack of halfpence, or copper money, paid to him for one of his grandest works.

On the other hand, Mengs, his most devoted admirer, who made every possible inquiry concerning him, contends that he was of a good family, and lived in opulence; that he had every advantage of education, both general and professional; that he had been at Rome and Florence, and had, consequently, seen the works of Da Vinci, Michael Angelo, and Raphael; that he studied philosophy, mathematics, painting, sculpture, and architecture, and conversed familiarly with the most famous professors of his time.

"Of chiaroscuro on the grandest scale, as it extends to the regulation of the whole of a work, he was certainly the inventor. Antecedently to him, no painter had attempted, or even imagined, the magic effect of this principle, which is strikingly predominant in all that remains of Coreggio, from his widely-extended cupolas to the smallest of his oil paintings: its sway was uncontrollable, parts were enlightened, extended, curtailed, obscured, or buried in the deepest shade ; even correctness of form, propriety of action, and characteristic attitude, were occasionally sacrificed. To describe his practice, will be in a great degree to repeat general observations on chiaroscuro in its enlarged sense. By classing his colours, and judiciously dividing them into few and large masses of bright and obscure, gently rounding off his light, and passing, by imperceptible degrees, through pellucid demi-tints and warm reflections, into broad, deep, and transparent shade, he artfully connected the fiercest extremes of light and shadow, harmonized the most intense opposition of colours, and combined the greatest possible effect with the sweetest and softest repose imaginable. The same principle of easy gradation seems to have operated as his guide in respect to design, as well as in colouring and chiaroscuro. By avoiding straight lines, sharp angles, all abrupt breaks, sudden transitions, and petty inflexions, and running by gentle degrees from convex to concave, and *vice versa*, together with the adoption of such forms and such attitudes as admitted this practice in the highest degree, he gave his figures that ease, elegance, and flexibility, that inimitable grace, which, in honour of the inventor, has since obtained the appellation of Coreggiesque."

This rare union of grace, harmony, and effect, forms the skill of Coreggio, which, while it operates, suspends judgment and disarms criticism. Entranced and overcome by pleasing sensation, the spectator is often compelled to forget incorrectness of drawing, and deficiency of expression and character. These defects, however, it has already been observed, are but occasional; and though, in comparing him with Raphael, it may justly be said, that the one painted best the effects of body, and the other those of mind, it must also be acknowledged that modesty, sweetness, and the effusions of maternal tenderness, have never been more forcibly expressed than by the pencil of Coreggio.

The turn of his thoughts, also, in regard to particular subjects, was often in the highest degree poetical and uncommon: of which it will be sufficient to give, as an instance, his celebrated Notte, or painting of the Nativity of Christ, in which the circumstance of his making all the light of the picture emanate from the child, striking upward from the beautiful face of the mother, and in all directions, on the surrounding objects, may challenge comparison with any invention in the whole circle of art, both for the splendor and sweetness of the effect, which nothing can exceed, and for its happy appropriation to the person of Him who was born to dispel the clouds of ignorance, and diffuse the light of truth over a darkened world!

This circumstance, at once sublime, beautiful, and picturesque, is one of those rare instances of supreme felicity by which a man may be said to be lost in his own glory. The thought has been seized with such avidity, and produced so many imitations, that no one is accused of plagiarism. The real author is forgotten; and the public, habituated to consider the incident as a part of the subject, have long ceased to inquire when or by whom it was invented.

The harmony and the grace of Coreggio are proverbial: the medium which, by breadth of gradation, unites two opposite principles, the coalition of light and darkness, by imperceptible transition, are the element of his style. This inspires his figures with grace, to this, their grace is subordinate: the most appropriate, the most elegant attitudes were adopted, rejected, perhaps sacrificed to the most awkward ones, in compliance with this imperious principle, parts vanished, were absorbed, or emerged in obedience to it. This unison of the whole predominates over all that remains of him, nor have his imitators attained the same effect. The harmony of Coreggio, though assisted by exquisite hues, was entirely independent of colour; his great organ was chiaroscuro in its most extensive sense: compared with the expanse in which he floats, the effects of Leonardo da Vinci are little more than the dying ray of evening, and the concentrated flash of Giorgione, discordant abruptness. The bland central light of a globe, imperceptibly gliding through lucid demi-tints into rich reflected shades, composes the spell of Coreggio, and affects us with the soft emotions of a delicious dream.

Though, perhaps, we should be nearer the truth by ascribing the cause of Coreggio's magic to the happy conformation of his organs, and his calm serenity of mind, than to Platonic ecstasies, a poet might at least be allowed to say, "that his soul, absorbed by the contemplation of infinity, soared above the sphere of measurable powers, knowing that every object whose limits can be distinctly perceived by the mind, must be within its grasp; and, however grand, magnificent, beautiful, or terrific, fall short of the conception itself, and be less than sublime." In this, from whatever cause, consists the real spell of Coreggio. He is, no doubt, in the whole of his character, one of those very few artists of the first class; and, not to mention any other of his admirable works, his picture of St. Jerome, in the academy of Parma, is, as far as it goes, and for an agreeable union of all the parts of the art, perhaps superior to any other picture in the world.

In the invention of this work, which exhibits St. Jerome presenting his translation of the Scriptures by the hand of an angel, to the infant seated in the lap of the Madonna, the patron of the piece is sacrificed in place to the angelic group which occupies the middle. The figure that chiefly attracts, and has, by its suavity for centuries attracted, and still absorbs the general eye, is that charming one of the Magdalen, in a half-kneeling, half-recumbent posture, pressing the foot of the infant Jesus to her lips. By doing this, the painter has, undoubtedly, offered to the Graces the boldest and most enamoured sacrifice which they ever received from art.

FRA BARTOLOMEO DI ST. MARCO.

Fra Bartolomeo di St. Marco, (or Baccio Della Porta,) was born in the territory of Savignano, near Florence, in 1469. At an early age he was placed under Cosimo Roselli, at Florence, who happening to live near the gate of St. Peter, his pupil received the name of Baccio Della Porta. Here he continued for some years, studying the works of his master, and those of Leonardo da Vinci, whose grandeur of relief and chiaroscuro he greatly admired.

His early performances were small, but exquisitely finished. He gave a noble proof of his powers in the Last Judgment, painted in fresco, for the chapel of St. Maria Nuova. About this time he contracted an intimacy with the famous monk, Jerome Savanarola, who afterwards suffered at the stake, which circumstance so much affected the painter that he took the habit of St. Dominic, in 1500, and was afterwards called Il Frate.

In 1504, he became acquainted with Raphael, who instructed him in colouring, for which he received in return some lessons in perspective. Soon after this he went to Rome, where the works of Michael Angelo and Raphael both astonished and depressed him so much, that he was almost ready to abandon his art in despair. While here he only painted the two figures of St. Peter and St. Paul, which were long preserved in the Quirinal Palace.

On his return to Florence his spirits revived, and he painted several splendid altar-pieces for the churches of his order. His design approached that of Raphael; and he was even superior in boldness of relief, and strength of colouring. Among his most celebrated pictures was a St. Sebastian, a St. Mark, Marriage of St. Catharine, the Four Evangelists, and the Assumption. He died in his convent of St. Mark, in 1517.

MICHAEL ANGELO.

Michael Angelo Buonaroti, of the noble house of Canossa, was born in the year 1475, in the castle of Caprese, on the Arno. His predilection for art was so strong that he prevailed with his father to place him with Ghirlandaio. He early attracted the attention of Lorenzo de Medicis, who fostered his genius with a generosity and sympathy that the artist never forgot. Poet, painter, sculptor, and architect, he excelled in every branch of art; yet, in his declining days, he regretted not having devoted himself wholly to sculpture.

"The genius of this great man," says Opie, "made an entire change in modern art; to the little and meagre he gave grandeur and amplitude; to the confused and uninteresting he gave simplicity and effect; and to the feeble and unmeaning he stamped energy and character. Raphael, his greatest cotemporary and rival, thanked God for having been born in an age which boasted of such a man; and Reynolds, the greatest painter and critic of our times, prides himself on the capability of feeling his excellence, and declares that the slightest of his perfections ought to confer glory and distinction enough to satisfy an ambitious man."

Michael Angelo having observed the great deficiency of Albert

Durer's rules for drawing, resolved to write a complete treatise on the anatomy and proportions of the human figure, and to compose a theory founded on the knowledge and experience acquired by long practice, for the benefit of all future artists. That this resolution was never carried into effect must ever be regretted, as an incalculable and irreparable loss to the arts; for certainly never man, before or since, (at least in modern times,) was so perfectly qualified for the task.

He was indefatigable in his practice, and in the study both of nature and the works of the ancients, and this was continued through his whole life, even to extreme old age; the poorest of men, as he observed of himself, did not labour from necessity more than he did from choice; indeed, from all that is related of him, he appears not to have had the slightest conception that his art was to be acquired by any other means than incessant and unwearied diligence, though, as Sir Joshua Reynolds justly remarks, he, of all men that ever lived, might have advanced the strongest pretensions to the efficacy of genius and inspiration.

The principal work of Michael Angelo in the way of painting, consists of a series of pictures painted on the ceiling and part of the walls of the Pope's chapel, commonly called the Cappella Sistina. The subjects, (taken from the sacred records,) beginning with the Creation, and ending with the Last Judgment, seem to have been chosen for the purpose of exhibiting the history of man, as he stands in relation to the Creator, and of showing his origin, progress, and the final dispensations of Providence respecting him.

He avoids, on all occasions, a multiplicity of objects, and a multiplicity of parts. He knew, as a great critic has judiciously remarked, that, in poetry and painting, many little things do not make a great one; and he has, therefore, rejected all unnecessary subdivisions and unessential particularities; hence the bold swell and flow of his line, uninterrupted by useless breaks and petty inflections; hence the unincumbered breadth of his surfaces, on which the eye rests unfatigued and unperplexed by impertinent differences and trivial distinctions; and hence the fewness and largeness of the parts, both in respect to his figures and his compositions, at once so simple and so impressive.

The same method obtains with him in the intellectual as in the practical parts of the art. In his manner of conceiving his subject and telling his story, he equally avoids all petty and commonplace details of circumstances, ingenious artifices, unimportant shades of character, and merely curious varieties of expression, which arrest and attract the attention of the spectator, and weaken the force of the general effect: essence, not individuality; sentiment, not incident; man, not men, are his objects; and like the Satan and Death, of Milton, he meditates no second stroke, but hastens, by one sure blow, to effect his purpose.

As his profound knowledge of the human figure taught him what to reject, so it likewise taught and enabled him to mark the essential forms with unexampled force and precision: possessed himself, he instantly possesses the spectator with a complete idea of his object. As in the drawing of his figures there is more knowledge and precision, so in their actions and attitudes there is more vigour and unity than is seen in any other modern painter. By this is meant, that the situation and turn of every limb is more correspondent with the whole, is more perfectly informed with the same mind, and more exactly bears its part in the general feeling; and hence it is, that though Raphael often exceeds him in the variety of his characters, the particular expression of passion, and what may be called the dramatic effect of his pictures, yet, in giving the appearance of thought, capacity, and dignity, he is altogether unrivalled and unapproached

Unison of parts.—Derelictions, dangerous.

This perfect unity or concurrence of every feature, joint, and limb, in the same feeling, united to the breadth and boldness of his style of drawing, is what constitutes the intellectual energy of his figures, and gives them that air of inspiration and of belonging to a higher species of beings, which Sir Joshua Reynolds notices with such admiration. Wrapped and absorbed themselves, they instantly communicate the same sensations to the beholder, who, awe-struck while he gazes on them, dares not think them on a level and of the same rank with himself.

Such is his figure of the Creator, borne aloft on clouds, dividing light from darkness. Such when, descending on attendant spirits, he imparts the electric spark of vitality and immortality to the newly-formed Adam, or, with a word, calls forth the adoring Eve from the side of her sleeping mate. Such are the majestic forms of the prophets Isaiah, Ezekiel, Jeremiah, Zechariah, and Joel. And such, though wild and haggard, the form of the Cumean Sibyl, and many others, if not all, of that sublime and inimitable circle: all of them, more or less, in louder or lower tones, proclaim the imagination that conceived, and the hand that formed them, were divine. These are some of the principal features of the style of Michael Angelo; a style in which knowledge, energy, and simplicity bear equal parts; which unravels perplexity, gives the appearance of ease to difficulty, and imparts dignity and sentiment to every object it embraces. Though the sublime in poetry and painting so overpowers, and takes such absolute possession of the whole mind, that, while the work is before us, no room is left for the ungracious and ungrateful task of criticism, yet, in cooler moments, it cannot, it must not, be denied, that Michael Angelo had derelictions and deficiencies too great to be overlooked, and too dangerous to be excused; that he was sometimes capricious and extravagant in his inventions, and generally too ostentatious of his anatomical knowledge; that he wanted the vigorous tone of colour and force of chiaroscuro necessary to complete the effect of his design; and that, from aiming always to be great, he often violated propriety, neglected the proper discrimination of character, and not seldom pushed it into monotony and bombast. It has been pleaded, in mitigation, that great painters, like great poets,

> "sometimes gloriously offend,
> And rise to faults true critics dare not mend;"

that his errors flowed from the same source as his beauties; and were often such as none but himself was ever capable of committing, and such as could never have occurred to a mean or vulgar mind.

"Sublimity of conception, grandeur of form, and breadth of manner," says Fuseli, "are the elements of Michael Angelo's style. By these principles he selected or rejected the objects of imitation. As painter, as sculptor, as architect, he attempted, and above any other man succeeded, to unite magnificence of plan and endless variety of subordinate parts with the utmost simplicity and breadth. His line is uniformly grand; character and beauty were admitted only as far as they could be made subservient to grandeur. The child, the female, meanness, deformity, were by him indiscriminately stamped with grandeur. To give the appearance of perfect ease to the most perplexing difficulty, was the exclusive power of Michael Angelo. He is the inventor of epic painting, in that sublime circle of the Sistine chapel which exhibits the origin, the progress, and the final dispensations of theocracy. He has personified motion in the groups of the cartoon of Pisa; embodied sentiment on the monuments of San

Lorenzo; unravelled the features of meditation in the Prophets and Sibyls of the Sistine chapel; and, in the Last Judgment, with every attitude that varies the human body, traced the master-trait of every passion that sways the human heart. In painting he contented himself with a negative colour, and as the painter of mankind, rejected all meretricious ornament. The fabric of St. Peter, scattered into infinity of jarring parts by Bramante and his successors, he concentrated; suspended the cupola, and to the most complex, gave the air of the most simple of edifices. Such, take him all in all, was Michael Angelo, the salt of art."

RAPHAEL.

Raphael Sanzio d' Urbino, was born in 1483. At about the age of fourteen he became the pupil of Perugino, In this school he studied with indefatigable diligence, and imitated his master so closely that their works could hardly be distinguished, the one from the other; a circumstance, however, which only served to rivet the affection of Perugino more firmly for his scholar, while Raphael strove to repay his regard by unwearied assiduity and endeavours to excel.

Raphael had three styles: his Perugino, his Florentine, and his Roman.

The genius of Raphael was not of that phosphoric kind that blazes out of itself without foreign help. His manner, at the commencement of his career, was dry, minute, and hard to excess; precisely like that of his master, Pietro Perugino, in whose footsteps he appeared, for a time, to be going on, without a conception of his own powers, or those of the art. A visit to Florence, however, soon enabled him to leave his master at an humble distance. Seizing every opportunity of improvement, as he rolled on, he increased every moment in size and splendor; he mended his style of design, improved his colouring, and acquired composition. But it was not until after he had been introduced to the sight o' Michael Angelo's works, in the Capella Sistina, that he completely freed himself from the defects of his first manner. Henceforward his style of design became original, and truly his own; not the vehicle of those awe-creating and terrific energies, conceived only by Michael Angelo, nor of the more exquisite beauty and elevated refinement of the antique, but the medium of natural forms, well chosen, indeed, and united to an invention, expression, grace, and propriety such as, in an equal degree, never before or since fell to the lot of one man.

But however great and various his powers, his peculiar strength, that in which he has never yet been rivalled, and never can be surpassed, was expression. To this all his efforts tended; for this he invented, drew, and composed, and exhausted nature in the choice of subjects to display it: every effect of mind on matter, every affection of the human soul, as exhibited in the countenance, from the gentlest emotion to the utmost fury and whirlwind of contending passions; from the demoniac phrensy of the possessed boy, in the transfiguration, to the melting rapture of the virgin mother contemplating her divine offspring, may be found so faithfully and energetically represented on his canvass, that we not only see, but feel, and are, by irresistible sympathy, made partakers of his well-imaged joys and sorrows. By this he attracts every eye, warms every heart, and sways it to the mood of what he likes or loathes. This is what has made him, if not the greatest, certainly the most interesting and the most universally admired of all modern painters, and rendered his name, in the general mouth, synonymous with perfection.

The history of no man's life affords a more encouraging and instructive example than that of Raphael. The path by which he ascended to eminence is open, and the steps visible to all. He began with apparently no very uncommon fund of ability; but, sensible of his deficiencies, he lost no opportunity of repairing them. He studied all the artists of his own and the preceding times; he penetrated all their mysteries, mastered all their principles, and grafted all their separate excellencies on his own stock. His genius, like fire, embraced and gathered strength from every object with which it came in contact, and at last burst forth in a flame, to warm, enlighten, and astonish mankind.

Perfect human beauty he has not represented; no face of Raphael's is perfectly beautiful; no figure of his, in the abstract, possesses the proportions that could raise it to a standard of imitation: form to him was only a vehicle of character or pathos, and to those he adapted it in a mode and with a truth which leaves all attempts at emendation hopeless. His invention connects the utmost stretch of possibility with the most plausible degree of probability, in a manner that equally surprises our fancy, persuades our judgment, and affects our heart. His composition always hastens to the most necessary point as its centre, and from that disseminates, to that leads back, as rays, all secondary ones. Group, form, and contrast are subordinate to the event, and commonplace is ever excluded. His expression, in strict unison with, and decided by character, whether calm, animated, agitated, convulsed, or absorbed by the inspiring passion, unmixed and pure, never contradicts its cause, equally remote from tameness and grimace; the moment of his choice never suffers the action to stagnate or expire; it is the moment of transition, the crisis big with the past and pregnant with the future. If separately taken, the line of Raphael has been excelled in correctness, elegance, and energy; his colour far surpassed in tone, and truth, and harmony; his masses in roundness, and chiaroscuro: in effect, considered as instruments of pathos, they have been equalled; but in composition, invention, expression, and the power of telling a story, he has never been approached.

"In Raphael's figures," says Barry, "the energy of action and expression always arises out of the occasion, and are happily and justly proportioned to it. This discretion appears often wanting in Michael Angelo. The energy and expression of his figures, cannot always be accounted for from the character and occasion; and even when they can, some of them appear to have more than the occasion calls for. Besides this admirable discretion and judgment, in which Raphael appears almost unique, (as Da Vinci has unavoidably done so little,) there is a general air of urbanity diffused over Raphael's figures, which seems to have been derived from his general observations on the antique statues and basso-relievos; I say, general observations, for indeed they appear nothing more, and he seems never to have paid much attention to an exquisite degree of beauty, or of elevated character. He however says, in a letter to Count Baldassare Castiglione: 'To paint a beautiful woman I must see several, with this condition, that your excellence may be near me to select the most beautiful. But as there are few good judges, and few beautiful women, I have recourse to a certain ideal in my mind.'"

GIORGIONE.

Giorgione Barbarelli del Castel Franco, was born at Castel Franco, in the Venetian territory, in 1478, and learned the art of painting from Giovanni Bellini, though in a few years he proved far superior to his master. He carefully studied the works of Leonardo da Vinci, and from them derived his first notions of the force of well-adapted lights and shadows, to add life and spirit to the figures; till, by frequent experiments, he produced such a new and animated style of colouring, as rendered him more admired than all the artists who had gone before him; and he still added to his taste and judgment by a diligent study of nature, which he imitated with remarkable fidelity in all his compositions. He was one of the first who observed the powerful effect of strong lights opposed by strong shadows, which he practised with astonishing success; and from him, Titian studied and improved that enchanting part of painting, till he excelled Giorgione. His taste in design is delicate, somewhat resembling that of the Roman school, though he frequently seems more attentive to the roundness, than the correctness of his figures. His pencil was light, easy, and free; his knowledge of chiaroscuro extensive; and his carnations had more the appearance of real flesh than of being a fine imitation of it. His landscapes, also, are exquisite; and he found out some secret to keep his colours fresh and lively, especially the greens.

Vasari thus descants on one of his productions: "In the school of San Marco he painted the story of the ship which conducts the body of St. Mark through a horrible tempest, with other barges assailed by furious winds; and besides, groups of aërial apparitions, and various forms of fiends, who vent their blasts against the vessels, that, by dint of oars and energy of arms, strive to force their way through the mountainous and hostile waves which threaten to submerge them. You hear the howling blast, you see the grasp and fiery exertion of the men, the fluctuation of the waves, the lightning that bursts the clouds, the oars bent by the flood, the flood broken by the oars, and dashed to spray by the sinews of the rowers. What more? In vain I labour to recollect a picture that equals the terrors of this; whose design, invention, and colour, make the canvass tremble! Often when he finishes, an artist, absorbed in the contemplation of parts, forgets the main point of a design, and as the spirits cool, loses the vein of his enthusiasm; but this man, never losing sight of the subject, guided his conceit to perfection."

The effect of this work, when it drew such a stream of eulogy from lips else so frugal in Venetian praise, may be guessed at from the impression it makes in its present decay; for even now, it might defy the competition of the most terrific specimens in chiaroscuro, the boat of Charon, in Michael Angelo's Last Judgment, perhaps only excepted.

PORDENONE.

Among the followers of Giorgione, one of the most celebrated was Il Pordenone. Though he had never visited Florence or Rome, he excelled in invention, design, spirit, mechanism of colour, rapidity of execution, powerful relief, and chiaroscuro. Other followers of Giorgione imitated more or less his manner, but Pordenone resembled him in genius and vigour. He painted many pictures, in oil colours, of great merit; but his greatest excellence was in fresco, in which he executed many works at Friuli, Mantua, Genoa, Cremona, and Florence. Some of them, it is true, like many others of the Venetian painters, are sketchy and almost slovenly; but still they exhibit a mind capable of grappling with all the difficulties of the art. Others again, such as those of St. Maria di Campagna, and the Sposalizio di St. Caterina in Piacenza, are carefully finished, and of the highest excellence, in colour, composition, and design. Indeed, he has carried force and brilliancy of colour as far as it is possible. In aërial perspective, he cannot be surpassed. His female figures are often strikingly beautiful, and his general forms noble and well defined. The keen rivalship between him and Titian, benefited both—a rivalship reflecting no small glory on Pordenone, as it secured to him the next place after Titian, in an age so fertile in great artists.

TITIAN.

Tiziano Veccelli, sometimes called Da Cadore, was born in 1480, at the castle of Cadore, in Friuli. He studied under Zuccati and Bellini. But the works of Giorgione, who arrived in Venice about the year 1507, so warmed and captivated him, by the unusual boldness and richness of his style, that immediately turning out of doors all that he had learned in the school of Bellini, he began afresh; and such was the assiduity with which he applied himself to the study and practice of the new manner, that from the humble imitator he very soon became the successful rival of Giorgione.

The style of Titian may be divided into three periods: when he copied; when he imitated; when he strove to generalize, to elevate, or invigorate the tones of nature. The first is anxious and precise, the second is beautiful and voluptuous, the third sublime.

"Titian in colouring," says Opie, "may be regarded as the father of modern art. He first discovered and unfolded all its charms, saw the true end of imitation, showed what to aim at, when to labour, and where to stop; and united breadth and softness to a proper degree of finishing. He first dared all its depths, contrasted all its oppositions, and taught colour to glow and palpitate with all the warmth and tenderness of real life ; fiee from tiresome detail or disgusting minutiæ, he rendered the roses and lilies of youth, the more ensanguined brown of manhood, and pallid coldness of age, with truth and precision ; and to every material object, hard or soft, rough or smooth, bright or obscure, opaque or transparent, his pencil imparted its true quality and appearance to the eye, with all the force and harmony of light, shade, middle tint, and reflection, by which he so relieved, rounded, and connected the whole, that we are almost irres.stibly tempted to apply the test of another sense, and exclaim,

> "Art thou not, pleasing vision! sensible
> To feeling as to sight?"

Though gifted with a perfect knowledge of all the qualities and powers of colour, he never overstepped the modesty of nature, and made that ostentatious and meretricious use of it so censurable in many of his followers. In his works, it is modest without heaviness, rich without glaring, and transparent without flimsiness. Like a great orator, he never sacrifices the end to the means, subjugates sense to sound, or diverts the attention of the spectator from the subject to himself.

At an early period he mounted the throne of portrait painting, where, in the opinion of many, he still keeps his seat, unshaken, notwithstanding the violent attacks made on him at different times, by Vandyke, Rembrandt, and Reynolds. He combines resemblance with dignity, costume with taste, and art with simplicity; and equally delights the physiognomist, the artist, the antiquary, and the connoisseur. He was the inventor of all that is simple and captivating, or sublime and energetic, in landscape; and, in short, his powers changed the whole appearance of modern colouring, and still continues to influence its style.

Titian, like his cotemporaries, began his career by merely copying nature, as she happened to present herself, without choice or selection, and laboured for a time in the labyrinth of littleness, meanness, and deformity; but a hint from Giorgione soon taught him that taste was as requisite as industry, that labour might be misapplied, and truth itself become uninteresting, unnatural, and disgusting; that hairs, pores, pimples, warts, stains, freckles, and all the train of nauseous minutiæ, on which inferior artists waste their puny powers, are incompatible with the true end of imitation; that the detail must be sunk in the essential and predominant qualities of bodies; and that the business of painting, like that of poetry, is not to give a feeble catalogue of particulars, but a characteristic, comprehensive, and animated impression of the whole. By the operation of this principle, extended from the parts to the individual, from the individual to the group, and thence to the entire composition, he reached the last and greatest excellence of colouring—that of giving the ruling passion or sentiment of his subject in the prevailing tone or predominant hue of his piece.

From Titian we may learn what may be usefully applied, not only to artists, but to men in all situations, and to all professions—that it is never too late to improve; for at the age of seventy, and considerably upwards, we find him still rapidly advancing in his art. He had, it is true, at an early period, acquired breadth and grandeur in respect to colour, but he was not so happy as to burst the shackles of meanness and emancipate himself from littleness, in respect to design, character, and invention, till very late in life. All obstacles, however, at length gave way to his powers and perseverance, and his latter works are not only remarkable for the most truly historic and awful tones of colour, for a freedom and felicity of execution beyond even the great promise of his former time, but also a picturesque boldness and sublimity of conception, an energy of action and expression, and a learned and grand style of design, second to none but Michael Angelo. Those, therefore, who have seen the majestic figure of Abraham about to offer up Isaac, his Cain and Abel, h.s David adoring over the headless trunk of Goliah, and his astonishing picture of the Death of Peter the Martyr, in which there is very nearly a complete union of all the excellencies of the art, will judge of the infinite importance of appropriate colour and execution to design, and be ready to cry out, with a certain critic, that, "if Titian was not the greatest painter, he certainly produced the best pictures in the world." Nature and fortune were equally kind to Titian; he had not to complain of having fallen on evil days and evil tongues. Honoured by the great, and his society courted by all the eminent men of his time, Titian was not more happy in his genius than in all the circumstances of his life, which, prolonged to an almost patriarchal extent, in uninterrupted health and with little abatement of vigour, was brought at last to a period by the plague, at the end of ninety-nine years.

Titian laboured first to make fac-similes of the stuffs he copied, before he changed them into drapery, and gave them local value and a place. He learned first to distinguish tint from tint, and give the skeleton of colour, before he emboldened himself to take the greatest quantity of colour in an object for the whole: to paint flesh which abounded in demi-tints, entirely in demi-tints; and to deprive of all, that which had but a few. It was in the school of deception he learned the difference of diaphanous and opaque, of firm and juicy colour; that this refracts and that absorbs the light ; and hence their place, those that cut and come forward first, and those which more or less partake of the surrounding medium, in various degrees of distance. It was here he learned the contrast of the tints, of what is called warm and cold, and, by their balance, diffusion, echo, to poise a whole. His eye as musical—if I may be allowed the metaphor—as his ear, abstracted here, that color acts, affects, delights, like sound ; that stern and deep-toned tints rouse, determine, invigorate the eye, as warlike sound or a deep base the ear ; and that bland, rosy, grey, and vernal tints, soothe, charm, and melt, like a sweet melody.

Such were the principles whose gradual evolution produced that coloured imitation, which, far beyond the fascination of Giorgione, irresistibly entranced every eye that approached the magic of Tiziano Veccelli. To no colourist, before or after him, did Nature unveil herself with that dignified familiarity in which she appeared to Titian. His organ, universal and equally fit for all her exhibitions, rendered her simplest, and her most compound appearances with equal purity and truth. He penetrated the essence and the general principle of the substances before him, and on these established his theory of colour. He invented that breadth of local tint which no imitation has attained, and first expressed the negative nature of shade. His are the charms of glazing, and the mystery of reflexes, by which he detached rounded, corrected, or enriched his objects. His harmony is less indebted to the force of light and shade, or to the artifices of contrast, than to a due balance of colour, equally remote from monotony and spots. His tone springs out of his subject—grave, gay, minacious, or soothing; his eye tinged nature with gold, without impairing her freshness, and she dictated his scenery. Landscape, whether it be considered as the transcript of a spot, or the rich combination of congenial objects, or as the scene of a phenomenon, as subject and as background, dates its origin from him. He is the father of portrait painting, of resemblance with form, character with dignity, and costume with subordination.

TINTORETTO.

Giacomo Tintoretto was born in Venice, in 1512. He was the pupil of Titian, who became so jealous of his powers that, it is said, he dismissed him from his school.

Tintoretto formed the plan of establishing a new school of art, by uniting the beauties of the Venetian harmony of colours with the Florentine dignity of design. The idea was a noble one, but though he partly succeeded, he failed in carrying his project to perfection, by the want of patience in the exercise of his talent. No less fertile in conception, than prompt in execution, his works rose with magical illusion under his rapid pencil. He was called the Furious Tintoretto, and the Lightning of the Pencil.

His manner of painting was bold, with strong lights opposed by deep shadows; his pencil wonderfully firm and free; his disposition good; his execution easy; and his touch lively, and full of spirit. His local colours are true and well understood, and the carnations of his best pictures approach near to those of Titian.

"Of all the extraordinary geniuses," says Vasari, "who have practised the art of painting, for wild, capricious, extravagant, and fantastical inventions, for furious impetuosity and boldness in the execution of his works, there is none like Tintoretto; his strange whimseys are even beyond extravagance, and his works seem to be produced rather by chance than in consequence of any previous design."

The nocturnal studies of Tintoretto from models and artificial groups, have been celebrated; these, prepared in wax or clay, he arranged, raised, suspended, to produce masses, foreshortening, and variety of effect. It was thence he acquired that decision of chiaroscuro unknown to more expanded daylight, by which he divided his bodies, and those wings of obscurity and light, by which he separated the groups of his composition; though the mellowness of his eye nearly always instructed him to connect the two extremes by something intermediate, that partook of both, as the extremes themselves by the reflexes with the background of the scenery. The general rapidity of his process, by which he baffled his competitors, and often overwhelmed himself, did not, indeed, always permit him to attend deliberately to this principle, and often hurried him into an abuse of practice, which, in the lights, turned breadth into mannered or insipid flatness, and in the shadows, into total extinction of parts. Of all this he has, in the schools of San Rocco and Marco, given the most unquestionable instances; the Resurrection of Christ and the Massacre of the Innocents, comprehend every charm by which chiaroscuro fascinates its votaries. In the Vision, dewy dawn melts into deep but pellucid shade, itself rent or reflected by celestial splendor and angelic hues: while in the Infant Massacre at Bethlehem, alternate sheets of stormy light and agitated gloom, dash horror on the astonished eye. His stormy brush swept individual woe away in general masses. Two immense wings of light and shade divide the composition, and hide the want of sentiment in tumult.

He pursued, however, another method to create, without more assistance from chiaroscuro than individual light and shade, an effect equivalent, and perhaps superior to what the utmost stretch of his powers could have produced. In the Crucifixion, of the

Albergo, the ominous, terrific, and ensanguined hue of the whole—the disastrous twilight, that indicates some more than mortal suffering, electrifies the spectator at the first glance, and is such an instance of the powerful application of colouring to expression, as has probably never been exceeded, except by Rembrandt, in the bloodless, heart-appalling hue, spread over his Belshazzar's Vision of the Handwriting on the Wall.

Tintoretto died in the year 1594.

PAUL VERONESE.

Paolo Cagliari, usually called Paul Veronese, was the son of a sculptor at Verona, and was born there, in the year 1532. He studied painting under his uncle, Antonio Badile; but among all the eminent artists of his time, he attached himself most to the manner of Titian. His composition was grand, his designs noble, and executed with truth and spirit; yet some critics think there is a want of delicacy in his expression, either of the subject in general, or of the passions, though taken from nature. The draperies of his figures are modern, after the fashion of his day, or the modes of such eastern people as resorted to Venice. But they are grand, rich, lively, and diversified; and Sandrart observes, that in the distribution of the folds, he adhered in some degree to the manner of Durer, whose designs he had studied in his youth. His heads are often graceful; but in the extremities of his figures, and the outlines of his naked forms, he is often incorrect, nor are his attitudes always well chosen. His works, however, display a lively imagination, fertile conception, a light and pleasing pencil, and a firm and spirited execution.

There is a delightful harmony in his tints, particularly in his draperies. One of his great faults was that of overloading his pictures with ornaments, and those frequently without due regard to the subjects represented.

For the whole economy and practical conduct of a picture, no man is more worthy attention. His tints, though often not equal in value to those of Titian, are, however, equally true, and necessarily much more variegated, from the great extent of his subjects. He has shown a most exquisite sensibility in according his almost endless variety of broken tints with the portions of pure vivid colour which accompany them; and the harmony resulting from all those variegated masses of colour, together with the light, easy, graceful, spiritual manner in which the whole is conducted, leaves nothing further to be wished for in this part of the art.

His taste was better adapted to large than small compositions; for though in the latter his merit in colouring and design was evident, yet in the former, he displayed all the fire of his imagination, and the fertility and magnificence of his invention. In most of his large works, he was either the associate or competitor of Tintoretto; nor was the pre-eminence of either ever determined. If Tintoretto was allowed to imitate nature with superior force and vivacity, and more truth of colour, Veronese was acknowledged to have a finer invention, more grace in his figures, more dignity in his characters, and more elegance.

Paul Veronese died in 1588, at the age of fifty-six.

THE CARACCI.

Lodovico Caracci was born at Bologna, in the year 1555. It is remarkable, that notwithstanding the pre-eminence which this great master attained, he was so unpromising at first as to receive the nick-name of Ox from his fellow-students. If he had less fire in his compositions than Annibale or Agostino, he surpassed them in grace, grandeur, and sweetness. In religious subjects, particularly, he excelled them both ; and, after the manner of his favourite Coreggio, he gave a wonderful grace to his Madonnas. Simplicity and elegance distinguished all his designs; his touch is lively, his expression good, the airs of his heads are graceful, his figures are marked with a fine outline, and his general composition is sublime. His breadth of light and shadow, the simplicity of his colouring, and the solemn effect of that twilight, which seems diffused over his pictures, is suited to the grave and dignified subjects he generally treated. In conjunction with Agostino and Annibale, he laid the foundation of that school, which has been so highly celebrated, and even to this time distinguished by the title of the Academy of the Caracci; and thither all students, who gave hopes of their becoming masters, resorted to be instructed in the true principles of painting. The Caracci taught freely those things that were proportionate to the talents and qualifications of their disciples.

Their academy was sometimes called the eclectic school, which by selecting the beauties, correcting the faults, supplying the deficiencies, and avoiding the extremes of the different styles, attempted to form a perfect system. But as the mechanical part was their only object, they did not perceive that the projected union was incompatible with the leading principle of each master.

It is observed that the manner of all the Caracci is the same; the only difference that can be perceived among them, seems to arise from their diversity of temper and disposition. Annibale had more fire, more boldness and singularity of thought than the others ; and his designs were more profound, his expressions more lively, and his execution firmer. His genius was better adapted to poetical and profane subjects than sacred; though when he attempted the latter he generally succeeded. His taste for composition was considerably promoted by his studies at Rome, as appears in the Farnesian Gallery; and though the design is loaded, yet it has so much elegance, that it often pleases even those whose critical judgment prevents them from approving it. His manner shows a mixture of the antique, of nature, and of the manner of Buonaroti. He forsook that of Bologna, and adopted the Roman manner entirely: the former was soft and mellow, and the latter more exact, but less delicate in the colouring; so that the pencilling in the last works of Annibale is neither so tender nor so agreeable as in his first. He had an admirable genius for landscape; the forms of his trees are fine, and in all his objects after nature there is a character that distinguishes them strongly.

Few of the pictures of Agostino are to be met with, and it is thought that several of those which he did finish, pass for the works of his brother, Annibale. The happy effect of the school of the Caracci is proved by many artists who were formed in it; among whom were Guido, Dominichino, Albano, Lanfranco, and others

GUIDO.

Guido showed in youth a rare talent for art; was proud and ambitious of distinction, and aspired to something new and grand. In consequence of a hint thrown out by Annibale, he resolved to adopt a style the very reverse of that of Caravaggio; instead of a concentrated and falling light, he chose one open and brilliant; to the fierce he opposed the tender; to his dusky colours, the clear and distinct; to his low and vulgar forms the beautiful, graceful, and select. Beauty, grace, and sweetness were his aim; and he sought them in design, touch, and colouring. He began by making use of white lead, (a colour dreaded by Lodovico,) from the conviction that it was durable, which turned out to be well founded. But it excited the scorn of his fellow-pupils, as if he had presumed to separate himself from the Caracci, and return to the feeble and nerveless manner of the past century. Nor was such remonstrance without effect; he adhered to the principles of his school, but tempered it by the admixture of more tenderness; and, by gradually increasing the latter quality, he reached, in a few years, that style of delicacy and sweetness which it was his object to attain. He had, consequently, two manners; the first, in the opinion of Malvasia, the more pleasing; the second, the more learned. In neither did he lose sight of the facility which conferred a charm on his works; and, above all, he delighted in beauty—more especially of youthful heads. His study of the beautiful was formed on select nature, Raphael, and the antique statues, medals, and gems. The Venus de Medici and Niobe were his favourite models. Nor did he overlook the beauties of Coreggio, Parmegiano, and Veronese. Like the Greeks, he formed an abstract and ideal beauty of his own, which he modified to suit his purpose. In copying from nature, which he occasionally did, he so improved and beautified it as to attract the highest admiration. The same principle he applied to drapery, and the nude. Neither grief, sadness, nor terror impairs the beauty of his figures; he turns them on every side, places them in every attitude, yet they are still beautiful. What variety in his beauty—in the airs of his heads, the style of the hair, the folds of the drapery, the arrangement of the veils and vestments! He shows equal variety in the heads of old men, animating them with bold and expressive touches, and few lights. Some of his paintings are of inferior merit, not from want of ability, but from carelessness and haste, to supply his losses at play, to which he was much addicted. Yet with all his genius and excellence, it must be confessed, that the constant repetition of sweetness and smiles, however varied, wearies the eye and palls upon the taste. If Caravaggio went to the extreme in coarseness, materialism, and fierceness, he goes to the other in ideality, beauty, and delicacy.

DOMINICHINO.

Dominichino (Domenico Zampicri) seemed at first of a sluggish genius, but was profound, accurate, and diligent. He is correct in design, true in colouring, rich in impasto, and learned in the theory of the art. After some years study in Bologna, he visited Parma, and went to Rome, where Annibale, having completed his instruction, placed him among his assistants. Like Paul Veronese, he introduced beautiful and appropriate architecture. His compositions, attitudes, and expressions are so true to nature, that they tell their own story without the help of an interpreter. Among his most celebrated works are the Flagellation of St. Andrew, the Communion of St. Girolamo, and the Martyrdom of St. Agnes. The St. Girolamo is generally reckoned the best picture in Rome, after Raphael's Transfiguration. An imitation of Coreggio may be detected in his attitudes, but the forms are different. If he excels in oil-colours, he is still greater in fresco. Incredible as it may seem, such works were so vilified and abused by his cotemporaries, that he was thrown out of employment, and on the point of abandoning painting for sculpture. In invention he was not so great as in the other branches of the art. Diffident of his own powers, he was in the practice of borrowing from other masters, some not the most eminent, which exposed him to the bitter censure of his rivals, and the imputation of plagiarism. Lanfranco, his chief detractor, made a parade of his own fertility of invention and celerity of execution, contrasted with the slowness and irresolution of his rival. But if Dominichino was an imitator, he was not a servile one; if he was slow in execution, his works have stood the test of time and impartial criticism; while those of his detractors have fallen to their proper level, his, have proportionably risen in estimation.

ALBANI.

Francesco Albani adopted the same principles, and trod the same path, as his intimate friend Dominichino. They resembled each other in general style and colouring, only the carnations of Albani were deeper, and his colours less affected by his grounds. In originality of invention he is superior to Dominichino; and in representing females and children he surpasses, in the opinion of Mengs, every other painter. He delighted in subjects from the ancient mythology: Venus asleep, Diana in the Bath, Danaë, Galatea and her Sea Nymphs, Europa, &c. He was designated the Anacreon of painting. He occasionally veils his subjects in an ingenious allegory, as in the Four Ovals of the Elements, in the Borghese Palace, which he repeated in the Royal Gallery of Turin. His pictures were frequently of the cabinet size. He was husband of a beautiful wife, and the father of a numerous family, remarkable for their beauty, who were always at hand to furnish him with models. He introduced architecture and landscape, the latter full of verdure, freshness, and serene beauty He often repeated his compositions, making his pupils copy them, and afterwards retouching them with his own hand. His religious pieces were few, and in the same taste; troops of ministering angels supplied the place of the cupids. The school of his rival, Guido, censured his style as weak and effeminate, inelegant in his male, and monotonous in his youthful figures. There are, however, several of his paintings in oil as well as fresco, in different parts of Italy, at Florence, Bologna, Osimo, Rimini, &c, which prove that he had the talent for works of a higher style, though his inclination led him to an humbler department.

POUSSIN.

Nicolas Poussin was born at Audely, in Normandy, in the year 1594; and though a Frenchman, was grafted on the Roman stock. He studied under Quintin Varin, a French painter of mediocrity. He found on his arrival in Italy, that he had more to unlearn than to follow, of his master's principles, renounced the national character, and not only, with the greatest ardour, adopted, but suffered himself to be wholly absorbed by the antique. Such was his attachment to the ancients, that it may be said he less imitated their spirit, than copied their relics, and painted sculpture; the costume, the mythology, the rites of antiquity, were his element; his scenery, his landscapes, are pure classic ground. He has left specimens to show that he was sometimes sublime, and often in the highest degree pathetic; but history, in the strictest sense, was his property, and in that he ought to be followed. At first he endeavoured to imitate the colouring of Titian; but when he became an enthusiastic admirer of Raphael and the antique, his tone altered, and his carnations had no longer the warmth which distinguished his early productions.

In perspective and architecture he was perfectly accomplished; and this enabled him to give a captivating air of grandeur to his landscapes, the scenes and situations of which were highly pleasing, and received peculiar beauty from the novelty of the objects introduced, the variety of the trees, buildings, and other ornaments; every part being lightly and delicately touched, and exhibiting equal truth and judgment. By his predominant attachment to the antique, the historical compositions of Poussin are very accurate, and the airs and attitudes of his figures are also generally beautiful, though not always graceful; for by neglecting to study nature with due attention, his forms want that variety which alone gives entertainment and delight. It is remarked by a judicious critic, that, "though Poussin abstracted the theory of his proportions from the antique, he is seldom uniform and pure in his style of design, ideal only in parts, and oftener so in female than in male characters; he supplies antique torsoes with limbs and extremities transmitted from the model. As a colourist he was extremely unequal; into the Deluge and the Plague of the Philistines he transfused the very hues of the elements whose ravages he represented, while numbers of his other pictures are deformed by crudity and patches. His excellence in landscape is universally acknowledged, and when it is the chief object of his picture, precludes all censure; but considered as the scene or background of an historic subject, the ease with which he executed, and the predilection which he had for it, often made him give it an importance which it ought not to have; it divides our attention, and from an accessory becomes a principal. Poussin died at Rome, in 1665, aged seventy-one.

CLAUDE LORRAINE.

Claude Gélée was born at Lorraine, in 1600, but is usually ranked among Italian artists. In the early part of his life he showed no symptoms of that astonishing genius, which, in his more advanced years, attracted the admiration of the world. He was very little indebted to any master for instruction, except Angostino Tassi, from whom he learned the rules of perspective, and the method of preparing his colours. But though at first he with difficulty comprehended the rudiments of his art, yet in the progress of his studies his mind expanded, his ideas improved, his imagination became more lively, and his industry was indefatigable. He searched for true principles, by an incessant examination of nature, usually studying in the open fields, where he frequently continued from sunrise till the dusk of the evening, sketching whatever he thought beautiful or striking. Every curious tinge of light, on all kinds of objects, he marked in his sketches with a similar colour, by which means he gave his landscapes such an appearance of nature, as has rarely been equalled by any artist.

Sandrart relates that Claude used to explain to him, as they walked through the fields, the causes of the different appearances of the same prospect, at different hours of the day, from the reflections or refractions of light, from dews or vapours in the evening or morning, with all the precision of a philosopher. He worked on his pictures with great care, endeavouring to bring them to perfection by touching them over and over again; and if the performance did not answer his idea, he would alter, deface, and repaint it several times, till it corresponded with the image pictured in his mind. But whatever struck his imagination while he observed nature abroad, was so strongly impressed on his memory, that on his return home he never failed to make the happiest use of it. His skies were warm and full of lustre, and every object is properly illumined. His distances are admirable, and in every part a delightful union and harmony never fail to excite our admiration. His invention is pleasing, his colouring delicate, and his tints have such an agreeable sweetness and variety as to have been but imperfectly imitated by the best subsequent artists, and have never been equalled. He frequently gave an uncommon tenderness to his unfinished trees, by glazing; and in his large compositions, which he painted in fresco, he was so exact, that the distinct species of every tree might readily be distinguished.

SALVATOR ROSA.

This famous painter was born at Naples, in 1614. He was brought up with Francesco Francanzano, a painter to whom he was related; but while with him, was forced, for a livelihood, to sell his drawings about the streets. But after he became celebrated, he would sell none of his paintings but at an exorbitant price. A person of great wealth had been long treating with him for a large landscape, and every time he came Salvator raised the price one hundred crowns. The gentleman expressed his surprise, but the painter told him that with all his riches he could not purchase it, and to put an end to his importunities, destroyed the picture before his eyes.

He lived to the age of 59. In the sister arts of poetry and painting, he was esteemed one of the most excellent masters that Italy produced in the seventeenth century. In the former, his province was satire; in the latter, landscapes, battles, and seaports with figures. Though the talent of Salvator was principally adapted to small pictures, he filled one of a large size with strikingly sublime objects, of which the Conspiracy of Cataline, in the gallery of Florence, is a proof. But his great excellence lay in landscape; and he delighted in representing scenes of desolation, solitude, and danger; gloomy forests, rocky shores, lonely dells leading to caverns of banditti, Alpine bridges, trees scathed by lightning, and skies lowering with thunder. His figures are wandering peasants, forlorn travellers, shipwrecked sailors, or robbers intent upon prey. He also painted sorcerers and apparitions, of which the principal is the Witch of Endor.

Flemish, Dutch, and Spanish Schools.

THE Flemish school is characterized by splendor of colour, magical chiaroscuro, and learned design; by grandeur of composition, a certain nobleness of air, and strong and natural expression. Such qualities are confined to those artists who devoted themselves to the historical, but as the Flemish school was equally eminent in the subordinate departments, its characteristics, as regards the latter, are nearly identical with the Dutch school, recognizing as their sole guide, individual and common nature—often the lowest and ugliest In chiaroscuro, and all the requisites of harmony of colour, they equal the excellence of the Flemish and Venetian schools. In impasto, delicacy of touch, contrast, and gradation of tints, exemplified in their treatment of marine-pieces, landscapes, and animals, the Dutch school has not a rival.

Until lately, the Spanish school was little known or appreciated. To those who have not had an opportunity of seeing the *chefs-d'œuvre* of the great masters of Spain, the extensive gallery of Spanish pictures, established by Louis Phillipe, of France, must be particularly interesting. It contains a miscellaneous collection of the different masters, including specimens of Murillo, Morales, Zurbaran, Ribera, Cano, Herrera, Gomez, &c. The moment we enter, we feel that we are among a new people, whose life and character are strongly depicted in the works before us. Every thing bespeaks a grand and solemn nation—the dignified outlines, the monastic saints, the melancholy beauties, the proud forms of the men, the stern severity, the dark and vigorous chiaroscuro—all breathing the sad and solemn legends of history.

DURER.

Albert Durer was born at Nuremburg, in 1471. As an engraver, he is generally allowed to have been the best of his time; but as a painter, it is observed that he studied only nature in her unadorned state, without attending to those graces which that study might have afforded him, by a judicious choice. His imagination, however, was lively, his composition grand, his execution happy, and his pencil delicate. He finished his works with exact neatness, and was particularly excellent in his Madonnas, but would have done better if he had not encumbered them with heavy draperies. Though he surpassed the painters of his own nation, he could not avoid their defects—such as dryness and formality in the outlines, the want of a just degradation of the tints, an expression without agreeableness, and draperies broad in their folds, but stiff in the forms.

Ingenuity.—Colour.—Father of the German school.

"The indiscriminate use of the words genius and talent," says Fuseli,* "has perhaps nowhere caused more confusion than in the classification of artists. Albert Durer was, in my opinion, a man of great ingenuity, without being a genius. He studied, and as far as his penetration reached, established certain proportions of the human frame, but he did not invent a style; every work of his is a proof that he wanted the power of imitation, of concluding from what he saw to what he did not see, that he copied rather than selected the forms that surrounded him, and without remorse tacked deformity and meagreness to fulness, and sometimes to beauty. Such is his design. In composition, copious without taste, anxiously precise in parts, and unmindful of the whole, he has rather shown us what to avoid than what to follow. He sometimes had a glimpse of the sublime, but it was only a glimpse: the expanded agony of Christ on the Mount of Olives, and the mystic conception of his figure of Melancholy, are thoughts of sublimity, though the expression of the last is weakened by the rubbish he has thrown about her. His Knight, attended by Death and the Fiend, is more capricious than terrible; and his Adam and Eve are two common models shut up in a rocky dungeon. If he approached genius in any part of art, it was in colour. His colour went beyond his age, and as far excelled in truth and breadth of handling, as Raphael excels him in every other quality. I speak of easel-pictures. His drapery is broad, though much too angular, and rather mapped than folded. Albert is called the father of the German school, though he neither reared scholars, nor was imitated by the German artists of his or the succeeding century."

* Many of the criticisms on the works of the Old Masters in this volume, are adopted from Fuseli.

RUBENS.

Peter Paul Rubens was, according to some accounts, a native of Antwerp; but others say, that his father removing to Cologne, to avoid the calamities of a civil war, his son was born there, in 1577. His family was respectable, and he received a very liberal education. Discovering an early turn for painting, he attached himself to Otho Venius, or Octavio Van Veen, who was a man of learning, an accomplished artist, and of an amiable disposition. From this preceptor Rubens acquired that taste for allegory which distinguished him so remarkably through life, though it certainly did not constitute his highest merit. After continuing with this instructor for four years, he was told very candidly by him that he could teach him no more, and that nothing remained for his improvement but a journey to Italy.

Endowed with a full comprehension of his own character, he wasted not a moment on the acquisition of excellence incompatible with its fervour, but flew to the centre of his ambition, Venice, and soon compounded from the splendor of Paolo Veronese and the glow of Tintoretto, that florid system of mannered magnificence which is the element of his art, and the principle of his school. He first spread that ideal pallet, which reduced to his standard the variety of nature, and once methodized, while his mind tuned the method, shortened or superseded individual imitation.

Rubens is not one of those regular and timid composers, who escape censure and deserve no praise. He produces no faultless monsters; his works abound with defects, as well as beauties, and are liable, by their daring eccentricities, to provoke much criticism. But they have, nevertheless, that peculiar property, always the companion of true genius, that which seizes on the spectator, commands attention, and enforces admiration in spite of all their faults.

The productions of Rubens seem to flow from his pencil with more than freedom, with prodigality—his mind was inexhaustible, his hand was never wearied; the exuberant fertility of his imagination was, therefore, always accompanied by a correspondent spirit in the execution of his work:

> "Led by some rule which guides but not constrains,
> He finish'd more through happiness than pains."

No man ever more completely laid the reins on the neck of his inclinations—no man ever more fearlessly abandoned himself to his own sensations, and depending on them, dared to attempt extraordinary things, than Rubens. To this, in a great measure, must be attributed that perfect originality of manner, by which the limits of the art may be said to be extended. Endowed with a full comprehension of his own character, he waited not a moment for the acquisition of what he perhaps deemed incompatible excellence—his theory once formed, he seldom looked abroad for assistance; there is, consequently, in his works, very little that appears to be taken from other masters, and if he has occasionally stolen any thing, he has so well digested and adapted it to the rest of his composition, that the theft is not discoverable. But though it must be allowed that he possessed, in many respects, the true art of imitation; though he looked at nature with a true painter's eye, and saw at once the characteristic feature by which every object is distinguished, and rendered it at once on canvass with a vivacity of touch truly astonishing; though his powers of grouping and combining his objects into a whole, and forming his masses of light and shade, and colour, have never been equalled; and though the general animation and energy of his attitudes, and the flowing liberty of his outline, all contribute to arrest the attention, and inspire a portion of that enthusiasm by which the painter was absorbed and carried away—yet the spectator will at last awake from the trance, his eyes will cease to be dazzled, and then he will not fail to lament that such extraordinary powers were so often misapplied, if not entirely cast away; he will inquire why Rubens was content to want so many requisites to the perfection of art; why he paid no greater attention to elegance and correctness of form—to grace, beauty, dignity, and propriety of character; why every subject, of whatever class, is equally adorned with the gay colours of spring, and every figure in his compositions indiscriminately fed on roses. Nor will he be satisfied with the ingenious, but surely unfounded apology, that these faults harmonize with his style, and were necessary to its complete uniformity; that his taste in design appears to correspond better with his colouring and composition, than if he had adopted a more correct and refined style of drawing; and that, perhaps, in painting, as in personal attractions, there is a certain agreement and correspondence of parts in the whole together, which is often more captivating than mere regular beauty.

His universality is another striking trait in the character of Rubens. In the smallest sketch, the lightness and transparency of his touch and colour are no less remarkable than the sweeping rapidity and force of his brush in his largest works; and in all kinds of subjects, he equally keeps up his wonted superiority. His animals, particularly his lions and horses, are so admirable, that it may be said that they were never properly, at least poetically, painted but by him. His portraits rank with the best works of those painters who have made that branch of art their sole study. The same may be said of his landscapes; and, though Claude Lorraine finished more neatly, as became a professor of a particular branch, yet there is such an airiness and facility in the landscapes of Rubens, that a painter would as soon wish to be the author of them as of those of Claude, or any other artist whatever.

Rubens, like Titian, was caressed, honoured, employed, and splendidly rewarded by several crowned heads, and even deputed, in a ministerial capacity, by the king of Spain, to make confidential overtures to the court of London, where he was knighted by Charles I., and had every possible mark of respect shown to him, on account of his unrivalled excellence in his profession. At his return to Flanders he was honoured with the post of secretary of state, and in that office he continued till his death, which was brought on by the gout, at the age of sixty-three. He is said to have shown the ruling passion strong in death, lamenting that he should be taken off just as he had begun to be able to paint, and understand his art. He died in 1640.

REMBRANDT.

Rembrandt Van Ryn was born at a village near Leyden, in 1606. His real name was Gerretsz, but he obtained that of Van Ryn from the place where he spent the youthful part of his life, which was on the borders of the Rhine. He was at first placed under Jacob Van Zwanenburg, with whom he continued three years, and gave such proofs of uncommon talents as surprised his instructor. After this he studied under Peter Lastman, but staid no longer than six months with him; and for the same length of time was the scholar of Jacob Pinas; from whom, it is said, he acquired that taste for strong contrasts of light and shadow, which he ever afterwards so happily cultivated. He, however, formed his own manner entirely, by studying and imitating nature, which he copied in its most simple dress, without any attention to elegance of choice. But though it was not his talent to select what was most beautiful or graceful, yet he had an amazing power of representing every object, with such truth, force, and life, as nothing but nature itself can equal. By the advice of a friend, Rembrandt was prevailed on to carry one of his first performances to the Hague, where he offered it to a dealer, who instantly gave him a hundred florins for the picture. This incident laid the foundation of his fortune; for it not only served to make the public acquainted with his abilities, but contributed to make him more sensible of his merit. His style of painting, in the first years of his practice, was very different from that of his latter time; for his early performances were finished highly, and with a neat pencil, resembling those of Mieris; but he afterwards assumed a style of colouring and handling as opposite to it as possible—strong, bold, and with a degree of astonishing force; in which he has not been excelled by any artist. As he advanced in the art, he took liberties with the pencil, wrought with all the broad fullness of the brush, and left the touch undisturbed; he even employed the stick, the pallet-knife, or his fingers accordingly as they were most capable of producing the effect he desired, when viewed at a proper distance. The invention of Rembrandt was very fertile, and his imagination lively and active; but his composition, notwithstanding its remarkable strength of expression, was destitute of grandeur; and though his genius was full of fire, yet he wanted elevation of thought, and had little or no notion of grace or elegance. It has been said, that if he had visited Rome, his taste would have been proportionably refined, and that the knowledge of the antique, added to his other eminent qualifications, might have produced a master equal to the most exalted character. This conclusion, however, may be doubted, when the prevalence of habit is considered; and that his mind was stored with gross ideas of objects, to which he had been familiarized from his infancy. It deserves observation, also, that though he furnished himself with the finest Italian prints, drawings, and designs—many of them taken from the antiques—he never improved his taste by the study of them. He had, indeed, more delight in contemplating his own repository of old draperies, armour, weapons, and turbans, which he jocularly called his antiques, than he ever felt from surveying the works of the Grecian artists, or the compositions of Raphael. His colouring is surprising and his carnations are as true, fresh, and perfect, as those in the works of Titian, or any other master; with this difference, that the colouring of Titian will admit of the nearest inspection, whereas that of Rembrandt must be viewed at a convenient distance: and then an equal degree of union and harmony may be observed in both.

Being at one time reproached for the boldness and roughness of his manner of laying on the colours, he replied, "I am a painter and not a dyer."

In richness and truth of colouring, in copiousness of invention and energy of expression he equalled the greatest of his predecessors; and whatever he attempted, he rendered with a degree of truth, of reality, of illusion, that defies all comparison. By these powers he seemed to be independent of his subject. It mattered not what he painted, his pencil, like the finger of Midas, turned every thing he touched into gold; it made defects agreeable, gave importance to trifles, and begat interest in the bosom of barrenness and insipidity itself.

But, though thus gifted to dwell with nature in her simplest retirement, he was no less qualified, with a master's hand anu poet's fire, to follow and arrest her in her wildest flights. All that was great, striking, and uncommon in her scenery, was familiar to him; yet he chiefly delighted in obscurity and repose. Mystery and silence floated round his pencil, and dreams, visions, witcheries, and incantations, he alone, with no less magic power, rendered probable, awful, and interesting. In short, so great and original were his powers, that he seems to be one who would have discovered the art had it never before existed.

Rembrandt, with all his powers, is a master whom it is exceedingly dangerous to imitate. His excellencies are so fascinating that we are apt first to forgive, and lastly, to fall in love even with his faults; or, at least, to think the former cheaply purchased with the incumbrance of the latter.

He was so exact in giving the true resemblance of the persons who sat to him, that he distinguished the predominant feature and character, in every face, without endeavouring to improve or embellish it. Many of his heads display such a minute exactness, as to show even the hairs of the beard, and the wrinkles of age; yet, at a proper distance, the whole has an astonishing effect, and every portrait appears as if starting from the canvass. Thus, a picture of his maid-servant, placed at the window of his house at Amsterdam, is said to have deceived the passengers for several days.

The etchings of Rembrandt are exceedingly admired, and collected with great care and expense, for the cabinets of the curious, in most parts of Europe. He had spirit in every stroke of the graver, as in the markings of his pencil; there seems not to be a single touch that does not produce expression and life.

Rembrandt died at Amsterdam, in 1674; or, according tc other accounts, in 1688

KUYP.

Albert Kuyp (or Cuyp) was the eldest son of Jacob Cuyp, the landscape painter, and was born at Dort, in 1606. He received no instruction but from his father, though his manner was very different, being abundantly neater; nor was his pencilling so rough and bold. The father principally adhered to one or two species of animals; but to Albert, oxen, sheep, cows, horses, fruit, landscape, smooth water, or ships and boats, were all equally familiar. He excelled in every thing that he attempted to represent, and painted every object in the same free and natural manner; always lovely and true in his colouring, as well as clear and transparent. He observed attentively even the particular times of the day, to express the various diffusions of light on his objects, with all the truth of nature; and in his pictures, the morning, attended with its mists and vapours, the clear light of noon, and the saffron-coloured tints of the evening, may readily be distinguished. He likewise excelled in moonlight pieces; some of them being so admirably expressed, that the glittering reflection of the lunar beams on the surface of the water, appears more like nature than an imitation of it. But though he painted every variety of scenery, whether of land or water, well, he enchanted most by his winter pieces.

His studies were entirely after nature; and most of his land scapes were sketched from scenery in or about the city of Dort He died at Dort, in 1667.

TENIERS.

David Teniers, the Young, as he is called, to distinguish him from his father, was born at Antwerp, in 1610, and was principally instructed by his father, David, whose taste of design he always followed; but he was afterwards the disciple of Adrian Brouwer; and he had also the advantage of receiving great improvement, particularly in colouring, from Rubens. At first his merit was so little regarded, that he was often under the necessity of going to Brussels to dispose of his pictures, on which occasions he was sometimes mortified to find the paintings of inferior artists preferred to his own. But this cloud dispersed when the Archduke Leopold William, chancing to see some of his pieces, was so struck with them, that he immediately appointed Teniers his principal painter, and made him one of the gentlemen of his bedchamber, presented him with a chain and medal of gold, and gave him the direction of his gallery.

He studied nature in every form; and as he generally composed his subjects from persons of low stations, he accustomed himself to frequent their meetings at sports, feasts, and pastimes, by which means he had an opportunity of remarking the simplicity of their manners, and the various actions, attitudes, characters, and passions of every age, and of both sexes. He had a lively invention and ready execution; his pencil is free and delicate; the touching of his trees is light and firm; his skies are admirable, and though not much varied, are clear and brilliant; and the expression of his figures, whether mirthful or grave, in anger or good humour, is uncommonly striking. His pictures are generally clear in all their parts, with a beautiful transparence; and he had the art of relieving his lights by the disposition of others, without employing deep shadows, which yet produced the intended effect very happily. This practice he is supposed to have derived from Rubens, who remarked, that strong oppositions were not always necessary to produce an effect in a picture, which observation that great artist knew to be just, from studying the colouring of Titian. Teniers was remarkable for another excellence, and that was the power of imitating the works of the greatest painters that Italy, or any other country, produced. The power of his pencil was incredible; he knew how to adapt it to a variety of eminent artists, whose touch and colouring were exceedingly difficult; and yet he gave to his imitations so strong a character of originality, as to leave it doubtful whether they were not really painted by the very artists, of whose manner of thinking, composing and pencilling, they were only imitations, or what the Italians call Pasticci. His principal subjects are landscapes, with small figures, corps-de-garde, merry-makings, fairs, shooting at butts, playing at bowls, and the diversions, sports, or occupations of villagers; but his small pictures are preferable to his large ones. Some connoisseurs have objected to Teniers, that his figures are short and clumsy, with too much sameness in their countenances and habits; but it ought to be considered that as he designed every object after the life, and formed his ideas from scenes with which he was most conversant, his forms are exactly those of his models. The pictures of Teniers are on a low scale of colour, but the reverse of insipidity, from the delicacy of execution, and the due degree of sharpness in the touches, which give character and animation. He was remarkably expeditious, and could finish a picture full of figures, and of the middle size, in one day. This accounts for the great number of his works, which, however, brought extraordinary prices. He died at Brussels, in 1694.

MURILLO.

Bartolomeo-Estevan Murillo, the greatest of all Spanish painters, was born at Seville, in 1613. He received his first instructions in the art from his relation, Juan del Castillo; but the latter having gone to settle at Cadiz, Murillo was obliged, for the means of subsistence, to have recourse to painting banners and small pictures for exportation to America. In that line he obtained full employment, and began to distinguish himself as an able colourist. He was still very young, when he happened to see some of the works of Pedro de Moya, which being painted in the style of Vandyke, inspired him with the desire of imitating that great artist. In 1646 he finished painting the little cloister of St. Francis, and the manner in which he executed it produced sentiments of the greatest astonishment among his countrymen. His picture of the Death of Santa Clara, and that of St. James distributing Alms, served to crown his reputation. In the first he showed himself a colourist equal to Vandyke; and in the second, a rival of Velasquez. They obtained him a multitude of commissions, which were not long in procuring him an independent fortune. His success, however, never led him to be careless of his reputation; he gradually perfected his manner, by giving more boldness to his pencil, and without abandoning that sweetness in his colouring, which distinguished him from all his rivals, increasing its strength, and giving greater freedom to his touch. To the greatest merits as an historical painter, Murillo joined that of equal excellence in flowers and landscape. All his works afford incontestable proofs of the perfection to which the Spanish school had attained, and the real character of its artists; for, as Murillo never quitted his native country, he could not be influenced by any foreign style; and this originality of talent places him in the first rank among the painters of every school. He has neither the charming dignity of Raphael, the grandeur of Caracci, nor the grace of Coreggio; but as a faithful imitator of nature, if he is sometimes vulgar and incorrect, he is always true and natural; and the sweetness, brilliancy, freshness, and harmony of his colouring, make us forget all his defects.

RUYSDAEL.

Jacob Ruysdael, was born at Haerlem in 1636, and though it is not known by whom he was instructed, yet it is said that at the age of twelve some of his productions surprised the best artists.

The merits of Ruysdael as a landscape painter are of the highest description. His grounds are agreeably broken; his skies are clear; his trees are delicately handled; every leaf is touched distinctly, and with great spirit. He perfectly understood the principles of chiaroscuro and perspective; his distances have always a fine effect, and his manner of light and shadow are distributed with such judgment, and contrasted with such harmony, that the eye and the imagination are equally delighted. His works are distinguished by a natural and pleasing tone of colour; a free, light, firm, and spirited pencil; and an agreeable choice of situations. His general subjects were views of the banks of rivers; hilly grounds, with natural cascades; a country interspersed with cottages and huts; solemn scenes of woods and groves, with roads through them; windmills and water-mills: but he rarely painted any subject without a river, brook, or pool of water, which he expressed with truth and transparency.

He likewise excelled in representing torrents and impetuous falls of water; in which subjects the foam of the one, and the pellucid appearance of the other, were described with force and grandeur. Most of the choice collections in England are adorned with the works of this master. He died in 1684.

BOTH.

John Both was born at Utrecht, in 1610, and was the disciple of Abraham Bloemart, who at the same time instructed Andrew, the brother of John. To perfect themselves in design the brothers went to Rome, where they resided many years. John excelled in landscape, in which he rose almost to the highest perfection; he made the style of Claude Lorraine his model; and his works are sometimes mentioned in competition with those of that great master. The warmth of his skies, the judicious and regular receding of his objects, and the sweetness of his distances, afford the eye a degree of pleasure, superior to that we feel in viewing the works of almost any other artist. The figures of his landscapes were inserted by his brother Andrew. The colouring of John Both obtained for him the distinction, which he still possesses, of being called Both of Italy. By some connoisseurs he is censured for having too much of the tawny in his colouring, and that his foliage is too yellow, approaching to saffron; but this is not a general fault in his pictures, and though some perhaps may be liable to that criticism, he corrected the error.

The two brothers assisted each other until the death of John, in 1650, when Andrew left Italy and settled in his native place, but he was so affected by the death of his brother that he survived him only a few years; dying in 1656.

Deschamps states that Andrew died in Italy, and that John returned to Utrecht, where he practised his art, and employed Polembourg in painting the figures.

BERCHEM.

Nicolas Berchem, (or Berghem,) was born at Haerlem, in 1624, and was taught the first principles of painting by his father, Peter Van Haerlem, an artist of no great note, who painted still-life. Nicolas, however, was afterwards successively the disciple of Grebber, Van Goyen, Mojaart, Jan Wils, and Weeninx. Berchem was distinguished for his landscapes and cattle. He possessed a clearness and strength of judgment, and a wonderful power and ease in expressing his ideas; and though his subjects were of the lower kind, yet his choice of nature was judicious, and he gave to every subject as much of beauty as it would admit. The leafing of his trees is exquisitely and freely touched; his skies are clear; and his clouds float lightly, as if supported by air. The distinguishing characters of his pictures are the breadth and just distribution of the lights; the grandeur of his masses of light and shadow; a natural ease and simplicity in the attitudes of his figures, expressing their several characters; the just gradations of his distances; the brilliancy and harmony, as well as the transparency, of his colouring; the correctness and true perspective of his design; and the elegance of his composition. One of his best pictures, was a view of a mountainous country, enriched with a variety of cattle, and painted for the chief-magistrate of Dort. At the same time the burgomaster bespoke a landscape of John Both, and agreed to pay eight hundred guilders to each artist; but to excite an emulation he promised to pay a considerable premium to the one whose performance should be adjudged the best. When they were finished, there appeared such an equality of merit in them, that the generous magistrate presented them with an equal sum above that he had agreed on. He died in 1689.

GOTTFRIED MIND.

This celebrated cat painter was born at Berne, in Switzerland, in 1768. We are not informed how his attention was first directed to the study and delineation of cats, and occasionally of bears, but he became devoted to them with that earnestness and zeal that always ensures success. He was termed the Raphael of cats. No painter before him had ever succeeded in representing with so much nature and spirit, the mingled humility and fierceness, suavity and cunning, which the appearance of this animal presents, or the grace of its various postures in action or repose. Kittens he particularly delighted to represent. He varied, almost to infinity, their fine attitudes, while at play around the mother, and represented their gambols with inimitable effect. Each of his cats, too, had an individual character and expression, and was, in fact, a portrait which seemed animated; the very fur appeared so soft and silky as to tempt a caressing stroke from the beholder.

In time, the merits of Mind's performances came to be so well understood, that travellers made it a point to visit him, and obtain, if possible, his drawings, which even sovereigns sought for, and amateurs treasured carefully in their portfolios.

His attachment was unbounded to the living animals he so much delighted to represent. Mind and his cats were inseparable

Minetta, his favourite, was always near him when at work, and he seemed to carry on a sort of conversation with her by gestures and by words. Sometimes his cat occupied his lap, while two or three kittens were perched on each shoulder, or reposed in the hollow formed at the back of his neck, while sitting in a stooping posture at his table. He would remain for hours in this position without stirring, for fear of disturbing the beloved companions of his solitude, whose complacent purring seemed to him an ample compensation for the inconvenience. Not at any time a good-humoured man, he was particularly surly if disturbed by visitors when thus situated.

Symptoms of madness having been manifested among the cats of Berne, in the year 1809, the magistrates gave orders for their destruction. Mind exhibited the greatest distress when he heard of this cruel mandate. He cherished his dear Minetta in secret; but his sorrow for the death of eight hundred cats, immolated to the public safety, was inexpressible, nor was he ever completely consoled. To soothe his regret, and as if to reproduce the victims with his pencil, he began to paint cats with increased diligence; and he amused himself during the long evenings of the ensuing winter by cutting chestnuts into miniature figures of cats and bears. These trifles were executed with such astonishing address, that, notwithstanding his dexterity, he was unable to supply the demand for them. His death took place at Berne, in 1814.

French School.

SIMON VOUET.

Simon Vouet is generally regarded as the founder of the French school. Many and conflicting are the opinions of his professional merit; and among his detractors, his countrymen are foremost and loudest. Felibien, one of his countrymen, and one of the most temperate, after enumerating the important works he painted, both in France and Italy, and the distinguished honours he received in both countries, mentions that Charles I. of England was so pleased with his pictures that he expressed a strong wish to have him in England. He continues, "Il ignorait la perspective, et ne savait ni l'union et l'amitié des couleurs, ni l'entente des ombres et des lumières. Ce qu'il y a de plus estimer dans les tableaux est la beauté et la fraîcheur de son pinceau." Lairesse, on the other hand, so learned in his principles and practice of colouring, says that Vouet was celebrated for his profound knowledge of the science of reflexes, in which he has not only surpassed all the French, but the Italians also. When director of the Academy of St. Luke at Rome, Vouet was much employed in that city, where many of his works may be found, particularly in the Barberini palace. His pictures, indeed, have always been esteemed in Italy; nor did that esteem cease after his death, for he was the only foreigner whom Armidei has placed among the celebrated painters of the seventeenth century, whose lives and portraits he published in quarto, at Rome, in 1731.

LE SIEUR.

Le Sieur exhibits first-rate genius in composition, design, and expression; but, in the generality of his pictures, his colouring is hard and crude, his chiaroscuro defective, and the general effect without keeping, or contrast. The few finished works which this great artist has left—such as the Preaching of St. Paul, and the Descent from the Cross, afford, in the opinion of M. Burtin, convincing proofs that he was in a fair way of becoming as great in colour as he was in design. Had not a premature death arrested his career before he had an opportunity of visiting Italy, he would, in all probability, have rivalled the first masters of the art. Nicolas Poussin and Claude Lorraine, though claimed by the French, are more properly classed under the Roman school, where they studied, practised, and passed the best part of their lives. Indeed Poussin was so disgusted with the bad taste of his countrymen, who could not appreciate his works, that he left France and settled in Italy.

CHARLES LE BRUN.

Charles Le Brun, of Scottish descent, likewise the pupil of Vouet, was the most eminent and popular painter of his time. In the higher qualities of the art, his works will not bear a comparison with Le Sieur. Yet he had great talent, a powerful and inventive genius, was intimately acquainted with all the branches of decorative art, and well versed in history and poetry. His manners were polished and agreeable. He wrote two treatises: one on physiognomy, and the other on the passions. He died at Paris, in 1690.

From the end of the seventeenth, to the concluding quarter of the eighteenth century, the French school, in common with the other schools of Europe, fell into comparative decline.

The recent French school took its rise from DAVID, and his pupils LE GROS, GERARD, GERODET, &c., but their celebrity has already greatly declined. David was born at Paris in 1750. His first great work was the Horatii and Curatii, which attracted much attention, and called forth the admiration of his countrymen. It was followed by Belisarius, and the Death of Socrates. He likewise distinguished himself in portrait. He produced a series illustrating the Coronation of Napoleon, besides numerous portraits of him as consul and emperor, particularly that representing him on horseback at the celebrated passage of the St. Bernard. During the reign of the hundred days, Napoleon conferred on him the command of the Legion of Honour. On the second restoration of Louis XVIII., he took refuge in Brussels, where he painted his Cupid and Psyche, and formed a school. He was a great and original artist, eminent in design, and full of energy, forcible, though hard and glaring in his colouring. In composition, attitude, and expression, he was rather strained and theatrical—faults which are less obvious to his countrymen than to strangers. Moreover his works embodying, as many of them do, the scenes of the Revolution, and the consular and imperial governments, must always possess an interest independent of their intrinsic merits.

Gros and Horace Vernet were the first to emancipate themselves from the style of David. Much it is true, of the vehement, theatrical, and glaring, still remains, but, on the whole, a very great and important revolution has been effected. Retaining the correct drawing of David and his school, they have improved his cold and harsh colouring, and have introduced into their compositions truth, energy, sentiment, and poetry. Among the principal artists of the modern school may be mentioned, DELAROCHE, INGRES, HORACE VERNET, PRUDHON, DELACROIX, ARY SCHEFFER, &c.

The German School of Painting.

THE present German school of painting is of very recent date. Forty years ago it had no existence ; it is only within a few years that its productions began to be known to other countries of Europe. It is founded partly on the old German school, from which it derives a certain hardness and precision of manner ; partly on the Italian, especially the older masters preceding Raphael ; with much that is original.

The German school comprehends the schools of Berlin, Dusseldorf, Munich, Stuttgard, Nuremburg, Augsburg, Ratisbon, Carlsruhe, Prague, and Vienna ; of which that of Munich is the most distinguished. The school of Munich, and that of Cornelius, are, in a manner, synonymous terms. All the artists are not his pupils, for many are his cotemporaries, yet he has mainly contributed to the grandeur and originality of historical painting. His powerful genius is equally great, whether he selects the romantic or the classical. His style is serene, chaste, and elevated —inspired by poetry, especially the Epic, which is his natural element. Schnorr is more Teutonic ; the romantic poetry of the heroic and chivalric times having impressed a decided character on his genius. His frescoes are distinguished for composition, grace, and delicate sentiment. He has occasionally painted in oil colours, but his chief occupation has been the composition of drawings for fresco painting. HENRY HERZ is devoted to sacred and Christian subjects; religious sentiment being the predominant character of his genius. His great work, which was exclusively confided to him by the king, is the series of frescoes from the Old Testament in the chapel of All Saints. In style they have a strong analogy to the works of Giotto and the older masters preceding Raphael, as well as the pictures and mosaic of the Lower Empire. His object is to represent religion in all its simplicity and solemnity, divested of human passion, and irrespective of beauty and grace, or the æsthetical principle of the antique. He has been engaged in completing his magnificent Last Supper in fresco, in the refectory of the Benedictine convent, whose church will be the basilica, now almost finished. HERR CASPER* is engaged on the interior of the temple, with a fresco of Stephen Stoned. One of the greatest compositions of the German school is the Combat of the Huns by KAULBACH, a pupil of Cornelius, painted for Count Raczynski, and now in his possession. This was followed by his grand work of the Destruction of Jerusalem.

The school of Düsseldorf excels in genre landscape, humorous subjects, and scenic representations of popular authors. It has likewise attained eminence in marine pieces, and architectural painting.

"The chief characteristic of the Düsseldorf school," says a contributor to a recent Bulletin of the Art-Union, "is the strict attention paid to the elementary principles of painting, and more particularly to drawing. The primary class consists of the very youngest beginners, who are employed, under the direction of a professor, in the simplest branches of instruction. After having

* 1848, Cleghorn.

acquired a certain degree of familiarity with the use of the crayon, and drawing objects in nature, the student prepares several drawings of plaster casts, carefully finished and modelled, which are presented for the inspection of a committee formed of the Faculty of the Academy, who have a session about twice in each month, and decide whether the candidate be sufficiently advanced to qualify him for a place in the next higher class—namely, the Antique school. For admission into the Antique class, it is necessary that the candidate should possess no inconsiderable knowledge in drawing. Skilful mechanical execution has but little weight in the decision of the judges. Some of the most slovenly drawings are sometimes preferred to those of a very exquisite finish. Accuracy of outline, and perfect acquaintance with the modelling of the object, are all-important; and the judges to whose criticism these drawings are submitted, are those who have passed through the same trials themselves, and whose experienced eyes not even the smallest inaccuracy escapes. One or two hours are usually devoted, daily, to a lecture on anatomy or perspective, alternately—Professor Mücke giving instructions in the former, and Professor Weigman in the latter department. The study of anatomy, as pursued in this school, is one peculiarly adapted to the purposes of artists. It has been much simplified of late years, and is strictly confined to that portion of anatomical knowledge which bears upon the external form. The lectures are amply illustrated, by drawings from the bones and muscles.

"During the winter, two hours are employed on each of the six evenings of the week, in drawing from the living model. For this purpose, subjects are provided by the academy. Several rows of benches are arranged in an amphitheatre, rising one above another, and so illuminated by gas, that the flame by which the model is lighted comes only from one point, and is thrown strongly upon his body, by means of a tin reflector. The drawings of the students are similarly lighted—there being a separate jet for each three or four persons, the light of which is so thrown as not to interfere with the lighting of the model. About ten or twelve hours are devoted to one drawing, and each professor takes his turn in the arrangement of the figure in a suitable position. This class is thrown open to all members of the academy—indeed, we do not know that it is closed to any artist.

"The greatest liberality prevails in the management of the entire establishment. A delightful relation exists between the professors and students; and previous to the late political disturbances, which have tended somewhat to disturb the general harmony of feeling, a charming 'esprit du corps' prevailed among the painters. Of late years there has been a line of distinction, too strongly marked, between the older and junior artists. This, however, was perhaps to have been expected, as the rapid increase of their numbers precludes the possibility of an universal acquaintance.

"There are three painting classes, independent of the landscape school, &c. Professors Sohn and Hildebrandt each have charge of one, and the director, Von Schadow, of the third or higher class. These classes are visited by their respective superintendents on alternate days. The professor examines the paintings of each student separately, points out the faults, and commends the merits, and these criticisms are always made with the models before him. After having attained a certain degree of proficiency in painting heads, in the two junior classes, the student is admitted to the higher class, under the supervision of director Von Schadow, where he begins to paint one of his own compositions. This is the last department previous to his being invested with the dignity and title of 'Meister Maler.'

"Among those who rank highest in the Düsseldorf school, LESSING, TIDEMANN, HUBNER, CAMPHAUSEN, JORDAN, RITTER, and SCHRÔDTER, stand conspicuous for composition and figures, and the two ACHENBACHS, Professor SCHIRMER, GUDE, WEBER, and SAAL, in landscape

"The Antique school embraces three large rooms or halls, in the lower part of the Academy building, in which are placed carefully selected collections of plaster casts, mostly from well-known antique statues. There are, however, casts from nature—hands, arms, legs, &c. The drawings are made upon a tinted paper, (stretched upon a wooden frame,) with black and white crayons. In making them, the stump is much used. To give an idea of the care with which they are executed, it will be only necessary to say, that two or three days are sometimes employed in completing the outline of a single head. It is studied in every feature, placed in every light, and observed from every point of view, and by touch as well as sight. To a person unaccustomed to such scrupulous care, this apparently exaggerated caution becomes almost ridiculous; but it is only by such assiduous attention to the 'finesses' of drawing, that one is enabled to arrive at a just appreciation of those niceties, which, when combined, form the beauty of the whole. The time usually devoted to the studying and careful drawing of a head, averages about two weeks. After having drawn a number of heads, varying according to the progress and perseverance of the student, from six to twelve, the study of the hand and foot is taken up. The Academy is provided with a number of plaster casts, of feet, hands, and limbs, taken from nature, as well as anatomical casts, displaying the arrangement of the sinews, &c. A similar careful study of the other parts of the body having been made, the student selects one of the full-length figures, of which he makes a drawing, at first of small size. Having drawn a sufficient number of these to give him a tolerable idea of the human form, he is directed by the professor to prepare his 'cartoon.' No student of the Academy is admitted from the Antique into the Painting class, until he shall have made such a cartoon (the size of life, or the actual size of the original statue) as shall meet with the entire approbation of the professor. In the preparation of this drawing, students are sometimes diligently occupied whole months."

A notion prevails at Munich that a spectator should be able quickly and easily to comprehend the subject of a picture; a notion referable to their national proneness to abstraction and analysis. Count Raczynski denies the necessity of this instant comprehension of subjects of art. He asserts, that in those who are gifted with a sense of beauty and love of the arts, emotion always precedes reasoning; and, on the contrary, when a spectator at first sight of a picture, begins to analyze its subject, either he is not endowed with that instinctive feeling which enables him to comprehend art, or the work he contemplates expresses nothing. After this feeling has been gratified, it is natural to wish to ascertain whether the subject has been well treated; but with a man of taste this criticism will not be considered the most important point and still less will his attention be first directed to it.

British Painters.

THE arts, in the early part of the thirteenth century, showed but few symptoms of vitality in England.* Henry III. employed many artists, both native and foreign, in ornamenting his palaces and cathedrals; but the multifarious occupations of the artist of this period, precluded the idea of superior excellence in any branch—he was, at the same time, goldsmith jeweller, armorer, saddler, sculptor, architect, and painter. The illuminated manuscripts of these times, throw some light upon the state of the arts. They are remarkable for brilliancy and delicacy of tint, and though not devoid of a fanciful grace, deal little in expression or sentiment.

Tapestry was introduced into England at an early period. The earliest record of it is in the reign of Henry VIII. The high-born dames of the land worked at it with their own hands, as the princesses of the east and the ladies of Greece. It undoubtedly fostered a love for painting, though its grotesque mixture of mythological subjects and Romish superstition, could have done little towards cultivating the taste and refining the sensibilities. The written direction of Henry VIII. for his own monument, speaks for the taste of the times: "The king shall appear on horseback, of the size of a goodly man, while over him shall appear a venerable image, holding the king's soul in his left hand, with his right hand extended in the act of benediction." It was to be of bronze, and was commenced, but the work was stopped by the parsimony of Elizabeth; but whether the king's

* This section is abridged from Cunningham's Lives of British Artists.

soul was duly portrayed or not, is not ascertained. It was in the reign of this monarch that HANS HOLBEIN came to England ; he was the first artist of distinction that practised in that country. He excelled in portraits. These were once very numerous in England, but some were destroyed in the civil wars, and some sold out of the country by the Puritan's Parliament, and many were burned in the palace of Whitehall. He made drawings of the principal characters of the court of Henry VIII., to the number of eighty-nine, which are now in the Royal Gallery. "A great part of these drawings," says Horace Walpole, "are exceedingly fine, and in one respect preferable to the finished pictures, as they are drawn in a bold and free manner. And though they have little more than the outline, being drawn with chalk upon paper stained of a flesh colour, and scarce shaded at all, there is a strength and vivacity in them equal to the most perfect portraits." There is no evidence that Elizabeth had much taste for painting ; but she loved pictures of herself. In them she could appear really handsome ; yet, to do the profession justice, they seem to have flattered her less than her dependants ; there is not a single portrait of her that one can call beautiful. The profusion of ornaments with which they are loaded, are marks of her fondness for dress ; while they entirely exclude all grace, and leave no more room for the painter's genius than if he had been employed to copy an Indian idol, totally composed of hands and necklaces—a pale Roman nose, a head of hair loaded with crowns and powdered with diamonds, a vast ruff, a vaster farthingale, and a bushel of pearls, are the features by which every one knows the portrait of Queen Elizabeth.

Towards the close of Elizabeth's reign, HILLIARD and OLIVER began to distinguish themselves, and they are probably the earliest natives of England who have any claim to the name of artist.

The former was the son of the queen's goldsmith, and was allowed to study from the heads of Holbein The parentage of the latter is unknown; "nor is it of any importance," says Walpole, "for he was a genius, and they transmit more honour by blood than they can receive." Hilliard enjoyed the protection of the court, and became popular; Oliver obtained the patronage of the nation, and merited all which they bestowed. The chief merit of Hilliard is that he helped to form the taste and discipline the hand of Oliver. The works of the latter are all miniatures; in the estimation of judges, they rival those of Holbein.

VANDYKE went to England in 1632; but, being unnoticed, soon returned to the continent. When Charles I., learning what a treasure he had lost, prevailed on him to return, he eventually knighted him, and bestowed on him a pension. He painted portraits almost exclusively; there are more than two hundred now in Great Britain. "No one," says Canning, "has yet equalled him in manly dignity; in the rare and important gift of endowing his heads with power to think and act. With all his vigour, he has no violent attitudes, no startling postures—all is natural and graceful. Whatever his figures do, they do easily—there is no straining. Man, in his noblest form and attitudes, was ever present to his fancy. He strikes his subjects clearly and cleverly out; he disdains to retire into the darkness of backgrounds, or to float away the body into a cloud or a vapour. All his men are of robust intellect, for he is a painter of mind, more than of velvet or silk; yet he throws a cloak over a cavalier with a grace few have attained. His ladies are inferior to his men; they seldom equal the fresh innocent loveliness of nature."

GEORGE JAMESON, of Aberdeen, born on the same day on which Mary, queen of Scots, was beheaded, was a fellow-pupil with Vandyke, under Rubens. He was the first native of Great

Britain who excelled in painting the size of life. His portraits are sometimes mistaken for Vandyke's.

When Charles I. visited Scotland, in 1633, "the magistrates of Edinburgh," says Mr. George Chalmers, "desirous to pay a compliment to the king's taste in painting, begged of Jameson to allow them the use of as many of the portraits done by him as could be gathered together. These were hung on each side of Netherbow Port, through which the royal cavalcade was to pass. This exhibition so attracted the king's attention, that he stopped his horse for a considerable time, and expressed his admiration of the good painting, and remarked the likeness of some of those they represented. This was a lucky circumstance for Jameson, for the king, while at Edinburgh, sat for a full-length picture; and having heard that Jameson had been accustomed to wear his hat while at work, by reason of a complaint in his head, his majesty very humanely ordered him to be covered; which privilege he ever after thought himself entitled to, in whatever company he was." To reconcile conflicting accounts we must have recourse to tradition, which avers that Jameson, to render the pageant prepared for the king's entrance more attractive, introduced the real and imaginary line of Scottish monarchs, from Fergus the First, welcoming Charles to the throne of his ancestors. These rude and hasty works, having fulfilled their purpose, were probably thrown aside with the other lumber of the pageant. The notice of a king, and such a judge too as Charles, must have been favourable to the fortunes of the painter; it is even said to have given new vigour and purity to his style. "His best works," says one of his biographers, "were from thence to his death." Having obtained the sanction of the chief authority at that time in art, he wrought with confidence; and the confidence of genius inspired his drawing, and gave a freer glow to his colouring.

LELY, a foreigner, who next became celebrated in the art, painted a portrait of Cromwell, who gave him these unwonted directions: "I desire you will use all your skill to paint my picture truly like me, and not flatter me at all; but remark all those roughnesses, pimples, warts, and every thing, as you see me; otherwise I never will pay you one farthing for it." When the softer customers of the court of Charles II. sat to the same painter, they laid his talents under no such restrictions. He seemed to consider himself chief limner at the court of Paphos. He, however, did not dedicate his pencil wholly to the condescending beauties of the court of Charles; he preserved the features of statesmen who contrived to walk uprightly in those slippery times: nor did he neglect the men of genius who flourished in his day. He painted Clarendon, Cowley, Butler, Selden, and Otway. He formed a gallery of the works of Vandyke and other eminent artists, which were sold at his death for twenty-six thousand pounds. He maintained the state of a gentleman, and preserved the dignity due to art in his intercourse with the court.

Shortly after the death of Sir Peter Lely, arrived KNELLER, one of the four foreign artists to whom the English nation is indebted for the fine portraits of many eminent persons, who lived prior to the days of Reynolds, on whom his mantle is said to have fallen. Sir Godfrey Kneller died in 1723. His numerous works are almost exclusively portraits; and over whatever he produced, he threw an air of freedom and a hue of nature not unworthy of Vandyke. All the sovereigns of his time, all the noblemen of the court, all the men of genius in the kingdom, and almost all the ladies of rank or of beauty in England, sat to him for their portraits.

HOGARTH.

Wm. Hogarth, the first English painter of note, was born in London, in 1697. He says of himself: "As I had naturally a good eye and fondness for drawing, shows of all sorts gave me uncommon pleasure when young, and mimicry, common to all children, was remarkable in me. An early access to a neighbouring painter drew my attention from play; and I was at every possible opportunity employed in making drawings. I picked up an acquaintance of the same turn, and soon learned to draw the alphabet with great correctness. My exercises, when at school, were more remarkable for the ornaments which adorned them, than for the exercises themselves. In the former, I soon found that blockheads, with better memories, would soon surpass me; but for the latter I was particularly distinguished.

His father lived by his pen, and William shrewdly perceiving that learning brought his father little honour and less pecuniary profit, he requested to be taken from school, and apprenticed to a silver-plate engraver. But he soon found this business too limited for his genius. "I determined," says he, "that silver-plate engraving should be followed no longer than necessity obliged me to it. Engraving on copper was, at twenty years of age, my utmost ambition. To attain this it was necessary that I should learn to draw objects something like nature, instead of the monsters of heraldry, and the common methods of study were much too tedious for one who loved his pleasure and came so late to it; for the time necessary to learn in the usual mode would leave me none to spare in the ordinary enjoyments of life. This led me to consider whether a shorter road could not be found. The early part of my life had been employed in a business rather detrimental than advantageous to those branches of the art which I wished to pursue and have since professed. I had learned by practice to copy with tolerable correctness in the ordinary way, but it occurred to me that there were many disadvantages attending this method of study, as having faulty originals, &c., and even when the pictures or prints to be imitated were by the best masters, it was little more than pouring water out of one vessel into another. Many reasons led me to wish that I could find a shorter path—fix forms and characters in my mind—and instead of copying the lines, try to read the language, and, if possible, find the grammar of the art, by bringing into one focus the various observations I had made, and then trying by my power on the canvass how far my plan enabled me to combine and apply them to practice. For this purpose I considered what various ways, and to what different purposes, the memory might be applied, and fell upon one most suitable to my situation and idle disposition; laying it down first as an axiom, that he who could by any means acquire and retain in his memory perfect ideas of the subjects he meant to draw, would have as clear a knowledge of the figure, as a man who can write freely hath of the twenty-five letters of the alphabet, and their intimate combinations. I had early acquired the habit of retaining in my mind' eye, without coolly copying it on the spot, whatever I intended to imitate. Sometimes, but too seldom, I took the life for correcting the parts I had not perfectly enough remembered, and then I transferred to my own compositions. I have ever found studying from nature the shortest and safest way of obtaining knowledge in my art. A choice of composition was the next thing to be considered, and my constitutional idleness naturally led me to the use of such materials as I had previously collected; and to this I was further induced by thinking that if properly combined, they might be made useful to society, though similar subjects had often failed in writing and preaching." The following story is related of his first attempt at satire: One summer day, during his apprenticeship, he went with three companions to Highgate, and the weather being warm and the way dusty, they went into a public-house, and called for ale. There happened to be other customers in the house, who to free drinking added fierce talking, and a quarrel ensued. One of them, on receiving a blow on the head with a quart pot, looked so ludicrously rueful, that Hogarth snatched out a pencil, and sketched him as he stood. It was very like and very laughable, and contributed to the restoration of order and good humour.

Hogarth turned his attention at one time chiefly to painting portraits, but he soon became tired of an occupation in which he was obliged to humour the vanity of his sitters by gross flattery, or incur their displeasure. He thus expresses his disgust: "For the portrait of Garrick, as Richard, I received more than any English artist ever before received for a single portrait, and that, too, by the sanction of several painters who were consulted about the price. Notwithstanding all this, the current remark was, that portraits were not my province; and I was tempted to abandon the only lucrative branch of the art; for the practice brought the whole nest of phizmongers on my back, where they buzzed like so many hornets. I sometimes declared I would never paint another portrait, and frequently refused when applied to; for I found, by mortifying experience, that whoever will succeed in this branch, must adopt the mode recommended in Gay's Fables, and make divinities of all who sit to him." Whether or not this childish affectation will ever be done away, is a doubtful question: none of those who have attempted to reform it have yet succeeded; nor, unless portrait painters in general become more honest and their customers less vain, is there much reason to expect they ever will. Hogarth thus describes the style which was most congenial to his mind, and in which he so well succeeded: "Those subjects that will both entertain and inform the mind, bid fair to be of the greatest public utility, and must, therefore, be entitled to rank in the highest class. If the execution is difficult, though that is but a secondary merit, the author has a claim to a higher degree of praise. If this be admitted, comedy in painting, as well as in writing, ought to be allotted the first place, as most capable of all these perfections, though the sublime, as it is called, has been opposed to it. Ocular demonstration will carry more conviction to the mind of a sensible man, than all he would find in a thousand volumes, and this has been attempted in the prints I have composed. Let the decision be left to any unprejudiced eye; let the figures in either pictures or prints be considered as players, dressed either for the sublime—for genteel comedy or farce—for high or low life. I have endeavoured to treat my subjects as a dramatic writer; my picture is my stage, my men and women my players, who, by means of certain actions and gestures, are to exhibit a dumb show."

The first works which seem to have created a sensation in the public mind, were the Harlot's Progress, a series of six scenes; and the Rake's Progress, in eight. Hogarth, as the engraver of his own paintings, reaped a double profit; and "the boldness, originality, and happy handling of those productions, made them general favourites, and by the aid of the graver they were circulated over the island with the celerity of a telegraphic dispatch. In 1736 he produced the Sleeping Congregation, in which the very genius of Slumber seems to preside No one has escaped his influence except the preacher, who seems to be giving forth the very essence of poppies, and the clerk, who has one eye still open.

The Distressed Poet appeared about the same time. No one can look upon it without mingled feelings of compassion and humorous delight. While the laborious "fine phrensy" of the poet excites our mirth, our sympathy is enlisted for his gentle wife, who anxiously endeavours to quiet the noisy milk-woman, that her husband may profit by the fit of inspiration, which has, perhaps, been long looked for.

The Enraged Musician, and the Strolling Players, followed; then came Marriage à-la-Mode, in six scenes. The first represents the contract between the parents. The young lord, a fop in his dress, and something of a fool in his looks, gazes at his person in the glass, and practises with his snuff-box infinitely more to his own satisfaction than to that of his intended—who turns half from him in scorn—plays with her wedding-ring, and listens, as well as offended pride will allow, to the words of Mr. Silvertongue, a smooth and insinuating lawyer. Beside them are two spaniels, coupled contrary to their inclinations, and pulling different ways—symbolical of the happiness to be expected from the approaching union. Then come contention and hatred in the following scenes. The husband pursues a course of gambling and dissipation. His wife, to resent his conduct, frequents the gaming-table, and listens to the eloquence of the lawyer, till both fortune and reputation are ruined. At length we find her kneeling before her husband, who has just received a sword-thrust from the injurious lawyer. The last scene is in the house of the lady's father, where she expires, holding the fatal vial of laudanum in her hand. Her child clings about her neck, and her sordid wretch of a father, removes a valuable ring from her finger. Such is the outline of a dramatic story, which it would require a volume to describe—so great, so various, and so lavish is its wealth of satire and pathos—with such waste of ornament, such overflowing knowledge of life, nature, and manners, has Hogarth emblazoned this domestic tragedy.

Next came the Industrious and the Idle Apprentice, then the March to Finchley, Beer Street, Gin Lane, France and England, the Cockpit, the Election, in four scenes, &c. His last work was entitled, Credulity, Superstition, and Fanaticism.

WILSON.

Richard Wilson, the first British landscape-painter of note, was born in Wales, in 1713. His love of art appeared early, and, attracting the attention of his uncle, he was placed under the care of a portrait painter in London. In his thirty-sixth year he was enabled, by his own savings and the aid of his friends, to go to Italy, where his talents procured him notice, and his company was courted by men of sense and rank. He continued the study and practice of portrait painting, and it is said with fair hopes of success, when an accident opened another avenue to fame, and shut up the way to fortune. Having waited one morning, till he grew weary, for the coming of Zucarelli, the artist, he painted, to beguile the time, a scene from the window of his friend, with so much grace and effect, that Zucarelli was astonished, and inquired if he had studied landscape. Wilson replied that he had not. "Then I advise you," said the other, "to try, for you are sure of great success." The counsel of one friend was confirmed by the opinion of another. This was Vernet, a French painter; a man whose generosity was equal to his reputation, and that was very high. One day, while sitting in Wilson's painting-room, he was so struck with the peculiar beauty of a newly-finished landscape that he desired to become the proprietor, and offered in exchange one of his best pictures. This was much to the gratification of the other; the exchange was made, and with a liberality equally rare and commendable, Vernet placed it in his exhibition-room, and when his own productions happened to be praised or purchased by English travellers, the generous Frenchman used to say, "Don't talk of my landscapes alone, when your own countryman, Wilson, paints so beautifully."

These praises, and an internal feeling of the merits of his new performances, induced Wilson to relinquish portrait painting and proceed with landscape. He found himself better prepared for this new pursuit than he had imagined; he had been long insensibly storing his mind with the beauties of natural scenery, and the picturesque mountains and glens of his native Wales had been to him an academy when he was unconscious of their influence.

After a residence of six years abroad he returned to England to try his fortune with his own countrymen; and the commencement was promising. But the love of landscape painting spread very slowly—so slow, that after the sale of a few of his works among the more distinguished of the lovers of art, he could not find a market for the fruits of his study, and had the mortification of exhibiting pictures of unrivalled beauty before the eyes of his countrymen in vain. He soon began to feel that, in relinquishing portrait painting, he had forsaken the way to wealth and fashionable distinction, and taken the road to certain want and unprofitable fame. Wilson had a poet's eye and a poet's feeling; he selected his scenes with judgment, and spread them out in beauty and in all the fresh luxury of nature. He did for landscape what Reynolds did for faces—with equal genius, but far different fortune. A fine scene, rendered still more lovely by the pencil of the artist, did not reward its flatterer with any of its productions, either of oil, or corn, or cattle. Kneller was one day conversing about his art, when he gave the following neat reason for preferring portraiture: "Painters of history," said he, "make the dead live, and do not begin to live themselves until they are dead. I paint the living, and they make me live." As Kneller found dead men indifferent paymasters, so inanimate nature proved but a cold patroness to Wilson.

His process of painting was simple; his colours were few, he used but one brush, and worked standing. He prepared his palette, made a few touches, then retired to the window to refresh his eye with natural light, and returned in a few minutes and resumed his labours. Buchy called on him one day and found him at work; he seized his visitor by the arm, hurried him to the remotest corner of the room, and said, "There, look at my landscape; this is where you should view a painting, if you wish to examine it with your eyes and not your nose." He was then an old man; his sight was failing, his touch was unsure, and he painted somewhat coarsely, but the effect was wonderful. He, too, like Reynolds, had his secrets of colour, and his mystery of the true principle in painting, which he refused to explain, saying: "They are like those of nature, and are to be sought for and found in my performances." Of his own future fame, he spoke but seldom, for he was a modest man; but when he did speak of it he used expressions which the world have since sanctioned. "Buchy," he said, "you will live to see great prices given for my pictures, when those of Barret will not bring one farthing." A small estate became his by the death of a brother; and, as if nature had designed to make some amends for the neglect of mankind, a profitable vein of lead was discovered on his grounds.

His residence stood among fine green hills, and old romantic woods, picturesque rocks, verdant lawns, deep glens, and the whole was cheered with the sound as well as the sight of running water. He was now in affluence—was loved and respected by all around him—and, what was as much to him or more, he was become a dweller among scenes such as had haunted his imagination, even when Italy spread her beauty before him. He wrought little and walked much; the stone on which he loved to sit, the tree under which he shaded himself from the sun, and the stream on the banks of which he commonly walked, are all remembered and pointed out by the peasantry. But he wanted what wealth could not give—youth and strength to enjoy what he had fallen heir to. His strength failed fast; his walks became shorter and less frequent; and the last scene he visited was where two old picturesque fir-trees stood, which he loved to look at and introduce into his compositions. Walking out one day, accompanied by his favourite dog—whether exhausted by fatigue, or overcome by some sudden pain—Wilson sank down and found himself unable to rise. The sagacious animal ran home, howled, pulled the servants by their clothes, and at last succeeded in bringing them to the aid of his master. He was carried home, but he never fairly recovered from the shock. He complained of weariness and pain, refused nourishment, and languished and expired in May, 1782, in the sixty-ninth year of his age. As a landscape painter the merits of Wilson are great; his conceptions are generally noble, and his execution vigorous and glowing; the dewy freshness, the natural lustre, and harmonious arrangement of his scenes, have seldom been exceeded. He rose at once from the tame insipidity of common scenery into natural grandeur and magnificence; his streams seem all abodes for nymphs, his hills seem fit haunts for the muses, and his temples worthy of the gods. His whole heart was in his art, and he talked and dreamed landscape. He looked on cattle as made only to form groups for his pictures, and on men as they composed harmoniously. One day, looking on the fine scene from Richmond terrace, and wishing to point out a spot of particular beauty to the friend who accompanied him, "There," said he, holding out his finger, "see near those houses—there, where the figures are." He stood for some time by the waterfall of Terni in speechless admiration, and at length exclaimed, "Well done, water, well done." In aërial effect he considered himself above any rival. When Wright of Derby offered to exchange works with him, he answered, "With all my heart; I'll give you air, and you will give me fire." Wilson has been styled the English Claude, and though inferior in sublimity, he excelled that master in effects of dewy freshness and quiet evening lights.

SIR JOSHUA REYNOLDS.

Sir Joshua Reynolds was born at Plympton, in Devonshire, in 1723. His inclination to idleness as to reading, and industry in drawing, began to appear early. When he was some eight years old, he read "The Jesuit's Perspective" with so much care and profit, that he made a drawing of Plympton school, a plain Gothic building, raised partly on pillars, in which the principles of that art were very tolerably adhered to. The approbation of his father, with his own natural love of art, induced him more and more to devote his time to drawing, and neglect his duties at school. He drew likenesses of his sisters and of various friends of his family; his proficiency increased with practice, and his ardour kept pace with his growing skill. Of boyish productions no specimen is preserved; he himself probably destroyed them, being little pleased with what he had done; but it is inconceivable that a youth like this, who gave so little of his leisure to other knowledge, should have executed nothing worthy of remembrance at the age of nineteen. There is no doubt that, as soon as he had a fair field for the display of his talents, he showed a mind stored with ready images of beauty, and a hand capable of portraying them with truth and effect. He was sent to London on the 14th of October 1781, and on the 18th of the same month, the day of St. Luke, the patron saint of painters, he was placed under the care of Mr. Hudson. While he remained with Mr. Hudson he went to a sale of pictures, and just before the auctioneer commenced he observed a great bustle at the door, and heard "Pope! Pope!" whispered round the room. All drew back to make way for the poet to pass, and those who were near enough held out their hands for him to touch as he went along. Reynolds held out his, and had the honour of a gentle shake, of which he was ever after proud. This was one of the early anecdotes of his life which he loved to relate; it shows the enthusiasm of the painter, and the popularity of the great poet. He continued for two years in the employment of Hudson, and acquired with uncommon rapidity such professional knowledge as could then and there be obtained. He painted during that period various portraits, of which he never gave any account, and made many sketches and studies which would require a minute description to be comprehended. It is enough to say, that in general they contained the germ of some of his future graces, and displayed considerable freedom of handling and truth of delineation. Among the productions most worthy of remembrance was the portrait of an elderly servant woman of Hudson's. It was accidentally exhibited in Hudson's gallery, and obtained general applause. This was more than the old man could endure. Without any warm words a separation took place, and Reynolds returned to Devonshire; here he passed three years in company, from which, as he informed Malone, little improvement could be gained.

When he was twenty-two years old, Reynolds and his two youngest sisters took a house at the town of Plymouth Dock: here he occupied the first floor, and employed his time in painting portraits. It must be confessed that many of his productions, up to this period, were carelessly drawn, in common attitudes, and undistinguished by those excellences of colouring and power of expression which have made his name famous. His old master, Hudson, was still strong within him. One hand was hid in the unbuttoned waistcoat; the other held the hat; and the face was looking forwards with that vacant listlessness which is the mark of a sitter who conceives portrait painting to resemble shaving, and that the *sine qua non* is to keep his features stiff and composed. One gentleman desired to be distinguished from others, and was painted with his hat on his head; yet so inveterate had the practice of painting in one position become, that—if there be any truth in the story—when the likeness was sent home, the wife discovered that her husband had not only one hat on his head, but another under his arm.

Rome, which is in reality to painters, what Parnassus is in imagination to poets, was frequently present to the fancy of Reynolds; and he longed to see with his own eyes the glories of art, of which he had heard so much. He went to Rome in 1749. Of his first impressions in the Metropolis of Art, he has left a minute account. "It has frequently happened," says he, "as I was informed by the keeper of the Vatican, that many of those whom he had conducted through the various apartments of that edifice, when about to be dismissed, have asked for the works of Raphael, and would not believe that they had already passed through the rooms where they are preserved ; so little impression had these performances made on them. One of the first painters of France once told me that this circumstance happened to himself; though he now looks on Raphael with that veneration which he deserves from all painters and lovers of art. I remember very well my own disappointment when I first visited the Vatican : but, on confessing my feelings to a brother student, of whose ingenuousness I had a high opinion, he acknowledged that the works of Raphael had the same effect on him, or rather that they did not produce the effect which he expected. This was a great relief to my mind, and on inquiring farther of other students, I found that those persons only who, from natural imbecility, appeared to be incapable of relishing those divine performances, made pretensions to instantaneous raptures on first beholding them. All the undigested notions of painting which I had brought with me from England, where the art was in the lowest state it had ever been in, (it could not, indeed, be lower,) were to be totally done away and eradicated from my mind. It was necessary, as it is expressed, on a very solemn occasion, that I should become *as a little child.* Notwithstanding my disappointment, I proceeded to copy some of those excellent works. I viewed them again and again ; I even affected to feel their merit and admire them more than I really did. In a short time, a new taste and a new perception began to dawn upon me, and I was convinced that I had originally formed a false opinion of the perfection of art, and that this great painter was well entitled to the high rank which he holds in the admiration of the world.

The truth is, that if these works had really been what I expected, they would have contained beauties superficial and alluring, but by no means such as would have entitled them to the great reputation which they have borne so long, and so justly obtained."

"He contemplated with unwearied attention and ardent zeal the various beauties which marked the style of different schools, and different ages. It was with no common eye that he beheld the productions of the great masters. He copied and sketched in the Vatican such works of Raphael and Michael Angelo as he thought would be most conducive to his future excellence, and by his well-directed study acquired, while he contemplated the best works of the best masters, that grace of thinking, to which he was principally indebted for his subsequent reputation as a portrait painter." After an absence of nearly three years, he returned to England; and, after visiting Devonshire for a few weeks, he established himself as a professional man in London. He found such opposition as genius is commonly doomed to meet with, and does not always overcome. The boldness of his attempts, the freedom of his conceptions, and the brilliancy of his colouring, were considered as innovations upon the established and orthodox system of portrait manufacture. The artists raised their voices first; and of those, Hudson, who had just returned from Rome, was loudest. His old master looked for some moments on a Boy, in a turban, which he had just painted, and exclaimed: "Reynolds, you don't paint so well as when you left England!" Ellis, an eminent portrait-maker, who had studied under Kneller, lifted up his voice next: "Ah! Reynolds, this will never answer! Why, you don't paint in the least like Sir Godfrey." The youthful artist defended himself with much ability, upon which the other exclaimed in astonishment, at this new heresy in art,

"Shakspeare in poetry, and Kneller in painting!" and walked out of the room. The contest with his fellow-artists was of short continuance. The works which had gained him celebrity, were not the fortunate offspring of some happy moment, but of one who could pour out such pictures in profusion. Better ones were not slow in coming.

The Royal Academy was planned in 1768. A list of thirty members was made out; and West called on Reynolds, and succeeded in persuading him to join them. He ordered his coach, and, accompanied by West, entered the room where his brother artists were assembled. They rose up to a man, and saluted him president. He voluntarily imposed on himself the task of delivering discourses, for the instruction of students in the principles of their art. They were delivered during a long succession of years, in a manner cold, and sometimes embarrassed, and even unintelligible. A nobleman, who was present at the delivery of the first of the series, said: "Sir Joshua, you read your discourse in so low a tone, I scarce heard a word you said." "That was to my advantage," replied the president, with a smile. The king, to give dignity to the Royal Academy of Great Britain, bestowed knighthood on the president; and seldom has any such distinction been bestowed amid more universal approbation. He died in 1792, in the sixty-ninth year of his age. Sir Joshua has a three-fold claim on posterity: for his discourses, his historical and poetical paintings, and his portraits.

The portraits of Reynolds are equally numerous and excellent; and all who have written of their merits, have swelled their eulogiums, by comparing them with the simplicity of Titian, the vigour of Rembrandt, and the elegance and delicacy of Vandyke. Certainly, in character and expression, and in manly ease, he has never been surpassed. He is always equal; always natural, graceful, unaffected. His boldness of posture, and his singular freedom of colouring, are so supported by all the grace of art, by all the sorcery of skill, that they appear natural and noble. Over the meanest head he sheds the halo of dignity; his men are all nobleness, his women all loveliness, and his children all simplicity; yet they are all like the living originals. He had the singular art of summoning the mind into the face, and making sentiment mingle in the portrait.

The admirers of portrait painting are many, and it is pleasant to read the social and domestic affections of the country in these innumerable productions. In the minds of some, they rank with historical compositions; and there can be no doubt that portraits, which give the form and the soul of poets, and statesmen, and warriors, and of all whose actions or whose thoughts lend lustre to the land, are to be received as illustrations of history. The most skilful posture and the richest colouring cannot create the reputation which accompanies genius, and we turn coldly away from the head which we happen not to know, or to have heard of. The portrait of Johnson has risen to the value of five hundred guineas, while the heads of many of Sir Joshua's grandest lords remain at their original fifty.

Of historical and poetic subjects he painted upwards of one hundred and thirty They are chiefly in England; and in the galleries of the titled or opulent. The names of a few of the most famous may interest the reader: Macbeth and the Witches; Cardinal Beaufort; Holy Family; Hercules strangling the Serpents; The Nativity; Count Ugolino; Cymon and Iphigenia; The Fortune-teller; Garrick between Tragedy and Comedy; The Snake in the Grass; The Blackguard Mercury; Muscipula, Puck; Mrs. Siddons as the Tragic Muse; The Shepherd Boy; Venus chiding Cupid for Casting Accounts, &c.

GAINSBOROUGH.

Thomas Gainsborough, the celebrated landscape-painter, was born at Sudbury in the year 1727. In his case also, "the boy was father of the man." At ten years old he had made some progress in sketching, and at twelve he was a confirmed painter. A beautiful wood of four miles in extent is shown, in Suffolk, whose ancient trees, winding glades, and sunny nooks inspired him, while he was but a schoolboy, with a love of art. Scenes are pointed out where he used to sit and fill his copybooks with pencillings of flowers and trees, and whatever pleased his fancy; and it is said that those early attempts of the child bore a distinct resemblance to the mature works of the man.

On one occasion he was concealed among some bushes in his father's garden, making a sketch of an old fantastic tree, when he observed a man looking most wistfully over the wall at some pears, which were hanging ripe and tempting. The slanting light of the sun happened to throw the eager face into a highly picturesque mixture of light and shade, and Tom immediately sketched his likeness, much to the poor man's consternation afterwards, and much to the amusement of his father, when he taxed the peasant with the intention of robbing his garden, and showed him how he looked. Gainsborough, long afterwards, made a finished painting of the Sudbury rustic—a work much admired among artists—under the name of Tom Peartree's portrait. He loved to exercise his powers in those hasty things: and from the unembarrassed freedom of mind and hand with which he produced them, they take rank with his happiest compositions.

Of those early sketches made in the woods of Sudbury, few now exist, though they were once very numerous. No fine clump of trees—no picturesque stream—no romantic glade—no cattle grazing, nor flocks reposing, nor peasants pursuing their pastoral or rural occupation—escaped his diligent pencil. Those hasty sketches were all treasured up as materials to be used when his hand should have become skilful; he showed them to his visitors and called them his riding-school. As his reputation rose, he became less satisfied with those early proofs of talent, and scattered them with a profuse hand among friends and visitors. To one lady he made a present of twenty; but so injudiciously were those precious things bestowed, that the lady pasted them round the walls of her apartment, and as she soon after left London, they became the property of the next inhabitant. His first drawing was a clump of trees—he long retained it, and one of his biographers says it was a "wonderful thing."

At an early age he married and settled at Ipswich, thence he removed to Bath, and in his forty-seventh year he removed to London, where he continued his career in portraiture and landscape, with fresh feeling and increasing success. Among those who sat to him was the Duchess of Devonshire—then in the bloom of youth, at once the loveliest of the lovely, and the gayest of the gay. But her dazzling beauty, and the sense which she entertained of the charms of her looks and her conversation, took away that readiness of hand, and hasty happiness of touch, which belonged to him in his ordinary moments The portrait was so little to his satisfaction, that he refused to send it to Chatsworth. Drawing his wet pencil over the mouth which all who saw it thought exquisitely lovely, he said, "Her grace is too hard for me." The picture, it is supposed, was destroyed. Among his papers were found two sketches of the Duchess,—both exquisitely graceful.

He had customers who annoyed him with other difficulties

than too radiant loveliness. A certain lord came for his portrait; and that all might be worthy of his station, he had put on a new suit of clothes, richly laced, and a well-powdered wig. He put on also a practised look of such importance and prettiness, that the artist, who was no flatterer, either with tongue or pencil, began to laugh, and was heard to mutter, "This will never do." The sitter having composed himself in conformity with his station, said, "Now, sir, I beg you will not overlook the dimple in my chin!" "Confound the dimple in your chin," said Gainsborough; "I shall neither paint the one nor the other." And he laid down his brushes, and refused to resume them.

Nature sat to him in all her attractive attitudes of beauty; and his pencil traced, with peculiar and matchless facility, her finest and most delicate lineaments. Whether it was the sturdy oak, or the twisted eglantine, the mower whetting his scythe, the whistling ploughboy, or the shepherd under the hawthorn in the dale—all came forth equally chaste, from his inimitable and fanciful pencil.

The dates of Gainsborough's various productions, cannot now be ascertained: he never put his name to his compositions, and very seldom even the date. He knew that his own happy character was too strongly impressed on his works to be denied; and probably thought that the excellence of a painting had nothing to do with the day or the year of its execution. The Woodman with his Dog in a Storm, was one of his favourite compositions. There is a kind of rustic sublimity, new to English painting, in the heavenward look of the peasant, while the rain descends and the lightning flies. The same may be said of the Shepherd Boy in the Shower; there is something inexpressibly mournful in the looks of both. The former unfortunately perished; but the sketch remains, and shows it to have been a work of the highest order. He valued it at one hundred guineas, but could find no purchaser while he lived. His widow sold it for five hundred guineas, after his death, to Lord Gainsborough, whose house was subsequently burned to the ground. Another of his own chief favourite works, was the Cottage Girl with her Dog and Pitcher.

Like Reynolds, he painted standing, in preference to sitting; and the pencils which he used had shafts sometimes two yards long. He stood as far from his sitter as he did from his picture, that the hues might be the same. He generally rose early, commenced painting between nine and ten o'clock, wrought for four or five hours, and then gave up the rest of the day to visits, to music, and to domestic enjoyment. He loved to sit by the side of his wife, during the evenings, and make sketches of whatever occurred to his fancy; all of which he threw under the table, except such as were uncommonly happy, and those were preserved, and either finished as sketches, or expanded into paintings.

He died in 1788, in the sixty-first year of his age. When he felt his end approaching, he sent for Reynolds, with whom he had been unable to live in peace. But in the hour of death all petty animosities and rivalries were forgotten, and the last words of Gainsborough were addressed to Sir Joshua: "We are all going to heaven, and Vandyke is of the company."

His drawings are numerous and masterly—no artist has left behind him so many exquisite relics of this kind. "I have seen," said his friend Jackson, "at least a thousand, not one of which but possesses merit, and some in a transcendent degree." Many of them are equal, in point of character, to his most finished performances. They have all great breadth and singular freedom of handling. His sketches of ladies are very fine. The Duchess of Devonshire is shown in side view and in front; she seems to move and breathe among the groves of Chatsworth. The names of many are lost, but this is not important. New light, however, has lately been thrown on those perishable things, by the painter's grand nephew, Richard Lane, in whom much of the spirit survives. He has copied and published some twenty-four of those fine sketches.

The chief works of Gainsborough are not what is usually called landscape ; for he had no wish to create gardens of paradise, and leave them to the sole enjoyment of the sun and breeze. The wildest nooks of his woods have their living tenants, and in all his glades and his valleys we see the sons and daughters of men. A deep human sympathy unites us with his pencil, and this is not lessened because all his works are stamped with the image of old England. His paintings have a national look. He belongs to no school ; he is not reflected from the glass of man, but from that of nature.

" It is certain," says Reynolds, " that all those odd scratches and marks, which, on a close examination, are so observable in Gainsborough's pictures, and which, even to experienced painters, appear rather the effect of accident than design—this chaos, this uncouth and shapeless appearance—by a kind of magic, at a certain distance, assumes form, and all the parts seem to drop into their proper places, so that we can hardly forbear acknowledging the full effect of diligence, under the appearance of chance and hasty negligence." That Gainsborough himself considered this peculiarity in his manner, and the power it possesses in exciting surprise, as a beauty in his works, may be inferred from the eager desire, which we know he always expressed, that his pictures, at the exhibition, should be seen near as well as at a distance.

There is a charm about the children running wild in the

landscapes of Gainsborough, which is more deeply felt by comparing them with those of Reynolds. The children of Sir Joshua are indeed beautiful creatures—free, artless, and lovely; but they seem to have been nursed in velvet laps, and fed with golden spoons. There is a rustic grace, an untamed wildness about the children of the latter, which speak of the country and of neglected toilets. They are the offspring of nature, running free among woods as wild as themselves. They are not afraid of disordering their satins, and wetting their kid shoes. They roll on the green sward, burrow like rabbits, and dabble in the running streams, daily. In this the works of Reynolds and Gainsborough differ; but they are both unlike the great painters of Italy. The infants of Raphael, Titian, or Coreggio, are not meant for mortals, but for divinities.

WEST.

Benjamin West was born in the year 1738, at Springfield, Pennsylvania. In his seventh year little Benjamin was placed by the cradle to watch the sleeping infant of his eldest sister while his mother gathered flowers. As he sat by the cradle, the child smiled in sleep; he was struck with its beauty, and seeking some paper, drew its portrait in red and black ink. His mother returned, and snatching the paper, which he sought to conceal, exclaimed to her daughter, "I declare, he has made a likeness of little Sally!" She took him in her arms and kissed him fondly.

When he was some eight years old, a party of roaming Indians paid their summer visit to Springfield, and were much pleased with the rude sketches which the boy had made of birds and fruits and flowers, for in such drawings many of the wild Americans have both taste and skill. They showed him some of their own workmanship, and taught him how to prepare the red and yellow colours with which they stained their weapons ; to these his mother added indigo, and thus he was possessed of the three primary colours. The Indians unwilling to leave such a boy in ignorance of their other acquirements, taught him archery, in which he became expert enough to shoot refractory birds, which refused to come on milder terms for their likenesses. The future President of the British Academy, taking lessons in painting and in archery from a tribe of Cherokees, might be a subject worthy of the pencil.

The wants of West increased with his knowledge. He could draw, and he had obtained colours, but how to lay those colours skilfully on, he could not well conceive. A neighbour informed him that this was done with brushes formed of camel's hair ; there were no camels in America, and he had recourse to the cat, from whose back and tail he supplied his wants. The cat was a favourite, and the altered condition of her fur was imputed to disease, till the boy's confession explained the cause, much to the amusement of his father, who, nevertheless, rebuked him, but more in affection than in anger. Better help was at hand. He received as a present a box of paints and brushes, with canvass prepared for the easel, and six engravings by Grevling. West placed the box on a chair at his bedside, and was unable to sleep He rose with the dawn, carried his canvass and colours to the garret, hung up the engravings, prepared a palette, and commenced copying. So completely was he under the control of this species of enchantment, that he absented himself from school laboured secretly and incessantly, and without interruption for several days, when the anxious inquiries of the schoolmaster sent his mother to his studio with no pleasure in her looks. But her anger subsided as she looked upon his performances. He had avoided copying, and made a picture composed from two of the engravings, telling a new story, and coloured with a skill and effect which was in her sight surprising. Sixty-seven years after this piece was exhibited in the same room with the sublime painting of Christ Rejected, and the painter then declared "that there were inventive touches of art in this juvenile essay, which, with all his subsequent knowledge and experience, he had not been able to surpass." His future career became the subject of anxious deliberation. His father resolved upon submitting the matter to the Society to which he belonged.

The spirit of speech first descended on one John Williamson "To John West and Sarah Pearson," said this western luminary, "a man-child hath been born, on whom God hath conferred some remarkable gifts of mind, and you have all heard that, by something amounting to inspiration, the youth has been induced to study the art of painting. It is true that our tenets refuse to own the utility of that art to mankind, but it seemeth to me that we have considered the matter too nicely. God has bestowed on this youth a genius for art—shall we question His wisdom? Can we believe that He gives such rare gifts but for a wise and good purpose? I see the Divine hand in this; we shall do well to sanction the art and encourage this youth."

Benjamin was summoned, and took his station in the middle of the room, his father on his right hand, and his mother on his left, while around him flocked the whole Quaker community. One of the women now spoke, but Williamson's words are alone remembered. "Painting," said he, "has been hitherto employed to embellish life, to preserve voluptuous images, and to add to the sensual gratifications of man. For this we classed it among vain and merely ornamental things, and excluded it from among us. But this is not the principle, but the misemployment of painting

In wise and pure hands it rises in the scale of moral excellence, and displays a loftiness of sentiment and a devout dignity worthy of the contemplation of Christians. I think genius is given by God for some high purpose. What the purpose is, let us not inquire—it will be manifest in His good time and way. He hath, in this remote wilderness, endowed with the rich gifts of a superior spirit this youth, who has now our consent to cultivate his talents for art—may it be demonstrated in his life and works that the gifts of God have not been bestowed in vain, nor the motives of the beneficent inspiration, which induces us to suspend the strict operation of our tenets, prove barren of religious or moral effect!" "At the conclusion of this address," says Galt, "the women rose and kissed the young artist, and the men, one by one, laid their hands on his head."

That this scene made a strong impression on the mind of West, we have his own assurance; he looked upon himself as expressly dedicated to art. He established himself in Philadelphia, as a portrait painter, in the eighteenth year of his age. After painting the heads of all who desired it, he went to New York, hoping to raise a sufficient sum to take him to Rome. Ere long, one of the Allans of Philadelphia, offered him a passage to Leghorn. It happened that a New-York merchant, of the name of Kelly was at that time sitting to West for his portrait. To this gentleman the artist spoke of his intended journey. Kelly paid for his portrait, gave him a letter to his agents in Philadelphia, shook him by the hand, and wished him a good voyage. When the letter of Kelly was presented, it was found to contain an order from that generous merchant to his agent to pay him fifty guineas—a present to aid in his equipment for Italy. The plodding citizens of New York rose in the painter's estimation fifty per cent.

When it was known that a young American had come to study Raphael and Michael Angelo, some curiosity was excited among the Roman virtuosi. The first fortunate exhibiter of this lion from the western wilderness, was Lord Grantham. He invited West to dinner, and afterwards carried him to an evening party, where he found almost all those persons to whom he had brought letters of introduction. Among the rest was Cardinal Albani. "I have the honour," said Lord Grantham, "to present a young American, who has letters for your eminence, and who has come to Italy for the purpose of studying the fine arts." The Cardinal knew so little of the New World, that he conceived an American must needs be a savage. "Is he black or white?" said the aged virtuoso, holding out both his hands, that he might have the satisfaction of touching this new wonder. Lord Grantham smiled, and said, "He is fair—very fair." "What, as fair as I am?" exclaimed the prelate. The complexion of the churchman was a deep olive—that of West more than commonly fair; and as they stood together the company smiled. "As fair as the cardinal," became for a while proverbial.

Others, who had the use of their eyes, seemed to consider the young American as at most, a better kind of savage, and accordingly were curious to watch him. They wished to try what effect the Apollo, the Venus, and the works of Raphael would have upon him; and "thirty of the most magnificent equipages in the capital of christendom, and filled with the most erudite char acters in Europe," says Galt, "conducted the young Quaker to iew the masterpieces of art." It was agreed that the Apollo should be first submitted to his view. The statue was enclosed in a case, and when the keeper threw open the doors, West unconsciously exclaimed, "A young Mohawk warrior!" The Italians were surprised and mortified with the comparison of their noblest statue to a wild savage; and West, perceiving the unfavourable impression, proceeded to remove it. He described the Mohawks—the natural elegance, and admirable symmetry of their persons—the elasticity of their limbs, and their motions free and unconstrained. "I have seen them often," he continued, "standing in the very attitude of this Apollo, and pursuing with an intense eye the arrow which they had just discharged from the bow." The Italians cleared their moody brows, and allowed that a better criticism had rarely been pronounced. West was no longer a barbarian.

He waited on Lord Grantham. "I cannot," said he, "produce a finished sketch, like the other students, but I can paint a little, and if you will do me the honour to sit for your portrait, that I may show it to Mengs, you will do me a great kindness." His lordship consented, the portrait was painted, and the name of the artist being kept secret, the picture was placed in the gallery of Crespigni, where artists and amateurs were invited to see it. It was known that Mengs was painting Lord Grantham's portrait, and to him they ascribed the picture, though they thought the colouring surpassed his other compositions. Dance, an Englishman of sense and acuteness, looked at it closely. "The colouring surpasses that of Mengs," he observed, "but the drawing is neither so good nor so fine." The company engaged eagerly in the discussion. Crespigni seized the proper moment, and said, "It is not painted by Mengs." "By whom, then?" they exclaimed, "for there is no other painter in Rome capable of doing any thing so good." "By that young gentleman," said the other, turning to West, who sat uneasy and agitated. The English held out their hands; the Italians ran and embraced him.

The story of his success with the portrait of Lord Grantham

found its way to Allan, in Philadelphia, when he was at dinner with Governor Hamilton. "I regard this young man," said the worthy merchant, "as an honour to his country; and as he is the first that America has sent out to cultivate the fine arts, he shall not be frustrated in his studies, for I shall send him whatever he may require." "I think with you, sir," said Hamilton, "but you must not have all the honour to yourself. Allow me to unite with you in the responsibility of the credit." Some time afterwards, when West went to take up ten pounds from his agents, the last of the sum with which he had commenced his studies, one of the partners opened a letter, and said, "I am instructed to give you unlimited credit; you will have the goodness to ask for what sum you please." It is not without cause that Mr. Galt says, "The munificence of the Medici was equalled by these American magistrates."

West, with recovered health and a heavier purse, was now able to follow the counsel of Mengs; he visited Florence, Bologna, and Venice.

On the 20th of June, 1763, West arrived in London. Allan, Hamilton, and Smith, his early and steadfast friends, happened to be there: they welcomed him with open arms. At this time he had no intention of remaining in England, nor of practising his profession for the time that he stayed. He visited the collections of Hampton Court, Windsor, and Blenheim; residing some time at Reading with Thomas West, the half-brother of his father, and looked at the vanities of Bath in the middle of its season. By degrees he began to love the land and the people. He was introduced to Reynolds; and a letter from Mengs made him acquainted with Wilson. Intercourse with artists, and an examination of their works, awakened his ambition; he consulted no one, but took chambers in Bedford-street, Covent-

Garden, and set up his easel. When his determination was known, his brethren in art came round him in a body, welcomed him with much cordiality, and encouraged him to continue his career as an historical painter. Reynolds was devoted to portraits; Hogarth on the brink of the grave; Barry engaged in controversies in Rome; Wilson neglected; Gainsborough's excellence lay in landscape; and the prudent American saw that he had a fair field and no opponents.

This successful beginning, and the promise of full employment, induced him to resolve on remaining in the Old Country.

Dr. Drummond, the archbishop of York, a dignified and liberal prelate, invited West to his table, conversed with him on the influence of art, and on the honour which the patronage of genius reflected on the rich; and opening Tacitus, pointed out that fine passage where Agrippina lands with the ashes of Germanicus. He caused his son to read it again and again, commented upon it with taste and feeling, and requested West to make him a painting on that subject. The artist went home; it was then late; but before closing his eyes he formed a sketch, and carried it early next morning to his patron, who, glad to see that his own notions were likely to be embodied in lasting colours, requested that the full size work might be proceeded with.

The archbishop sought and obtained an audience of his majesty, George III., then young and unacquainted with cares; informed him that a devout American and Quaker had painted, at his request, such a noble picture, that he was desirous to secure his talents for the throne and country. The king was much pleased with the story, and said, "Let me see this young painter of yours, with his Agrippina, as soon as you please."

The king received West with easy frankness, assisted him to place the Agrippina in a favourable light, removed the attendants, and brought in the queen, to whom he presented our Quaker. He related to her majesty the history of the picture, and bade her notice the simplicity of the design and the beauty of the colouring. "There is another noble Roman subject," observed his majesty, "the departure of Regulus from Rome—would it not make a fine picture?" "It is a magnificent subject," said the painter. "Then," said the king, "you shall paint it for me." He turned with a smile to the queen, and said, "The archbishop made one of his sons read Tacitus to Mr. West, but I will read Livy to him myself—that part where he describes the departure of Regulus." So saying, he read the passage very gracefully, and then repeated his command that the picture should be painted.

West had the good fortune to maintain his influence at Windsor. When the king grew weary of courts, and camps, and battles, the observing artist took new ground, and appealed to the religious feelings of his royal patron. He suggested to the king a series of pictures on the progress of revealed religion: a splendid oratory was projected for their reception; and half a dozen dignitaries of the Church were summoned to consider the propriety of introducing paintings into a place of worship. After some deliberation, Bishop Hurd delivered, in the name of his brethren and himself, their unanimous opinion that the introduction of religious paintings into his Majesty's Chapel would in no respect whatever violate the laws and usages of the Church of England. "We have examined, too," continued Hurd, "thirty-five subjects which the painter proposed for our choice, and we feel that there is not one of them but may be treated in a way that even a Quaker might contemplate with edification." The king conceived this to be an ironical allusion to West, and was a little nettled. "The Quakers," he replied, "are a body of Christians for whom I have a high respect. I love their peaceful tenets and their benevolence to one another; and, but for the obligations of birth, I would be a Quaker." The bishop bowed submissively and retired.

No subtle divine ever labored more diligently on controversial texts, than did our painter in evolving his pictures out of the grand and awful subject of revealed religion. He divided it into four dispensations—the Antediluvian, the Patriarchal, the Mosaical, and the Prophetical. They contained in all thirty-six subjects, eighteen of which belonged to the Old Testament, the rest to the New. They were all sketched, and twenty-eight were executed, for which West received in all twenty-one thousand seven hundred and five pounds. A work so varied, so extensive, and so noble in its nature, was never before undertaken by any painter. But the imagination of West was unable to cope with such glorious themes; the soft, the graceful, and the domestic were more suited to his talents.

He was now moving in the first circles, and the word of West was the courtly sanction in matters of taste. His various and extensive works left little leisure for the acquisition of extra-professional knowledge, but he made the little that he did know go far; and found means to pass with men of some discernment as a silent person of fair education who did not wish to throw any wisdom away. The royal favour was much, and he had besides a certain quiet air of natural dignity in his manner.

The death of Reynolds vacated the president's chair, and no one then living was more worthy to fill it than Mr. West.

The new president delivered many discourses, all more or less distinguished for plain practical sense; but he had no unstudied felicities of phrase, little vigour of thought, or happiness of illustration—he was cold, sensible, and instructive; and the student, who may learn from his pictures the way to manage a difficult subject, and from his life the art of employing his time, can hardly be expected to re-read his discourses.

He rose early—studied before breakfast—began to work at one of his large pictures about ten—painted with little intermission till four—dressed and saw visitors, and having dined, recommenced his studies anew. His works were chiefly historical; he dealt with the dead; and the solitude of his gallery was seldom invaded by the rich or the great, clamouring for their portraits.

When he succeeded to the president's chair, the king wished to confer upon him the distinction of knighthood. The royal sword had probably never been laid on the shoulder of a Quaker, and curiosity was excited. The duke of Gloucester called on West from the king to inquire if this honour would be acceptable. "No man," said Benjamin, "entertains a higher respect for political honours and distinctions than myself, but I really think I have earned greater eminence by my pencil already than knighthood could confer on me. The chief value of titles is to preserve in families a respect for those principles by which such distinctions were originally obtained—but simple knighthood to a man who is at least as well known as he could ever hope to be from that honour, is not a legitimate object of ambition. To myself, then, your highness must perceive the title could add no dignity, and as it would perish with myself, it could add none to my family. But were I possessed of fortune, independent of my profession, sufficient to enable my posterity to maintain the rank, I think that with my hereditary descent and the station I occupy among artists, a more permanent title might become a desirable object. As it is, however, that cannot be; and I have been thus explicit with your royal highness that no misconception may exist on the subject." The duke took West by the hand, and said, " You have justified the opinion which the king has of you; he will be delighted with your answer."

Christ healing the Sick was painted for the Philadelphia hospital. When exhibited in London, the crush to see it was very great—the praise it obtained was very high—and the British Institution offered him three thousand guineas for the work: West accepted the offer, for he was far from being rich,—but on condition that he should be allowed to make a copy, with alterations, for his native place. He did so; and when the copy went to America, the profits arising from its exhibition, enabled the committee of the hospital to enlarge the building and receive more patients.

The success of this piece impressed West with a belief that his genius appeared to most advantage in pictures of large dimensions, and that royal commissions had hitherto interposed between him and fortune. His mind, from long contemplation, was familiar with subjects of gigantic proportions; and he soon sketched out several, and finished some. But there was no market for them. Few were tempted to become purchasers, though many were edified with the Descent of the Holy Ghost on Christ at the Jordan, the Crucifixion, the Ascension, and the Inspiration of St. Peter—all large pictures.

As old age benumbed his faculties, and began to freeze up the well-spring of original thought, his daring intrepidity seemed but to grow and augment. Immense pictures came crowding upon his fancy, and he was the only person who appeared insensible that such were too weighty for his handling. It was evident that all this was soon to cease, that he was suffering a slow and general and easy decay. The venerable man sat in his study among his favourite pictures, a breathing image of piety and contentment, awaiting calmly the hour of his dissolution. Without any fixed complaint, his mental faculties unimpaired, his cheerfulness uneclipsed, and with looks serene and benevolent, he expired, 11th March, 1820, in the eighty-second year of his age. He was buried beside Reynolds, Opie, and Barry, in St. Paul's cathedral. The pall was borne by noblemen, ambassadors, and academicians; his two sons and grandson were chief mourners; and sixty coaches brought up the splendid procession.

West's kindness to young artists was great—his liberality seriously impaired his income—he never seemed weary of giving advice—intrusion never disturbed his temper—nor could the tediousness of the dull, ever render him impatient or peevish. Whatever he knew in art he readily imparted—he was always happy to think that art was advancing, and no mean jealousy of other men's good fortune ever invaded his repose.

As his life was long and laborious, his productions are very numerous. He painted and sketched in oil upwards of four hundred pictures, mostly historical and religious, and he left more than two hundred original drawings in his portfolios. His works were supposed by himself, and for a time by others, to be in the true spirit of the great masters, and he composed them with the serious ambition and hope of illustrating Scripture, and rendering gospel truth more impressive. In all his works the human form was exhibited in conformity to academic precepts—his figures were arranged with skill—the colouring was varied and harmonious—the eye rested pleased on the performance, and the artist seemed to the ordinary spectator, to have done his task like one of the highest of the sons of genius. But below all this splendor there was little of the true vitality—there was a monotony, too, of human character—the groupings were unlike the happy and careless combinations of nature, and the figures seemed distributed over the canvass by line and measure, like trees in a plantation.

In his Death on the Pale Horse, and more particularly in the sketch of that picture, he has more than approached the masters and princes of the calling. The Battle of La Hogue has been praised as the best historic picture of the British school. Many of his single figures, too, are of a high order. There is a natural grace in the looks of some of his women which few painters have ever excelled.

West was injured by early success, he obtained his fame too easily—it was not purchased by long study and many trials—and he rashly imagined himself capable of any thing.

BARRY.

James Barry was born in Cork, on the 11th of October, 1741. There is no decided information concerning the subjects which employed his boyish pencil. We know that ere he left his native city he had painted, in oil colours, Æneas escaping from the Burning of Troy, Susanna and the Elders, Daniel in the Lion's Den, and Abraham's Sacrifice; but whether these were copies or originals is not mentioned.

His father's name had not been heard of beyond Cork; it was soon to be known in remote parts, and received with a favour which must have fallen on Barry like a shower upon a summer drought. There is a tradition in the Irish Church concerning the conversion of a king of Cashel, by the eloquence of St. Patrick. The barbarian prince, when the apostle concluded his exhortation, called loudly to be baptized; and such was the hurry of the one, and the fortitude of the other, that though the saint, in planting his iron-shod crosier in the ground, struck it unwittingly through the royal convert's foot, he uttered not one murmur, nor yet moved a muscle, but, conceiving it to be a part of the ceremony, stood and was baptized. "The moment of baptism," says Dr. Fryer," rendered so critical and awful, by the circumstance of the king's foot being pierced with the spear, is that which Mr. Barry chose for a display of his art; and few stories, it is presumed, have been selected with greater felicity, or with greater scope, for the skill and ingenuity of the artist. The heroic patience of the king, the devotional abstraction of the saint, and the mixed emotions of the spectators, form a combined and comprehensive model of imitation, and convey a suitable idea of the genius of one, who, self-instructed, and at nineteen, conceived the execution of so grand a design."

With this work in his hand, Barry went to Dublin, and placed it among the paintings collected for exhibition, by the Society for the Encouragement of Arts, &c. The picture was exhibited and admired; but so little was such a work expected from a native artist, that when the name of the painter was demanded, and he stepped modestly forward, no one would believe him; his brow glowed, he burst into tears, and hurried out of the room. All this was observed by Edmund Burke, one of the greatest and best-hearted of all the sons of genius. He sought the young artist out, commended and encouraged him, laid down the natural rules of composition, and directed his attention to what was pure and poetical. One of those incidents which biographers love to relate, and the world indulgently believes, is said to have happened at the very first interview between these two youthful adventurers. They had plunged into controversy in the first hour of their friendship, and Barry, in aid of his argument, quoted a passage from the "Essay on the Sublime and Beautiful," then published without the author's name. Burke refused to bow to the authority of a performance which he called slight and unsubstantial; and the fiery Barry exclaimed: "Do you call that a slight and unsubstantial work, which is conceived in the spirit of nature and truth, is written with such elegance, and strewn all over with the richness of poetic fancy? I could not afford to buy the work, sir, and transcribed it every word with my own hand." Burke smiled, and acknowledged himself the author. "Are you!" exclaimed Barry, embracing him, and holding up the copy which he had made of the work.

In his twenty-third year Barry went to London, on the invitation of Burke, who introduced him to Athenian Stewart, whose conversation confirmed him in his love for the ancients, and to Sir Joshua Reynolds, in whose works he studied delicacy of style, propriety of character, and force of light and shade. "If I should chance to have genius, or any thing else," he observes, in a letter to Dr. Sleigh, "it is so much the better; but my hopes are grounded on an unwearied, intense application, of which I am not sparing. At present, I have little to show that I value; my work is all underground, digging and laying foundations, which, with God's assistance, I may hereafter find the use of. I every day centre more and more upon the art; I give myself totally to it: and, except honour and conscience, am determined to renounce every thing else. Though this may appear enthusiastic, or rather extravagant, it is really the state of my mind."

Barry pursued his studies in London for a year, when Burke generously fitted him out for his journey to Rome, and settled an annual pension on him during the period of probationary study.

Barry failed to discover in the compositions of the illustrious masters of Italy, the entire proportion, and grace, and simplicity of the Grecian sculpture. He was too ardent in his nature to keep this to himself; he preached this unheard-of heresy in Rome with the fervour of a devotee; and thus unbosomed himself to

Burke: "I see," he said, "in no part of Raphael's work, any figure that I may call truly and correctly beautiful, like the Antinous, or the Venus of Medici; or any that is truly good, like the bust of Alexander. Michael Angelo appears still less near the standard than Raphael. He is infinitely above Raphael in knowledge and correctness; yet his ostentation and show of this, and Raphael's art of concealing, bring them nearly to a level; fewer have attained Michael Angelo's merits than Raphael's, though no one has come near the latter on the whole."

"At Nitri," he says in one of his letters, "are monuments which give me heartfelt pleasure. One is a piece of raw hide, a little broader than the sole of the foot, tied on after the manner of the ancient sandal. I bought a pair of them, and will show you the villany of our Gothic shoes, which, by the line which the termination of the upper leather makes upon the stocking, cuts off the foot from the leg, and loses that fine idea of one limb, which is kept up in this vestige of a sandal."

On his arrival in England he was warmly welcomed by Burke; and measuring himself at once with the most lovely of all Grecian productions, he painted Venus rising from the Sea. This picture was allowed by both friends and foes to be an exquisite one; but he painted it in vain; it excited no lively sympathy—no fresh emotion; the subject had been exhausted by sculptor and painter. The great artists of Greece and Italy wrought in the spirit of their age and country; they sought at home for subjects of high character, yet familiarly known. But the heathen gods on Barry's canvass, appealed to no popular sympathy—to no national belief—to no living superstition. The mob marvelled what they meant, and the learned had little to say.

The vehement temper of Barry led him to waste his time in

continued broils with his brother artists, and kept him involved in pecuniary difficulties. The high distinction which he claimed, as follower of the grand style, rendered it necessary, he imagined, that he should vindicate his title. He determined to offer his pencil to the Society of Arts; and applied to adorn their great room at the Adelphi with a series of historical paintings, all from his own hand, and wholly at his own expense. When he made this magnificent offer, he had but sixteen shillings in his pocket; and was aware that if this offer was accepted, he must steal time from sleep to supply him with the means of life.

He had now ample room and verge enough to exhaust his powers of imagination, and exhibit all his knowledge and skill. The subject which he selected was Human Improvement. He divided the whole into six compartments. "We begin," says the artist, describing his own conceptions, "with man in a savage state, full of inconvenience, imperfection, and misery, and we follow him through several gradations of culture and happiness, which, after our probationary state here, are finally attended with beatitude or misery.

The first picture represents Orpheus as the founder of Grecian civilization; uniting in one character the legislator, divine, philosopher poet, and musician. He stands in a wild and savage country, surrounded by people as uncultivated as their soil, to whom, as messenger of the gods, he is pouring out his song of instruction, accompanied by the music of the lyre. The hearers of this celestial delegate are armed with clubs, and clad in the skins of wild beasts; they have courage and strength, by which they subdue lions and tigers; but they want wisdom for their own protection and for that of their offspring. In illustration of this, a matron is seen, at a little distance from the door of her hut, milking a goat, while her children are about to become the prey of a lion ; two horses are run down by a tiger ; and a damsel, carrying a dead fawn, leans on the shoulder of her male companion. In the distance, Ceres descends on the world ; and by the side of Orpheus, lie paper, an egg, a bound lamb, and materials for sacrifice.

The second piece exhibits a dance of youths and maidens round the terminal figure of Pan. On one side appears the father of the harvest feast, with a white staff or rustic sceptre in his hand, accompanied by his wife ; on the other is a group of peasants, carousing amid rakes and ploughs, and fruits and flowers ; while behind the whole, two oxen are seen drawing a load of corn to the threshing-floor. Ceres, Bacchus, and Pan, overlook from the clouds this scene of innocent festivity. A farm-house, with all its inn-door and out-door economy, is there. Love, too, and marriage mingle in the scene ; children abound ; rustic games are not forgotten ; and aged men repose on the ground, applauding sports in which they can no longer participate.

The third picture—the crowning the victors in the Olympian games—shows the judges seated on a throne, bearing the likenesses of Solon, Lycurgus, and other legislators, and trophies of Salamis, Marathon, and Thermopylæ. Before them pass the victors crowned ; people are crowding to look on them. The heroes, poets, sages, and philosophers of Greece are present. Pindar leads the chorus ; Hiero, of Syracuse, follows in his chariot ; Diagorus, the Rhodian, is borne round the stadium on the shoulders of his victorious sons ; Pericles is seen speaking to Cimon ; while Socrates, Anaxagoras, and Euripides listen, and Aristophanes laughs and scoffs.

The fourth piece descends to modern times, and the scene is laid at home. The Thames triumphs in the presence of Drake,

Raleigh, Cabot, and Cook. Mercury, as Commerce, accompanies them; and Nereids are carrying articles of manufacture and industry. Some of these demi-celestial porters are more sportive than laborious, and others more wanton than sportive. As music is connected closely with all matters of joy and triumph, Burney, the composer, accompanies Drake and Raleigh, and cheers them with his instruments.

The fifth picture is the meeting of the members of the Society of Arts, discoursing on the manufactures, commerce, and liberal pursuits of the country, and distributing the annual premiums. It is an assemblage of the chief promoters of the institution, male and female, with the gratuitous addition of Johnson and Burke.

The sixth picture is a view of Elysium. Mental Culture conducts to Piety and Virtue, and Piety and Virtue are rewarded by Immortal Happiness. In a picture forty-two feet long, the artist brings together the chief of the distinguished men of various nations, in one connected group, over which a splendor is shed, from between the wings of angels.

Those who have examined these extraordinary works, will hardly dispute that the artist grappled with a subject too varied, complicated, and profound, for the pencil. The moral grandeur of the undertaking, and the historical associations which it awakened, together with the room which it afforded for the display of imagination, imposed upon the ardent and indiscriminating Barry, and he propably began in the belief that the subject would unfold and brighten upon him by degrees.

A young lady of great wit and beauty, went to see the Elysium. She looked earnestly for a while, and said to Mr. Barry: "The ladies have not arrived in this paradise of yours." "Oh, but they have, madam," said the painter, with a smile;

" they reached Elysium some time ago, but I could find no place so fit for creatures so bright and beautiful, as behind yon very luminous cloud—they are there, and very happy, I assure you." On these six pictures Barry spent six years, instead of three as he had originally contemplated. A miscalculation that involved him in many difficulties, out of which he strove to extricate himself by uncommon frugality, self-denial, and labour during the periods he should have reserved for repose. He gave his day to the Adelphi, and much of the night to hurried drawing and hasty engravings, by the profits of which he sustained life.

His character, and whole system of in-door economy, were exhibited in a dinner he gave Mr. Burke. No one was better acquainted with the singular manners of this very singular man than the great statesman. He wished, however, to have ocular demonstration how he managed his household concerns in the absence of wife or servant, and requested to be asked to dinner. "Sir," said Barry, "you know I live alone; but if you will come and eat a steak with me, you shall have it tender and hot, and from the most classic market in London—that of Oxford." The day and the hour came, and Burke arriving at No. 36 Castle-street, found Barry ready to receive him. He was conducted into the painting-room, which had undergone no change since it was a carpenter's shop. On one of the walls hung his large picture of Pandora, and round it were placed the studies of the six pictures of the Adelphi. There were likewise old straining frames, old sketches, and a printing-press, on which he printed his plates with his own hands. The labours of the spider, too, abounded, and rivalled in extent and colour pieces of old tapestry.

Burke saw all this, and yet wisely seemed to see it not. He observed, too, that most of the windows were broken or cracked, that the roof, which had no ceiling, admitted the light through many crevices in the tiling, and that two old chairs and a deal table composed the whole of the furniture. The fire was burning brightly; the steaks were put on to broil, and Barry having spread a clean cloth on the table, put a pair of tongs in the hand of Burke, saying, "Be useful, my dear friend, and look to the steaks, while I fetch the porter." Burke did as he was desired. The painter soon returned with the porter in his hand, exclaiming, "What a misfortune! the wind carried away the fine foaming top, as I crossed Titchfield-street." They sat down together; the steak was tender, and done to a moment; the artist was full of anecdote, and Burke often declared that he never spent a happier evening in his life.

That Barry failed to reap the harvest which his qualities and attainments promised, must be imputed mainly to his infirmity of temper; but partly also to what he so often complained of—the unawakened taste of his country for works of an historical character. Other reasons, however, may be assigned for Barry's want of success. His first picture, the Legend of St. Patrick, was right—it was one of his own island's traditions—in it he heard the voice of nature, and he who obeys her, will seldom fail. But afterwards, the miracles of Greece and the Vatican oppressed and enthralled his fancy. The artist who disdains to work in the spirit of his own country, will rarely work well in the spirit of any other. The names of Barry's pictures will tell where his heart was—Pandora, or the Heathen Eve; the Conversion of Polemon, in the presence of Xenocrates; the Birth of Venus; Philoctetus in Lemnos; Jupiter and Juno—and many more. Fondness for such subjects had long since fallen asleep, and it was not in the power of Barry to awaken it. To be truly classic, he should have done for Britain what the artists of old did for Greece. Their works are classical—not from being the offspring of a classic land, but because they were the embodied poetry of its actual beauty and sentiment. Subjects of ordinary emotion had no charms for him : he loved to contemplate what was solemn and terrible ; and his mind teemed with magnificent undertakings, which he wanted time or talent to realize. The multitude of his sketches, and the small number of his finished works, attest his immoderate ambition, and his deficiency in some of those high qualities which, like the key-stone of an arch, is necessary to the completion of whatever is vast or grand.

RUNCIMAN.

Alexander Runciman was born at Edinburgh in 1736. When some six years old, he began to make rude drawings ; and before he was twelve, had shown such a decided inclination to painting, that his father was induced to encourage him. After painting twelve years in his mother country, he visited Rome, where he remained five years, and practised his hand and eye, morning, noon, and night, in drawing from the antique, copying the best works of the old masters, and assiduous study of those paintings of an historic order which are scattered profusely through the Italian galleries.

Historical painting had become the confirmed idol of Runciman, since he had beheld the wonders of the Sistine ; and he was no sooner settled in the north, than he submitted the design of a great national work to Sir J. Clerke—namely, to embellish his hall at Pennycuick with a series of paintings from Ossian. This was agreed to at once. The poems ascribed to the blind old man of Morven, were at that time in all the full-blown splendor of fame. The singular boldness of the style, the wildness of the imagery, the deep heroic and chivalrous feelings which they breathed, rendered them universal favourites.

There are twelve principal paintings, representing some of the finest passages of the poems:—1. Ossian singing to Malvina: "Daughter of the hand of snow, I was not so mournful and blind when Everallan loved me." 2. The Valour of Oscar: "Behold, they fall before my son, like the groves in the desert, when an angry ghost rushes through the night, and takes their green heads in his hand. Cairbar shrinks from Oscar's sword, and creeps in darkness behind his stone. He lifted up his spear in secret and pierced my Oscar's side." 3. The Death of Oscar: "We saw Oscar on his shield; we saw his blood around; silence darkens every face; each turns his face and weeps; the king strives to hide his tears." 4. Death of Agendecca: "'Bring hither,' says Starno, 'Agendecca to her lovely king of Morven.' She came with red eyes of tears; she came with her loose and raven locks; Starno pierced her side with steel; she fell like a wreath of snow, which slides from the rocks of Ronan." 5. The Hunting of Catholda: "Many a hero came to woo the maid, the stately huntress of Termoth wild; but thou lookest careless from thy steps, high-bosomed Strina Donna," &c.

Those who examine the works of Runciman, with a wish to find beauties rather than faults, will not look in vain. Certainly true genius for art is present in most of his performances. Brown, his scholar and his friend, an able artist, thus writes regarding the merits of his master: "His fancy was fertile, his discernment of character keen, his taste truly elegant, and his conception always great. Though his genius seems to be best suited to the grand and serious, yet many of his works amply prove that he could move with equal success in the less elevated line of the gay and the pleasing. His chief excellence was composition, the noblest part of the art, in which it is doubtful if he had any living superior."

COPLEY.

John Singleton Copley, was by the most credible accounts born in Boston, Mass., in 1737. Be that as it will, he was educated in America, and to her he owes his first inspiration in art. This came upon him, it seems, early enough : when some seven or eight years old, he was observed to absent himself from the family for several hours at a time, and was traced to a lonely room, on whose bare walls he had drawn, in charcoal, a group of martial figures, engaged in some nameless adventure. Boston, at this period, had neither Academy of Arts, nor private instructors. Copley had, therefore, to educate himself. Of Copley's very early works no better account can be rendered, than that they were chiefly portraits and domestic groups, to which the wild wood scenery of America usually formed backgrounds.

In his thirty-seventh year he visited Rome, and after about a year's travel he settled in London. In February, 1783, the king sanctioned his election as a royal academician.

By this time Copley's name had been established by works of eminent merit ; among the first of which was "The Death of Chatham." The chief excellence of this picture, is the accurate delineation of that impressive event, and the vast number of impressive heads, all portraits, with which the House of Lords is thronged ; its chief fault is an air of formality, and a deficiency of deep feeling : yet, it must be owned, that those who are near the dying statesman are sufficiently moved. The picture was so much admired, that the artist was emboldened to have an engraving made from it of unusual size, viz. : thirty inches long and twenty-two inches and a half high, by the hand of Bartolozzi. The artist could not but feel gratified with the united thanks of Washington and Adams, to whom he had presented two of the prints: "This work," says the former, "highly valuable in itself, is rendered more estimable in my eye, when I remember that America gave birth to the celebrated artist who produced it." "I shall preserve my copy," said the latter, "both as a token of your friendship, and as an indubitable proof of American genius."

He died in the seventy-eighth year of his age, in 1815. He was long in quest of, and he wrote out receipts for composing those lustrous hues in which Titian and Coreggio excelled. For the worth of his discoveries, rather look at his works than read his receipts; of all that he ever painted, nothing surpasses his Boy and Squirrel, for fine depth and beauty of colour; and this was done, probably, before he heard the name of Titian pronounced. His Samuel reproving Saul for sparing the People of Amalek, is a fine piece of colouring, with good feeling and good drawing too. He shares with West, the reproach of want of natural warmth; and uniting much stateliness with little passion. As to his personal character, it seems to have been in all essential respects that of an honourable and accomplished gentleman.

Copley's eminent son, Lord Lyndhurst, still inhabits the artist's house in George-street, Hanover Square; and all must consider it as honourable to this noble person, that he has made it his object to collect the works of his father's pencil, wherewith to adorn the apartments in which they were conceived and produced.

ROMNEY.

George Romney was born at Beckside, in Lancashire, in 1734. His works are of two kinds, history and portrait; in both of which he attained, in the eyes of many, great distinction, and during his day ranked with the foremost. In his portraits there appears such skill in drawing, such accuracy in delineation, and such clear and natural colouring, as in a great measure justify the taste of those who crowded to his easel, and considered him as the rival of Reynolds, and the chief painter of his day. In his portraits Romney missed, certainly, the grace and ease, and the fine flush of colouring, which have brought lasting fame to Reynolds; and he wanted, moreover, his illustrious rival's exquisite prudence in handling the costume of the day, so as to soften down the capes and cuffs and buttons. There appears, however, traces of great dignity and manliness in all his heads; and in some, a certain touch of poetic loftiness, of which Reynolds has furnished hardly an example.

His historical and domestic pictures, finished and unfinished, deserve a more minute examination; they embrace a wide range of reading and observation; and are numerous beyond all modern example. "Most of these," says Flaxman, "were of the delicate class, and each had its peculiar character. Titania, with her Indian votaress, was arch and sprightly; Milton, dictating to his daughters, solemn and interesting. Several pictures of Wood Nymphs, and Bacchantes charmed by their rural beauty, innocence, and simplicity. The most pathetic, perhaps, of all his works, was never finished: Ophelia, with the flowers she had gathered in her hand, sitting on the branch of a tree, which was breaking under her, while the melancholy distraction visible in her lovely countenance accounts for the insensibility to her danger. Few painters have left so many examples in their works, of the tender and delicate affections; and several of his pictures breathe a kindred spirit with the Sigismonda of Coreggio. His cartoons, some of which have unfortunately perished, were examples of the sublime and terrible; at that time perfectly new in English art. As Romney was gifted with peculiar powers for historical and ideal painting, so his heart and soul were engaged in the pursuit of it, whenever he could extricate himself from the importunate business of portrait painting. It was his delight by day, and study by night: and for this his food and rest were often neglected. His compositions, like those of the ancient pictures and basso-relievos, told their story by a single group of figures in the front; while the background is made the simplest possible, rejecting all unnecessary episode and trivial ornament, either of secondary groups or architectural subdivision. In his compositions, the beholder was forcibly struck by the sentiment at the first glance, the gradations and varieties of which he traced through several characters, all conceived in an elevated spirit of dignity and beauty, with a lively expression of nature in all the parts.

FUSELI.

Henry Fuseli was born in 1741, at Zurich. He made great progress in learning: having overleaped the first difficulties, he became an ardent devourer of the classics; but it was only or chiefly to find in the poetry of Greece and Rome, vivid images of life and daring flights of imagination.

The time which the school demanded was thus spent by one who could do in minutes what would have cost his fellows hours;

for the rest of the day he had other occupation. As soon as he was released from his class, he withdrew to a secret place to enjoy unmolested the works of Michael Angelo, of whose prints his father had a fine collection. He loved, when he grew old, to talk of those days of his youth, of the enthusiasm with which he surveyed the works of his favourite masters, and the secret pleasure which he took in acquiring forbidden knowledge. With candles which he took from the kitchen, and pencils which his pocket-money was hoarded to procure, he pursued his studies till late at night, and made many copies from Michael Angelo and Raphael, by which he became familiar, thus early, with the style and ruling character of the two great masters of the art.

Lavater presented Fuseli with a card on which he had inscribed in German, "Do but the tenth part of what you can do." "Hang that up at your bed-head," said the physiognomist, "obey it, and fame and fortune will be the result."

He lived in England for several years, and found his way to the studio of Sir Joshua Reynolds; to him he submitted several of his drawings. The president looked at them for some time, and then said, "How long have you studied in Italy?" "I never studied in Italy; I studied at Zurich; I am a native of Switzerland; do you think I should study in Italy? and, above all, is it worth while?" "Young man," said Reynolds, "were I the author of these drawings, and were offered ten thousand a year not to practise as an artist, I would reject the proposal with contempt." This very favourable opinion from one who considered all he said, and was so remarkable for accuracy of judgment, decided the destiny of Fuseli, and he forsook for ever the hard and thankless trade of literature.

The first effort of his pencil was Joseph interpreting the Dreams of Pharaoh's chief Baker and Butler. Of his studies in the numerous galleries of Italy he has left a minute account. He refused to follow the common method of laboriously copying the chief pictures of the great masters, with the hope of carrying away their spirit as well as the image of their works. He sought to animate his own compositions by contemplating rather than transcribing theirs. With the reputation of an eight years' residence in Rome upon him, he commenced his professional career, and the beginning was auspicious.

The first work that proved that an original mind had appeared in England was the Nightmare, exhibited in 1782. "The extraordinary and peculiar genius which it displayed," says one of his biographers, "was universally felt, and perhaps no single picture ever made a greater impression in this country." A very fine mezzotinto engraving of it was made by Raphael Smith, and so popular did the print become, that, although Mr. Fuseli received only twenty guineas for the picture, the publisher made five hundred by his speculation." This was a subject suitable to the unbridled fancy of the painter, and perhaps to no other imagination has the fiend which murders our sleep appeared in a more poetical shape.

Shakespeare presented a whole world to the eye of art; and to embody the whole or any considerable portion of his visions, would demand a combination of powers not to be hoped for. As might have been expected, Fuseli grappled with the wildest passages of the most imaginative plays; and he handled them with a kind of happy and vigorous extravagance which startled common beholders.

The Tempest, the Midsummer Night's Dream, King Lear, and Hamlet suggested the best of the eight Shakespearian pictures which he painted; and of these, that from Hamlet is certainly the noblest. It is indeed, strangely wild and superhuman; if ever a spirit visited the earth it must have appeared to Fuseli. The majesty of buried Denmark is no vulgar ghost, such as scares the belated rustic, but a sad and majestic shape with the port of a god ; to imagine this required poetry, and in that our artist was never deficient. He had a fine taste in matters of high import ; he drew the boundary line between the terrible and the horrible, and he never passed it ; the former, he knew was allied to grandeur, the latter to deformity and disgust. An eminent metaphysician visited the gallery before the public exhibition ; he saw Fuseli's picture of the Ghost in Hamlet, and declared that it haunted him round the room.

The Milton gallery of paintings was commenced in 1790, completed in 1800, and contained in all forty-seven pictures from the works of the illustrious poet. To this task the artist brought many high powers; but when the doors of the Milton gallery were opened to the world, it was seen that the genius of Fuseli was of a different order from that of Milton. To the severe serene majesty of the poet the intractable fancy of the painter had refused to bow ; the awful grandeur of the realm of perdition, and the sublime despair of its untameable tenant, were too much for him, though he probably thought them too little. He could add fury to Moloch and malignity to Beelzebub ; but he fell below the character of terrible daring, enduring fortitude, and angelic splendor, which mark the arch-apostate of Milton. The most visible want is in that grave and majestic solemnity with which the poet has invested all that he has touched ; and the chief excellences to be set against this prevailing defect are, a certain aërial buoyancy, and a supernatural glow of colour which, in some of these pieces, fill the imagination of the observer, and redeem, in so far, the reputation of Fuseli.

In the original sketch of the guardian angels forsaking our first parents after the fall, they were represented as rising on wings. He looked earnestly at his sketch, and exclaimed—for he generally thought aloud—"They *shall* rise without wings." He tried and succeeded.

It pleased Fuseli to be thought one of those erudite gentlemen whom the poet describes—

"Far seen in Greek—deep men of letters."

When thwarted in the Academy, and that was not seldom, his wrath aired itself in a polyglot. "It is a pleasant thing and an advantageous," said the painter on one of those occasions, "to be learned. I can speak Greek, Latin, French, English, German, Danish, Dutch, Icelandic, and Spanish, and so let my folly or my fury vent through nine different avenues."

When Barry lost the professorship of painting, in the year 1799, it was bestowed by acclamation on Fuseli, and as his mind was overflowing with knowledge of all kinds, he found little difficulty and much pleasure in fulfilling the duties of his new station. During his professorship he delivered twelve lectures; of which the following are considered the best: On Ancient Art, On the Art of the Moderns, Invention, Composition, and Expression. In these lectures he has poured out learning, observation, and feeling with a lavish hand, and there is an original power in his diction, such as no man has exhibited before or since in a language not his own.

Having conceived an affection for the poetry of Gray—which, however, was confined chiefly to the translations—he painted the Bard, the Descent of Odin, and the Fatal Sisters He was fond, indeed, of the wild mythology of the Scandinavians, and numerous traces of the impression which it had made on his mind might be pointed out in his paintings and in his sketches. His Thor Battering the Serpent was such a favourite that he presented it to the Royal Academy as his admission gift. With quiet beauty and serene grace he knew not how to begin; the hurrying measures, the crowding epithets, and startling imagery of the northern poetry suited the intoxicated fancy of Fuseli.

From 1817 to 1825, Fuseli exhibited at the Academy twelve pictures, and neither the fervour of his fancy nor his skill of hand had failed him in the least. Of his twelve pictures, six were received with much approbation—Perseus starting from the cave of the Gorgons; the Lady and the Infernal Knight, in Theodore and Honoria; Dante, descending into Hell, discovers in a whirlwind the forms of Paolo and Francesca; an Incantation, from Theocritus; Theseus, Ariadne, and the Minotaur; and Comus, from Milton. These works attest his love of poetic art, and his resolution to die as he had lived—in the service of the loftier muses. "I have been a happy man," said Fuseli, "for I have been always well, and always employed in doing what I liked;" a boast which few men of genius can make. When work with the pencil failed, he lifted the pen, and as he was ready and clever with both, he was never obliged to fill up unemployed time with jobs which he disliked.

Fuseli died at the age of 84, in the year 1825.

His main wish was to startle and astonish—it was his ambition to be called Fuseli the daring and the imaginative, the illustrator of Milton and Shakespeare, the rival of Michael Angelo.

His sketches are very numerous, amounting to eight hundred, and show the varied knowledge and vigorous imagination of the man. He busied himself during his hours of leisure with making sketches and drawings from scenes which had occurred in his reading, or had arisen on his fancy; in this manner he illustrated the whole range of poetry, ancient and modern.

Scattered among those sketches, we are sometimes startled by the appearance of a lady floating gracefully along in fashionable attire—her patches, paint, and jewels on—and armed for doing mischief among the sons of modern men. There is no attempt at caricature; they are fac-similies, and favourable ones, of existing life and fashion. Their presence among the works we have described jars upon our feelings; they are out of keeping with the poetic simplicity of their companions, and look as strange as court ladies would do taking the air with Apollo or the dying Gladiator. They do, however, what the painter meant. They tell us how contemptible every thing is, save natural elegance and simple grandeur, and that much which gives splendor to a ball or levee will never mingle with what is lofty or lasting.

COSWAY.

Richard Cosway was born in the year 1740, at Tiverton, in Devonshire. His father, who was master of the public school there, saw, with astonishment, his son, at the age of seven years, neglecting his lessons, and devoting all his time to what he called the idle pursuit of drawing. His skill became so great, that in the course of a few years he obtained no less than five premiums, some of five and one of ten guineas, from the Society of Arts. The first was conferred when he was but fourteen years old; the last when he was under four-and-twenty.

He seems not to have coveted earnestly the applause which follows the painting of works of a high historic order, though he tried his success in that unprofitable style, as well as Barry and

Fuseli. He aspired rather to reign king in the little pleasing paradise of miniature. To gratify the ladies, by the softer graces of his pencil, was, he thought, honour enough, and in that kind of flattery, no one excelled him.

Cosway married Maria Hadfield, a native of Italy, but of English parentage; who, besides her wit and beauty, had such taste and skill in art, as rendered her worthy of the notice of Reynolds and Fuseli, when but eighteen years old. She was educated in a convent, where she learned music and drawing. On her return home, she studied painting, went to Rome for a time, and became acquainted with the best artists.

Her foreign manner and extreme youth induced Cosway to keep his wife at home until she learned the language; and, by intercourse with intimate friends, acquired a knowledge of society. She studied art, too, under her new instructor; and with such success, that almost the first time she was seen in public, she was pointed out as the lady who had painted some of the most lovely miniatures in the Royal Academy Exhibition. Her reputation was made at once; nothing was talked of but the great youth and the great talent of Mrs. Cosway; and one-half of the carriages which stopped at her husband's door, contained sitters ambitious of the honours of her pencil. The painter, however, was too proud a man to permit his wife to paint professionally. This, no doubt, was in favour of domestic happiness, but much against her success in art. The impulse which professional rivalry gives was wanting; and on works which were only to be seen by a few, she wrought with less feeling and care, than is generally bestowed on paintings which challenge public examination.

The climate of England impaired the health of Mrs. Cosway, and, accompanied by her brother, she visited Italy, where she remained nearly three years, expecting, every spring and autumn, the coming of her husband. At length she returned. But she neither found health nor happiness in London—the illness and death of an only daughter threw her upon art once more. To mitigate her grief she painted several large pictures for chapels, and afterwards went to France, without regard to the war, which had commenced between that country and England, and executed what she considered her masterpiece, a work containing all the pictures in the gallery of the Louvre. The turn which the war took, interfered with her stay at Paris; and she was persuaded by Cardinal Fesch to establish a college, for the education of young ladies, at Lyons. This plan was interrupted; and, with her husband's approbation, she passed into Italy, and formed a college at Lodi, similar to that which she planned at Lyons. On the establishment of peace she returned to England.

The latter years of Cosway were passed in pain, bodily and mental. A paralytic stroke deprived him of the use of his right hand, and with it cut off one chief source of pleasure, the power of drawing. His wife watched patiently over him, and tried to render pleasant the many sad hours he was now obliged to spend without other solace; and by her assiduity and tenderness, atoned for the years she had spent out of his household, making experiments in pictures and ladies' colleges. She considered her solicitude to be amply rewarded by the feeling of performing her duty, and by hearing her husband speak of art. His conversation to her, at least, was gay and imaginative. He loved to look at his collection of drawings, at his old armour, at his innumerable curiosities, and to talk of the ancient masters of the calling, and imagine what they would now say, were they to revisit the earth, and see the civilized, grown savage, and the savage, grown civilized. He sometimes startled such visitors as did not know his way, by saying, with a serious air, that he had just had an interview with Praxiteles and Apelles, and the former recommended a closer study of the living figure in the English Academy; and the other, a less gaudy style of colour. These things, to the dull and unimaginative, sounded strange and ridiculous.

He died in 1821, aged eighty years. His accomplished wife returned to her beloved Lodi, where she finally established her ladies' college.

NORTHCOTE.

James Northcote was born at Plymouth, in Devonshire, in the year 1746. His progress in youth was slow, and all that he produced was laboriously done; he had no first outflashings; he grew quietly up into eminence year by year. His desire to be an artist of distinction arose from the fame of Reynolds, whose friendship with the family of the Mudges made him much talked of in Devonport; and his first attempts are said to have been portraits and outlines, which some blamed, and more commended. He was sixteen years old, and irrecoverably an artist, when Sir Joshua Reynolds visited Devonport, accompanied by Dr. Johnson. "I remember," said Northcote, "when he was pointed out to me at a public meeting, where a great crowd was assembled; I got as near to him as I could from the pressure of the people, to touch the skirt of his coat, which I did with great satisfaction to my mind." This is sufficiently enthusiastic, and shows the resolute liking which already possessed him for painting.

With the year 1771, the fortune of Northcote began to dawn. Sir Joshua Reynolds was prevailed on to admit him into his house as a student, and to give him all the advantages of his gallery. He also attended the Royal Academy, where he drew from sculpture, and afterwards from the living model.

Of his studies under the eye of Sir Joshua, he relates that, for the sake of practice, he painted the portrait of one of the female servants. The likeness was so strong, that it was recognized by a large macaw, which Reynolds introduced into several of his pictures. The bird had no good-will to the maid-servant, and the moment he saw her portrait, he spread out his wings, and ran in fury and bit at the face. Perceiving that he made no impression, he struck at the hand, and then looked behind, and lowering his wings, walked off. Sir Joshua observed, "that it was as extraordinary an instance as the old story of the bunch of grapes."

Northcote set out for Italy in 1777. When he reached Rome, he went to the Sistine chapel, and paid homage, as his master had done, to the presiding spirit of the place. The more he studied, the more he was convinced that little was lasting which had not its source in science and poetry; and he surrendered his feelings freely to this new impulse. With all his enthusiasm, he perceived, what few artists have done, namely: that neither repetitions of the antique would do in sculpture, nor imitations of Raphael in painting. "It is easy," said he, "to imitate one of the old masters. If you would last, you must invent something. To do otherwise, is only to pour water from one vessel to another, that becomes staler every time. We are tired of the antique; the world wants something new, and will have it; no matter whether it be better or worse, if there is but an infusion of new life and spirit, it will go down to posterity. There is a Michael Angelo; how utterly different from the antique, and in some things how superior! There is his statue of Cosmo de Medici leaning on his hand, in the chapel of St. Lorenzo at

Florence. I declare it has that look of reality in it, that it almost terrifies one to be near it! Is it not the same with Titian, Coreggio, and Raphael? These painters did not imitate one another, but were as unlike as possible, and yet they were all excellent. Originality is neither caprice nor affectation. It is an excellence that is always to be found in nature, and has never had a place in art before."

In 1783 Northcote sent his first pictures to the exhibition. One was Beggars with Dancing Dogs; a second was Hobinella, from Gay's "Shepherd's Week;" and a third was the Village Doctoress. The work which made the most favourable impression on the public mind, was Argyle visited, while asleep in Prison, by his Chief Enemy. There is an air of tranquillity and innocence about the slumbering nobleman, and of awe and mingled remorse and admiration in his foe. "When I found that others saw this look in the sketch I had made, I left off. By going on, I might lose it again. There is a point of felicity, which, whether you fall short of or have gone beyond it, can only be determined by the effect on the unprejudiced observer. You cannot always be with your picture, to explain it to others; it must be left to speak for itself. Those who stand before their pictures, and make fine speeches about them, do themselves a world of harm: a painter should cut out his tongue."

From 1800, for the space of twelve years, Northcote exhibited some sixty out of the numberless portraits which he painted.

Though the love of historic painting was well nigh extinct in the land, Northcote was slow or unwilling to abandon a line of study which had brought him into fame. His picture of the Vulture and Snake has been commended by all critics, and admired by all spectators. The former seems to be uttering that sharp, shrill cry, which announced his love of carnage; and the latter raises his slim and speckled neck and prepares for resistance. The picture of Prospero and Miranda, is from that fine scene in the Tempest, where the father relates to his daughter the cause of his exile. Miranda is supposed to be saying:

"You have often
Begun to tell me what I am; but stopp'd
And left me to a bootless inquisition;
Concluding—Stay, not yet."

Had something of the wildness of Fuseli mingled with the composition of Northcote, we might, perhaps, have had in him a great painter. As it is, one finds in almost all his historical compositions little of that vital fire, without which the fairest forms are but clods of the valley, and the most gorgeous draperies, but a waste of colour.

Northcote died in 1831. Of his system and habits of study, something may be said. He was an early riser; remained long at his easel; sought models in all things to aid his conception; and was long in pleasing himself with his outline or his colours. He attained all by a slow, protracted, and laborious process.

BLAKE.

William Blake, a native of London, was born in 1757. At ten years of age, he became an artist, and at twelve a poet. At fourteen he was apprenticed to an engraver.

Though Blake lost himself often in the enchanted regions of song, he was always at work. "Were I to love money," he said, "I might roll in wealth; my business is not to gather gold, but to make glorious shapes expressing godlike sentiments." His wife, whom he married at twenty-six, believed him to be the finest genius in the world; to the wildest flights of his imagination she bowed the knee and was a worshipper. She learned, what a young and handsome woman is seldom apt to learn, to despise gaudy dress, costly meals, pleasant company, and agreeable invitations. She found out the way to be contented and happy at home. She wrought off her husband's plates from the press, coloured them with a neat hand, made drawings much in the spirit of his style, and almost rivalled him in all things, save in the power which he possessed of seeing visions of any individual, living or dead, whenever he chose to see them. As he drew the figure, he meditated the song which was to accompany it; and the music to which the verse was to be sung, was the offspring too of the same moment. Of his music there are no specimens, he wanted the art of noting it down. We have lost melodies of real value, if they equalled many of his drawings.

The first fruits of his genius were the "Songs of Innocence and Experience." A work original and natural, and of high merit, both in poetry and painting. It consists of from sixty-five to seventy scenes, presenting images of domestic sadness and fireside joy, the gayety, innocence, and happiness of childhood. Every scene has its poetical accompaniment, curiously interwoven with the group or landscape. The designs are highly poetical, more allied, however to heaven than to earth, indicating a better world and fuller happiness than mortals enjoy. By frequent indulgence in these imaginings, he gradually began to believe in the reality of what dreaming fancy painted. Of these imaginary visitations he made good use, when he invented his truly original and beautiful mode of engraving and tinting his plates. He was meditating, he said, on the best means of multiplying the sixty-five designs of his "Days of Innocence," and felt sorely perplexed. At last he was made aware that the spirit of his favourite brother Robert was in the room. To him he applied for counsel, the celestial visitor advised him at once. "Write," he said, "the poetry and draw the designs upon the copper with a certain liquid, (which he named, and which Blake ever kept secret;) then cut the plain parts down with aquafortis, and this will give the whole, both poetry and figures, in the manner of a stereotype." The plan recommended by this gracious spirit was adopted; the plates were engraved, and the work printed off. The artist then added a peculiar beauty of his own. He tinted both the figures and the verse with a variety of colours, among which, while yellow prevails, the whole has a rich and lustrous beauty, to which I know little that can be compared. The size of these prints is four inches and a half high, by three inches wide. Sad to say, the original genius of Blake was always confined, through poverty to small dimensions.

The most propitious time for those "angel-visits," was from nine at night, till five in the morning; and so docile were his spiritual sitters, that they appeared at the wish of his friends.

Blake was requested to draw the likeness of Sir William Wallace—the eye of Blake sparkled, for he admired heroes. "William Wallace," he exclaimed, "I see him now there, there, how noble he looks—reach me my things!" Having drawn for some time, with the same care of hand and steadiness of eye, as if a living sitter had been before him, Blake stopped suddenly, and said, "I cannot finish him—Edward the First has stepped in between him and me." "That's lucky," said his friend, "for I want the portrait of Edward too." Blake took another sheet of paper, and sketched the features of the Plantagenet; upon which his majesty politely vanished, and the artist finished the head of Wallace. "And pray, sir," said a gentleman who heard Blake's friend tell the story, "was Sir William Wallace an heroic-looking man? And what sort of a personage was Edward?" The answer was: "There they are, sir, both framed and hanging on the wall behind you, judge for yourself." "I looked," says my informant, "and saw two warlike heads of the size of common life, that of Wallace was noble and heroic, that of Edward, stern and bloody. The first had the front of a god, the latter the aspect of a demon. I have sat beside him from ten at night till three in the morning, sometimes slumbering, and sometimes waking, but Blake never slept; he sat with pencil and paper drawing portraits of those whom I most desired to see. I will show you some of these works." He took out a large book filled with drawings, opened it and continued, "Observe the poetic fervour of that face—it is Pindar, as he stood a conqueror in the Olympic games. And this lovely creature is Corinna, who conquered in poetry in the same place. There, that is a face of a different stamp—can you conjecture who it is?" "Some scoundrel, I should think, sir, "There now—that is a strong proof of the accuracy of Blake—he is a scoundrel indeed: the very individual task-master whom Moses slew in Egypt. This head speaks for itself. It is the head of Herod."

He closed the book, and taking out a small panel from a private drawer, said: "This is the last which I shall show you; but it is the greatest curiosity of all. Only look at the splendor of the colouring, and the original character of the thing!" "I see," said I, "a naked figure, with a strong body and a short neck, with burning eyes which long for moisture, and a face worthy of a murderer, holding a bloody cup in his clawed hands, out of which he seems eager to drink. I never saw any thing so strange, nor did I ever see any colouring so curiously splendid—a kind of glistening green, and dusky gold, beautifully varnished.

But what in the world is it?" "It is a ghost, sir—the ghost of a flea—a spiritualization of the thing.' "He saw this in a vision, then," I said. "I'll tell you all about it, sir. I called on him one evening, and found him unusually excited. He told me he had seen a wonderful thing—the ghost of a flea! 'And did you make a drawing of him?' I inquired. 'No, indeed, I wish I had,' said he; 'but I shall if he appears again!' He looked earnestly into a corner of the room, and then said: 'Here he is—reach me my things—I shall keep my eye on him. There he comes! his eager tongue whisking out of his mouth, a cup in his hand to hold blood, and covered with a scaly skin of gold and green.' As he described him so he drew him."

Had Blake always thought so idly, and wrought on such visionary matters, this memoir would have been the story of a madman, instead of the life of a man of genius, some of whose works are worthy of any age or nation. Even while he was indulging in these laughable fancies, and seeing visions at the request of his friends, he conceived, and drew, and engraved one of the noblest of all his productions—the "Inventions for the Book of Job." He accomplished this series in a small room, which served him for kitchen, bed-chamber, and study, where he had no other companion but his faithful Katharine, and no larger income than some seventeen or eighteen shillings a week. Of those Inventions, as the artist loved to call them, there are twenty-one, representing the man of Uz sustaining his dignity amid the inflictions of Satan, the reproaches of his friends, and the insults of his wife. It was in such things that Blake shone; the Scripture overawed his imagination, and he was too devout to attempt aught beyond a literal embodying of the majestic scene. He goes step by step with the narrative; always simple, and often sublime; never wandering from the subject, nor overlaying the text with the weight of his own exuberant fancy. He reached the age of seventy-one years, and died in 1826.

Blake was a most splendid tinter, but no colourist, and his works are all of small dimensions; and therefore confined to the cabinet and portfolio. His happiest flights, as well as his wildest, are thus likely to remain shut up from the world. If we look at the man through his best and most intelligible works, we shall find, that he, who could produce the "Songs of Innocence and Experience," the "Gates of Paradise," and the "Inventions of Job," was the possessor of very lofty faculties, with no common skill in art; and, moreover, that, both in thought and manner of treatment, he was a decided original. Ten thousand authors and artists rise to the proper, the graceful, and the beautiful, for ten who ascend into "the heaven of invention." A work, whether from poet or painter, conceived in the fiery ecstasy of imagination, lives through every limb, while one elaborated out of skill and taste only, will look, in comparison, like a withered and sapless tree beside one green and flourishing. Blake's misfortune was that of possessing this precious gift in excess. His fancy overmastered him; until he at length confounded "the mind's eye" with the corporeal organ, and dreamed himself out of the sympathies of actual life.

His method of colouring was a secret which he kept to himself, or only communicated to his wife. "His modes of preparing his grounds," says Smith, in his supplement to the "Life of Nollekens," "and laying them over his panels for painting, mixing his colours, and manner of working, were those which he considered to have been practised by the early fresco-painters, whose productions still remain, in many instances, vividly and permanently fresh. His ground was a mixture of whiting and carpenter's glue, which he passed over several times in the coatings; his colours he ground himself, and also united with them the same sort of glue, but in a much weaker state. He would, in the course of painting a picture, pass a very thin transparent wash of glue water over the whole of the parts he had worked upon, and then proceed with his finishing.

OPIE.

John Opie was born near Truro, in Cornwall, in 1761. At the age of twelve, he had mastered Euclid, and was considered so skilful in arithmetic and penmanship, that he commenced an evening school for the instruction of the peasants of the parish of St. Agnes.

When yet very young, we find him commenced portrait painter, by profession, and wandering from town to town in quest of employment. "One of these expeditions," says Prince Hoare, "was to Padstow, whither he set forward, dressed, as usual, in a boy's short jacket, and carrying with him all proper apparatus for portrait painting. Here, among others, he painted the whole household of the ancient family of the Prideaux, even to the dogs and cats of the family. He remained so long absent from home, that some uneasiness began to arise on his account; but it was dissipated by his returning, dressed in a handsome coat, with very long skirts, with lace ruffles, and with silk stockings. On seeing his mother, he ran to her, and taking out of his pocket twenty guineas, which he had earned by his pencil, he desired her to keep them; adding, that in future he should maintain himself. In the twentieth year of his age he formed the resolution of visiting London, and set out for the great city under the protection of Wolcot.

The wealthy and titled houses, who professed taste and virtù, and were absolute in art and literature, came swarming out to behold the "Cornish Wonder," for as such the patron announced the painter. The novelty and originality of manner in his pictures, added to his great abilities, drew a universal attention from the connoisseurs, and he was immediately surrounded and employed by all the principal nobility of England.

The first use he made of his success, was to spread comfort around his mother; and then he proceeded with his works and his studies, like one resolved to deserve the distinction which he had obtained. When his works were unstudied, their applause was deafening; when they were such as really merited a place in public galleries, the world, resolved not to be infatuated twice with the same object, paid him a cold, or at least very moderate attention.

The ladies who sat for their portraits, he found more difficult to deal with than the great leader of the Whigs. There was, at first, a want of grace and softness in his female heads. He felt this early, and laboured to amend it; but it is said that he did not wholly succeed until after his second marriage. "Opie," said one of his brethren, when he exhibited some female portraits, soon after that event, "we never saw any thing like this in you before—this must be owing to your wife;" and it is likely that the compliment, though paid probably in jest, was nevertheless just. The habitual ruggedness of his personal manners yielded to the winning and graceful tact of Amelia Opie, and it is easy to believe that her presence might have the same influence upon his pencil.

OWEN.

William Owen was born at Ludlow, in Shropshire, in the year 1769. He made his appearance before the public in 1792, when he sent the Portrait of a Gentleman, and a View of Ludford Bridge, in Shropshire, to the Somerset-house exhibition; in the latter his early haunts were remembered. These were probably well received; for, in the succeeding exhibition, he had no less than seven portraits: one was a Lady of Quality, and two were Clergymen, but to none of them was a name attached.

Owen carried on the painting of portraits to a great extent, during a period of twenty-seven years. Men of all ranks, and ladies of all conditions, flocked to his easel. He rose early—wrought late; drew, painted, touched, finished, framed, packed, and when these were out of the house, fresh heads appeared. The monotony was sometimes too much for him. He has been known to turn a portrait from the easel, postpone the coming of a dozen sitters, single out some little happy theme, and in the course of a week dash it on the canvass, in all the truth and charm of nature embellished by art; this put him in good humour with himself and with his destiny, and happy was he who sat for his portrait next.

Men's living looks, with the memory of them, die away and are forgotten, but the sentiment and natural action belong to all times; and in these, artists who desire the praise of posterity, must put their trust. A Cupid, painted by Owen for Sir Thomas Heathcote, was called an exquisitely finished thing; and it was so; but the god of love had lost a little of his power in painting as well as poetry; and he who complains of the darts and flames of Cupid has, by the universal consent of all misses above seventeen, been voted affected and pedantic. In a better taste was the Fortune-teller and Lady; it was easy to see the insidious poison of the tawny sibyl's tongue stealing through the frame of her victim—so lovely and so innocent were her looks, that they attracted a crowd in the exhibition from morning till night. The Cottage Door was another of his happy little hits; so was the Children in the Wood, a piece of which it is praise sufficient to say that it breathes all over the simple pathos of the old melting ballad. Towards the close of his career such things grew less frequent; portraiture, with its temptations of pleasing society, prompt payment, and ready made-looks, which cost imagination nothing, prevailed. The Boy and Kitten, his admission present to the Royal Academy, though mentioned last, was an early performance, and may rank with some of his best.

He died in the fifty-sixth year of his age, in the year 1825.

LAWRENCE.

Sir Thomas Lawrence, principal painter to the king, and president of the Royal Academy, was born in 1769, in Bristol, within a few doors of the birthplace of Robert Southey. At the age of nine without the least instruction from any one, he was capable of copying historical pictures in a masterly style, and also succeeded amazingly in compositions of his own, particularly in that of Peter denying Christ. In about seven minutes he scarcely ever failed of drawing a complete likeness of any person present, which had generally much freedom and grace, if the subject permitted.

When Lawrence was about ten years old, or little more, his

father failed in his business, and it occurred to him in his hour of distress that he might derive solid advantage from the talents of his youngest son. He made the first experiment upon Oxford. The boy had not been unnoticed by the chiefs of the university who stopped at Devizes on their way to Bath ; and when he appeared in that city, and announced himself as a portrait painter, many sitters flocked to him. "He took the likenesses," says his biographer, "of the most eminent persons at Oxford ; but his pencil was not confined to grave sexagenarians ; for many of the younger nobility and gentry were anxious to have their portraits taken by the phenomenon : and the female beauty of this dignified city, and its wealthy neighbourhood, equally pressed upon his talents."

When the Oxford harvest was reaped and gleaned, the Lawrences hastened to Bath, and hired a house at the rate of a hundred pounds a year. Here, however, as art was not so certain as to be trusted to, lodgers were admitted ; the sisters of the young artist were placed at respectable boarding-schools, and all was prosperous and happy. Sitters were numerous, and those who at first considered him as a curiosity, began to recognize the presence of real taste and elegance in his pictures. His price, a guinea at first, was soon raised to a guinea and a half ; his portrait of Mrs. Siddons, as Zara, was admired and engraved ; his fame spread far and wide ; Sir Henry Harpur desired to adopt him as his son ; and Hoare, the painter, saw something so angelic in his looks, that he proposed to paint him as a Christ. His portraits of those days were graceful fac-similies of his sitters ; in course of time he learned how to deal with a difficult face, and evoke beauty and delicacy out of very ordinary materials.

The prettinesses of pencilling, and the delicacies of manner, of Lawrence, are note-worthy, inasmuch as they show the man in the child; in these he excelled more when he became eminent than in grand harmony of colouring and masculine energy of thought.

He had not then learned the art, in which he afterwards became a master, of softening the geometrical lines and manifold points of modern dress into something like elegance; the broad and innumerable buttons, the close-fitted capes, peaked lapels and hanging cuffs, and pointed skirts of these our latter days, are sorely in the way of a young artist who thinks of Michael Angelo and the antique, and dreams of his profession like a poet. Nor were the dresses of the women less extravagant than those of the men: their hair frizzed, and filled with pomatum and powder; a wide hat and enormous feather stuck on the top of the head; a close-cut riding-jacket, wide at the shoulders, and pinched at the waist so tightly, that, with the expanding petticoat and spreading hat, they looked like sand-glasses, and were assuredly frights, either in life or in painting. In such things the early works of Lawrence abounded—and no wonder, when he dedicated his whole youth to portraiture; and was, therefore, obliged to take sitters as they came, dressed as fashion or their own fancies dedicated. His studio, before he was twelve years old, was the favourite resort of the beauty, and fashion, and taste of Bath; young ladies loved to sit and converse with this handsome prodigy, men of taste and virtù purchased his crayon heads, which he drew in vast numbers, and carried them far and near, even into foreign lands, to show as the works of the boy-artist of Britain. His father, the public, and his own love of display, all conspired to make him a coxcomb; but his natural good sense, now strengthening every day, and his genius expanding with his growth, carried him safely over those shoals and quicksands on which so many lesser spirits have been shipwrecked.

With his seventeenth year, the true fame of Lawrence commences; for then he first used oil colours, and began to free himself from the captivating facilities of crayons. All this was not to be done as soon as he wished. He desired to become a great artist; but it was necessary meanwhile to live, and moreover to study the best works; and this he accomplished without abandoning portraiture.

In 1787, Lawrence went to London, and took handsome apartments in Leicester Fields. The fame of Sir Joshua Reynolds rendered the situation popular, nor had the name of Hogarth ceased to be remembered; that of Lawrence was now added, though at first with but indifferent success. He opened an exhibition of his works, over which his father presided; but the charm which his extreme youth had bestowed was gone, and little was made by the wondrous "boy painter."

One of his reasons for going to London was, that he might study in the Royal Academy; and on the 13th of September, 1787, he took his place as a student; his large bright eyes, his elegant form, his long and plentiful hair, flowing down upon his shoulders, and a certain country air which London is long in removing made many look at him oftener than once.

It had been long rumoured that Lawrence was busied on a grand poetic piece. The subject was, however, left a secret until the exhibition of 1797, when it was found to be Satan calling to his Legions.

"Awake, arise, or be for ever fallen."

The next year he exhibited Coriolanus at the hearth of Aufidius; Rolla, Cato, and Hamlet, all followed in the train of Coriolanus. The Rolla, a splendid picture, is perhaps a little melo-dramatic; but so is the play in which Rolla appears. The colouring is fine, and the drawing nearly faultless. The Cato will never be named as one of the painter's finest works: Kemble is trying with all his might to put on the looks of the last of the Romans—but he fails. It is far otherwise with Hamlet; a work of the highest kind—sad, thoughtful, melancholy; with looks conversing with death and the grave; a perfect image of the prince of the great dramatist. This picture Lawrence himself placed above all his works except the Satan; but it far surpasses the Satan in propriety of action, accuracy of expression, and grandeur of colouring. The light touches the face and bosom and falls on the skull on which he is musing. It is one of the noblest paintings of the modern school.

Of the male portraits of this time, the most remarkable was that of the eloquent Curran; under mean and harsh features, a genius of the highest order lay concealed, like a sweet kernel in a rough husk; and so little of the true man did Lawrence perceive in his first sittings, that he almost laid down his palette in despair, in the belief that he could make nothing but a common or vulgar work. The parting hour came, and with it the great Irishman burst out in all his strength; he discoursed on art, on poetry, on Ireland; his eyes flashed, and his colour heightened, and his rough and swarthy visage seemed in the sight of the astonished painter to come fully within his own notions of manly beauty. "I never saw you till now," said the artist, in his softest tone of voice; "you have sat to me in a mask; do give me a sitting of Curran the orator." Curran complied, and a fine portrait with genius on the brow was the consequence.

Lawrence died in 1830, in the sixty-first year of his age. He was buried with many honours in St. Paul's cathedral, beside his eminent brethren—Reynolds, Barry, and West.

On being asked how many hours he had ever painted without ceasing, he said thirty-seven; and that was on the portrait of Lord Thurlow. He began at seven in the morning, painted all day and all night, and all the next day till eleven on the following night; "by this time," said he, "I could not distinguish one colour from another; remember, too, I was standing or walking all the while, for I never paint sitting."

As a portrait painter, his merits are of a high order. He has been called the second Reynolds; not from being an imitator of the style of that great master, but from possessing very largely the same singular power of expressing sentiment and feeling, and of giving beauty and often dignity to his productions. He resembled him less in breadth and vigour than in the freedom and elegance of his attitudes, in his skilful impersonation of human thought, and in the exquisite grace and loveliness with which he inspired all that he touched. One age of the great men, and the courtly beauties of England, will live to posterity on the canvass of Reynolds; another will do so on that of Lawrence.

BIRD.

Edward Bird was born at Wolverhampton, in the year, 1772. The family tradition says that he began to sketch at three or four years of age. He would stand on a stool, chalk outlines on the furniture, and say, with childish glee, "Well done, little Neddy Bird!" He would be up at the dawn to draw figures upon the walls, which he called French and English soldiers.

His first attempt worthy of notice, was in his fourteenth year—this was the imaginary interview between the Earl of Leicester and the daughters, whom Miss Lee has conferred on Mary Queen of Scots, in her novel of "The Recess."

When his father saw that his love of drawing and sketching was incurable, he began to grow anxious to turn it to some account, but could think of nothing better than apprenticing him to a maker of tea-trays—these accordingly it became the boy's business to embellish. Long after, when his name was in the ranks of acknowledged genius, he was on a tour in France with several companions, and at Boulogne drank tea off a beautiful tray which excited their notice and praise. Bird looked at it and smiled; when they had recommenced their journey, one of his friends said, "I did not think they could have made such trays in France." "It was not made here," said Bird, "it was made at Birmingham, for I painted it." One of the party was with difficulty restrained from turning back and buying it.

His first successful work, if we measure success by the applause of the world, was called Good News. The Choristers Rehearsing and the Will followed, and received equal praise, and, what was not less fortunate, obtained purchasers of high distinction.

The Royal Academy soon after conferred honour on themselves by enrolling our self-taught artist among their number.

His next work was his most poetical, and decidedly his best one. This is a representation of the Field of Chevy Chase, on the day after the battle. It is painted in the mournful spirit with which the glorious old ballad concludes, and cannot well be looked on without tears. These are the words imbodied:

"Of fifteen hundred Englishmen
Went home but fifty-three;
The rest were slain at Chevy Chase
Under the greenwoode tree.

"Next day did many widows come
Their husbands to bewayle;
They washed their wounds with brinish tears,
But all would not prevail.

"Their bodies in purple blood
They bare with them away;
They kist their dead a thousand times
Ere they were clad in clay."

Of this heroic ballad, which Sir Philip Sydney said roused him like the sound of a trumpet, and which Ben Johnson affirmed was worth all his dramas, the people of England are great admirers, and among the peasantry of the south, it is almost the only one known. When they saw a painting which gave a life-like and touching picture of a scene often present to their fancy, they were loud in its praise. Lady Percy is, with perfect propriety, made a visitor of the fatal field: she appears in deep agony beside the body of her lord.

Bird's chief merit as an artist lay in natural and touching representations of homely and social things. Nor was he less skilfu in subjects where the interest was confined to a single figure with little action. When he happened to meet an original-looking personage, young or old, his practice was to make a rude sketch on the spot—return to his study—assign to the figure some characteristic employment—expand it upon the canvass, and give it all the charm of colouring. He painted such works with astonishing rapidity; the picture existed complete in his mind, and an effort of art and memory produced it. During the stormy season of 1812 he was in London—found a famishing match girl in the street—painted her in character in three days, and sold the work for thirty guineas. An old man seeking alms came in his way; of him, too, he took a characteristic likeness—half real and half imaginative, and with equal success. Accurate copies of nature he disliked; he took a poetic license with his subjects. "He could," said one of his admirers, "extract delight and joy out of any thing." The Gipsy Boy, the Young Recruit, Meg Merrilies, Game at Put, and various other paintings, are instances of his skill in adapting living life to the purposes of art. In this respect he resembled Opie. When one of his friends congratulated him on the rapidity with which he dashed off his lesser, but his happier works, Bird said: "Yes, I can do them quickly; but it will not do to tell the world how soon I can paint such things." They who believe that what is done well cannot have been done quickly, are often mistaken

During one of his visits to London, Bird sat for his bust to Chantrey. These visits to London, and his admiration of the historical pictures of the great painters, wrought a sore change on Bird; he forsook that style of art, natural to his feelings, and dedicated his pencil to far other aspirations. He became affected with a kind of Scripture mania. He thought only of sublime passages in the Bible, and scenes of religious tragedy, which the Reformation furnished. The Fortitude of Job, the Death of Saphira and others, found admirers and purchasers. There is considerable talent in these paintings, and some pathos; but they are deficient in that regal loftiness of look which the subjects require.

The early works of Bird have an original and unborrowed air, which mark an artist who thought for himself, and sought the materials of his pictures in the living world around him, rather than in the galleries of art.

Those who wish well to the fame of Edward Bird, will speak of his paintings of humble life, and seek to forget not only those mistaken efforts of his declining hand, but even his historical productions, with the single exception of Chevy Chase.

BURNET.

Art has its early victims, as well as poetry. Chatterton and Kirke White gave no greater promise of excellence in verse, than did Bonnington and Liversage in painting. To these names we may add that of James Burnet, a young landscape painter of no common powers. He was born at Musselburg, in 1788. His mind early took a turn towards art. In Wilkie and the Dutch masters he perceived something entirely after his own heart. He loved the vivid human character in the former ; and of the latter, Potter and Cuyp became his favourites. He had sought what he wanted, in the academy, but found it not ; he therefore determined, like Gainsborough, to make nature his academy ; and with a sketch-book and pencil, he might be seen wandering about the fields, around London, noting down scenes which caught his fancy, and peopling them with men pursuing their avocations, and with cattle of all colours, and in all positions. The first fruit of all this preparation was the picture of Cattle going out in the Morning. There is a dewy freshness in the air ; and the cattle, released from their stalls, seem to snuff the richness of the distant pastures, and acknowledge the loveliness of the day. His next picture was superior even to this. "In his Cattle Returning Home in a Shower, he has introduced," says an excellent judge, "every thing that could in any way characterize the scene. The rainbow in the sky, the glittering of the rain upon the leaves, the dripping poultry under the hedge, the reflection of the cattle upon the road, and the girl with her gown over her shoulders—all tend, with equal force, to illustrate the subject." This picture placed him in the first rank, as a pastoral painter. Others followed, of equal or superior truth and beauty.

He felt that the excellence which he coveted could only be obtained by much study of nature. It was his practice to write down on the spot (when he had made a sketch) his observations regarding the future handling of the picture in oil. In a memorandum respecting distances, he writes : " Extreme distance ought generally to be of the same tint as the sky with which it unites ; and as it approaches the middle ground, the strata appear interspersed with touches of light and dark, such as the lights upon the tops of the houses, with their shadows. Be particular in marking the buildings with a firmer line than the trees. Never admit colour into your distance, when in the direction of the light. Scumble a little with purple and grey at the bottom of your trees, losing their forms at the base. In a side light, the objects are coloured where the light shines upon them ; while the shadows are all of one tint—even red is grey in the shadow. But when the light is behind you, every object is made out with its proper colour." The same clear, simple mode of instruction, distinguishes all he says regarding the treatment of that unstable element, water. "To paint water well, it ought, if possible, to be painted at once with a full pencil and a quantity of vehicle. The colours reflected in the water appear more pleasing from their possessing a rich pulpy substance ; and also from their sweetly melting into each other. In painting water, particular attention should be paid to the place and distance, as it alters much according to the situation. Objects near the foreground raise their reflections when they touch aught, but are often lost when they come to the bottom of the picture ; while, on the contrary, objects in the distance show their reflection stronger as they approach towards you. This arises from the waves, conveying the reflection, being larger and less under the influence of perspective than when they touch the distant object. The sky being of a receding character, all those points which contribute to give it such character, should be the study of the painter. Mere white, for example, will seldom keep its place in a sky, but ought to be used in foreground objects, for the purpose of giving a retiring quality to the lights in the sky and distance. Softness of form also aids in giving the sky a retiring character, although it is necessary to give a little sharpness, to prevent the sky appearing what is termed woolly; yet very little is sufficient to give firmness to the whole. Clouds are much more opaque in the north than in the south, as the light shines upon them in the one situation, and through them in the other. Their form alters much, too, according to the time of day. At noon they are round, and more like those of Wouvermans; in the evening they are more like those of Cuyp, especially about an hour before the sun goes down."

Burnet died at the early age of twenty-eight years, in 1816.

He had a fine eye, and an equally fine feeling, for the beauties of landscape. His knowledge of nature was extensive and minute. He had watched the outgoings and incomings of shepherds and husbandmen, had studied flocks and herds, and as the memoranda which we have quoted show, had made himself acquainted with much that lends lustre to landscape. To such feeling for the rural and picturesque, he added an excellent eye for colour. He could employ, at will, either the bold, deep tones of Rembrandt, or the silvery and luminous tones of Cuyp. To those who know the difficulty of guiding the eye from one extreme to another, this will be deemed great praise. He had much poetical feeling; there is nothing coarse or common in his scenes. His trees are finely grouped; his cows are all beautiful; they have the sense to know where the sweetest grass grows. His milkmaids have an air of natural elegance about them; and his cowboys, even, are not without grace.

HILTON.

William Hilton was born at Lincoln, in 1786. He early applied himself to the study of general literature, as well as the productions of his favourite art. Perhaps this training of the taste by general study, is too much neglected by students in art, but it is only from a well-cultivated field that we are to look for an abundant crop.

From 1806 to 1814, when he was elected an associate of the Royal Academy, Hilton exhibited eight pictures: Cephalis and Procris, from Ovid; Venus carrying the wounded Æneas from battle; Ulysses and Calypso; the Good Samaritan; John of Gaunt reproving Richard II.; Christ restoring Sight to the Blind; Mary anointing the Feet of Jesus; and Miranda and Ferdinand bearing the Log; large pictures, possessing much dignity of expression, finely drawn, skilfully arranged, and softly and harmoniously coloured. In the three following years, he exhibited the Raising of Lazarus, Una with the Satyrs, and Ganymede. In 1819 he was chosen a Royal Academician. When in 1821, he exhibited his very vivid and poetic picture of Nature blowing Bubbles for her Children, it was thought that the tide of opinion had turned in his favour, for every eye was on it, and commendation flowed from every lip. This he followed up by four great pictures: Venus in search of Cupid surprises Diana at her Bath; Comus and the Lady in the Enchanted Chair, a scene worthy of the poet; Love taught by the Graces; and Christ crowned with Thorns, a superior work, purchased by the British Institution, in 1825, in which the meekness and beautiful resignation of the Saviour were in strict keeping with Scripture history.

On the resignation of Thompson, in 1826, he was appointed keeper of the Royal Academy, an office to which a small pension and good apartments were attached. From this period to 1839, he painted and exhibited ten pictures; three of which were Scriptural, one historic, and the rest poetic. The Crucifixion Abraham's Servant meeting Rebecca; the Angel releasing Peter from Prison; Serena rescued by Sir Calepine, now in the National Gallery; Una seeking shelter in the Cottage of Corecea; Nymphs and Cupid; Edith and the Monks finding the Body of Harold; and the Infant Warrior, which proved to be his last effort. He died in 1839.

HAYDON.

R. B. Haydon was born in 1786, at Plymouth. In 1807, he sent his first work, Joseph and Mary, resting with the Infant Saviour after a day's journey, on the road to Egypt, to the Academy exhibition. Anastasius Hope became the purchaser. Urged on by his acquired reputation, he produced the following year, his celebrated picture of Dentatus, the story of which was well told It was purchased by Lord Mulgrave, while yet upon the easel.

His talents and ardent character, had obtained for him many friends. Sir George Beaumont gave him a commission for a subject from Macbeth. His Judgment of Solomon was sold for seven hundred guineas. His Alexander returning in triumph, after having vanquished Bucephalus, found a purchaser at five hundred guineas, in the earl of Egremont, and his Venus and

Anchises, was purchased for two hundred guineas, by Lord De Tabley. Flushed with success, he renewed his application for admission to the Royal Academy, and for two successive elections, received not a vote in his favour.

"For twenty-one years," says he, writing of the members of the Royal Academy, "there has not been an affection they have not lacerated—an ambition they have not thwarted—a hope they have not blasted—a calumny they have not propagated—a friendship they have not chilled, or a disposition to employ me, they have not tampered with."

His next great work, Christ's Entrance into Jerusalem, now the property of the Philadelphia Academy of Fine Arts, was begun in 1814, and exhibited in 1820. He was proud of this picture, the central portion of which is deserving of all praise, and although it remained upon his hands, he commenced another of the same character, Christ in the Garden, and a third in the same high walk, Christ Rejected.

He now became involved in debt, and was for a time an inmate of the King's Bench prison, where he witnessed the celebrated Mock Election, which took place there in July, 1827; and being struck with the picturesque character of the scene, he imbodied it on canvass, and found a purchaser in George IV. His friends also assisted him; and, once more at ease, he commenced a picture of Eucles, a subscription being set on foot to take it off his hands by a public raffle. Sir Walter Scott interested himself in the subscription, and also sat to him for his portrait.

The success of the Mock Election, a work he tells us, of four months, justified another attempt in the same line; and he next produced, Chairing the Members, a scene from the Mock Election. It was exhibited at the Bazaar, in Bond-street, in 1829, and found a purchaser at three hundred guineas, in Mr. Francis, of Exeter. Another picture of the same period, was Pharaoh dismissing Moses, at the dead of night, after the Passover; bought by Mr. Hunter, an East India merchant, for five hundred guineas. This was followed by Napoleon musing at St. Helena, of which he painted three copies; one for Sir Robert Peel, a second for the duke of Devonshire, and a third for the duke of Sutherland. This work was popular as an engraving; but a second picture of the same character, the Duke of Wellington on the Field of Waterloo, was much inferior in execution. His last works were Curtius leaping into the Gulf, and Uriel and Satan. On the morning of his death, he had been working on a picture of Alfred, and the Trial by Jury. He came to his end by his own hand, in 1846.

ETTY.

William Etty was a native of the city of York, where he was born, in 1787. He says, in an autobiographical letter addressed to a relative: "My first panels, on which I drew, were the boards of my father's shop floor; my first crayon a farthing's white chalk; but my pleasure amounted to ecstasy when my mother promised me that next morning, if I were a good boy, I should use some colours, mixed with gum water. I was so pleased I could scarcely sleep. On the eighth of October, 1798, just half a century ago, at the tender age of eleven and a half years, I was sent abroad into the world, and put an apprentice to a letter-press printer, as a compositor, at Hull, to which business I served seven full years, faithfully and truly, and worked at it three weeks as journeyman; but I had such a busy desire to be a painter, that the last years of my servitude dragged on most heavily. I counted the years, days, weeks, and hours, till liberty should break my chains and set my struggling spirit free! That hour, that golden hour of twelve on the twenty-third of October, 1805, I watched on the dial-plate of Hull high church, and felt such a throb of delight as for seven long years I had been a stranger to.

"I worked for three weeks as a journeyman printer, waiting with anxious expectation each morning a summons from London, either from my dear brother Walter, or your noble and beloved grandfather, my dear uncle, William Etty, of the firm of Bodley, Etty, and Bodley, 31 Lombard-street; himself a beautiful draughtsman in pen and ink, and who, if he had studied engraving, would have been in the first rank. He smiled on and patronized my juvenile and puny efforts, but saw enough to convince him that my heart was in it alone. These three benevolent individuals—my uncle and brother and Mr. T. Bodley—united hand in hand to second my aspiring and ardent wishes; and having painted in crayons a head of your dear mother, Mrs. Clarke, and also two successful crayon heads of my uncle's two favourite cats, I was encouraged in this my darling pursuit, and the sun of my happiness began to shine.

"And here I will beg to say—because I hope it will have an influence, on the younger aspirants in the art, and I can give the experience of a long life—that I strongly and strenuously recommend to their notice, that however I might at times, and who does not? forget my duty to my God and Maker, yet it was impressed on my mind by my dear parents, and echoed feelingly in my own heart, a love and fear of Almighty God, and a reference of every action to His divine will; a confidence in His friendly mercy, a fear of offending Him, and I may safely say, I never for one moment forgot the path of virtue without the bitterest feeling of remorse, and an ardent desire to return to it, the only path of sunshine, happiness, and peace. My sincere wish, in whatever station of life I was placed, was to be actuated by an honest desire to do my duty to God and man, and whatever deficiency may have arisen, this was my only principle of action, and one I can confidently recommend to the young, who are desirous of raising the reputation of themselves or their country, whether in the arts or in any other liberal pursuit.

"My first academy was in a plaster-cast shop, kept by Granelli, in that lane near Smithfield, immortalized by Dr. Johnson's visit to see the "Ghost." I drew, in heat and cold; sometimes the snow blowing into my studio under the door, white as the casts. There I studied and drew the Cupid and Psyche, after the antique, well enough to take to Mr. Opie, to whom I had a respectable letter of introduction; then, with palpitating heart and admiring feeling, I approached the dread study of this truly great and powerful artist. He encouraged me, and gave me a letter to another great and powerful genius, Fuseli, who admitted me as a probationer in dear Somerset House. With a flannel vest tied round his waist, and an eagle eye, he received me in that magic circle of unearthly creations peculiarly his own.

"I drew in the Royal Academy; here was an event in my life, so long looked for and hoped for. Poor dear Collins and I entered the Academy as probationers the same week. We drew the Laocoon side by side, with many now no more; poor Haydon, ardent, mistaken in some respects, but still glorious in his enthusiasm, drew at the same time, his zeal and that of Hilton in the cause of historic art, urged me to persevere, and by their example and precept, I certainly benefited and was encouraged."

After a year's study with Sir Thomas Lawrence, for several years he pursued his studies with perseverence and ardour before success dawned upon him. Etty thus writes of his labours at this period: "I lit the lamp at both ends of the day. I studied the skeleton, the origin, and insertion of the muscles: I sketched from Albinus. I drew in the morning, I painted in the evening; and, after the Royal Academy, went and drew from the prints of the antique statues of the Capitolina, the Clemintina, Florentine, and the other galleries, finishing the extremities in black-lead pencil, with great care. This I did at the London Institution, in Moorfields. I returned home; kept in my fire all night, to the great dismay of my landlord, that I might rise next morning before daylight to draw; in short, I worked with such energy and perseverance to conquer my radical defects, that at last a better state of things began to dawn, like the sun through a November fog; and though I did not get a medal, from an informality on my part, I gained it, in point of fact, for my picture was esteemed the best; and Mr. West said of it—it would one day be sold for a Titian. I had what was better, a high compliment paid me, from the president's chair, by Sir Martin Shee, on my copy of the Ganymede of Titian. I then sent a small picture to the British Gallery, highly finished and carefully wrought; it made a considerable noise. I sent a larger the same year to the Royal Academy; it made a still greater noise. The Coral Finders, the Cleopatra, were sent the next year, Sir Francis Freeling being my patron. It made a great impression in my favour. Sir Thomas said, jocularly, to me of it: 'They (the public) leave Marc Antony,' meaning himself, 'whistling in the market-place, and go to gaze on your Cleopatra.' The old Times even, deigned to notice me, though as much in the shape of a castigation as in any other; but still the Times noticed me. I felt my chariot wheels were on the right road to fame and honour, and I now drove on like another Jehu!"

In 1822, he visited Italy. He thus writes of Venice: "Venezia, caro Venezia! thy pictured glories haunt my fancy now. Venice, the birthplace of colour, the hope and idol of my professional life! I felt at home most at Venice, though I knew not a soul. I soon began my labours, in sucking like a bee the sweets of Venetian colour. Nostro Paolo—divine! Nostra Tintoretto! Tiziano! the grand Tiziano Vecelli, Bassano, Bonifacio, and all the radiant glories of that beloved city, which seemed to love and cherish me as I loved it. Its grand and glorious Academia, where the godlike statuary, after the antique, stand in a circle, and hold their council. It is one of the best appointed, and most complete academies in Europe. Here I studied, and they did me the honour to elect me an Honorary Academician. Charleston, America, gave me the first diploma; Venice, the second; England, the third; last not least in my estimation.

"Behold me, then, after a year's sojourn in dear Venice, and with labour infinite, returning back to Florence, to copy Titian's celebrated Venus, as large as life; after difficulties were surmounted, I was allowed to copy it; and brought it, and numerous copies and studies—studies of all the numerous works I had set my mind to do—and, having got with difficulty through the various doganas and states and snowy mountains and seas, I brought them in safety—stopping and copying and painting, in the Louvre, as I returned in 1824, having spent about two years in Italy and France.

"Pandora, formed by Vulcan, and crowned by the Seasons, from Hesiod, claimed my first attention; and a picture of eight or nine figures, with accompaniments, was begun and finished in a few weeks, and sent to the exhibition of the Royal Academy: my dear master, Sir Thomas Lawrence, bought it, and the Royal Academy elected me an Associate for it." "Strike while the iron is hot," was the advice of Sir Thomas Lawrence; and the picture last named was followed by nine colossal paintings: Woman pleading for the Vanquished, Judith, and Joan of Arc, each in three pictures; Benaiah, Origin of Marriage, and Ulysses and the Syrens. "It was my desire," he says, "to paint three times three." This was the mere outset; the productions of his long and industrious lifetime were exceedingly numerous. His works were chiefly from poetic and historic subjects.

Etty died in 1849, of a disease of the heart, in the sixty-third year of his age. "Etty was an enthusiast in his art, but his enthusiasm was not of that fitful kind which comes and goes where and when it wills; it was steady, continuous, and abiding; cheering and lighting him through many a toilsome path, till he had reached the highest point of all his greatness. He lived just long enough to witness the triumph of his genius over prejudice and narrowness of mind, and has left behind him a name to which his fellow-countrymen may point with pride and exultation."

Of the present British school of painting, Cleghorne says: Deprived of national patronage, British painters have not succeeded in forming a religious and historical school, properly so-called; still isolated attempts may be made by such artists as Barry, Hilton, and Haydon, whose enthusiasm prompted them to sacrifice their private interests to their love of high art, but such attempts, like exotics transplanted to an ungenial soil, soon languish and droop. The painters of the present day have, however, attained great excellence in a style which rising above the domestic and genre, borders closely on the historical, for examples of which, generally executed in the cabinet Poussin size, reference may be made to the works of Eastlake, Maclise, Sir

William Allan, Mulready, Leslie, George Harvey, Ward. Thomas Duncan, &c. In the first line of portrait, we find Pickersgill, Leslie, Philips, Watson Gordon, Partridge Landseer, Francis Grant, Count D'Orsay, Buckler, &c. In rural subjects, equestrian, hunting, and animal compositions, the works of Edwin Landseer, Mulready, Wetherington, Cooper, and Francis Grant, are distinguished for beauty and truth.

"Of living Scotch artists, Mr. Watson Gordon is distinguished for pure, chaste, and vigorous colouring, truth of character, wonderful relief, and close adherence to nature. His portraits attract much attention in the exhibitions of Trafalgar Square. In the difficult department of battle-pieces, Sir William Allan has been very successful. His Battle of Preston, and Battle of Waterloo, are pictures that may vie with any similar works of modern times. The latter, on its first exhibition in London, was purchased by the duke of Wellington. As a proof of his versatility of talent, we may refer to his naval picture of Nelson boarding the San Nicolas, at the battle of St. Vincent. In landscape, the Rev. John Thomson, of Duddingston, D. O. Hill, Horatio Macculloch, George Simpson, John A. Houston, Montague Stanley, J. Giles, E. T. Crawford, A. Perigal, are well known for their eminence in their different styles. The marine-pieces of Montague Stanley, J. F. Williams, and E. T Crawford, are full of truth and character. Of amateur contributors in landscape, Miss Frances Stoddart takes the first place for picturesque sylvan scenery, beauty of colour, and delicacy of touch. Miniature is successfully cultivated by J. Faid, Kenneth Macleay, Mrs. Musgrave, H. J. Stiwart, B. W. Crombie, &c."

American Painters.

THE first easel set up in the North American Colonies, was that of JOHN WATSON,* a Scotchman, who settled, as a portrait painter, at Perth Amboy, in 1715. The only token of his success is that he amassed considerable wealth by his profession, but none of his paintings are now to be found.

JOHN SMYBERT, also of Scotland, settled in Boston in 1728. He served his time with a house-painter, but finally went to Italy, where he spent three years in copying the works of Raphael, Titian, Vandyke, &c. His talents attracted the attention of Dean Berkeley, afterwards bishop of Cloyne, who persuaded him to accompany him to America, where he intended to establish a university for instructing the savages in Christian duties and civil knowledge, and Smybert was to be professor general of the fine arts. The scheme was abandoned, but Smybert remained in Boston. "We see," says Dunlap, "the influence of Smybert and his works upon Copley, Trumbull, and Allston. Copley was a youth of thirteen, at the time of Smybert's death, and probably had instructions from him—certainly from his pictures. Trumbull having retired from the army, resumed the study of painting, in Boston, in 1777, amidst the works of Copley, and in the room which had been built by Smybert, and in which remained many of his works. And Allston says, in a letter to a friend, after speaking of the paintings of Pine, "But I had a higher master in the head of Cardinal Bentevoglio,

* This account of American artists is chiefly drawn from Dunlap's Arts of Design in the United States.

from Vandyke, in the college library, (Cambridge,) which I obtained permission to copy, one winter vacation. This copy from Vandyke was by Smybert, an English painter, who came to this country with Dean, afterwards Bishop Berkeley. At that time, it seemed to me perfection; but when I saw the original, some years afterwards, I had to change my notions of perfection; however, I am grateful to Smybert for the instruction he gave me—his work rather."

It is thus that science, literature, and art, are propagated; and it is thus that we owe, perhaps, the colouring of Allston to the faint reflection of Vandyke in Smybert. The best portraits which we have of the eminent magistrates and divines of New England and New York, who lived between 1725 and 1751, are from his pencil.

MATHEW PRATT.

Mathew Pratt was born in 1734, and at the age of fifteen was placed an apprentice to his uncle, James Claypole, from whom—to use his own words—he learned all the different branches of the painting business, particularly portrait painting, which was his favourite study from the age of ten years. This allusion to the different branches of the painting business, shows plainly the degraded state of the arts, at that time, in this country.

Mr. Pratt afterwards studied with Benjamin West. He remained in England four years—eighteen months of that time being spent in the practice of his profession in the city of Bristol. In 1768 he returned to Philadelphia. Many of his portraits extant prove him to have been an artist of talent and capacity. Among these I would notice, as works praised by competent judges, a portrait of the duke of Portland, and one of the duchess of Manchester; also a Scripture piece, and the London School of Artists, and a full-length portrait of Governor Hamilton.

Devotedly attached to his profession, and governed by the spirit of the times, feeling that the legitimate path of the limner could not support an increasing family, Mr. Pratt painted at intervals a number of signs, some of which, until within a few years, have been hanging in Philadelphia. Perhaps the best among them was the representation of a cock in a barn-yard, which for many years graced a beer-shop in Spruce-street; the execution of this was so fine, and the expression of nature so exactly copied, that it was evident to the most casual observer that it was painted by the hand of a master. On the picture of the grand convention of 1788, which was first raised as a sign on the corner of Fourth and Chesnut streets, Mr. Pratt gave portraits of most of the distinguished men assembled on that occasion, and for some time the streets were filled with crowds occupied in identifying likenesses.

After a life spent principally in the cultivation of the arts, of which he was in this country a most effective pioneer, he died in 1805, aged seventy years.

CHARLES WILSON PEALE.

Charles Wilson Peale was born at Chesterton, on the eastern shore of Maryland, in 1741. Going to Norfolk when a youth, he saw the paintings of Mr. Frazier, and he thought he could do as well if he tried. On going home, he painted a portrait of himself which attracted much attention, and induced him to decide to make painting his profession. Forty years after this portrait was found tied up as a bag, containing a pound or two of whiting.

Peale went to Philadelphia, procured materials for portrait painting, and a book to refer to for instruction, "The Handmaid of the Arts," and set up as a painter. In 1770 he visited London, where West received him frankly as a pupil. His scanty funds were soon exhausted, and West received him into his house, that he might not lose the opportunity of improvement. He remained in London four years.

In 1776, Peale established himself in Philadelphia. He joined the army as a captain of volunteers, and was present at the battles of Trenton and Germantown. While in camp, he found time to exercise his pencil, and painted the likenesses of many officers. His son Rembrandt Peale asserts that his father painted a miniature of General Washington at a farm-house in New Jersey, and that during a sitting the general received a letter announcing the surrender of Cornwallis. Mr. Peale had his table and chair near the window, and Washington was seated on the side of the bed, the room being too small for another chair. It was an interesting moment, but the sitting was continued, as the miniature was intended for Mrs. Washington. But as Washington was at Yorktown when the surrender took place, it is probable that the incident belongs to an earlier period of the war, and that the name of Burgoyne should be substituted for that of Cornwallis.

From 1779 to 1785, Mr. Peale applied himself assiduously to painting; but about that time some bones of a mammoth being brought to him, the idea of forming a museum occurred to his active mind, and this new pursuit engaged all his thoughts.

In all attempts to introduce the arts of design, and the cultivation of science, Peale did his part, as far as possible, and always honourably. He died in 1827, at the age of eighty five.

To sum up the trades, employments, and professions of Mr. Peale, as his biographer in the "Cabinet of Natural History" has done. He was a saddler, harness-maker, clock and watch maker, silversmith, painter in oil, crayons, and miniature, modeller in clay, wax and plaster; he sawed his own ivory for his miniatures, moulded the glasses, and made the shagreen cases; he was a soldier, a legislator, a lecturer, a preserver of animals, a dentist. and a mild, benevolent, and good man.

GILBERT STUART.

Gilbert Stuart was born at Narraganset, in Rhode Island, in 1756. The first instruction he received, was from Mr. Alexander, an amateur painter, who visited Newport, when our artist was eighteen years of age. Mr. Alexander was so well pleased with his talents, that he took him with him, on his return to Scotland, but his friend dying soon after his arrival in his own country, Gilbert made his way home again, and commenced portrait painting in New York. He painted about this time a striking portrait of his grandmother, who had been dead eight or ten years. This faculty of drawing upon his memory for a correct portrait, was one of the distinguishing characteristics of Stuart.

At the age of twenty-four, the young painter was received as a pupil by West, in 1778. At this age he had painted his own portrait, to the great excellence of which Dr. Waterhouse bears ample testimony. He says, "it is painted in the freest manner, with a Rubens' hat;" and in another place, says, "that Stuart in his best days, said he need not be ashamed of it."

"On one occasion," says Mr. Dunlap, "as I stood by his easel, and admired the magic of his pencil, he amused me and my companion, whose portrait he was painting, by the following anecdote of himself and his old master." 'Mr. West,' said he, 'treated me very cavalierly on one occasion, but I had my revenge. It was the custom whenever a new Governor-General was sent out to India, that he should be complimented by a present of his majesty's portrait, and Mr. West, being the king's painter, was called upon, on all such occasions. So when Lord —— was about to sail, the usual order was received. My old master who was busily employed on one of his ten-acre pictures, thought he would turn over the king to me. He never could paint a portrait. "Stuart," said he, "it is a pity to make the king sit again for his picture; there is the portrait of him, that you painted, let me have it for Lord ——: I will retouch it, and it will do well enough." So the picture was carried down to his room, and at it he went. He worked at it all that day. The next morning, "Stuart," said he, "have you your palette set?" "Yes, sir." "Well, you can soon set another, let me have the one you have prepared; I can't satisfy myself with that head." I gave him my palette, and he worked the greater part of that day. In the afternoon, "Stuart," says he, "I don't know how it is, but you have a way of managing your tints different from every one else, here, take the palette and finish the head." "I can't indeed, sir, as it is, but let it stand until the morning, and get dry, and I will go over it with all my heart." I went into his room bright and early, and by half-past nine I had finished the head. When West saw it he complimented me highly; and I had ample revenge for his "It will do well enough."' "

Before Stuart left the roof of his benefactor and teacher, he painted a full-length portrait of him, which elicited great admiration. It was exhibited at Somerset House, and the young painter paid frequent visits to the exhibition rooms. It happened one day that, as he stood surrounded by artists and students, near his master's portrait, the original came in and joined the group. West praised the picture, and, addressing himself to his pupil, said: "You have done well, Stuart—very well; now all you have to do, is to go home and do better." He uniformly said, that nothing could exceed the attention of that distinguished artist to him. And when West saw that he was fitted for the field—armed and prepared to contend with the highest and best—he advised him to commence his professional career, and pointed out the road to fame and fortune.

In 1782, in pursuance of Mr. West's advice, Stuart commenced painting as a professional artist.

The following anecdote was told by Judge Hopkinson. Lord Mulgrave employed Stuart to paint the portrait of his brother, General Phipps, previous to his going abroad. On seeing the picture, which he did not until it was finished, Mulgrave exclaimed, "I see insanity in that face!" The general went to India, and the first account his brother had of him was that of his committing suicide from insanity. It is thus that the real painter dives into the recesses of his sitter's mind, and displays strength or weakness upon the surface of his canvass, while the mere mechanic makes a map of a man.

The love of his own country, his admiration of General Washington, and the very great desire he had to paint his portrait, were his inducements to turn his back on his good fortune in Europe. Accordingly, in 1793, Mr. Stuart embarked for his native land, and took up his abode for some months in New York. Thence he proceeded to Philadelphia, for the purpose so near his heart, of painting a portrait of Washington. This he accomplished in 1794, but not being satisfied with the expression, he destroyed it, and the president consented to sit again. In the second portrait, he was eminently successful. He painted it on a three-quarter canvass, but only finished the head. It now adorns one of the rooms of the Boston Atheneum.

After the removal of Congress to Washington, Stuart followed, and resided there until 1805, and then removed to Boston, where he resided until his death. If we judge by the portrait of the Hon. John Quincy Adams, the last he painted, his powers of mind were undiminished to the last, and his eye free from the dimness of age. The picture was begun as a full-length, but death arrested the hand of the artist, after he had completed the likeness of the face; and proved that at seventy-four he painted better than in the meridian of life. This picture has been finished, that is, the person and accessories painted, by that eminent and highly-gifted artist, Thomas Sully; who, as he has said, would have thought it little less than sacrilege to have touched the head.

Mr. Stuart died in 1828, in the seventy-fifth year of his age.

"The narrations and anecdotes with which his knowledge of men and of the world had stored his memory," says Washington Allston, "and which he often gave with great beauty and dramatic effect, were not unfrequently employed by Mr. Stuart in a way, and with an address, peculiar to himself. From this store it was his custom to draw largely while occupied with his sitters —apparently for their amusement; but his object was rather, by thus banishing all restraint, to call forth, if possible, some involuntary traits of natural character. But these glimpses of character, mixed as they are in all men with so much that belongs to their age and associates, would have been of little use to an ordinary observer ; for the faculty of distinguishing between the accidental and the permanent, in other words, between the conventional expression which belongs to manners, and that more subtle indication of the individual mind, is indeed no common one : and by few, if indeed by any, has this faculty been possessed in so remarkable a degree. It was this which enabled him to animate his canvass—not with the appearance of mere general life, but with that peculiar distinctive life which separates the humblest individual from his kind. He seemed to dive into the thoughts of men—for they were made to rise and speak on the surface. Were other evidences wanting, this talent alone were sufficient to establish his claims as a man of genius ; since it is the privilege of genius alone to measure at once the highest and the lowest. In his happier efforts no one ever surpassed him in imbodying, if we may so speak, these transient apparitions of the soul. Of this, not the least admirable instance is his portrait of President Adams, whose bodily tenement at the time seemed rather to present the image of some dilapidated castle than the habitation of the "unbroken mind;" but not such is the picture : called forth from its crumbling recesses, the living tenant is there —still ennobling the ruin, and upholding it, as it were, by the strength of his inner life. In this venerable ruin will the unbending patriot and the gifted artist speak to posterity of the first glorious century of our republic.

"In a word, Gilbert Stuart was, in its widest sense, a philosopher in his art ; he thoroughly understood its principles, as his works bear witness—whether as to harmony of colours, or of lines, or of light and shadow—showing that exquisite sense of a whole which only a man of genius can imbody.

"Jealousy was unknown to him, but where praise was due he gave it freely, and gave too with a grace that showed that, loving excellence for its own sake, he had a pleasure in praising it. To young artists he was uniformly kind and indulgent, and most liberal of his advice, which no one ever properly asked but he received, and in a manner no less courteous than impressive."

WILLIAM DUNLAP.

William Dunlap was born at Perth Amboy in 1766 His father, a retired British officer, removed to New York, when that city was in possession of the English. The heart of the boy had from early childhood been turned towards art, and with some difficulty a teacher was procured. In his own words, " William Williams undertook the task ; I went to his rooms, and he put a drawing-book before me, such as I had possessed for years : after a few visits the teacher was not to be found. I examined his portraits, tried his crayons, and soon procured a set, and commenced painting portraits, beginning with my father's. From painting my relations, I proceeded to painting my young companions, and having applications from strangers, I fixed my price at three guineas a head. I thus commenced portrait painter in 1782, by no means looking to it as a means of subsistence, but living as the only and indulged child of my parents, and doing as it seemed best unto me. Thus passed life until the age of seventeen. About this time I took up my abode at Mr. John Van Horne's, by invitation, within a short distance of the head-quarters of the commander-in-chief, near Princeton, New Jersey He frequently called, when returning from his ride, and passed an hour with Mrs. Van Horne and the ladies of the family, or with the farmer, if at home. I was, of course, introduced to him. I had painted the portraits of Mr. and Mrs. Van Horne, and they were admired far beyond their merits, and shown to all visitors. I had with me a flute and some music books, and one morning as I copied notes and tried them, the general and his *suite* passed through the hall, and I heard him say, 'The love of music and painting is frequently found united in the same person.' The remark is commonplace, but it was delightful to me at the time.

"The assertion that this great man never laughed must have arisen from his habitual, perhaps natural reservedness. But I remember, during my opportunity of observing his deportment, two instances of unrestrained laughter. The first, and more moderate, was at an anecdote from Judge Peters. The second was on witnessing a scene in front of Mr. Van Horne's house. A black boy had been ordered to catch a young porker, and was in full but unavailing chase, when the master and myself arrived from a walk. 'Stand away,' said Van Horne, and, throwing off his coat and hat, he undertook the chase, determined to run the pig down. His guest and his negroes stood laughing at his exertions, and the pig's manifold escapes. Shouts and laughter at length proclaimed the success of the *chasseur*, and while he held the pig up in triumph, the big drops coursing from forehead to chin, amidst the squealing of the victim, the stentorian voice of Van Horne was heard, 'I'll show you how to run down a pig;' and as he spoke, he looked up in the face of Washington, who, with his *suite*, had trotted their horses into the court-yard, unheard amidst the din of the chase, and the shouts of triumphant success. The ludicrous expression of surprise at being so caught, with his attempts to speak to his heroic visitor, while the pig redoubled its efforts to escape by kicking and squealing, produced as hearty a burst of laughter from the dignified Washington as any that shook the sides of the most vulgar spectator of the scene.

"My friend, Van Horne, requested the general to sit to me, and he complied. This was a triumphant moment for a boy of seventeen ; and it must be remembered that Washington had not then been 'hackneyed to the touches of painter's pencil.' I say a triumphant moment ; but one of anxiety, fear, and trembling.

'I was soon quite at home at head-quarters. To breakfast and dine, day after day, with the general and Mrs. Washington, and members of congress, and to be noticed as the young painter, was delicious. The general's portrait led to the sitting of the lady. I made what were thought likenesses, and presented them to Mr. and Mrs. Van Horne, taking copies for myself.

"It was now decided that I should go to London in the spring, and the winter was passed in making preparations for the voyage.

"My first portrait in oil was made for the assistance of a sign-painter, probably in 1782. Delanoy had undertaken to paint the head of Sir Samuel Hood, one of the lions of the day, and found himself puzzled to make a likeness that the sailors would acknowledge. In this dilemma he came to me. I took his palette, and with a bold brush dashed in the red face and hair of the naval hero. The sign swung amidst the acclamations of the Jack tars. A more inveterate likeness did not exist in the collection of Charles Surface ; and yet I have recognized my first oil portrait, somewhat improved, in the 'British Portrait Gallery,' under the title of Lord Hood.

"In preparation for my departure for Europe, which had been determined upon, I painted my second oil picture, a full length of Washington. I placed my hero on the field of battle, at Princeton. I did not take the liberty to throw off his hat, nor did I omit the black and white cockade ; but in full uniform, booted and spurred, he stood most heroicly alone ; for the figures in the background I had thrown to a most convenient distance. There was General Mercer, dying in precisely the same attitude that West had adopted for Wolfe—two authors may think alike. A great deal of smoke completed the picture; which, with a copy of a print, served as my credentials to Benjamin West, who had consented to receive me.

"On my arrival, having procured London-made clothes, and sent forward my pictures, Captain Lawrence, my father's friend, accompanied me to Newman-street, and guided me through a long gallery, hung with sketches and designs, and then through a lofty antechamber, filled with gigantic paintings, to the inner painting-room of the artist. After my first introduction, Mr. West led us back to the room we had passed through, where my specimens were deposited. He first examined my drawing in India ink. I awaited my sentence. 'This is very well.' I felt that all was safe. 'But it only indicates a talent for engraving.' I sank from summer heat to freezing point—my friend seized the painting and unrolled it on the floor. The artist smiled—the thermometer rose. 'This shows some talent for composition.' He appeared pleased, and looking at the distant figures, smiled to see an awkward imitation of his own General Wolfe, dressed in blue, to represent the death of General Mercer; and the Yankees playing the part of the British grenadiers, and driving the red-coats before them. I was encouraged. We were directed to 84 Charlotte-street, Rathbone-place, where rooms had been engaged for me. Mr. West offered his casts for my practice, when I should be ready to draw.

"After seeing the lions of the Tower, and other parts of London, I sat down to draw in black and white chalks from the bust of Cicero; and having mastered that, in every point of view, I drew from the Fighting Gladiator, and my drawing gained me permission to enter the Academy of Somerset House. I know not why—perhaps because I was too timid and awkward to introduce myself, or to ask Mr. West to introduce me; but I never made use of the permission. I had an awe of distinguished men that caused many weaknesses in my conduct; a bashfulness that required encouraging, at the same time that I was first and boldest among my companions—but so it was; I went with my portfolio, port-crayon, chalks, and paper, and delivered them to the porter, made an excuse for not going in, and walked off. I never entered the school, nor saw my portfolio again.

"The drawings above mentioned, and a few pictures in oil, executed under the direction of Mr. Davy, who taught me to set a palette, as he had been taught in Rome, were all the records of my exertions to become a painter which the year 1784 produced.

"During this period of my life I was a favourite with my companions. I was by them supposed to possess humour and wit. I could sing to please my associates, but I did nothing to satisfy the man who had it in his power to serve me. My follies and my faults were reported and exaggerated to Mr. West, and as he saw no appearances of the better self which resided in me, (for there was a better self,) he left me to my fate.

"About this time I painted several portraits, and composed some historical pieces, the subject of one of which, and the only one which attained any thing like a finish, was from Hoole's Ariosto. I had attempted to represent Feran gazing with horror upon the ghost, who rises from the water with the helmet in his right hand, and points to it with his left. The steel armour of Feran had received a touch from my friend Raphael West. The ghost I had studied from the looking-glass. When I showed this picture to West I unexpectedly heard him say to one present,

'That figure is very good,' and turning towards him, I was on the point of saying, 'Rafe helped me with the armour,' when to my surprise I found that he pointed to the ghost, for which I had been my own model. On the same occasion, I showed the great painter a portrait I had painted. It was freely touched, well coloured, and full of expression—better than any thing I had done, by far. He gave it due praise, but observed, 'You have made the two sides of the figure alike; each has the same sweeping swell—he looks like a rolling-pin.' I might have said truly that it was characteristic—but I took the lesson in silence, and made no defence, although I knew that my subject was, in fact, 'like a rolling-pin.' Silence, in this instance, may have been commendable; but my habit of silence, in presence of those whom I considered my superiors, was very detrimental to me. The person who asks for information gains it; the questioner may be at times irksome, but that is for want of tact. He should be a judicious questioner and a good listener. I stood in the presence of the artist and wondered at his skill, but I stood in silence, abashed, hesitating—and withdrew unenlightened—discouraged by the consciousness of ignorance and the monomaniacal want of courage to elicit the information I eagerly desired. Let every student be apprised that those who can best inform him, are most willing to do so

"This life of unprofitable idleness was terminated by a summons to return home, brought by Captain Watson, who informed me that my passage was paid, and that he should sail in August. Thus ended a residence in London, of sufficient length to have made a man of feebler abilities than my own, a painter; but my character was at first mistaken. I was discouraged, and led astray; and gave up the pursuit of my profession, for the pursuits which youth, health, and a disposition to please and be pleased presented to me. In August, 1787, I embarked, to return home, in the same ship, that brought me, all alive with the best disposition to improve myself, to the metropolis of Britain, in 1784.

"In due time, my pictures, canvasses, colours, &c., were landed, and I was installed as a portrait painter, in my father's house, and had sitters, but I felt my own ignorance. By degrees, my employers became fewer, my efforts were unsatisfactory to myself. I sought a refuge in literature, and, after a year or two, abandoned painting, and joined my father in mercantile business.

"In 1805 I engaged in theatrical speculations, and became a bankrupt. I next turned my attention to miniature painting, and found that I could make what were acknowledged likenesses. I was in earnest, and, although deficient even in the knowledge necessary to prepare ivory for the reception of colour, I improved, as it was necessary to make exertion to procure money for my family.

"After various vicissitudes, and changes of occupation, at the age of fifty-one I became permanently a painter. In a sick chamber, and in aiding to re-establish the American Academy of Fine Arts, many months now passed away. I was elected a director and keeper, had a salary of two hundred dollars a year, and rooms for painting assigned me; and painted, in 1817 and 1818, many portraits."

But business failing in New York, Mr. Dunlap spent the three following years chiefly in Norfolk and Montreal He returned to New York in 1821. "To paint a great picture," he continues, "now occupied all my thoughts. I purchased of my friend Sully, a canvass 18 feet by 12, but where was I to put a thing of that size, and have a proper light on it.

"I raised my canvass in the garret of a house I occupied in

Leonard-street, with conflicting lights all below the centre of the cloth, and thus proceeded with my work all through a hot summer, sometimes discouraged, but generally pleased to see effects produced which I had thought beyond my power. In November I took down my canvass, and packed it for the purpose of transportation to Norfolk, where I purposed to pass a third winter, and I knew I had a better place than my garret to work on my picture, as well as a better prospect of lucrative employment while finishing it.

"On the 3d of June, 1822, I left Norfolk, I presumed for the last time. I engaged a young Irishman, who aspired to be a painter, to take charge of the Christ Rejected, and shipped it by the way of Baltimore for Philadelphia. I had reason to be satisfied with the impression made upon the public, and the surprise it excited among the artists.

"On the 23rd of February, 1824, I purchased a large unprepared cloth, and having nailed it to the floor of the garret, I gave it several coats of white lead, which being dry, I proceeded to outline the Bearing of the Cross, from the sketch previously made. So *high* and so *low* was the commencement of this my second big picture.

"My next exertion as an artist was the composition of a third picture, connected with the Crucifixion, which I called Calvary. This winter and spring I finished the sketch in oil, probably my best composition. Before transferring it to the large canvass, I painted from nature the principal figures and groups separately. I had none of that facility which attends the adept in drawing, and now felt the penalty of my folly, when I had the Royal Academy of England at my command, and the advice of the best historical painter of the age always ready to instruct me—and both neglected. I now, as for some years previous, studied the casts from the antique, and improved; but my drawing remained deficient. I had neglected 'the spring of life,' and it never returned.

"I also determined to make a picture from the etched outline of West's Death on the Pale Horse, before the Calvary, I exerted myself for that purpose, and making an arrangement with the directors of the American Academy of Fine Arts, for the use of the gallery, I opened the picture to the public in less than three months from the commencement of the outline.

"In November, I became acquainted with the person and paintings of Mr. T. Cole. I did the best I could to make the public acquainted with the extraordinary merit of his pictures—even then, and it is among the few of my good deeds; he has proved more than I anticipated, and I have been repaid by his friendship, and gratified by his success.

"In 1826 the National Academy of Design was created, composed of, and governed by artists only. I became an active member, being elected an academician. In the spring I continued to paint studies from nature, for the Calvary, and likewise painted several portraits. In May, the National Academy opened their first annual exhibition, which has increased in interest yearly.

"From my journal I extract an entry not made for the public eye :—

"'Thursday, 19th Feb., 1829.—I am this day 63 years of age, active, and, I think, stronger than a year ago. I believe I am improving as an artist. As a man, I hope I am—but it is little. May God receive my thanks for His blessings, and may His will be done.'

"In March, my Calvary was exhibited in Washington with praise and profit."

JOHN TRUMBULL.

Trumbull was born in Lebanon, Connecticut, and was the son of Jonathan Trumbull, first governor of that state, of the name. When at college, he ransacked the library for books on the arts, among others he found "Brook Taylor's Jesuit's Perspective made easy." This work he studied faithfully, and copied all the diagrams: he also copied a picture belonging to the college of an Eruption of Mount Vesuvius, painted by an Italian; also, a copy of Vandyke, the Head of Cardinal Bentevoglio, and Nicolas Coypell's Rebecca at the Well. He did these in oil, obtaining his colours of a house-painter.

Before he went to college he obtained a book called the "Handmaid of the Arts." He somewhere picked up the title page, and sent to London for the book. Copley was then in Boston, and young Trumbull's first visit to that distinguished artist, happened to be made at a time when he was entertaining his friends, shortly after his marriage. He found him in a suit of crimson velvet, with gold buttons; and the elegance of his style, and his high repute, impressed the future artist with grand ideas of the life of a painter.

The works of Smybert, Blackburn, and Copley, at Boston, so immediately under the eye of the young man, doubtless strengthened the desire to become a painter; and on his return to Lebanon, he made his first attempt at composition.

After leaving college, he painted the Battle of Cannæ, which shows the bent of his mind, being particularly struck with the character of Paulus Emilius. This picture is now at Yale College. He painted several other pictures; among them one of Brutus condemning his Sons. What has become of that is unknown. Very soon after, all other subjects were absorbed in the stirring incidents of the times. He served about two years in the army as an adjutant-general, with the rank of colonel. He resigned his commission in 1777, and after two or three years' study in Boston, he proceeded to London, and became the pupil of Benjamin West. For three months he pursued his studies uninterruptedly, when falling under suspicion as an American spy, he was imprisoned for eight months.

It was during this confinement, that Mr. Trumbull, among other pictures, copied that beautiful copy of the St. Jerome, which is mentioned in the "Life of West," as being executed by him from the exquisite original of Coreggio, at Parma. Mr. Trumbull's is, perhaps, equal to his master's, and certainly one of the gems of the art.

In June, at which time a change had taken place in the affairs of the two countries, and the government began to relax their severity; Trumbull was admitted to bail by a special order of the king in council, on condition of quitting the kingdom within thirty days, and not to return during the war. His securities were West and Copley. Consequently he returned home greatly changed and disappointed. In the spring of 1783, the news arrived of the preliminaries of peace having been arranged, and in January, 1784, Trumbull landed in Portsmouth, England, and immediately proceeded to London, where he was again kindly received by Mr. West, pursued his studies indefatigably, and in 1785, had made such progress as to copy for Mr. West his celebrated picture of the Battle of La Hogue. An original composition of his own, was painted immediately afterwards, and he chose for his subject Priam bearing back to his palace the body of Hector, the figures about ten inches in height. The picture is now in the possession of the widow of Mr Gore, to whom it was presented, at Waltham, near Boston, and is devised to Harvard College, where the painter was educated. It is in miniature oil, a style in which Mr. Trumbull afterwards excelled as an historical painter. The figures were of a size similar, or nearly so, to those in his Bunker Hill, and Death of Montgomery.

"The composition, colouring, and touch of Mr. Trumbull's Bunker Hill," says Mr. Dunlap, "are admirable. The drawing and attitudes of the figures, though excellent, are inferior to his next picture, of the same miniature size, the Death of Montgomery at Quebec. The figures are accurately drawn, and the attitudes finely diversified. The chiaroscuro is perfect. These two beautiful little pictures were carried to Washington, in 1816, and shown to the members of congress, as inducements to employ the painter in patriotic works for the capitol: but, although their merits gained employment for the artist, the senators and representatives saw at once, that such subjects were not fitted for the decoration of the rotunda. Had the Battle of Bunker Hill represented the true point of time; the triumph of our militia and gallant leaders, over the disciplined veterans of Britain, there can be no doubt that the picture would have been copied for the nation.

The fourth and last historical painting which Mr. Trumbull finished, under the eye of West, was the Sortie from Gibraltar; it is, perhaps, the best of his works.

The immense traffic in prints which had been established by England, presented a field for the accumulation of wealth. To paint a series of pictures on subjects connected with the American Revolution, was a speculation worthy of attention; and to do it in copartnership with European engravers, and spread prints of the size of the original pictures, was a feasible project, offering both fame and fortune.

The present constitution of the United States had been framed, and the first session of congress had been appointed to be held in New York, in December, 1789. The time had therefore arrived for proceeding with the American pictures. (He had already obtained a portrait of Mr. Adams, in London, and Mr, Jefferson sat to him for his, in Paris.) He sailed for America, and arrived in New York in November, 1789; and proceeded to paint as many of the heads of the signers of the Declaration of Independence as were present.

These portraits of such persons as had been in congress at the signing of the Declaration of Independence, or of such as had afterwards signed it, and of Washington for the battles of Trenton and Princeton, are among the most admirable miniatures in oil that ever were painted. The same may be said of the portraits in the small picture of the Surrender of Cornwallis.

In the summer of 1790 he painted the full-length portrait—in the council room, City Hall, New York—of General Washington, of the size of life; and in 1791, that of Governor George Clinton, in the same room. In 1792 he painted another full-length of Washington, for the city of Charleston, with a horse, and a view of that city in the distance. He painted another at the same time, which is now at the college at New Haven, to which it was presented by the State Society of the Cincinnati. The latter is considered as the finest portrait of Washington in existence. It represents him at the most critical moment in his life—on the evening before the battle of Princeton—meditating his retreat before a superior enemy. At the time this picture was painted, Signor Ceracchi executed a bust, of which there is a colossal cast in the collection of the American Academy of the Fine Arts The best evidence that can be given of the correctness of both these productions of art, is to be found in the close resemblance they bear to each other, although executed by differ ent hands and in materials so dissimilar.

A few other portraits were painted about this time ; but the years '91, '92, and '93, were principally spent in painting original portraits for the historical pictures. In the accomplishment of this great design he travelled from New Hampshire to Charleston, South Carolina. The head of General Lincoln, at the surrender of Yorktown, was painted at Boston. Edward Rutledge, Hayward, and William Washington, were painted in Charleston. The heads painted at this period are in the small set of pictures now at New Haven. They are the originals of the whole work, and were all painted from the living men.

In 1794 Mr. Trumbull accompanied Mr. Jay, who was appointed minister to Great Britain, as secretary. He visited Paris. and saw from the condition of the continent, that all hope of profit, from the sale of engravings, was at an end. His calculation had been on a more extensive demand, on the continent of Europe, for American historical pictures. The war had overwhelmed all Europe, and paintings and painters were not in demand ; in consequence of which, he gave up his professional pursuits and embarked in commerce, until August, 1796, when he returned to England. He was appointed one of the commissioners under the treaty then pending between Great Britain and the United States, which was not concluded until 1804, when he returned to America, and established himself on the corner of Pine-street and Broadway, New York, as portrait painter, in his second style. He stood alone in the northern and eastern division of the United States. Jarvis and Sully were then little known Stuart was at the seat of government. The wealthy citizens had their portraits painted, and the corporation of New York had their governors and mayors immor.alized by Trumbull.

EDWARD G. MALBONE.

Malbone was born at Newport, Rhode Island, in 1777. He discovered a propensity for painting very early, and it grew with his growth, and increased until it absorbed all other desires. His sister thus writes of him: "He could not have been more than six or seven years of age before any common observer must have noticed many peculiarities. He could find but little leisure for play, the intervals of his school hours being filled by indefatigable industry in making experiments, and endeavouring to make discoveries. He took great delight in blowing bubbles, for the pleasure of admiring the fine colours they displayed.

"He soon turned his attention to painting, copying any little picture that pleased him; making his own brushes, and preparing his colours even before he could discriminate between the different shades, having never seen a paint-box. He would gather stones on the beach, and with the few colours he could collect, labour until he could make them answer his purpose. He was naturally very absent, appearing to be wholly absorbed in his own reflections. We used to tease him to join in our plays, but he would remain inflexible, until we were induced to ridicule his stupidity, and laugh at his folly in spending all his time in ruminating over all the old pictures he could collect; he used to smile and reply, 'You may enjoy your mirth, but you shall one day see my head engraved;' nothing ruffled him or put him out of his course. About the age of eleven or twelve he commenced drawing figures of gods and goddesses, with India ink, upon ivory or bone, purchasing common breast-pins and expunging the devices to replace them with his own performances, but more frequently by sawing out the ivory or bone with his own hands, it being an article which Newport at that time could not furnish.

"At about sixteen he painted upon paper a likeness of Thomas Lawrence, which was so universally admired by all persons of taste who saw it, that his father could no longer shut his eyes to his decided talent. He sent the picture by a friend to Philadelphia, to a French artist, with a request that he would receive him as a pupil. He immediately replied, 'De boy would take de bread out of my mout.' Requiring several years' services and so exorbitant a sum of money, that his father did not think proper to comply, but waited for an opportunity of placing him to more advantage. But at seventeen he determined to throw himself upon his own resources. Communicating his plans to no one but myself, he proposed a visit to Providence, and immediately brought himself before the public as miniature painter, and so warmly was he received, that several weeks passed away before he apprised his father of the step he had taken. He now wrote a letter to my father and two to myself, which I regret that it is not in my power to forward, having sought for them in vain; they were worth preserving, as they expressed his hopes and views for the future so strongly, and at the same time with so much filial obedience to his father's wishes. Continuing pleased with his flattering reception, daily improving, and successful in his likenesses, he remained in Providence thirteen months, until he was recalled by the sudden illness of his father, which terminated in death before he reached home.

"In 1796, a friend advised his going to Boston; to this he acceded, and was there introduced to, and found friends in, many of the most distinguished characters. His natural refinement and engaging manners being so prepossessing, that letters of of introduction seemed hardly necessary; his Boston friends seemed to vie with each other in the exercise of their hospitality

"In May, 1801, he embarked for London, in company with Mr. Allston. His reception by the president of the Royal Academy was so flattering, that it could not fail to give him confidence in himself, holding out every inducement for him to remain in Europe; and having free access to the school of the arts, his improvement was very rapid. He now painted the Hours, and several female heads, which were highly eulogized by the president, Mr. West saying that no man in England could excel them, and that he had nothing to fear from professional competition; but his private affairs requiring his attention, he returned to Charleston in December of the same year."

Malbone had almost every kind of excellence which can be displayed in this kind of painting. He drew well and correctly, yet without tameness. He had acute discernment of character, and much power of expressing it. He had taste, fancy, and grace; and in the delineation of female beauty, or gay, innocent childhood, these qualities were admirably conspicuous. His preeminent excellence was in colouring, such was its harmony, its delicacy, its truth. His miniatures have most of the beauties of fine portraits, without losing any of their own peculiar character. He had the happy talent, among his many excellencies, of elevating the character without impairing the likeness: this was remarkable in his male heads; and no woman ever lost any beauty by his hand; nay, the fair often became fairer under his hand. To this he added a grace of execution all his own.

To all this he added the still rarer merit of originality; for he was almost a self-taught painter. Though whilst he was in England, he doubtless improved himself very much by the study of fine pictures, and the observation of the practice of West, and other great painters of the day, yet it has been said by artists, that the style and manner of his earlier and later works are substantially the same; and those painted after his return from Europe are only to be distinguished by their superior delicacy of taste, and greater apparent facility of execution.

The few pieces of larger composition, which his hurry of business left him time to complete, have the same character of grace and beauty.

He occasionally amused himself with landscape. His sketches in this way were but slight, and are valuable only as they show the extent of his powers. There is one little piece of his which is said to be mere sport of imagination. It possesses a singularly pleasing effect of pastoral sweetness. There is a fine miniature of Col. Scolbay, of Boston, in possession of his daughters. Stuart used to go, at least once a year, to see it, desiring them to take care of it, as it was decidedly the best miniature in the world.

In the latter years of his life, he tried his hand in oil painting, in which he made a respectable proficiency. That he did not attain to great eminence in this branch, was owing, not to any want of talent, but for want of leisure and health; for so much of his excellence was intellectual, and so little of it purely mechanical, that with requisite application, he could not have failed to acquire distinction in any department of the art.

Too close an application to his profession brought on a decline. He died at Savannah, in 1807, in the thirty-second year of his age.

WASHINGTON ALLSTON.

Allston was born in 1779, in the state of South Carolina The climate not agreeing with his constitution, he was sent, by the advice of physicians, at a very early age, (between six and seven,) to Newport, Rhode Island, and was there at school until 1796, when he was transferred to Harvard College, Cambridge, Massachusetts.

Mr. Allston, speaking of his boyhood, says: "My chief pleasure now was in drawing from prints—of all kinds of figures, landscapes, and animals. But I soon began to make pictures of my own, at what age, however, I cannot say. The earliest compositions that I remember, were the Storming of Count Roderick's Castle, from a poor, (though to me delightful) romance of that day, and the Siege of Toulon; the first in India ink, the other in water colours. To these succeeded many others, which have likewise passed into oblivion. Though I never had any regular instruction in the art, (a circumstance both idle and absurd to boast of,) I had much incidental instruction; which I have always through life been glad to receive from those in advance of myself.

"My leisure hours at college, were chiefly devoted to the pencil—t› the composition equally of figures and landscapes. I do not remember that I preferred one to the other; my only guide in the choice was the inclination of the moment. There was an old landscape in the house of a friend in Cambridge, that gave me my first hints in colour in that branch; it was of a rich and deep tone, though not by the hands of a master.

"In the colouring of figures, the pictures of Pine, in the Columbian Museum, in Bostoı, were my first masters. Pine had certainly, as far as I can recollect, considerable merit in colour. But I had a higher master in the head of Cardinal Bentevoglio, from Vandyke, in the college library, which I obtained permission to copy one winter vacation."

At the period of his return to South Carolina from college, in 1800, Mr. Allston painted a head of St. Peter, when he hears the cock crow, and one of Judas Iscariot. In 1801, at the age of twenty-two, he embarked with his friend Malbone for England. In one of his letters he says: "I arrived in England about the middle of June. The next year was the first of my appearing before the public, when I exhibited three pictures at Somerset House. The principal one, a French Soldier telling a Story, (a comic attempt;) a Rocky Coast, with Banditti; and a Landscape with Horsemen, which I had painted at college, as before alluded to. I received two applications for the French Soldier; which I sold to Mr. Wilson, of the European Museum, for whom I afterwards painted a companion to it, also comic—the Poet's Ordinary, where the lean fare was enriched by an incidental arrest."

After three years' residence in England, Mr. Allston passed over to France, and in the letter before mentioned, thus expresses his feelings on visiting the Louvre, that splendid accumulation of plunder: "Titian, Tintoretto, and Paul Veronese, absolutely enchanted me, for they took away all sense of subjects. When I stood before the Peter Martyr, the Miracle of the Slave, and the Marriage of Cana, I thought of nothing but of the gorgeous concert of colours, or rather of the indefinite forms (I cannot call them sensations) of pleasure with which they filled the imagination. It was the poetry of colour which I felt; procreative in its nature, giving birth to a thousand things which the eye cannot see, and distinct from their cause. I did not, however, stop to analyze my feelings—perhaps at that time I could not have done it. I was content with my pleasure without seeking the cause. But I now understand it, and I think I understand why so many great colourists, especially Tintoretto and Paul Veronese gave so little heed to the ostensible stories of their compositions. In some of them, the Marriage of Cana, for instance, there is not the slightest clue given by which the spectator can guess at the subject. They addressed themselves not to the senses only, as some have supposed, but rather through them to that region (if I may so speak) of the imagination, which is supposed to be under the exclusive dominion of music, and which, by similar excitement, they caused to teem with visions that 'lap the soul in Elysium.' In other words, they leave the subject to be made by the spectator, provided he possesses the imaginative faculty—otherwise they will have little more meaning to him than a calico counterpane."

In pursuing the subject, Allston says: "I am by nature, as it respects the arts, a *wide liker*. I cannot honestly turn up my nose even at a piece of still-life, since, if well done, it gives me pleasure. This remark will account for otherwise strange transitions. I will mention here a picture of a totally different kind, which then took great hold of me, by Ludovico Caracci. I do n t remember the title, but the subject was the body of the Virgin borne for interment by four apostles. The figures are colossal; the tone dark, and of tremendous depth of colour. It seemed, as I looked at it, as if the ground shook under their tread, and the air were darkened by their grief."

Mr. Allston spent about four years in Italy, the principal part of the time in Rome. His studies while there were not confined to drawing and painting. He made modelling in clay a separate branch of study, and devoted much time to it. He has said of this study, in after life: "I would recommend modelling to all young painters, as one of the best means of acquiring an accurate knowledge of the joints."

At Rome he became acquainted with Coleridge. It is only his own words that can do justice to his estimation of the great poet. In one of his letters, after mentioning a friend, he proceeds: "I have had occasion in former letters, more than once, to mention the name of another most valued friend, of whom I would gladly say more, did I not feel that it is not for me to do justice to his extraordinary powers. I would observe, however, that to no other man whom I have known do I owe so much, *intellectually*, as to Mr. Coleridge, with whom I became acquainted in Rome, and who has honoured me with his friendship for more than five-and-twenty years. He used to call Rome the silent city; but I never could think of it as such, while with him; for, meet him when and where I would, the fountain of his mind was never dry, but like the far-reaching aqueducts that once supplied this mistress of the world, its living stream seemed especially to flow for every classic ruin over which we wandered. And when I recall some of our walks under the pines of the Villa Borghese, I am almost tempted to dream that I have once listened to Plato, in the groves of the Academy. It was there he taught me this golden rule—*never judge of any work of art by its defects;* a rule as wise as benevolent; and one that, while it has spared me much pain, has widened my sphere of pleasure."

Mr. Allston returned to America, in 1809. When Robert W. Weir, Esq., of New York, was studying in Rome, many years after, the artists there asked him after an American painter, for whom they had no other name than the American Titian. When Weir mentioned the name of Allston, they exclaimed—"that's the man!" Sully and others say, that Allston's colouring is more like Titian than that of any modern artist.

After remaining in his native country three years, he returned to England; where the first work in which he engaged, was his great picture of the Dead Man revived by the touch of Elisha's Bones. He writes to a friend: "My progress in this picture was interrupted by a dangerous illness, which, after some months of great suffering, compelled me to remove to Clifton, near Bristol. It was first exhibited at the British Gallery—an institution patronized by the principal nobility and gentry—the Prince Regent then president; it there obtained the first prize of two hundred guineas. As I had returned to London chiefly to finish this picture, that accomplished, I went back to Bristol, where I painted, and left a number of pictures; among these were half-length portraits of my friend Mr. Coleridge, and my medical friend, Mr. King, of Clifton. I have painted but few portraits, and these I think are my best."

The great picture of the Dead Man restored to Life by touching the Bones of the Prophet Elisha, was put up in the Pennsylvania Academy of Fine Arts, in April, 1816, in a good light; and has been a source of delight to the citizens and artists. The size is 13 feet by 11. The passage on which it is founded is as follows: "And the bands of the Moabites invaded the land at the coming in of the year. And it came to pass, as they were burying a man, that, behold, they spied a band of men, and they cast the man into the sepulchre of Elisha; and when the man was let down, and touched the bones of Elisha, he revived." 2 Kings, chap. xiii. verses 20, 21.

The sepulchre of Elisha is supposed to be in a cavern among the mountains. In the foreground is the man at the moment of reanimation; in which the artist has tried, both in the action and colour, to express the gradual recoiling of life upon death. Behind him, in a dark recess, are the bones of the Prophet, the scull of which is marked by a preternatural light. At his head and feet are two slaves, bearers of the body; the ropes still in their hands, by which they have let it down, indicating the act that moment performed: the emotion in the figure at the feet is astonishment and fear, modified by doubt, as if requiring further confirmation of the miracle before him; while in the figure at the head, is that of unqualified, immoveable terror. In the most prominent group above is a soldier, in the act of rushing from the scene. The violent and terrified action of this figure was chosen to illustrate the miracle, by the contrast which it exhibits to that habitual firmness supposed to belong to the military character, showing his emotion to proceed from no mortal cause. The figure grasping the soldier's arm, and pressing forward to look at the body, is expressive of terror, overcome by curiosity. The group behind the soldier is composed of two men of different ages, earnestly listening to the explanation of a priest, who is directing their thoughts to heaven, as the source of the miraculous change. The boy clinging to the old man is too young to comprehend the miracle, but, like children of his age, unconsciously partakes of the general impulse. The group on the right forms an episode, consisting of the wife and daughter of the reviving man. The wife, unable to withstand the conflicting emotions of the past and the present, has fainted; and whatever joy and astonishment may have been excited in the daughter, are wholly absorbed in distress and solicitude for her mother. The young man, with out-stretched arms, actuated by impulse, announces to the wife, by a sudden exclamation, the revival of her husband; the other youth, of a mild and devotional character, is still in the attitude of one conversing—the conversation being abruptly broken off by his impetuous companion. The sentinels, in the distance, at the entrance of the cavern, mark the depth of the picture, and indicate the alarm which had occasioned this tumultuary burial.

In 1817, Mr. Allston was engaged on Jacob's Dream—"a subject," he writes, "I have long had in contemplation. It has been often painted before, but I have treated it in a very different manner from any picture I have ever seen; for instead of two or three angels, I have introduced a vast multitude; and instead of a ladder or narrow steps, I have endeavoured to give the idea of unmeasurable flights of steps, with platform above platform, rising and extending into space immeasurable. Whether this conception will please the matter-of-fact critics, I doubt; nay, I am certain that men without imagination will call it stuff! But if I succeed at all, it will be with those whom it will be an honour to please."

Mr. Allston's prize picture, "Uriel in the Sun," is in the collection of the Marquis of Stafford.

The poet-painter now became "homesick," as he says, and on the return of peace, as soon as his engagements permitted, left his English friends.

In 1818, Mr. Allston writes to his friend M'Murtrie, from Boston: "The success I have lately met with in England left me but one finished picture to bring with me, Elijah in the Wilderness, and which, had I remained a few weeks longer, I had the prospect of transferring to another proprietor. I have brought, however, several others on the stocks, some of which are considerably advanced, particularly Belshazzar's Feast, or the Handwriting on the Wall, sixteen feet by twelve in size, which is, I believe, several feet larger than the Raising the Dead Man. I purpose finishing it here. All the laborious part is over, but there still remains some six or eight months' work to do to it."

In a letter to a friend, Mr. Allston had said that it was not his wish to give a catalogue of all his pictures. He was afterwards prevailed on to give the following brief notice of a part of his works :—" I will mention only a few of the principal which I painted during my visit to England :—The Dead Man restored to life by the bones of Elisha. The Angel liberating Peter from Prison—this picture was painted for Sir George Beaumont, the figures larger than life, and is now in a church at Ashby de la Zouch. Jacob's Dream, in the possession of the earl of Egremont—there are many figures in this picture, which I have always considered one of my happiest efforts. Elijah in the Desert—this I brought to America, but it has gone back, having been purchased here by Mr. Labouchere, M.P. The Angel Uriel in the Sun, in possession of the marquis of Stafford—this is a colossal foreshortened figure, that, if standing upright, would be fourteen feet high, but being foreshortened occupies a space but of nine feet; the directors of the British Gallery presented me with a hundred and fifty guineas as a token of their approbation of Uriel. Since my return to America, I have painted a number of pictures, but chiefly small ones. These pictures being pretty well known here, I shall mention only a few of the larger ones : Jeremiah dictating his prophecy to Baruch ; Saul and the Witch of Endor ; and Spalatro's Vision of the Bloody Hand."

" The exhibition of Allston's Feast of Belshazzar," says a late writer, " has established an era in the history of painting. The point of time selected is that when Daniel is interpreting the mystic writing, which the astrologers, soothsayers, and Chaldeans could not read. In the foreground the chief personages are the King, Queen, Daniel, and four of the wisest magicians of Babylon. In their rear is a group of Jewish men and women, and beyond extend the banqueting-tables, which are sumptuously embellished with gold and silver vessels ; and on the sides are seated numerous guests of both sexes. In the distance, on an elevated platform, is a colossal golden statue of a Persian god, which is dazzlingly refulgent, from the intense flood of light that descends upon it from numerous brilliant lamps that are suspended around a circular opening in the ceiling, directly over the divinity. A host of idolators are assembled round the statue in various attitudes.

"Above the royal party is a spacious gallery thronged with spectators. The numerous massive columns, and other architectural appendages in the distance, are of richly variegated and polished marble : in the royal saloon they are of porphyry, but in an unfinished state. The spacious hall is illuminated by the supernatural beams which emanate from the inscription on the wall ; while the artificial light in the distance tinges with a mellow roseate radiance, like that of the glowing west on a summer's eve, the colonnades and entablatures of the vast area appropriated to the sacred image. There are more than sixty figures introduced, all elaborately executed.

"Near the centre of the group in the foreground stands the inspired Daniel, draped in a plain tunic of a sombre colour, over which is gracefully disposed an ample and appropriate mantle of dark blue. His face is turned towards Belshazzar, and with his left arm elevated, he is pointing towards the inscription, 'over against the candlestick, on the wall of the king's palace.' In his broad and massive forehead, projecting brows, and soul-penetrating eyes, as well as in his commanding attitude, we behold the undaunted prophet of the living God. Calmly he announces the startling interpretation of those blazing words, 'which when the king saw, written by the fingers of a man's hand, his countenance was changed and his thoughts troubled him, so that the joints of his loins were loosened and his knees smote together.'

"The first sentence, 'God hath numbered thy kingdom and finished it!' had fallen so like the crashing shock of a thunderbolt upon the ears of the horror-stricken monarch, that he has involuntarily thrown himself back upon his throne, in a posture of despair, and in his agony, he clenched with his right hand the side of his regal chair with such violent energy, that the fingers appear cramped and almost disjointed; as those of a man expiring in the pangs of a horrible death. As only the outlines of the head of the king remain, its contour, and the features are barely discernable; but the attitude of the whole figure, and the withdrawal of the right foot, as is evident from the folds of the drapery, and the extension of the left, with the toes contracted in that convulsive exertion which the hands so emphatically evince, give almost as complete a conception of the mental sufferings of the monarch, as could have been given if the face had been finished. The royal robe is of cloth of gold, and a crimson mantle with a broad green border is thrown over one side of the throne, which is supported by golden elephants standing on a base of verd-antique.

"On the left of the throne stands the queen, the mother of Belshazzar, gorgeously arrayed and flashing with jewels, while in her countenance is portrayed the conflicting emotions aroused by the fearful words of the prophet, while her attitude is expressive of a haughty struggle to receive the intelligence with becoming fortitude.

"On the extreme left, under the inscription on the wall, is a group of four soothsayers. One, who presents nearly a full view of his face, is looking at the chief among them, as if endeavouring to ascertain what was his interpretation, but there is also perceived, by the drawing down of the right corner of the mouth, in such a manner as to expose the clenched teeth, a deadly hatred, and a wrathful spirit of revenge for the indignity offered to the Persian astrologers. The second of the soothsayers is seen in profile, and by the contemptuously closed mouth, the protruding under lip, lowering brows, and malignant eyes sternly fixed upon Daniel, he betrays his utter scorn and proud defiance of a presumptuous rival for the confidence and favour of the court.

"The principal astrologer is of gigantic proportions, and towers above his exasperated compeers with such a diabolical expression as might well be presumed to denote a God-defying potentate of hell. The other has been only so far delineated as to prefigure the size and position, with the mere indication of the profile and features; but even in that, there is discoverable a steadfast look towards the prophet, and a stubborn disbelief in his revelations.

"Next to the soothsayers, yet, beyond them in the middle distance, sits an old man, who is evidently a Jew of distinction; leaning forward with his left hand a little raised, his lips slightly parted, and looking earnestly towards Daniel, while a gleam of triumph rests on his face. Next, on the right of the last, there is seated a younger man, who is thrown so entirely into the shade, that it requires a near approach to the painting to perceive his features, his flashing eyes are immoveably directed towards the king, and glare with the malignity of gratified revenge.

"On the left of Daniel, and in front of several superb Jewish women, who are anxious spectators of the wonderful scene before them, are two youthful females; one of whom, with an eager effort, yet timid expression, is leaning forward and cautiously extending her hand to touch the hem of Daniel's garment, an act of reverence peculiar to the Jews. The other has kneeled near the feet of the prophet, lowly bowed her head, and with clasped hands, and her eyes cast down, has assumed the humblest posture of self-abasement, and of the most profound veneration for the chosen messenger of the Almighty. In this surpassingly lovely girl are united all the most attractive attributes of beauty.

"A young man who forms a prominent figure in front of the group of Jews, which has been named, having been enabled from his advanced position, to perceive the sacred vessels on the banqueting-table, has turned his face towards the women in the rear, and extending his hand in such a manner as to invite their attention, points with the other to this revolting desecration of those sacred symbols of their faith.

"Behind the two attendants of the queen is a man standing quite alone, who, from costume and bearing, appears to be a Hebrew of the highest rank. He has just discovered the golden candlestick with the seven branches, which is placed over the throne, and so is he amazed and horror-stricken at the sacrilege, that he hears not the awful words of the prophet, nor heeds the startling scene around him.

"At the head of the table which is seen between the queen and Daniel, a princess who occupies the highest seat has fainted and a lady on her left has risen up, and leaning over her, is imploring assistance; but so wrapt in wonder are all the other guests, that no one regards them. Immediately below is a grandee of the empire, who is earnestly looking at, and eagerly listening to Daniel, utterly regardless of the effect which terror has produced so near him. His countenance has a stern and fearless expression; and he seems prepared to firmly hear and boldly meet, the worst that can be said or done. In a word, so diversified in expression, attitude, and costume, are the numerous figures of this stupendous work, that the resources of the art would seem exhausted in its production."

"Allston was a man of finished literary education, having studied and taken his degree at the university of Cambridge. The best authors in several languages were familiar to him, as much so as the great models in his art.

"Some of his published poems are not surpassed by any thing in American literature. Every reader is familiar with his magnificent ode to England and America. As a prose writer, he is chiefly known as the author of 'Monaldi.' There are paragraphs in that book in which the very soul of the writer seems to pour itself out in strains of the richest melody. There are innumerable passages of such graphic beauty as could only be traced by the hand that painted for all coming time Beatrice, Rosalie, and Amy Robsart.

"Mr. Allston's conversation was singularly attractive. The graces seeking a shrine, certainly chose his soul for a temple. His peculiar and striking personal appearance can never be forgotten. His tall and slender figure, his pale countenance, the towering pile of his forehead, his regular and pleasing features, his large hazel eye, the venerable locks that waved in the solemn beauty of silvered age from his shapely forehead—formed in their combination an image which he who has once seen can never forget.

"The serene close of his days gave the finishing touch to the picture of his life. He died sitting in the same chair from which he had so often delighted his friends by his conversation. Beautiful in death as he had been in life, he looked like some gracious work of art just beginning its silent immortality."

HENRY INMAN.

Henry Inman was born at Utica, in the state of New York, in 1801. His early delights were connected with pictures, and his first aspirations were for fame as an artist. About 1812, his parents removed to New York, and there he commenced the study of drawing, under a competent teacher.

When Westmüller's celebrated picture of Danäe was exhibited at Mr. Jarvis's rooms in Murray-street, young Inman visited it, and gives the following account of his first interview with Jarvis: "On my second visit, I saw Mr. Jarvis. He came in from his painting-room, with mahl stick in his hand and palette on his arm. I removed my hat, and bowed. At that time I regarded an artist with peculiar reverence. Without noticing my salutation, he walked rapidly up to me, and with his singular look of scrutiny, peered into my face. Suddenly he exclaimed, 'The very head for a painter!' He then put some questions to me, invited me below stairs, and permitted me to examine his portfolios. He shortly after called on my father, and proposed to take me as a pupil. I was at that time preparing for my entrance at West Point as a cadet, for which I had already obtained a warrant My father left the matter to myself, and I gladly acceded to the proposal. I accordingly entered on a seven years' apprenticeship with him."

Mr. Inman remained with Mr. Jarvis during the whole time of his engagement, and with him visited New Orleans and other cities.

About 1822 he commenced business for himself as portrait and miniature painter. In the latter style he was highly successful, though he soon abandoned it In 1825 Mr. Inman assisted in the formation of the National Academy of Design, of which he was the first vice-president. He held the office until 1831, when he removed to Philadelphia. About this time he painted full-length portraits of William Penn, Col. Varick, Chief-Justice Marshall, and other distinguished individuals.

After a residence of about a year in Philadelphia, Mr. Inman removed to Mount Holly, New Jersey. He thus wrote to a friend, before his removal: "I have always panted to live in the country, where I can be surrounded with something pleasanter to look upon than the everlasting brick walls of a city. I shall then be better enabled to withdraw myself gradually from mere face-making, to practice in the more congenial departments of art—namely, landscape and historical painting."

Mr. Inman resided at Mount Holly between two and three years, and removed to New York in October, 1837. At this time his popularity was at its height. His annual receipts, for the succeeding five years, were from eight to ten thousand dollars.

For some time Mr. Inman had been subject to annual attacks of severe illness, which were eventually found to proceed from an organic affection of the heart. The attacks gradually increased in violence; and becoming involved in pecuniary embarrassments, in 1844 he embarked for Europe, with the double object of benefiting his health and fulfilling several commissions for portraits and landscapes. While abroad he painted portraits of several distinguished persons: among them, Dr. Chalmers, for Mr. Lenox; the poet Wordsworth, for Prof. Reed; and Thomas B. Macaulay, for Mr. Carey. Forced to give up his project of visiting France and Germany, after a stay of eight months in England, he returned to New York.

His health now rapidly declined; still he continued, at

intervals, to use his pencil. His death, which occurred January 17, 1846, called forth an unusually deep expression of public feeling; the press, throughout the country, teemed with the warmest eulogies of his social character, and his artistic abilities.

The following effusion, which was written by Mr. Inman, about three years before his death, has been much admired:

"Now listless o'er time's sullen tide,
My bark of life floats idly on;
Youth's incense-laden breeze has died,
And passion's fitful gusts are flown.

"While sadly round her aimless course,
Now lowering brood the mental skies,
The past but murmurs of remorse,
And dim the ocean-future lies.

"And must this be?—my soul arouse!
See through the passing clouds of ill,
How fame's proud pharos brightly glows,
And gilds thy drooping pennant still.

"Stretch to thine oar, yon beam thy guide,
Spread to ambition's freshening gale;
Friendship and love are at thy side,
While glory's breathings swell thy sail."

Speaking of the versatility of Inman, Sully says: "I remember going round the exhibition of the National Academy, at Clinton Hall, New York, and, seeing a fine landscape, I asked, Who painted this? The answer was—Inman. Then I came to a beautiful group of figures. Ah, this is very fine! Who painted this?—Inman. Then some Indians caught my eye—

Inman. A little further on, and I exclaimed—This is the finest miniature I have seen for many a day! Who is this miniature painter?—Inman. His large portraits I was acquainted with, but this variety of style took me altogether by surprise."

Inman's portraits are characterized by great clearness in tinting, and an air of life and animation. He might have excelled in any branch of his art. His view of Rydal Water, from a spot near the residence of Wordsworth, is a picture of extreme beauty What he saw, he saw at a glance; and transferred it to the canvass with rapidity and surprising precision.

THOMAS COLE.

Thomas Cole was born in the year 1802. From his infancy, Cole was fond of drawing, and passionately devoted to the contemplation of fine natural scenery. An excessive diffidence, joined to his love of the combination of land, water, and sky, which the ordinary eye may be said not to see, caused him to avoid society, even of children of his own age—he sought and found in nature, the pleasure which seemed denied to him elsewhere. To ramble through the woods, or on the beautiful banks of the Ohio, indulging in day-dreams, was the apparently idle occupation of a most active mind—of one who has proved a most persevering and industrious practitioner of nature's lessons.

In a letter, he afterwards thus refers to this part of his life. "My school opportunities were small; reading and music were among my recreations; but drawing occupied most of my leisure hours. My first attempts were made from cups and saucers; from, them I rose to copying prints; from copying prints, to making originals.

"About the year 1820, Mr. Stein, a portrait painter, came to Steubenville. I became acquainted with him—saw him paint—and considered his works wonderful; I believe they were respectable. He lent me an English work on painting, (I have forgotten the title;) it was illustrated by engravings, and treated of design, composition, and colour. This book was my companion day and night—nothing could separate us—my usual avocations were neglected—painting was all in all to me. I had made some proficiency in drawing, and had engraved a little, both in wood and copper, but not until now, had my passion been fully aroused—my love for the art exceeded all love—my ambition grew, and in my imagination I pictured the glory of being a great painter. The names of Stuart and Sully came to my ears like the titles of great conquerors; and the great masters were esteemed above all earthly things.

"I had painted many landscapes, but had never drawn from nature, although I had looked on her with a loving eye. One of these landscapes Judge Tappan, of Steubenville, happened to see; and, being pleased with it, invited me to look at a copy he had made from Stuart. He lent me a palette, and gave me some excellent advice. This kindness I repaid ungratefully, for I unfortunately broke the palette; and, though I often met him in the street my excessive bashfulness prevented my making any explanation or apology for keeping it so long. This circumstance gave me much pain; and, though it may appear trivial, it marks my common conduct in those days, and is one of a thousand follies of that nature committed through diffidence."

In 1820, young Cole took up the palette to paint portraits. His father first submitted to the operation. It was pronounced like. Another and another succeeded; and the three, though painted unskilfully and without proper materials, gave satisfaction and encouragement, to the would-be-painter, to proceed in a path that he hoped would lead to the object of his wishes—the power to assist his beloved parents and sisters. But after a short career as a portrait painter, he took up the more congenial branch of his art.

In 1823 his family removed to Pittsburg. It was spring, and the young painter seemed to awake to the beauties of nature in landscape, and to feel not only his love for, but his power in that branch of the art. Heretofore he had been straying in a wrong path. He now began to make studies from nature; every morning, before it was light, he was on his way to the beautiful banks of the Monongahela, with his paper and pencils. He made small but accurate studies of single objects—a tree, a leafless bough, every ramification and twig was studied; and as the season advanced, he studied the foliage, clothed his naked trees, and by degrees attempted extensive scenes. He was now in the right path, and, what is most extraordinary, he had found the true way to pursue it.

The succeeding year he passed in Philadelphia; thence he removed to New York, whither his father's family had preceded him. Here he first met with that success which he merited, and in a few years he was enabled to visit Europe.

"I did not find England," says Cole, "so delightful as I anticipated. The gloom of the climate, the coldness of the artists, together with the kind of art in fashion, threw a tone of melancholy over my mind, that lasted for months, even after I had arrived in sunny Italy.

"Previous to going to Rome, I passed nine months in Florence, which I spent in studying the magnificent collections there, and in painting several pictures, among which was a Sunset on the Arno, and a wild scene for Mr. Gilmor, of Baltimore. The Arno was exhibited in the Academy of St. Luke, and seemed to attract attention. The Grand Duke is said to have been much pleased with it, but he did not buy it. I studied the human figure part of my time, and drew from the life, at the Academy; and painted my Dead Abel, which was intended as a study for a large picture, to represent Adam and Eve finding the body of Abel. I was about three months in Rome, where I had a studio in the very house in which Claude lived. Returning to Florence, I painted more pictures in three months, than I have ever done in twice the time before or since. In that three months I painted the Aqueduct picture, the View of the Cascatelles of Tivoli, Mr. Lord's picture of Italian Scenery, four small pictures for Mr. Tappan, a small view near Tivoli, and several others.

"The pictures of the great Italian masters gave me the greatest delight, and I laboured to make their principles my own; for these which have stood best the criticism of ages, are produced on principles of truth, and on no abstract notion of the sublime or beautiful. The artists were gifted with a keen perception of the beautiful of nature, and imitated it in simplicity and single-heartedness. They did not sit down, as the modern artist too often does, with a preconceived notion of what is or ought to be beautiful; but their *beau ideal* was the choicest of nature. They often introduced absurdities and things of bad taste in their pictures; but they were honest--there was no affectation. I do not believe that they theorized, as we do; they loved the beauty they saw around them, and painted it.

"It is usual to rank landscape as a lower branch of the art, below the historical. Why so? Is there a better reason than that the vanity of man makes him delight most in his own image? In its difficulty (though perhaps it may come ill from me, although I have dabbled a little in history) it is equal at least to the historical. There are certainly fewer good landscape pictures in the world, in proportion to their number, than of historical. In landscapes there is a greater variety of objects, textures, and phenomena, to imitate. It has expression also; not of passion to be sure, but of sentiment—whether it shall be tranquil or spirit-stirring. Its seasons, sunrise, sunset, the storm, the calm, various kinds of trees, herbage, waters, mountains, skies; and whatever scene is chosen, one spirit pervades the whole—light and darkness tremble in the atmosphere, and each change transmutes."

Cole returned to America in 1832. "That he would have been a great painter," says Bryant, "if he had never studied abroad—scarcely less great on that account—no man can doubt; but would he have been able to paint some of these pictures which we most value and most affectionately admire; that fine one, for example, the Ruins of Aqueducts in the Campagna of Rome, with its broad masses of shadow dividing the sunshine that bathes the solitary plain, strewn with ruins; its glorious mountains in the distance, and its silence made visible to the eye? Would he ever have given us a picture like that which bears the name of the Present, a scene of loveliness, popular with the reminiscences of days gone by; or a picture like that great final one of the Course of Empire? Cole owed much to the study of nature in the old world, but very little to its artists. He had a better teacher, and copied the works of a greater Artist. A year or two after his return he commenced his first series of large pictures, well known to the public."

The Course of Empire consists of a series of five pictures, and forms an epitome of the life of man. It is conceived* and executed

* The following criticisms are from the pen of C. Lanman, Esq.

in a manner which must convince the beholder that the artist possessed many of the attributes of the philosopher, the poet, and the Christian.

In the first picture, we have a perfectly wild scene of rocks, mountains, woods, and a bay of the ocean, reposing in the luxuriance of a ripe spring. The clouds of night are being dissipated by the rising sun. On the opposite side of the bay rises a lofty promontory crowned by a singular isolated rock. As the same locality is preserved in each picture of the series, this rock identifies it, although the position of the spectator changes in the several pictures. The chase being the most characteristic occupation of savage life, in the foreground we see an Indian clothed in skins, pursuing a wounded deer, which is bounding down a narrow ravine. On a rock in the middle ground, are other Indians with their dogs surrounding another deer. On the bosom of a little river below, are a number of canoes passing down the stream, while others are drawn up on the shore. On an elevation beyond these is a cluster of wigwams, and a number of Indians dancing round a fire. In this picture we have the first rudiments of society. In the canoes, huts, and weapons, we perceive that the useful arts have commenced, and in the singing which undoubtedly accompanies the dance of the savages, we behold the germs of music and poetry. The Empire is asserted to a limited degree, over sea, land, and the animal kingdom.

In the second picture we have the simple or Arcadian state of Society. The time of day is a little before noon, and the season, early summer. The "untracked and rude," has been tamed and softened. Shepherds are tending their flocks, a solitary ploughman, with his oxen, are turning up the soil; and in the rude vessels passing into the haven of a growing village, and in the skeleton of a bark, building on the shore, we perceive the commencement of commerce. From a rude temple on a hill, the smoke of sacrifice is ascending to the sky, symbolizing the spirit of Religion. In the foreground on the left, is seated an old man, who, by describing strange figures in the sand, seems to have made some geometrical discovery, emblematic of the infancy of science. On the right hand, is a woman with a distaff, about crossing a stone bridge, beside her, a boy is drawing on a stone the figure of a man with a sword ; and beyond these, ascending the road, a soldier is partly seen. Under some noble trees, in the middle distance, are a number of peasants dancing to the music of pipe and timbrel. All these things show us that society is steadily advancing in its march of usefulness and power.

Ages have passed away, and in the third picture we have a magnificent city. It is now mid-day, and early autumn. The bay is surrounded by piles of architecture, temples, colonnades, and domes. It is a day of rejoicing. The spacious harbour is crowded with vessels, war-galleys, ships, and barks, their silken sails glistening in the sunshine. Moving over a massive stone bridge, in the foreground, is a triumphal procession. The conqueror, robed in purple, is mounted on a car drawn by an elephant, and surrounded by captives and a numerous train of guards and servants, many of them bearing pictures and golden treasures. As he is about to pass the triumphal arch, beautiful girls strew flowers in his path ; gay festoons of drapery hang from the clustered columns ; golden trophies glitter in the sun, and incense rises from silver censers. Before a Doric temple, on the left, a multitude of white-robed priests are standing on the marble steps, while near them a religious ceremony is being performed before a number of altars. Near a statue of Minerva, with a victory in her hand, is a company of musicians, with cymbals and trumpets. From the lofty portico of a palace, an imperial personage is watching the procession, surrounded by her children, attendants, and guards. Nations have been subjugated, man has reached the summit of human glory. Wealth, power, knowledge, and taste, have worked together and accomplished the highest meed of human achievement and Empire.

In the fourth picture, a barbarous enemy has entered the once proud city ; a fierce tempest is raging ; walls and colonnades are lying in the dust, and temples and palaces are being consumed by the torch of the incendiary. The fire of vengeance is swallowing up the devoted city. An arch of the bridge, over which the triumphal procession had before passed, has been battered down, and broken pillars, ruins of war-engines, and the temporary bridge which had been thrown over, indicate that this had been the scene of direst contention. Now there is a terrible conflict on the bridge, the insecurity of which accelerates the horror of the struggle. Horses, men, and chariots, are precipitated into the raging waves. War-galleys are contending ; some in flames, and others sinking beneath the prow of a superior foe. Smoke and flames are issuing from the falling and prostrate edifices ; and along the battlements, and in the blocked-up streets, the conflict rages terribly. The foreground is strewed with the bodies of the dead and dying. Some have fallen into the basin of a fountain, tinging the water with blood. One woman is sitting in mute despair over the dead body of her son ; another leaping over a battlement to escape the grasp of a ruffian soldier ; and other soldiers drag a woman by the hair down the steps that form the pedestal of a mutilated colossal statue, whose shattered head lies on the pavement below. A barbarous enemy has conquered the city ; Carnage and Destruction have asserted their frightful Empire

The last and most impressive picture of the series is the scene of Desolation. The sun has just departed, and the moon is ascending the twilight sky over the ocean, near the place where the sun arose in the first picture. The shades of evening are stealing over the shattered and ivy-grown ruins of that once great city. A lonely column rises in the foreground ; on the capital a solitary heron has built her nest, and at the foot of it her mate is standing in the water.

The Doric temple and triumphal bridge may still be identified among the ruins which are laved by the waters of the tranquil sea. But though man and his works have perished, the steep promontory, with its isolated rock, still rears itself against the sky, unmoved, unchanged. Time has consumed the works of man, and art is resolving into its elemental nature. The gorgeous pageant has passed, the roar of battle has ceased, the multitude has mingled with the dust, the Empire is extinct.

The Voyage of Life is a series of four pictures, allegorically portraying childhood, youth, manhood, and old age. In the first we behold the dawn of a summer morning. A translucent stream is issuing from a deep cavern in the side of a mountain. Floating gently down the stream is a gilded boat, made of the sculptured figures of the Hours, while the prow is formed by the present hour, holding forth an emblem of Time. It is filled with flowers, and on these a little child is seated, tossing them with his upraised hands, and smiling with new-born joy, as he looks upon the unnumbered beauties and glories of the bright world around him ; while a guardian angel is at the helm, with his wings lovingly and protectingly extended over the child. Love, purity, and beauty emanate like incense from the sky, the earth, and water, so that the heart of the gazer seems to forget the world, and lose itself in a dream of heaven.

In the second painting, the Stream of Life is widened, and its current strong and irresistible, but it flows through a country of surpassing loveliness. The voyager, who is now a youth, has taken the helm into his own hands, and the dismissed angel stands upon the shore, looking at him with "a look made of all sweet accord," as if he said in his heart, "God be with thee, thoughtless mortal!" But the youth heeds not the angel, for his eyes are riveted on an airy castle pictured against the sky, dome above dome. The phantom of worldly happiness and worldly ambition has absorbed the imagination and eager gaze of the wayward voyager, and as he urges his frail bark onward, he dreams not of the dangers that may await him on the way. To the boat only a few flowers are now clinging, and we perceive that the castle in the air, apparently so real, has only a white cloud for its foundation, and that, ere long, the stream makes a sudden turn, rushing with the fury of a maddened steed down a terrible ravine. The moral of the picture it is needless to elucidate.

In the third of the series, the voyager is seen on the verge of a cataract, while a fearful storm rages around him. The rudderless bark is just about to plunge into the abyss below, while the voyager (now in the prime of manhood) is imploring the only aid that can avail him in the trying hour, that of Heaven. Demoniacal images are holding forth their temptations in the clouds around him, but he heeds them not. His confidence in God supports him; the previous agony of his soul is dispelled or subdued, by a reflection of celestial light, stealing through the storm, and by the smiles of his guardian angel, visibly stationed in the far off sky.

In the last scene of the allegory, the voyager, with hoary head, has reached that point where the waters of time and eternity mingle together—a bold conception, which is finely imbodied by the daring genius of the painter. The hour-glass is gone, and the shattered bark is ready to be drawn into the fathomless waters beneath. The old man is on his knees, with clasped hands, and his eyes turned heavenward, for the greenness of earth has for ever departed, and a gloom is upon the ocean of Eternity. But just above the form of the voyager is hovering his angel, who is about to transport him to his home, and, as the eye wanders upward, an infinite host of heavenly ministers are seen ascending and descending the cloudy steps which lead to the bosom of God. Death is swallowed up in life; the glory of heaven has eclipsed that of earth, and our voyager is safe in the haven of eternal rest.

The water in the first, second, and third pictures is very fine, the perspective and atmosphere in the second are masterly. In the first we are pleased with the simplicity of the composition; in the second, with the variety; in the third, with the suitableness of the gloomy storm, which helps to tell the story, and harmonizes with the scene; and in the fourth, with the management of the shadows, and the apparent reality of the light from heaven. This series belongs to the Rev. G. D. Abbott of New York.

The last, and in many respects the most impressive of Cole's productions, is a series of five pictures, entitled the Cross and the World. The designs or studies for these pictures were all executed, but owing to the untimely death of the artist, only two out of five were finished on a large scale. The idea is that two youths enter upon a pilgrimage, one to the Cross and the other to the World.

In the first picture the eye of the beholder is struck by the bold termination of a chain of mountains, with craggy peaks lost in the clouds The same lofty range is seen through the entire series. To the left, a straight and narrow pathway takes its way up a rugged gorge, down which beams a silvery light from a bright Cross in the sky. The path at first leads off through real flowers, betokening the early part of the Christian life, neither difficult nor uninviting. In the distance a dark mist, hovering over the track, conceals from the advancing wayfarer the real difficulties of his journey, and betokens the sorrows which necessarily befall him. To the right, a gracefully winding way, leads down into a gently undulating vale, Stretching forward through delightful landscapes, it finally fades away, and leaves the eye to wander on to the dim pinnacles and domes of a great city. A golden light falls through an atmosphere of repose, and lends warmth, softness, and beauty, as well to crag and precipice as to the rich valley. By-paths steal upon the sunny slopes of the mountain, inviting the traveller to the enjoyment of the prospect and the coolness of the waterfall. Vegetation of unnatural growth, and gorgeous and unreal flowers skirt the borders of the way. At the foot of the mountain stands Evangelist with the open Gospel. A little in advance are the waters symbolical of Baptism. Two youths, companions in the travel of life, having come to the parting of their road, are affectionately and earnestly directed to the shining Cross. While one, through the power of truth, enters with timid steps upon his holy pilgrimage, the other, caught by the enchantment of the earthly prospect, turns his back upon Evangelist and the Cross, and speeds forward upon the footpath of the World.

In the second picture, which symbolizes the trials of faith, we have a wild mountain region now opening upon the beholder. It is an hour of tempest. Black clouds envelop the surrounding summits. A swollen torrent rushes by and plunges into the abyss. The storm, sweeping down terrific chasms, flings aside the angry cataract, and deepens the horror of the scene below. The pilgrim, now in the vigour of manhood, pursues his way on the edge of a frightful precipice. It is a moment of imminent danger. But gleams of light from the shining Cross break through the storm, and shed fresh brightness along his perilous and narrow path. With steadfast look, and renewed courage, the lone traveller holds on his heavenly pilgrimage.

In the third picture, the beholder looks off upon an expanse of tranquil water. On the right are the gardens of pleasure, where the devotees of sensual delights, revel in all that satiates and amuses. Near a fountain, whose falling waters lull with perpetual murmurs, stands a statue of the goddess of love. An interminable arcade, with odorous airs and delicious shade, invites to the quiet depths of a wilderness of flowers. A gay throng dances upon the yielding turf, around a tree, to the sound of lively music. Near an image of Bacchus, a company enjoys a luxurious banquet.

On the left is the temple of Mammon, a superb and costly structure surmounted by the wheel of fortune. Beneath its dome, a curiously wrought fountain throws out showers of gold, which is eagerly caught by the votaries below. From the censers, rising here and there above the heads of the multitude, clouds of incense roll up and wreathe the columns of the temple. The trees and shrubbery of the adjacent grounds are laden with golden fruit. Far distant, in the middle of the picture, a vision of earthly power and glory rises upon the view. Splendid trophies of conquest adorn the imposing gateway, colonnades and piles of architecture stretch away in the vast perspective. At the summit of a lofty flight of steps stand conspicuous the throne and sceptre. Suspended in the air, at the highest point of human reach, is that glittering symbol of royalty, the crown. Between the beholder and this grand spectacle are armies in conflict, and a city in flames, indicating that the path to glory lies through ruin and the battle-field. To the contemplation of this alluring scene the pilgrim of the world, now in early manhood is introduced. Which of the fascinating objects before him is the one of his choice, is left to the imagination of the spectator. The picture symbolizes the pleasure, the fortune, and the glory of the World.

In the fourth picture, the pilgrim of the Cross, now an old man on the verge of existence, catches a first view of the boundless and eternal. The tempests of life are behind him; the world is beneath his feet. Its rocky pinnacles, just rising through the gloom, reach not up into his brightness; its mists, pausing in the dark obscurity, ascend no more into his serene atmosphere. He looks out into the infinite. Clouds—imbodiments of glory, threading immensity in countless lines, rolling up from everlasting depths—carry the vision forward towards the unapproachable light. The Cross, now fully revealed, pours its effulgence over the illimitable scene. Angels, with palm and crown of immortality, appear in the distance, and advance to meet him. Lost in rapture at the sight, the pilgrim drops his staff, and with uplifted hands sinks upon his knees.

In the last picture, desolate and broken, the pilgrim of the World, descending a gloomy vale, pauses at last on the horrid brink that overhangs the outer darkness. Columns of the temple of Mammon crumble; trees of the gardens of pleasure moulder in his path. Gold is as valueless as the dust with which it mingles. The phantom of glory—a baseless, hollow fabric—flits under the wing of death, to vanish in a dark eternity. Demon forms are gathering round him. Horror-stricken, the pilgrim lets fall his staff, and turns in despair to the long-neglected and forgotten Cross. Veiled in melancholy night, behind a peak of the mountain, it is lost to his view for ever.

The principal imaginative productions, besides those just described, are, the Departure and Return, which is a poetical representation of the feudal times ; the Cross in the Wilderness , Il Penseroso ; L'Allegro ; the Past and Present ; the Architect's Dream ; Dream of Arcadia ; the Expulsion of Adam and Eve ; and Prometheus Bound. The last-mentioned picture is owned in England, and is unquestionably one of the wildest and most splendid efforts of the painter's pencil. The scene represented is among the snow-covered peaks of a savage mountain-land, and to the loftiest peak of all Prometheus is chained. In the foreground is a pile of rocks and broken trees, which give a fine effect to the distant landscape ; while just above this foreground is a solitary vulture, slowly ascending to the upper air, to feast upon his victim. The idea of leaving the devouring scene to the imagination, could only have been conceived by the most accomplished artist. The time represented is early morning, and in the cold blue ocean of the sky is seen one brilliant star, which represents Jupiter, by whose orders Prometheus was chained to the everlasting rock.

This is most sublime, and possesses all the qualities which constitute an epic production. The unity of the design is admirable—one figure, one prominent mountain, a cloudless sky, one lonely star, one vulture, and one cluster of rocks for the foreground. It is also completely covered with an atmosphere which gives every object a dreamy appearance. In point of execution, there is no fault to be found with this glorious picture, and the idea of the poet could not have been better illustrated.

With regard to the actual views, and other less ambitious productions of Cole, we can only say that the entire number might be estimated at about one hundred.

"In July, 1841, Cole sailed on a second visit to Europe. On this occasion he travelled much in Switzerland, which he had never before seen, lingering as long as the limits of the time he had prescribed to himself would allow him, in that remarkable country; and filling his mind with its wonders of beauty and grandeur. From Switzerland he passed to Italy, whence he made an excursion to the island of Sicily, with the scenery of which he was greatly delighted. On its bold rocky summits, and in its charming valleys, he found everywhere scattered the remains of a superb architecture, and gazed without satiety upon the luxuriance of its vegetation, in which the plants of the tropics sprang intermingled with those of temperate climes."

It was after his return, in 1842, that he commenced the Pilgrim of the Cross and of the World, which was his last work. While engaged in painting this series, the summons of death came. He died in February, 1848.

In looking upon his better pictures of American scenery, we forget the pent-up city, and our hearts flutter with a joy allied to that which we may suppose animates the woodland bird, when listening in its solitude to the hum of the wilderness. Perpetual freedom, perpetual and unalloyed happiness, seem to breathe from every object which he portrays, and as the eye wanders along the mountain declivities, or mounts still farther up on the chariot-looking clouds, as we peer into the translucent waters of his lakes and streams, or witness the solemn grandeur of his forests, we cannot but wonder at the marvellous power of genius. His style is bold and masterly. While he did not condescend to delineate every leaf and sprig which may be found in nature, yet he gave you the spirit of the scene. To do this is the province of genius, and an attainment beyond the reach of mere talent. The productions of Cole appeal to the intellect more than to the heart, and we should imagine that Milton was his favourite poet. He loved the uncommon effects in nature, and was constantly giving birth to new ideas. He had a passion for the wild and tempestuous, and possessed an imagination of the highest order. He was also a lover of the beautiful, and occasionally executed a picture full of quiet summer-like sentiment. But his joy was to depict the scenery of our mountain-land, when clothed in the rich garniture of autumn. He was the originator of a new style, and is now a most worthy member of that famous brotherhood of immortals whom we remember by the names of Lorraine, Poussin, Rosa, Wilson, and Gainsborough.

C. VER BRYCK.

In compliance with a request of the National Academy of Design, the writer* has attempted a short memoir of Cornelius Ver Bryck. The life of an artist is proverbially barren of those stirring incidents and strange vicissitudes that interest the reading multitude, and to this the life of the subject of the present sketch forms no exception.

Mr. Ver Bryck was born at Yaugh Paugh, New Jersey, on the 1st of January, 1813. In childhood he discovered a predilection for the fine arts, which strengthened with his years, and at length led him to embrace the profession of an artist. In 1835 he studied for some time under Prof. Morse, then president of the National Academy. At the Academy of Design, he was distin-

* Thomas Cole, N. A.

guished for the ardour of his studies. His drawings from the antique showed a keen appreciation of character, and were executed in a vigorous manner. He obtained the prize of the silver palette soon after entering as a student. In the Academy exhibition of 1836, Mr. Inman called the attention of several artists, in his peculiar ominous and emphatic tone, to a picture exhibited by Ver Bryck. It represented an old Dutch Bible, with clasps, a skull, and other objects suggestive of serious feeling, painted with remarkable power. "Look," said Inman, "at the very dust which has collected on the old Bible—impossible for any one to paint better." This picture has since been presented, by a brother of the artist, to the New York City Gallery. It is an unpretending, low-toned picture, but whoever attentively observes it, will be interested in the solemn, still, and mournful air which is thrown around it by the "mysterious power of shade."

In the fall of 1837 he went to Mobile, for the benefit of his health; and a friend, to whom I am indebted for much of the information in this memoir, states, that he carried with him several pictures, among which were a Bacchante and a Cavalier, which were much admired. They were purchased at Tuscaloosa, Alabama. Early in the spring of 1838, he returned to New York. The next year, stimulated by the desire to behold with his own eyes the wonders of ancient art, and scenes that through history and poetry had long been familiar to his mind, he sailed for London, in company with his friends Huntington and Gray, and for a time enjoyed, as such a mind only can enjoy, the productions of the great masters; and the works of art to be found in London and Paris. But unfortunately his stay in the old world was short, for he was called home by the illness of a sister.

After his return, he was occupied in landscape and historical pictures. Among the latter was one whose subject was: "And one shall be taken and the other left." This picture was finely conceived; it represented a blessed spirit ascending towards heaven, with enraptured expression, in the midst of light; while below, in murky gloom, was seen one of the accursed ones, with demoniac face, descending.

His intimate friend, the Rev. Cleveland Coxe, at that time addressed a sonnet to him, which is introduced here, as characteristic both of the poet and painter:

"I'll spoil a sonnet, but—I'll tell thee now,
How much I love thy reveries and dreams,
Thy vein poetic, and thy darling themes,
Of dear pursuits, and stories that allow
The frequent laugh—though thou can'st weep, I trow—
And how I love to plot with thee, sweet schemes
Of future life, commingling the extremes
Of mirthful hours, and days of thoughtful brow;
For, like a strange chiaroscuro, thou
Hast in thy soul mysterious power of shade,
While thy warm heart of sunshine's self is made;
And if thou'lt labour out thyself enow
Upon thy canvass—all, I promise you,
Will love the picture, and the painter too."

In the year 1840 he was elected a member of the Academy, having previously been made an associate; a tribute due to his talent and character. For a few years he pursued his art, struggling with ill health and unfavourable circumstances, until 1843, when his friend Huntington, with his wife, who was the sister of one to whom Mr. Ver Bryck was deeply attached, proposed to visit Europe again. Suffering from disease, and in the hope that a voyage might restore him, Mr. Ver Bryck hastily determined to accompany his friend. To accomplish this was difficult, for the time was short; but his many warm friends interested themselves—a few commissions were obtained, and all necessary arrangements made.

Mr. Ver Bryck was married on the eve of sailing, and the party, after a favourable voyage, reached England the latter part of May. As far as health would permit, Mr. Ver Bryck enjoyed the scenery of the Isle of Wight and of England exceedingly: the cathedrals, castles, abbeys, and galleries filled his mind with delight; but, alas! neither the beauties of nature nor the charms of art could check the inroads of disease, and even the ever-hopeful eye of affection could perceive in him no change for the better, and with his wife he returned to New York in the autumn; but the air of his native country had no healing balm for him—he lingered through the winter, suffering much, but at times cheated into hope by the deceitful slumberings of his disease, until, on the 31st of May, 1844, his soul, which had been blessed and purified through religion, was freed from its mortal tenement.

It would almost seem, that the higher the intellectual qualities possessed by a man, the less fitted he is for encountering with success the stormy passage of life; that he whose mind is cast in nature's most finished mould—the mould of genius and taste—is least capable of withstanding the asperities of actual life, and we frequently find that the possessors of these fatal gifts become early tenants of the tomb. Of this class was Mr Ver Bryck: the flame burned too brightly, to burn long. Endowed with the keenest sensibilities, his heart responded to every call. The love of the beautiful was the law of his being; the beautiful in nature and art his chief joy. He felt a keen delight in natural scenery; a sight of the mountains moved him with unutterable thoughts, and he could truly say:

> "To me, the meanest flower that blows, can give
> Thoughts that do often lie too deep for tears."

Himself of poetic temperament, his taste for poetry was exquisite; but he loved most those ancient songs wherein simplicity of sentiment and style were combined with the mystic grandeur of olden time. He had a deep reverence for antiquity; and what poetical mind has not?—for it clothes the dim and shadowy forms of the past with drapery of its own.

Music was a passion with him; his voice was low but sweet, and he accompanied his songs on the guitar with great taste; and in his hours of quietness and solitude many a plaintive song of Ver Bryck's steals like an Æolian strain on the mind's ear of the writer of this memoir. Speaking, in a letter written during his last visit to England, of the pleasure he enjoyed in visiting Winchester cathedral, he says:

"We remained and heard the service chanted. To me it seemed very impressive—the sweet, plaintive tones of the boys—that long-drawn 'Amen,' so often repeated in rich harmony—the touching words of the psalm—'Have mercy on me, O Lord, for I am in trouble; mine eye is consumed for very heaviness—yea, my soul and my body.' I thought I had never heard true church music before." Alas! he could too well feel the words of the Psalmist, for disease was then consuming him.

With all his artistic feeling and enthusiasm for art, the productions of Mr. Ver Bryck's pencil were not numerous; and perhaps when we consider the obstacles that rose in his path, there will be little reason for surprise at this.

His landscapes, which were simple productions, views, or compositions, exhibiting nature in her tranquil aspects—as well as his historical pictures, too frequently remained without a purchaser. The high qualities of his works, which ought to have brought him encouragement and profit, were passed unnoticed by the multitude, and the coarse scenes of the tavern could frequently find purchasers, while the chaste works of Ver Bryck had no attractions. The hand of the artist is palsied if he once feels that his works produce no glow of sympathy in the minds of beholders. "Hope deferred maketh the heart sick," and this Ver Bryck had often felt.

Illustrative of the tone of his mind is a passage in one of his letters: "They may say what they will, of Hope and her pleasures. Oh! oft has she cheated me; but Memory—I love her, she is kind—doth she not make the pleasant seem more pleasant, the good better, the beautiful still more lovely? And even our past sorrows, she hath a way of softening them till they are almost sources of joy. A ruin, a pile of stones and mortar, are unsightly; but Time covers it with moss and ivy, and it is beautiful."

In another letter, he says: "I believe I am getting old, for my pleasures are more of Memory than of Hope."

But as the sands of life wasted away, the flame of Hope burned more brightly in his bosom, and lifted by religious faith above this shadowy vale of tears, his eye caught glimpses of a glorious future which made the past seem dim, and he longed to depart.

His mortal remains rest in Greenwood cemetery, in a spot chosen by himself, in a quiet dell, beneath the shade of trees, and when he was interred, flowers, which he loved so much, were growing near the grave; and as has been said of another spot where rests a child of genius, cut off also in the early promise of his years, "It might make one in love with Death, to think that one should be buried in so sweet a place."

It is ours to regret that disease and death should so soon have checked the development of powers which seem to have been of the highest order.

> "Peace! peace! he is not dead, he doth not sleep,
> He hath awakened from the dream of life.
> 'Tis we, who lost in stormy visions, keep
> With phantoms an unprofitable strife."

Sculpture.

SCULPTURE was practised at a very early period. The most common materials are marble, metals, wood, ivory, clay, and wax.

The first information we have of sculpture is in the time of Laban, who had images of his domestic gods. It probably preceded painting, and even drawing, which is a more abstract idea; the first essays being of the rudest possible character. The progressive advances in the art are evident from the remains still to be found in Egypt. At first they were mere outlines cut in the rock, next figures in very low relief, then more prominent and at length detached and entire. From these crude attempts among the learned and refined Greeks, even verging into supernatural beauty, sculpture reached its acme of perfection; when the whole circle of the sciences, especially anatomy, geometry, and mechanics, contributed to the development of the laws of motion and balance, and taught the proper play of the muscles.

Sculpture, of all the arts, requires the most scrupulous finish, and is scarcely excellent except when of the highest order. In painting, beauty of colour and well-conceived contrasts may atone for faults of design, even for distortions, if they are not in full view. But in sculpture, simplicity is the characteristic feature, and the slightest error is at once discoverable, and obtrudes itself upon the eye. Portrait statues or busts are not the least valuable productions of the chise.. When executed by the genuine artist, they transmit to posterity not only the features, but the very moral and intellectual uniqueness—the essential difference between the features they represent, and those of all the rest of mankind. They are superior to painted portraits, so far as the representation of intellect is concerned, though painting may be preferred for the expression of feeling, the acknowledged language of the eye.

To the representation of perfect quietude, or calm, self-inherent grandeur, perhaps sculpture, of all the arts, is best adapted. Poetry must give many nice strokes before it can give the expression of calm majesty; and in painting, colouring, however subdued, is almost incompatible with perfect ideal repose. But marble—pure, cold, impassive, insulated—beneath the touch of genius, becomes the very impersonation of passive majesty—of slumbering might.

The first essays of Grecian art, in the heroic age, prove they were neither stronger nor swifter in the race than other nations. But the improved imitation of nature, founded on the same principles of science, left their competitors at a distance not to be recovered; and the ability and zeal with which they pursued their advantage, gave them possession of the palm beyond dispute. In the institutions of Greece, the fine gymnastic exercises of boxing, running, wrestling, leaping, and throwing the spear, at the same time that they increased the strength and agility, exhibited all the various beauty of the human figure, diversified by all the difference of motion the several exertions could produce, with the multiplicity of anatomical changes in action and remission, occasioned by each exertion of body and limbs.

The Greeks added the cultivation of letters to their discoveries in science and improvement of philosophy. Hipparchus is said to have first made the Athenians acquainted with Homer's rhapsodies, (from which that people received their system of theology,) these were recited in the Panathenaic solemnities, and became so popular that they were continually quoted in the dialogues of Plato, and by succeeding writers. The poems of Hesiod, Sappho, Anacreon, and Simonides, are also believed to have been collected in a public library at Athens, at this time. Thus was infant art inspired by the spirit of poetry, and the effects of this inspiration are seen in the councils of the gods in the friezes of the Parthenon and the temple of Theseus, besides innumerable Homeric subjects on the painted vases and Greek basso-relievos of after ages.

The most numerous class of ancient statues was about the height of nature, or approaching to seven feet, which has been distinguished as the heroic size.

Statues were anciently appropriated to divinity. Portraits of men were not executed, unless for some illustrious cause which deserved perpetuity.

First, were the victorious contests in the sacred games, chiefly those of Olympia, where the custom was for all the conquerors to dedicate their statues, and those who were thrice victorious had exact portraits of their persons.

After the custom was adopted of bestowing this honour on distinguished merit, every battle increased heroic memorials; the porticoes, libraries, museums, and walks, were filled with statues of legislators, poets, philosophers, and all whose public spirit, or rare qualities had raised them to general notice and esteem. This increase of sculpture, extending over so considerable a portion of the globe known to the ancients, will account for the number of statues brought to Rome after the conquest of Greece.

Marcus Scaurus, when ædile, decorated his temporary theatre with three thousand statues. Two thousand were taken from the Volscians. Mummius, after the conquest of Achaia, is said to have filled the city. Lucullus brought many. Three thousand came from Rhodes—not fewer from Athens or Olympia—more are believed to have come from Delphi. Even after the terrific repetition of those conflagrations, which destroyed the noblest monuments in Rome, it was said that the city contained more gods than men.

The equestrian and pedestrian statues, trophies, and triumphal arches, which adorned the Roman forum, and the forum of Trajan—the innumerable sculptures in the imperial palace—in the baths of Dioclesian and Caracalla—the mausoleum of Augustus, and that of Hadrian—the files of patriots and heroes which lined the Flaminian way—were objects to fill the imagination, and occupy the mind. But neither the multitude of them, nor their magnificence, will produce any great impression on the painter or sculptor. He will keenly search out the rare specimens of excellence from among the hundreds of ordinary beauty.

In considering the impediments that prevented an earlier manifestation of the progress of modern art, and which were by some believed to be insurmountable, the following opinion, prevalent among the classical admirers of art, previous to the time of Winckleman and afterwards, deserves particular notice, which was, that the Christian religion afforded subjects less favourable to the painter or sculptor than the Pagan mythology; and although we hope this prejudice is diminished, yet it is not so entirely passed away as to render an inquiry into its merits wholly useless.

The ancient theory of personal beauty is, that it consists in a body and limbs accommodated to perform the various functions of life, under the government of the best principles of intelligence and will; in this definition the generality of moderns agree with the ancients. Here, then, we see that the artist is equally bound by the modern, as by the ancient practice, to make himself acquainted by physiological inquiry and philosophical reasoning, with the most perfect union of forms and sentiments for his studies.

Beauty is to be considered as pertaining to two orders of creation—the supernatural and the natural. In the Pagan mythology, the supernatural order consists of superior and inferior divinities, beatified heroes, and purified spirits. These have been represented by the ancients with a grandeur, perfection, and distinctness of character, by which we immediately recognize Jupiter from Hercules or Mercury, as we distinguish Cicero from Demosthenes, or Socrates from Zeno. The most elevated orders are more dignified in their characters, forms, and attitudes, while the younger deities are more remarkable for beauty in the bloom of youth, and a corresponding lightness of figure, and sprightliness of action; to these might be added an enumeration of distinctions both celestial and terrestrial. But the arts of design may exert their utmost efforts if employed on the personages and events of Divine revelation. The gradations of celestial power and beauty in the orders of angels and archangels, the grandeur and inspiration of prophets, according to the difference of mission, and the sanctity of apostles, have produced examples of grace, beauty, and grandeur of character, original in themselves, and not to be found in such variety among the remains of antiquity, as in works by the restorers of art in the fifteenth century.

We have subjects which, unknown to the Greeks and Romans, will employ the greatest powers, with the greatest advantage to the best faculties and dispositions of man, to his happiness, both present and future. It will be at once understood that the book which supplies these subjects is the sacred Scriptures.

The art of sculpture* imitates with more or less completeness the real bulk of objects, their substance and form, but it does not imitate their colour. This restriction is the result of a comprehensive view of imitation; it is by no means from actual impossibility, but because the end of genuine illusion would be defeated by the attempt. A statue coloured to the life might deceive the spectator for a moment, but he would presently discover, that life and motion were wanting; and the imitation would be consequently incomplete. Whatever is attempted by the arts, the perfection of style requires that the imitation, however really imperfect with reference to nature, or even with reference to other modes of representation, should suggest no want. The imagination then assents to the illusion, though the senses are far from being deceived.

As it is well known that the ancients occasionally added colour to their statues, it may be observed that the colours employed were probably never intended to increase the resemblance of the object to nature, they served only to insure distinctness, or were merely for ornament. The gilding of the hair, for instance, however objectionable, would not be condemned on the ground of its being too close an imitation of real hair. It would, indeed, soon be apparent that the differences which colours in nature present—for example, in the distinction of the face from the hair, and of the drapery from the flesh—require to be met in sculpture by some adequate or equivalent differences; hence, the contrasts

* The succeeding remarks are from Eastlake's "Contributions to the Fine Arts."

adopted were either greatly conventional or dictated such a choice of nature as was best calculated to supply the absent quality.

It will first be necessary to inquire what degree of resemblance was proposed in the imitation of the living form. In the fine examples of sculpture the surface of the skin, though free from minute accidents, is imitated closely. The polish is, however, uniform; first, because any varieties in this respect could not be distinguished at a due distance; and secondly, because a rough surface on marble in the open air is sure to hasten the corroding effect of time, by affording minute receptacles for dust or rain, while in interiors the rough portions would be soonest soiled.

In polishing the marble, the ancient sculptors were sometimes careful not to obliterate or soften too much the sharp ridges of the features, such as the edges of the eyelids, lips, &c. These sharpnesses were preserved, and occasionally exaggerated, in order to insure a distinct light and shade on the features at a considerable distance. Such contrivances, it is almost needless to say, were in a great measure dispensed with in statues intended for near inspection. Lastly, the marble received a varnish rather to protect the surface than to give it gloss.

These modes of finishing the surface are detailed, because it is of importance to remark, that this was the extent of the imitation. The varnish, doubtless, would give mellowness to the colour of the marble; but it may be assumed that a statue thus finished was nearly white.

The flesh is always the master-object of imitation in the antique statues; the other substances, drapery, armory, hair, or whatever they may be, are treated as accessories, to give value and truth to the naked. In nature it is possible for hair to be so smooth as to offer scarcely any difference in surface from flesh. Indiscriminate imitation in this particular, has also had its advo cates, and many Italian statues want colour to make the hair distinct from the face. The hair in the antique, whether crisp in its undulations, like that of the Venus of Milo; or soft, like that of the Medicean Venus; or bristled in unequal masses like that of the Dying Gladiator; or elaborately true, like that of the Lucius Venus; or whether even, as in the early Greek works, it is represented by undulating scratches, or by a series of regular curls, it is always more or less rough and channelled, so as to present a surface, sometimes from its deep shades almost approaching a mass of dark, opposed to the face. All this is only a judicious choice, and a skilful translation of nature.

In these and similar modes of distinction, as the accessories are treated in a relative and comparative manner; they cannot possibly approach so near to nature as the flesh. This relative effect is generally compatible with the admission of one or more of the proper qualities of the accessories; but it sometimes happens that, in them, the relative effect alone is studied. Thus, a detached portion of the hair of the Laocoon, or of the Dying Gladiator, would hardly be recognized for what it represents; the same might be said of detached portions of some draperies. This large principle of imitation is not to be recognized in less perfect examples of the art. The sculpture of the time of Hadrian, even when of colossal size, and requiring to be seen at some distance, is indiscriminately finished throughout. The master-object of imitation is consequently less effective.

The possibility of imitating drapery literally, accounts for some of the practices of the ancient sculptors, which, though judicious, have been sometimes objected to. Difficult as it may be supposed to be, to imitate a flexible substance in stone, the surface which drapery presents, in a quiescent state, may be copied in marble so as to produce illusion; for the surface being completely rendered, we have only to suppose the original drapery to be white, and the imitation in white marble is at once on a level with all absolute fac-similies. The consequence would be, that in a white marble statue with drapery thus literally copied from nature, we should immediately discover that the flesh was not of the natural colour, a discovery which we should never be permitted to make. The flesh from wanting colour, sets out with a departure from nature, and the conditions of imitation require that no other substance should surpass it in resemblance to its prototypes. As before observed, this generally follows when the accessories are treated in a merely relative manner. We should therefore pause before condemning the occasional squareness, straightness, and parallelism of the folds in some antique specimens, since this treatment not only serves to distinguish the drapery from the undulating outline and roundness of the limbs, but gives it that degree of conventional treatment, which prevents it from surpassing the flesh in mere truth of imitation. Thus the art is true to its own conditions; and this, at whatever cost attained, is necessary to constitute style.

The consequence of the direct and unrestrained imitation of the details is, that the flesh, however finished, looks petrified and colourless; for objects of very inferior importance, even to the buttons, are much nearer to nature. The objection to these details, from their unpleasant or unmeaning forms, is here left out of the account.

The boldness with which the ancient sculptors overcame difficulties is remarkable. Thus, to take an extreme case, rocks, which in marble can be easily made identical with nature, (thereby betraying the incompleteness of the art in other respects,) are generally conventional in fine sculpture—witness the basso-relievo of Perseus and Andromeda, and various examples in statues where rocks are introduced for the support of the figures. In order to reduce literal reality to the conditions of art, the substance is in this instance, so to speak, uncharacterized. The same liberty is observable in sculptured armour, as treated by the ancients. Sharpness is avoided; and the polish does not surpass, sometimes does not equal, that of the flesh. In like manner, steps, or any portions of architecture, are irregular and not geometrically true in their lines and angles. On a similar principle, probably, the inscriptions on the finest antique medals are rudely formed; for it cannot be supposed that the artists who could treat the figures and heads so exquisitely, could have been at a loss to execute mechanical details with precision.

In Canova's monument to the archduchess Maria Christina, at Vienna, figures are represented ascending real steps, and entering the open door of a real tomb—all executed with a builder's precision. It is plain that, to keep pace with the literal truth of these circumstances, the figures should at least have colour, life, and motion. The want of all these is injudiciously made apparent by the comparison in question, and some pains are taken to convince the spectator that he is looking at marble statues.

In the antique, on the contrary, it will generally be found that the employment of conventional methods (as opposed to the more direct truth of representation) increases in proportion, as objects are easily imitable, and consequently in danger of interfering with the higher aim.

The contrivances which are intended to give the impression of reality to the master-object of imitation, as exemplified in the best works of the ancients, thus point out the course to be pursued in the difficult treatment of statues in modern costume.

The very existence of imitation (however successful its results may be) depends on the condition, that its means should be different from those of nature. But sculpture, at the outset, gives substance for substance. A common quality being thus unavoidable, art is immediately on the watch to maintain its independence, by laying a stress on all the differences in its power, that are consistent with imitation. Accordingly, the form of the substance assumes peculiar beauty; it is thus removed, at least, from ordinary nature. The colour—in the imitation of the human figure—is altogether different from nature. Other qualities in the substance being given, the opposite qualities in nature are, in like manner, selected for imitation. The lifelessness, hardness, and rigidity of the material, point out the elastic surface of life and flexible substances, as the fittest objects for the artist's skill. Imitation is complete when we forget that the marble is white, lifeless, and inflexible. But if we are compelled to remember this, by the introduction of qualities common to nature and to the marble, (mere substance being already common) the first principle of art, as such, is violated. The selection of qualities differing from the nature of the material in which they are imitated, has, necessarily, its limits. Flying drapery, foliage, water, clouds smoke, are opposed, but may be too much opposed, to the artificial substance to render imitation possible. The spectator is, in this case, again reminded of the material.

Even in single figures, the distinction between the drapery and the flesh is chiefly expressed where they meet, and are immediately opposed to each other; in other parts remote from the flesh, the drapery exhibits nearly the same surface as the flesh. Again, where the drapery clings to the form, (a contrivance particularly objected to by Falconet,) it is the limb, rather than the drapery, which is apparent. There are, however, examples in the antique, where the entire surface of the drapery is plaited or channelled, so as to represent a general difference in its whole mass to the surface of the skin. Some figures of Amazons are thus treated; and in most female statues, the drapery being thin in texture, with minute folds, offers a constantly roughened surface, and insures a general opposition to the naked.

Costumes were represented more faithfully during the decline of art. It was the same in the ages of its immaturity. In Egypt the dresses were indiscriminately copied; and in the same proportion, imitation was imperfect, and taste undeveloped. The example is not without its use in other respects, for when the extreme warmth of the climate is considered, the multifarious Egyptian costumes are sufficient to prove that the civilized inhabitants of Greece and Italy were at least equally clad. The naked colossal statue of Pompey would have been as strange to the Romans, had they not been accustomed to similar works of art, as Canova's naked colossal Napoleon was to the Parisians. In the Panathenaic procession at Athens, as in all processions, the pomp of dress was the main part of the show. In the sculptured representation of this show, the elder functionaries have one loose garment becomingly thrown over the naked figure; and the Athenian cavaliers wear a still lighter mantle, which sometimes flowing from the shoulders in the breeze, shows their forms entirely undraped. The women, however, from motives which the Athenians never lost sight of, are fully but gracefully clad. With this exception, the peplon of Minerva was not more shorn of its embroidery in the marble, than the greater part of the figures were of their *real* costumes. It is necessary to compare the reality with the work of art, in order to be convinced that the difficulties of reconciling the style of sculpture with costume are not peculiar to modern times.

These two circumstances—the impossibility of absolute resemblance to nature in the principal object, and the extreme of such resemblance in many inanimate substances—define the style of sculpture; a style fully exemplified in the works of the ancients. On the authority of those works, it has been shown that this art, on the one hand, aims at the closest imitation of the living figure in its choicest forms; for such can best compensate for the want of colour, and enable the art to rival nature. In subordination to this, its first aim, sculpture affects the imitation of elastic and flexible substances generally. On the other hand, it is distinguished by the greater or less conventional treatment, or the entire omission of all particulars which are more literally imitable than the flesh. The instances of such conventional treatment, including alterations of costume, and omissions of various circumstances, which are observable in the sculpture of the Greeks, are perhaps the most remarkable liberties, with a view to consistency of style, which the history of art presents.

The Greeks, by selecting from a number of beautiful individuals those portions which they deemed most perfect, generalizing and reuniting them in conformity to an image in their own mind, produced that abstract ideal beauty, generally known by the term antique or ideal, a beauty and perfection of form which, though borrowed from nature in all its parts, is as a united whole superior to humanity. It is man represented according to the general laws of his species, rather than to the details, peculiarities, and imperfections of the individual. It is nature refined, exalted, and purified from her excrescences and defects. "Nature," says Flaxman, "has innumerable ends to accomplish; art but one—to produce ideal perfection and beauty."

The object of Grecian sculpture was to produce different degrees of the ideal, which approached, without passing the limits of divine beauty and majesty. The intermediate degrees of the ideal, which approached without passing the limits of divinity, were reserved for heroes—men whom antiquity delighted to exalt to the highest dignity of our nature. The heroic character was impressed, partly by idealizing the countenance and expression, yet retaining the resemblance, partly by increasing the stature, and heightening the swelling and action of the muscles; thus producing an augmented dignity, activity, and vigour. The only difference between a hero and one of the highest deities, was, that in the latter, the projections and square parts were rounded, the nerves and veins suppressed, so as to produce the most graceful elegance of form, in unison with a celestial spirit.

To perfect this ideal beauty, it became necessary to add the graces of expression and attitude. Yet aware, on the one hand, that expression and attitude, if pushed beyond a certain limit, detract from beauty and grace; and on the other, that beauty without expression and attitude is tame, and comparatively powerless, they steered a middle course between the two extremes—adopting chastened expression, repose, and decorum, combined with natural and unaffected gestures. A decency of motion and attitude is even observable in their Bacchante and dancing figures. In a word, dignity, grace, and a certain moral grandeur pervade all their works. In accordance with this principle, they uniformly gave to the higher class of deities, particularly to Jupiter, an expression of calm and majestic meditation, indicative of a mind wrapped up in itself, an energy of intellect elevated above human emotions and passions. The same exalted beauty, mental power, and sublime composure, may be traced through the whole Saturnian family. When the passions are represented, their visible signs are not such as to derange the dignity and beauty of the expression.

Whatever license may be permitted to the poet, the artist, more especially the sculptor, cannot carry the representation of the passions beyond a certain limit, without impairing all grace and beauty, outraging heroic dignity and decorum, and destroying the very interest and sentiment which it is intended to convey. In the Greek statuary, we observe no violent, cunning, malignant, ironical expression, no unseemly contortions of countenance. The movements and emotions are those of a man who knows how to control the fire of his passions; but allows certain flashes of them to escape, as it were, in spite of himself.

BASSO-RELIEVO.

There are three styles of relief. The highest is termed alto-relievo, in which some portions of the objects are often quite detached; the figures are usually half, or more than half, in relief. In basso-relievo the figures have a very slight projection from the background. Mezzo-relievo presents a medium between the two other styles. In the highest relief, however decided the shadows may and must of necessity be, on the plane to which the figure is attached, the light on the figure itself is kept as unbroken as possible; and this can only be effected by a selection of open attitudes; that is, such an arrangement of the limbs as shall not cast shadows on the figure itself. In basso-relievo the same general effect of the figure is given, but by very different means. Shadow is here the essential and only source of meaning and effect. The outline of the whole mass should be distinctly relieved, while those that come within should be very slightly marked, that the general effect of the whole may not be destroyed by confusing shadows; still, a very important figure may judiciously be raised even upon another, when the prominent idea of the subject may be thus more fully developed. Mezzo-relievo differs from both : it has neither the limited attitudes of the first, nor the distinct outline, and suppressed, internal markings of the second ; on the contrary, the outline is often less distinct than the forms within it, and hence it requires and is fitted for near inspection Its imitation may thus be more absolute, and its execution more finished, than either of the other styles.

Mezzo-relievo of the fullest kind was fitly employed (as well as alto-relievo, when in situations not exposed to accidents) to ornament tombs and sarcophagi. These works, placed in the open air, decorated the approaches to cities, as sepulchres were always without the walls. The Appian way was the most magnificent of these streets of tombs in the neighbourhood of Rome, and must have exhibited, literally, thousands of sepulchral monuments. Though, generally, the work of Greek artists, and often interesting from being copies of better works, now lost, the haste and inattention with which such prodigious numbers were executed, tended to degrade the style of their sculpture. In these relievi, even in the better specimens, buildings and other objects are occasionally introduced behind the figures, thus approaching the spurious style of relief in which the effects of perspective are attempted to be expressed. The greater part of what are called Roman bassi-relievi are of this kind, and may be considered a middle style between the pure Greek relievo and the modern Italian. It was from antique sarcophagi, fine in execution, but with these defects in style, that Niccoli da Pisa, in the thirteenth century, first caught the spirit of ancient art. Many of the works from which he is believed to have studied are still preserved in Pisa. In imitating the simplicity of arrangement, and, in a remote degree, the purity of forms which these works exhibited, the artist was not likely to correct the defects alluded to, which had been already practised in Italy and elsewhere. Various degrees of relief, background figures and objects, and occasional attempts at perspective, are found in the works of the Pisani and their scholars; yet, their works, which are to be regarded as the infancy of Italian art, and, which undoubtedly, are rude enough in workmanship and imitation, are purer in style than those of the succeeding Florentine masters, who attained so much general perfection in sculpture. The relievi of Donatello are mostly in the style called by the Italians stiacciato, (the flattest kind of mezzo-relievo, according to the definition before given,) which he probably adopted, as he worked in bronze, from the facility of casting; yet, in such a style, commanding little distinctness from its inconsiderable projection, he introduced buildings, landscape, and the usual accessories of a picture. But this misapplication of ingenuity was carried still further by Lorenzo Ghiberti, in the celebrated bronze doors of the Baptistry, or church of San Giovanni, at Florence, which exhibited such skilful compositions, in which the stories are so well told, and in the single figures are so full of appropriate action. In these works the figures gradually emerge from the stiacciato style to alto-relievo. They are among the best specimens of that mixed style, or union of basso-relievo, with the principles of painting, which the sculptors of the fifteenth century and their imitators imagined to be an improvement on the well-considered simplicity of the ancients. In these and similar specimens, the unreal forms of perspective buildings, and the diminished or foreshortened figures, which in pictures create illusion when aided by appropriate light and shade, and variety of hue, are unintelligible or distorted in a real material, where it is immediately evident that the objects are all on the same solid plane. Even Vasari, who wrote when this mixed style of relievo was generally practised, remarks the absurdity of representing the plane on which the figures stand ascending towards the horizon, according to the laws of perspective; in consequence of which "we often see," says he, "the point of the foot of a figure, standing with its back to the spectator, touching the middle of the leg, owing to the right ascent or foreshortening of the ground. Such errors," he adds, "are to be seen even in the doors of San Giovanni." Lorenzo Ghiberti, like other Florentine sculptors, first learned the practice of his art from a goldsmith, and the designs of the artist who competed with him for the honour of executing the doors of the San Giovanni, were submitted to the judgment of goldsmiths and painters as well as sculptors.

The taste of the Florentines in basso-relievo was thus greatly influenced by the prevalence of a style most applicable to the precious metals, in which a general sparkling effect is best insured by avoiding uniformly violent relief, which projects considerable shadows, and especially by avoiding unbroken flatness. The background is thus filled with slightly relieved distant objects, so as to produce everywhere a more or less roughened or undulating surface. The same end seems to have been attained in the antique silver vases, by the introduction of foliage. The style continued to be practised with occasionally greater absurdities than those before alluded to, and perhaps, less redeeming excellencies, till the close of the last century. The sculptor Falconet, says of the antique bassi-relievi, "that, however noble their composition may be, it does not in any way tend to the illusion of a picture, and a basso-relievo ought always to aim at the illusion." He leaves no doubt as to the literal meaning he intends, by citing the Italian writers who applied the term *quadro* indiscriminately to picture and basso-relievo. Sculpture in

England, was indebted principally to Flaxman for the revival of a purer taste in the application of basso-relievo to architecture. In works of decoration, intended to be executed in the precious metals, in which, as before observed, moderately embossed and general richness of surface is so desirable, in order to display the material as well as the work; he, however, united his own purity of taste and composition with an approach to the mixed style of relief practised by the Florentine masters, who, in this branch of sculpture, perhaps, never equalled his shield of Achilles.

Egyptian Sculpture.

THE Chaldeans, whose persons are deficient in grace and beauty, are supposed to have been the first sculptors. Specimens of this art, found in Egypt, are perhaps the most ancient extant. The dryness of the climate has preserved them wholly from the ravages of time

Owing to the prevalence of animal worship in Egypt, the most frequent and most successful performances of their artists were figures of animals.

In the history of Egyptian art, a distinction must be made between the old and the later styles. The former appears in the earliest monuments, down to the conquest of Egypt (525 B. C.) by Cambyses, who is supposed to have established the Mithratic worship in Egypt. What seems to have chiefly suggested this idea, is the discovery of a curious representation of a sacrifice to the sun, in an artificial cavern, near the ruins of Babien, in

Upper Egypt. It is hewn out of rock, in the middle of the mountain; it is above fifty feet wide, and as many in height, and between five and six feet in depth. The sun appears encompassed with rays, forming a circle fifteen or twenty feet in diameter. Two priests of the natural stature, their heads covered with long caps, terminating in points, stretch their hands towards the sun; the ends of their fingers touch the rays. Two little boys, clothed like the priests, stand by their sides, and reach to them two great goblets. Below the sun there are several lambs killed, and extended on piles, consisting each of ten pieces of wood; and below the piles are seven jars. On the other side of the sun, there are two women and two girls, in full relief, joined to the rock by parts of their backs and feet only. Behind and above these and the boys are several hieroglyphics. The tiara on the heads of the priests, very much resembles those of the Persians in a procession, in the bass-reliefs found at Chilminac, near Persepolis. The hawk and ibis are purely Egyptian. This is a very curious monument, and it is certainly very different from the other excavations of Upper Egypt.

The works of art in Egypt may be designated respectively, as the Old Egyptian, the Persian-Egyptian, the Grecian-Egyptian. and the Roman-Egyptian, or Roman imitations of the Egyptian manner.

The attitudes of their figures, whether sitting or standing, are awkward and unnatural—the bones and muscles feebly indicated; the eyes flat and oblique—not sunk as in the Grecian statues, but almost even with the head; the eyebrows, eyelashes, and the border of the lips marked by sunk lines; the nose thick and flat, the cheek-bones high; the chin small, receding, and pointed; the line of the mouth, at the angles, drawn upwards; the mouth always shut, and the lips full, and separated by a simple incision;

the ears placed very high; the heads of both sexes large and coarse; the feet broad, clumsy, and without articulation of the toes. The eyes are occasionally composed of different materials from the statues, such as metals and precious stones.

Their architectural relievi were cut or sunk in the stone, and then slightly relieved from the ground. Relievi, properly so called, were only executed by the Egyptians in bronze, cast in moulds. The period preceding the time of Cambyses, is considered by Memes, as the only period of real Egyptian sculpture. These remains may be classed under three divisions: colossal figures; figures about the natural size, single or in groups; and hieroglyphical and historical relievi. The colossal remains are very numerous. The sphinx is of most frequent occurrence, the dimensions varying from seventy to one hundred and twenty-five feet in length.

Of this era is the immense statue of red granite found on the site of the Memnonium, which was thrown down by Cambyses. Its stature is forty-six feet.

The space between the Memnonium and Medinet Abon, which is about a mile and a quarter, is covered with colossal fragments. Here appears to have been what Diodorus Siculus called the tomb of Osymandes. The palace of Medinet Abon has, still in a tolerable state of preservation, a peristyle, fifty-five paces long and sixty-five in breadth, formed of two rows of columns, placed on the four sides of the court. The columns are forty-five feet high, and seven in diameter; the materials good, and the execution fine. In the hieroglyphics, the large figures have two inches relief; the smaller ones, one inch. On the exterior of the palace-wall, a bass-relief represents a chase of lions, and an invasion of foreigners, whose dress very much resembles that of the Hindoos. The Egyptians oppose the descent by sea and land, and the barbarians seem to be routed. Under this is seen a marshalled army—some heavily armed, others armed in a lighter manner.

Many sculptures are found in the excavations of Philœ, Elephantis, Silulis, and at El Malook, in the tombs of the Theban kings. These excavations are often suites of magnificent chambers, hewn from white calcareous rock. A singular peculiarity marks the statues—a pilaster runs up behind each, the whole height, not only when the statue is connected with the surface of a wall, but also when it is wholly detached. Relievi are found in great abundance, occupying often the entire walls of the temples. In these, there is much skill in the mechanical workmanship, but they are very deficient as performances of art; proportion and perspective seem to have been utterly unknown.

Statues of wood have been discovered by modern travellers. Metal appears to have been sparingly used, at least only very small figures have been found, of a composition similar to the bronze of modern times. In the tombs small images of porcelain and terra-cotta are frequent.

The works of art produced by this nation were gloomy and grave, but full of deep sentiment, connected, by the hieroglyphics which covered them, with poetry and history, and with the belief of immortality. But as the kingdom of the dead seemed to them the true existence, so their art is more related to death than life: their figures are stiff and motionless, like mummies; even their images of Isis have this character.

Oriental Sculpture.

THE Persians, who loved splendor, ornamented their buildings with many sculptural decorations, as the ruins of Persepolis prove. In Assyria the art flourished under queen Semiramis. We find mention of brazen statues of Semiramis, Belus, and Ninus. In the mountains of Kurdistan, very ancient works of sculpture are found, which the inhabitants consider as the imagės of Chosroes and his beloved Shereen; he was surnamed the just, and is still cited as a model for kings. They are said to be the work of the poet and artist, Ferhad. The fancy of the Hindoos was very rich, but inclined towards the symbolical and allegorical, so that they never attained to a pure style of art. Their sculpture is highly expressive, exhibiting a mosaic of ideas, though almost destitute of beauty of form.

The excavations in the islands near Bombay abound with sculptures. Along the sides of the grand temple cut in the rock at Elephanta, are from forty to fifty colossal statues, from twelve to fifteen feet high, of good symmetry, and though not quite detached from the rock, boldly relieved; some have helmets of a pyramidal form, others crowns decorated with jewels and devices, and others have bushy ringlets of flowing hair. Many of them have four hands, some six, holding sceptres, shields, symbols of justice and religion, warlike weapons, and trophies of peace; some inspire horror, others have aspects of benignity. The face of the largest bust is five feet long, and the breadth across the shoulders is twenty feet.

At the west end of this great pagoda is a dark recess, 20 feet square, totally destitute of ornament; the altar is in the centre, and there are two gigantic statues at each of the four doors by which it is entered. The sculpture is good ; their heads are dressed like the other statues, and they wear rich collars, and have jewels in their ears.

In the excavations at Canana, in the island of Salsette, there are said to be not less than six hundred images. Besides colossal figures, the walls are covered with representations of men and women engaged in various actions. Along the cornice there are figures of elephants, horses, and lions, in bold relief; and above, as in a sky, genii and dewtah are seen floating in multitudes.

The art was evidently esteemed by the Hebrews, but chiefly as an auxiliary and ornament to architecture ; of this we have evidence in the temple of Solomon, in the construction of which, however, Phœnician artists were chiefly employed. The commerce and wealth of the Phœnicians were favourable to the arts, but there exists no genuine and proper specimens of their sculpture

Etruscan Sculpture.

THE Etruscans reached a high degree of civilization, and were particularly devoted to the cultivation of the fine arts, in which they attained an excellence only surpassed in grandeur by the monuments of Egypt, and in ideal beauty by those of Greece.

In their tombs and subterranean sepulchres, have been found most of their works of art now extant. Those of the great and wealthy may be regarded as subterranean museums, embracing painting and sculpture, besides innumerable other objects, illustrative of their mythology, usages, and habits. From these interesting sources of information, three important inferences have been drawn: that their religion was based on a belief of the immortality of the soul; a conviction of its responsibility beyond the grave for the deeds done in the body; and that the female was created as the companion, not the slave, of man, honoured in life as well as in death. They possessed a school of art remarkable for its nationality and beauty. Their works consisted of statues, both of marble and bronze, relievi, terra-cottas, paintings, vases, medals, coins, and engraved stones. Their statues and sculptures extant, at least those called Etruscan, resemble so closely the early and even later styles of the Greeks, that it is often impossible to pronounce with certainty as to their authenticity.

Winkelmann divides Etruscan art into three epochs—the first characterized by sharp lines, stiffness of attitude, forced action, no approach to beauty of feature, nor any indication of muscles. Some of the smaller figures, both in their features, hanging and attached arms, and parallel feet, have a strong resemblance to the Egyptian. But in spite of this rudeness of design in their sculpture, they contrived to give the most elegant and graceful forms to their vases. Winkelmann supposes that the second style commenced with the age of Phidias. It is characterized by an exaggerated indication and swelling of the muscles and articulations—the hair arranged in gradations—the movements affected, and sometimes forced. He thinks that up to this period they had an imperfect knowledge of Greek art. The third style was derived from the Greek colonists of Magna Græcia. It is very visible in the medals of the cities of the Campagna, the heads of the divinities bearing a perfect resemblance to the Greek statues. The medals of Capua represent Jupiter with the hair disposed in the sweeping manner of the Greeks. The most of their sepulchral urns, composed of alabaster of Volterra, are to be referred to this period.

Grecian Sculpture.

Of the rise of the art of sculpture in Greece, we have no data. The period of its predominance has been divided into four eras, though they are rather indefinite. The first may be said to have commenced about fourteen centuries before the Christian era—Dædalus, a native of Athens, then first raising the art from barbarous rudeness. The second commenced with Phidias, who lived about 450 B. C., and may be characterized as the period of the grand style. The third commences with Praxiteles, who lived about 360 B. C. The predominant trait of the style in this age, was beauty. The fourth commences with Lysippus, in the time of Alexander the Great, and extends to the subjugation of Greece by the Romans, soon after which the art rapidly declined. The characteristics of the style in this age, were gracefulness, and softness of expression.

FIRST PERIOD.

The first works must have been quite rude, as the artists were deficient in the theory of designing, and in mechanical skill, and were also destitute of the necessary instruments Accordingly, we find that the most ancient men and gods were scarcely any thing more than pillars or blocks, with the upper extremity formed into a sort of knob, or rounded, to represent a head. Such was the very ancient image of Cybele, brought to Rome from Persinus, in Phrygia. Gradually, the other parts of the body were more distinctly formed, at first, however. only indicated by lines; afterwards made more full and complete, yet not marked by significant action and attitude, but stiff, angular, and forced. This improvement was ascribed, among the Greeks, to Dædalus, who was on that account said to have formed living statues, and whose name was applied by the early Greeks to distinguished productions of art. In treating of him, it is requisite first to mention, that the statements of ancient writers respecting him cannot be understood as exhibiting the true history of an individual, but rather as obscurely intimating the origin and progress of the arts in Greece; and, in particular, the information which is afforded respecting the place of his birth, and the countries in which he lived, seems to reflect light on the districts in which the arts were first cultivated. In noticing the accounts which have reached us of the personal history of the artist Dædalus, the name itself first claims our attention. We learn from Pausanias, that all statues and images were anciently styled Dædalus. His performances were chiefly in wood, of which no fewer than nine, of large dimensions, are described as existing in the second century, which notwithstanding the injuries of fourteen hundred years, and the imperfections of early taste, seemed, in the language of Pausanias, to possess something of divine expression. Their author, as reported by Diodorus, improved upon ancient art, so as to give vivacity to the attitude, and an animated expression to the countenance. Hence, we are not to understand, with some, that Dædalus introduced sculpture into Greece, nor even into Attica; but simply that he was the first to form something like a school of art, and the first whose works excited the admiration of his own rude age, while they were deemed worthy of notice even in more enlightened times. Indeed, the details, preserved in the classic writers, that he raised the arms in varied positions from the flanks, and opened the eyes, before narrow and blinking, sufficiently prove the extent of preceding art.

The nephew of Dædalus, named Talus or Perdix, showed a great genius for mechanics; having, from the contemplation of a serpent's teeth, invented the saw, and applied it to the cutting of timber. Dædalus, jealous of his skill, and apprehensive of the rivalry of the young man, cast him down from the Acropolis and killed him. For this murder he was banished by the court of Areopagus, and he betook himself to Minos, king of Crete, for whom he built the Labyrinth. He also devised an ingenious species of dance for Ariadne, the daughter of that monarch; but, having formed the wooden cow for Pasiphaë, he incurred the displeasure of the king, and was thrown into prison. Having, by means of Pasiphaë, escaped from confinement, he determined to flee from Crete; but being unable to get away by sea, he determined to attempt flight through the air. He made, accordingly, wings of feathers united by wax, for himself and his son Icarus. They mounted into the air, but Icarus ascending too high, and approaching too near the sun, its heat melted the wax, and the youth fell into the sea, and was drowned. Dædalus arrived in safety in Sicily, where he was kindly received by Cocalus. It must be evident that under the name of this artist are concealed facts respecting the origin of Grecian art, which took its rise in Attica, and then spread, under different circumstances, into Crete and Sicily. Dædalus, which signifies ingenious invention, is by some supposed to be merely a personification of manual art.

During this epoch, schools of art were established at Sicyon, Corinth and Ægina. Many important improvements and discoveries were made during this period. "Rhœcus of Samos, 700 B. C., invented the art of moulding and casting statues in metal Theodorus and Telicles, his sons, travelled for the study of the art in Egypt. The former is reported to have made the statue of the Pythian Apollo for the temple of Samos, in two parts—one half at Ephesus, and the other at Samos—a manner of working which was, perhaps, possible in the condition of the Egyptian art. Dibutades invented the art of making portrait figures in baked earth, (*terra-cotta;*) his daughter, Callirhoe, suggested to him this idea, by drawing the profile of her lover's shadow, with coal, upon the wall. Euchirus, of Corinth, (663 B. C.,) accompanied Demaratus, the father of the elder Tarquin, to Italy, and is said to have introduced the art of modelling into Etruria; though others think that the Etruscans preceded the Greeks in this art. Dipœnus and Scyllis became the masters of a numerous school. Canachus was the greatest master of the Sicyonian school. Perillus made the famous brazen bull, a splendid masterpiece, for Phalaris, who ruled in Sicily, 564 B. C., in which the artist himself was burned. Among the principal works in stone, were those of Bathycles, of Amyche. Demeas, of Crotona, executed the statue of Milo. Iphicrates cast the brazen lioness, in commemoration of Leæna, who was privy to the conspiracy of her lover, Aristogiton, against Hipparchus, and who endured the torture till death, without confessing any thing. The artist gave no tongue to the lioness, in order to express the heroic silence of Leæna. Onatas, of Ægina, restored the statue called the Black Ceres of Phigalea. Agelades, of Argos, is considered to have been the master of Phidias, with whom began a new era in the art."

SECOND PERIOD.

Many favourable circumstances combined to promote the advancement of sculpture in Greece; the influence of a delightful climate upon physical and moral education; the constant views of beauty, not only in natural scenery, but especially in the human form, as produced among the Greeks; their peculiar religion, involving so much of poetry and imagination, and yet so addressed to the senses; the high honours and rewards bestowed upon artists; the various uses and applications of sculpture, and the flourishing condition of the other imitative arts, and of letters in general.

The occasions for the execution of statues in Greece were very frequent and various. Not only were the temples of the gods ornamented with their statues, and with sculptured representations of their mythological history, but works of this kind were required in great numbers for public squares, for private dwellings and gardens, country seats, walks, and for architectural ornaments in general. The portico at Athens, receiving its name Pœcile, from its variety of ornaments, was crowded with statues. To heroes, wise men, poets, and victors, statues were erected out of gratitude and respect; to princes, out of flattery. Thus did the statuary always find encouragement and reward for the exercise of his art, and for the application of all his talents, which were quickened and stimulated the more by emulation. Hence, from Phidias to Praxiteles, the art of sculpture obtained much higher excellence in Greece than among other nations. Its characteristic, at this period, was loftiness and grandeur in style;

yet this was accompanied with more or less of that want of softness and ease which marked the works of succeeding artists. There was a very rigid observance of outward proportion. The expression in gesture and attitude, was bold and significant, rather than captivating and pleasing.

PHIDIAS.

Nothing authentic is known of this artist in his earlier years, except that he was instructed in statuary by Hippias and Ageladas, and that when quite a youth he practised painting, and made a picture of Jupiter Olympus. He was an Athenian, and died 444 B. C. He brought to his profession a knowledge of all the finer parts of science which could tend to dignify and refine it. With the most exquisite harmonies of poetry, and the most gorgeous fictions of mythology, he was no less familiar than with geometry, optics, and history. From Homer, whose works he must have deeply studied, he drew those images of greatness, which he afterwards moulded in earthly materials with a kindred spirit. The circumstance which, by a singular felicity, not often accorded to genius, elicited the powers of Phidias, was the coincidence, in point of time, of the full maturity of his talents with the munificent administration of Pericles. Intent on his great national design of adorning Athens with the choicest specimens of art, this statesman saw in the genius of Phidias the means of giving form, shape, and completeness to the most glorious of his conceptions. He accordingly appointed this great sculptor the superintendent of all the public works then in progress, both of architecture and statuary, and well did the event sanction the choice. The buildings reared by the direction of Phidias, though finished within a comparatively short period, seemed built for ages, and, as was observed by Plutarch, had the venerable air of antiquity when newly completed, and retained all the freshness of youth after they had stood for ages. The beautiful sculptures on the frieze of the Parthenon were the work of Phidias and his pupils; while the statue of Minerva within the temple was wholly his production. This was indeed the most celebrated of all his works, if we except the Olympian Jupiter at Elis. Independently of the workmanship, the statue was of noble dimensions, and of the most costly materials. It was twenty-six cubits, or thirty-nine feet in height, and formed of ivory and of gold; being, most probably, composed originally of the former, and overlaid, in part, by the latter. The goddess was represented in a noble attitude—erect, clothed in a tunic reaching to the feet. On the head was a casque: in one hand she held a spear; in the other, which was stretched out, an ivory figure of Victory, four cubits high; while at her feet was a buckler, exquisitely carved, the concave representing the war of the giants, the convex the battle between the Athenians and the Amazons; the portraits of the artist and his patron were introduced among the Athenian combatants, one cause of the future misfortunes which envy brought upon the author. On the middle of the helmet a sphinx was carved, and on each of its sides a griffon. On the ægis, or breast-plate, was displayed a head of Medusa. The golden sandals were sculptured with the conflict between the Centaurs and Lapithæ, and are described as a perfect gem of minute art. On the base of the statue was represented the legend of Pandora's creation, together with the images of twenty deities.

The statue of the Olympian Jupiter graced the temple of that god at Olympia, in Elis and was chryselephantine, (made of gold and ivory,) like that of Minerva. Like that, too, the size was colossal, being sixty feet high The god was represented as sitting on his throne: in his right hand he held a figure of Victory, also made of gold and ivory; in his left, a sceptre, beautifully adorned with all kinds of metals, and having on the top a golden eagle. His brows were encircled with a crown, made to imitate leaves of olive; his robe was of massive gold, curiously adorned, probably by a kind of encaustic work, with various figures of animals, and also with lilies. The sandals, too, were of gold. The throne was inlaid with all kinds of precious materials—ebony, ivory, and gems—and was adorned with sculptures of exquisite beauty. On the base was an inscription recording the name of the artist. Lucian informs us that, in order to render this celebrated work as perfect in detail as it was noble in conception and outline, Phidias when he exposed it, for the first time after its completion, to public view, placed himself behind the door of the temple, and listened attentively to every criticism made by the spectators: when the crowd had withdrawn, and the temple gates were closed, he revised and corrected his work, wherever the objections he had just heard appeared to him to be well-grounded ones. It is also said, that when the artist himself was asked by his relation, Panænus, the Athenian painter, who, it seems, aided him in his work, whence he had derived the idea of this, his grandest effort, he replied, from the well-known passage in Homer, where Jove is represented as causing Olympus to tremble on its base by the mere movement of his sable brow. The lines in question, with the exception of their reference to the "ambrosial curls" and the brow of the god, contain no allusion whatever to external form, and yet they carry with them the noble idea of the Supreme Being nodding benignant assent with so much true majesty, as even to cause Olympus to tremble. Of this noble work Quintilian remarks, that it even added new feelings to the religion of Greece, and yet, when judged according to the principles of art, neither this nor the Minerva in the Parthenon possessed any strong claims to legitimate beauty. It does not excite surprise, therefore, to learn that Phidias himself disapproved of the mixed effect produced by such a combination of different circumstances, nor will it appear presumptuous in us to condemn these splendid representations. In these compositions, exposed, as they were, to the dim light of the ancient temple, and from their very magnitude imperfectly comprehended, the effects of variously reflecting substances, now in gloom, now glowing with unearthly lustre, must have been rendered doubly imposing. But this influence, though well calculated to increase superstitious devotion, or to impress mysterious terror on the bewildered sense, was meretricious, and altogether diverse from the solemn repose, the simple majesty of form and expression, which constitute the true sublimity of sculptural representations. In the time of Pausanias, there was still shown at Olympia, the building in which the statue of Jupiter was made, and the posterity of Phidias had charge of keeping the image free from whatever might sully its beauty.

According to Plutarch, his friendship and influence with Pericles, exposed the artist to envy, and procured him many enemies, who wishing, through him, to try what judgment the people would pass upon Pericles himself, persuaded Menon, one of his workmen, to place himself as a suppliant in the forum, and to entreat the protection of the state, while he lodged a complaint against Phidias. The people granted this request, Menon charged the artist with having embezzled a portion of the forty talents of gold with which he had been furnished for the decoration of the statue in the Parthenon. The allegation, however, was disproved in the most satisfactory manner; for Phidias, by the advice of Pericles, had put on the golden decorations in such a way that they could be easily removed without injury to the statue. They were accordingly taken off, and, at the order of Pericles, weighed by the accusers; and the result established the perfect innocence of the artist. His enemies, however, were not to be daunted by this defeat, and a new charge was in consequence, soon prepared against him. It was alleged that in his representation of the battle of the Amazons, on the shield of Minerva, he had introduced his own effigy, as a bald old man taking up a large stone with both hands, and a highly finished picture of Pericles contending with an Amazon. This was regarded as an act of impiety, and Phidias was cast into prison, to await his trial for the offence; but he died in confinement before his cause could be heard.

Besides his two masterpieces—Pallas Athene and the Olympian Jupiter at Elis—his Pallas of brass at Athens, his Venus, his Nemesis in the temple of Marathon, and his Amazon, remarkable for the beauty of her limbs, deserve particular mention

In the British Museum is a series of ancient sculptures, called the Elgin marbles, after the earl of that name by whom they were rescued from the barbarous hands of the Turks, and sold to the British government. These miracles of ancient art belonged originally to the temple of Minerva, (Parthenon,) and to some toher edifices on the Acropolis, at Athens. Their ancient history is well known; they were imagined and directed by Phidias, and executed in part by his chisel. "Every truth of shape, the result of the inherent organization of man as an intellectual being; every variation of that shape, produced by the slightest variation of motion, in consequence of the slightest variation of intention, acting on it; every result of repose on flesh as a soft substance, and on bone as a hard, both being influenced by the common principles of life and gravitation; every harmony of line in composition, from geometrical principle, all proving the science of the artist; every beauty of conception proving his genius; and every grace of execution proving that practice had given his hand power, can be shown to exist in the Elgin marbles." "There is a supposition," continues Haydon, "that feeling alone enabled the Greeks to arrive at such perfection: but, surely the capacity to feel a result is very different from power to produce the sensation of it in others, by an imitative art. After feeling a result, to produce the same effect in others, you must exercise your understanding, and practise your hand: you then begin immediately with the why and the wherefore; the how and the what; your understanding is thus stored with reasons and principles. The first requisite, of course, is a capacity to feel a result; the next, an understanding to ascertain the means of producing in others what you have felt yourself; and the third is the feeling again, to tell you when you have done what you wanted to do. The understanding being thoroughly stored with principles of the means of imitation, and the hand thoroughly ready from practice, a result is no sooner felt, than the understanding at once supplies the principle on which it is to be executed by imitation, and the hand instantly executes it, till at last, feeling, understanding, and hand go so instantaneously together, as not to be perceived, in their respective departments, by the possessor; and all resolve themselves into feeling, which at first was the instigator, and then becomes the director. A result having the appearance of being easily produced, induces the world to conclude that feeling alone is the cause; ignorant of what effects of the understanding and hand were at first requisite before they could so completely obey the feeling as to be identified with it. What previous study and preparation must have been requisite to bring into existence that divine form in a metope, grappling a Centaur by the throat, and heaving up his chest, and drawing in his breath, preparing to annihilate his enemy: or the one, in all the loosened relaxation of death, under the Centaur's legs, who prances in triumph; or the other, who presses forward, while he dashes back his opponent with a tendinous vigour, as if lightning dashed through his frame?" "The Elgin marbles," continues Haydon, "will as completely overthrow the old antique, as ever one system of philosophy overthrew another more enlightened: were the Elgin marbles lost, there would be as great a gap in art, as there would be in philosophy if Newton had never existed. Let him that doubts it, study them as I have done, for eight years daily, and he will doubt it no longer. They have thrown into light, principles which would **only** have been discovered by the inspiration of successive geniuses, if ever at all; because we had what the Greeks had not—an antique, and a system to mislead us, and misplaced veneration, and early habits, to root out. Such a blast will fame yet blow of their grandeur, that its roaring will swell out as time advances; and nations now sunk in barbarism, and ages yet unborn, will in succession be roused by its thunder, and refined by its harmony—pilgrims from the remotest corners of the earth will visit their shrine, and be purified by their beauty."

These works of the "marble-wise Phidias" have been in existence upwards of two thousand years, nor has time dealt hardly with them. It cannot but be regretted that their excellence was unappreciated during the night of barbarianism, which so long enveloped the world. They were—however indifferent may have been the Goths and the Turks—for more than seven hundred years, the admiration of the, ancient world; and have been regarded, by all competent judges, as inimitable. These celebrated relics of ancient art consist of several of the matchless statues which adorned the pediments of the Parthenon, at Athens; a number of the metopes, from the same temple, and about two hundred and fifty feet of the frieze; casts of all the sculptures of the temple of Theseus; a complete series of architectural drawings, containing accurate details of every building that can still be traced in Athens, or in the Peloponnesus; a great variety of fragments of sculpture, and embellishments of architecture; columns, capitals, friezes, inscriptions, &c.

The sublime style perfected by Phidias, seems almost to have expired with himself. Not that the art declined, but a predilection for subjects of beauty, and the softer graces, in preference to those of a more heroic and masculine character—with the exception of the grand relievi on the temple of Olympia—may be traced even among his immediate disciples. In the era and labours of Phidias, we discover the utmost excellence to which Grecian genius attained in the arts; and in the marbles of the British Museum, the former ornaments of the Parthenon, we certainly behold the conceptions, and in some measure, the very practice of the great Athenian sculptor. Of the intellectual character of these admirable performances, grandeur is the prevailing principle—the grandeur of simplicity and nature, devoid of all parade or ostentation of art; and their author, to use the language of antiquity, united the three characteristics, of truth, grandeur, and minute refinement; exhibiting majesty, breadth, gravity, and magnificence of composition, with a practice scrupulous in detail, and with truth of individual representation; yet in the handling, broad, rapid, and firm. This harmonious assemblage of qualities—in themselves dissimilar, and in their result the same—gives to the productions of this master an ease, a grace, a vitality, resembling more the spontaneous overflowings of inspiration, than the laborious offspring of thought and science.

ALCAMENES AND AGORACRITUS.

Alcamenes, of Attica, and Agoracritus, of Paros, were the favourite pupils of Phidias. The most celebrated works of the former were his Vulcan, his Olympian Conqueror, his Cupid, his Mars, and his Venus. The latter was a still greater favourite of Phidias; he contended with Alcamenes in the execution of a Venus, and was adjudged to be inferior by the Athenians, only out of partiality to their fellow-citizen. He transformed his Venus into a Nemesis, and sold it at Ramarus. Varro considered this statue the finest ever executed.

POLYCLETUS.

Polycletus was a native of Argos, and flourished about 430, B. C. He did not possess the grandeur of imagination which characterized his great predecessor; nor did he ever attempt, like him, to create images of the most powerful deities. It seems, indeed, that he excelled less in representing the robust and manly graces of the human form, than in the sweet, tender, and unconscious loveliness of childhood. In his works, however, he manifested an equal aspiration, after ideal beauty, with Phidias. He seems to have laboured to render his statues perfect in their kind, by the most scrupulous care in the finishing. Hence he is said to have observed that, "the work becomes most difficult when it comes to the nail." He formed a statue of a life-guardsman so marvellously exact in its proportions, and so exquisite in its symmetry, that it was called the Rule, and became the model whence artists derived their canons of criticism, which determined the correctness of a work. He executed also a statue of a youth binding a fillet, of so perfect a beauty that it was valued at the high price of a hundred talents. Another of his celebrated works represented two boys playing at dice, which was regarded with the highest admiration, in after days, at Rome, where it was in the possession of the Emperor Titus. Polycletus is said to have carried alto-relievo, which Phidias invented, to perfection. He discovered the art of balancing figures on one leg, and is said to have been so partial to this mode of representing the human form, that he almost invariably adopted it in his statues. He is accused, by Varro, of too great uniformity in his figures, and of the constant repetition of the same idea. Nothing could exceed the exactness of symmetry with which he framed his statues; but it seems they were destitute of passion, sentiment, and expression.

Like other statuaries of the same age, Polycletus was also distinguished as an architect, and erected a theatre, with a dome, at Epidaurus, on a piece of ground consecrated to Esculapius. This building, Pausanias pronounces to be superior, in respect of symmetry and elegance, to every other theatre, not excepting even those at Rome.

All ancient writers bestow the highest praise on Polycletus. Cicero pronounces his works absolutely perfect. Quintilian mentions the gracefulness of his productions; but intimates that they were deficient in majestic dignity.

MYRON.

Myron was a native of Eleutheræ, in Bœotia. He executed three colossal statues upon one pedestal—Minerva presenting the deified Hercules to Jupiter. The fertile genius of Myron was displayed in the choice of new and bold positions. He despised the softer forms of the Ephebi, and showed his skill in the representation of the most highly finished athletic forms. His Runner, his Slinger, and his Pancratists, are celebrated. His ideal of Hercules completed this class of forms. His Heifer, and his Sea Monster are famous among his animal forms. But one thing was wanting to this great sculptor—grace and expression; in this he was surpassed by his rival, Pythagoras, who introduced a softer style.

PYTHAGORAS.

Pythagoras was a native of Rhegium. He adopted the undulating line as the line of beauty, and first expressed the sinews and veins with accuracy. He erected the ideal of Apollo, in the position of an archer, who has just shot the serpent Python. This celebrated serpent sprung from the mud and stagnated waters which remained on the earth after the deluge of Deucalion. This monster abode in the vicinity of Delphi, and destroyed the people and cattle of the surrounding country. Apollo, on coming to Delphi, slew the serpent with his arrows; and, as it lay expiring, the exulting victor cried, "Now rot there on the man-feeding earth!" and hence, says the legend, the place and oracle received the name of Pytho. The Pythian Games were fabled to have been established in commemoration of this victory.

The Apollo Belvidere, which was found in the ruins of Actium, about twelve leagues from Rome, is supposed to be an imitation of the Pythian Apollo, by Pythagoras; and is esteemed one of the most sublime relics of ancient art.

THIRD PERIOD.

With Scopas and Praxiteles commenced a new era in the history of sculpture. The art was brought to its highest perfection—beauty being united with grace. The grand style was superseded by one of softer characteristics, while no less attention was paid to exactness and truth of form.

PRAXITELES.

The most probable opinion is, that Praxiteles was a native of Paros. In praising Praxiteles as an original inventor—as the discoverer of a new style—writers, very generally, have mistaken the influence exercised by his genius upon the progress and character of sculpture. Finding the highest sublimity in the more masculine graces of the art already reached—perceiving, also, that the taste of his age tended thitherward—he resolved to woo extensively the milder and gentler beauties of style. In this pursuit he attained eminent success. None ever more happily succeeded in uniting softness with force, or elegance and refinement with simplicity; his grace never degenerates into the affected, nor his delicacy into the artificial. He caught the delightful medium between the stern majesty which awes, and the beauty which merely seduces; between the external allurements of form, and the colder but loftier charms of intellectuality. Over his compositions he has thrown an expression, spiritual at once and sensuous; a voluptuousness and modesty which touch the most insensible, yet startle not the most retiring. The works which remain of this master, either in originals or in repetitions—the Faun; the Thespian Cupid, in the museum of the Capitol; the Apollo with a lizard, one of the most beautiful, as well as difficult specimens of antiquity—abundantly justify this character. He attained the perfect ideals of Diana and Bacchus. He formed the latter as a contrast to the Satyrs and Fauns, which have a rude and free expression; it was perpetual gayety personified, soft and tender, without being effeminate. The Diana of this artist expressed virgin modesty, with bold activity. Indeed he appears to have been the first, perhaps the sole master, who attained the true ideal on this subject, in the perfect union of yielding feminine grace with the dignity of intellectual expression. The group of Niobe is ascribed to this master. He reached the highest ideal of Eros or Cupid. The god of love was never represented by the ancients as an infant; the true infantile representation was not admitted until after the Christian era Eros always had the form of a boy approaching youth. His Venus of Cos and Cnidus are among his most celebrated works; the latter is probably the model of the Venus de Medicis. Nicomedes, of Bithynia, wished to purchase this admirable production of the chisel of Praxiteles, and actually offered to liquidate the debt of Cnidus, which was very considerable, if the citizens would cede it to him; but they refused to part with what they esteemed the glory of their city

SCOPAS.

The isle of Paros gave birth to Scopas, a sculptor in bronze and marble. This artist, assisted by his rivals Bryaxis, Timotheus, and Leochares, was employed in ornamenting the sepulchral monument, erected to the memory of her husband Mausolus, by queen Artemesia, and thence called Mausoleum. King Mausolus is said to have died in the year 353 B. C., and his wife was so disconsolate at the event that she perpetuated his memory by the erection of this magnificent monument, which became so famous as to be esteemed the seventh wonder of the world, and to give a generic name to all superb sepulchres. This edifice was, according to report, built by four different architects. Scopas erected the side which faced the east, Timotheus had the south, Leochares the west, and Bryaxis the north. Pythis was also employed in raising a pyramid over this stately monument, and the top was adorned by a chariot and four horses. The expenses of this edifice were immense, giving occasion to the philosopher Anaxagoras to exclaim, when he saw it, "How much money turned into stone!" This structure was nearly square; it was surrounded by thirty-six columns, and enriched by an immense number of sculptures. It was, according to Pliny, one hundred and eleven feet in circumference, and a hundred and forty feet high.

Scopas was employed also to contribute one of the thirty carved columns of the temple of Diana at Ephesus, the one which he executed being regarded as the most beautiful of all.

His most celebrated works are, his Furious Bacchante, (the head bending backward, united the highest beauty with Bacchanalian phrensy,) his Cupid, his Venus, and his group—the

Triumph of Achilles, whom Thetis is conducting, after his death, to the happy islands, in which the artist found an opportunity of introducing numberless Tritons, Nereids, and sea monsters in the most charming combinations. Many of his compositions were among the noblest ornaments of Rome in the days of Pliny.

FOURTH PERIOD.

Art could now only gain through grace and softness of execution, since the high ideal style was on the decline.

LYSIPPUS.

Lysippus, born at Sicyon, flourished about 324 B. C. He was at first a worker in brass, and then applied himself to the art of painting, until his talent and inclination led him to fix upon the profession of a sculptor. He is said to have been self-taught, and to have attained his excellence by studying nature alone. His talents were appreciated by his cotemporaries; the different cities of Greece were anxious to obtain his works, and Alexander is reported to have said that no one should paint him but Apelles, and no one represent him in bronze but Lysippus. He became a master of elevated portrait sculpture, and was particularly distinguished for his statues in bronze, which are said to have been superior to all other works of a similar kind. He introduced great improvements into his art, by making the head smaller, and giving the body a more easy and natural position, than was usual in the works of his predecessors. Pliny informs us that his statues were admired, among other things, for the beautiful manner in which the hair was executed. His reputation survived his death; many of his most valuable works were brought to Rome, in which city they were held in so much esteem, that Tiberius is said to have almost excited an insurrection by removing a statue of Lysippus, called Apoxyomenos, from the warm-baths of Agrippa to his own palace. Lysippus is said to have executed 610 statues, all of the greatest merit, many of which were colossal figures. Pliny, Pausanias, Strabo, and Vitruvius have presented long lists of his works; of which the most celebrated appear to have been several statues of Alexander the Great, executed at different periods of his life; a group of equestrian statues of the Greeks who fell at the battle of the Granicus; the Sun drawn in a chariot by four horses, at Rhodes; a colossal statue at Tarentum; a statue of Hercules at Alyzia, which was afterwards removed to Rome; and a statue of Opportunity, represented as a youth, with wings on his ancles, on the point of flying from the earth.

CHARES.

Chares was born at Lindus. He was a disciple of Lysippus, and celebrated as the maker of the Colossus at Rhodes. He was employed twelve years on this stupendous work. The statue was of brass, and dedicated to Apollo, the tutelary god of the Rhodians. It was upwards of one hundred feet in height; there were few persons who could encompass the thumb with their arms, and its fingers were larger than most statues. It was hollow, and in its cavities were large stones, placed there to counterbalance its weight, and render it steady on its pedestal. The Colossus is generally supposed to have stood with distended legs upon the two moles which formed the entrance of the harbour. As the city, however, had two harbours—the main one, and a second one much smaller, within which their fleets were secured, it seems more natural to suppose that this Colossus was placed at the entrance of the latter one, as the space between the legs at the base could not have greatly exceeded fifty feet; a space too narrow to be the entrance to the main harbour. There was a winding staircase within, reaching to the top of the statue, whence might be seen Syria and the ships that went to Egypt. It was erected 300 B. C., and, after having stood about fifty-six years, was thrown down by an earthquake, being broken off below the knees. In the year 672 of the Christian era, it was sold, according to Cedrenus, by the Saracens, who were masters of the island, to a Jewish merchant of Edessa, who loaded nine hundred camels with the brass.

AGASANDER.

Agasander and his sons Athenadorus and Polydorus, of Rhodes, produced the celebrated group of the Laocoon, about the time of Lysippus, according to the authority of some; others assign the reign of Titus. It represents Laocoon, a priest of Apollo, during the Trojan war. While offering a bullock to Neptune, accompanied by his two sons, two huge serpents issued from the sea and fastened upon his sons. While endeavouring to save them, Laocoon was himself wound in their folds, and the three were together crushed to death. The serpents were sent by Minerva, as a punishment to Laocoon for having dissuaded the Trojans from admitting into the city the fatal wooden horse which the Greeks had dedicated to Minerva.

The group represents the agonized father, and his youthful

sons, one on each side of him, writhing in the complicated folds of the serpents. Intense mental suffering is portrayed in the countenances, while the physical strength of all the three is evidently sinking under the irresistible power of the huge reptiles, wreathed round their exhausted limbs. One son, in whose side a serpent has fixed his deadly fangs, seems to be fainting; the other, not yet bitten, tries (and the futility of the attempt is faithfully shown) to disengage one foot from the serpent's embrace. The father, Laocoon himself, is mighty in his sufferings; every muscle is in extreme action, and his hands and feet are convulsed with painful energy, yet there is nothing frightful, disgusting, or contrary to beauty, in the countenance. Suffering is faithfully and strongly depicted there, but it is rather the exhibition of mental anguish than of the repulsive and undignified contortions of mere physical pain. The whole of this figure displays the most intimate knowledge of anatomy, and of outward form; the latter selected with discretion, and freed from any vulgarity of common individual nature. Indeed, the single figure of Laocoon may be fairly referred to, as one of the finest specimens existing of that combination of truth and beauty which is so essential to the production of perfect sculpture, and which alone can ensure for it lasting admiration. The youths are of a smaller standard than the proportion of the father—a liberty hardly justifiable, but taken probably with the view of heightening the effect of the principal figure. The right arm of Laocoon is a restoration. It is not certain what modern artist has the merit of this restoration, though it is thought that the arm it now bears was the plaster-model of Michael Angelo, who was charged with the task of adding a marble one, but left it unfinished in a fit of despair.

Gradually, Grecian art declined from its high excellence

The causes are obvious: the prevalence of luxury, and consequent corruption of morals; the internal changes and commotions, and the infringements upon civil liberty from the time of Alexander, and its final loss after the subjection of Greece to the Romans. There were, however, in this period, some skilful artists, as Arcesilaus and Pasitiles, who were led to Rome by the superior patronage that city afforded.

Had not the Ptolemies of Egypt and the Seleucidæ of Asia, shown themselves at this crisis the liberal patrons of art, Greek sculpture must have fallen, never to rise again. Under the successors of Alexander, in Egypt, Alexandria became a second Athens. The anatomical studies and dissections of Hierophilus and Eostratus in the Alexandrine school, introduced into the sculpture of this period a greater precision of anatomical detail, without injuring the breadth of the masses. As a proof of the number of Greek artists who flocked to that capital, and the splendid encouragement bestowed on art, it may be sufficient to allude to the magnificent pageant and cavalcade of Ptolemy Philadelphus, in which hundreds of statues were borne in the procession. In a large tent, prepared for the occasion, were to be seen the representations of animals of all kinds, executed by the most celebrated masters. To the same era may be referred the works of Grecian art, in Egyptian basalt and porphyry, which, from the specimens and fragments that remain, must have been in the finest style of art. The Seleucidæ of Asia were no less munificent; but whether from the remote situation of the city of Seleucia, or other causes, the arts never reached the same excellence as in Egypt. The epoch of art closed, both in Egypt and Asia, about the 124th Olympiad.

Roman Sculpture.

On the subjugation of the Greeks, their arts passed, as it were, into the hands of the Romans, by whom, however, sculpture was honoured and furnished with opportunities for its employment, rather than actually acquired and practised. In the early periods of the republic, distinguished merit was rewarded with statues, and the mythological system of worship afforded constant scope for the exercise of talent in that line. After the second Punic war, a great number of splendid works of sculpture were brought to Rome from captured cities—Syracuse, Capua, Corinth, and Carthage ; also from Etruria and Egypt. Greece abounded in the treasures of art, handed down to her from the renowned ages ; her temples and palaces were crowded with inestimable works, and the new rulers found the transfer of such productions a more expeditious and less hazardous process of acquisition than the tardy alternative of requiring original productions from cotemporary artists. These, therefore, being driven to mere expedients for a livelihood ; inferior classes of art became predominant. Among the artists who practised sculpture in Rome, we may mention Zenodorus, who, having cast a colossal Minerva in Cisalpine Gaul, was called to Rome by Nero, to make a colossal statue of himself, 110 feet high ; which was dedicated to the sun on the downfall of that emperor. The four beautiful horses of brass above the chief entrance of the church of St. Mark, at Venice, were also cast during the reign of this tyrant. One of the most perfect statues of the age of Hadrian, is Antinous, who, having cast himself into the Nile to fulfil an oracle and propitiate the gods in favour of Hadrian, the emperor, to testify his gratitude, erected numerous statues to his memory, and built a city, which he named after his favourite.

With the advancement of wealth, the Romans devoted greater and greater expense to the ornamenting of their temples, their public and private buildings, their gardens, and their grounds.

The Capitolium, (particularly the temple of Jupiter, included in it,) the Comitium, and the Rostra, were, in a special manner, adorned with statues. Inspectors were appointed, whose business it was to guard the edifices thus ornamented from injury and plunder, a duty afterwards assigned to a particular magistrate.

One great reason why the arts never attained the same high standard in Rome which they had reached in Greece, was, undoubtedly, because in Greece, the artist was not only incited to the utmost pitch of inspiration by the enthusiastic applause of his countrymen, and, above all, by the priceless crown of bay, the high award of the Olympic tribunal, that passed not as the jewelled diadem of kings, from head to head, but was hung up in the temple of Fame, never to fade, never to be alienated—was not only incited to exalted effort by the sympathy and admiration which his works elicited, but he was sustained and encouraged by the high personal esteem and appreciation which his talents procured him—by the influence and station which success brought him as a man, as well as an artist. The noblest names of Greece, were rendered brighter by the fame acquired in imbodying the refined conceptions of the mind in the workmanship of the hand; while in Rome, the artist was merged in his works, and these were mere appendages of pomp and luxury; hence few names of Roman artists have come down to us, while the galaxy of Grecian art is bright with stars of undying lustre.

In the last half of the second century after Christ, there was an obvious decline of good taste in sculpture, and soon after the middle of the third, the art was wholly prostrated, through political disasters, and other conspiring influences. Esteem for the art and its productions was lost, and many unfavourable circumstances happened, so that a number of the most valuable works of sculpture were mutilated, buried in ruins, or entirely destroyed. This resulted partly from the warlike character of the tribes that invaded Italy, partly from the avarice and rapacity of some of the later Roman emperors, from frequent earthquakes, or conflagrations, from the repeated capture and sacking of Rome and Constantinople, and from a mistaken zeal of many Christians against the preservation of heathen monuments. Notwithstanding all this ruin, many monuments of sculpture, and some of them of high excellence, have been preserved. Since the revival of the fine arts, which commenced in Italy, the last seat of ancient sculpture, these monuments have been diligently sought out, collected, and described. Yet most of them have suffered from time or accident, and very few are wholly free from mutilations.

Modern Sculpture.

The cathedral of Pisa, built by Buskettus, or Buschetto, was the second remarkable sacred edifice (St. Mark's in Venice being the first) raised after the destruction of the Roman power in Italy. Pisa has received the honour of being allowed by posterity to have taken the lead in restoring art; and, indeed, the traveller, on entering the city gates, is astonished by a scene of architectural magnificence and singularity not to be equalled in the world. Four stupendous structures of fine marble in one group: the solemn cathedral, in the general parallelogram of its form, resembling an ancient temple, which unites and simplifies the arched divisions of its exterior; the Baptistry, a circular building surrounded by arches and columns, crowned with niches, statues, and pinnacles, rising to an apex in the centre, terminated by a statue of the Baptist; the Leaning Tower, (which is thirteen feet out of the perpendicular,) a most elegant cylinder, raised by eight rows of columns surmounting each other, and surrounding a staircase; the Cemetery, a long square corridor of elegant pointed architecture, 400 by 200 feet, containing the ingenious works of the improvers of painting, down to the sixteenth century.

To describe the numerous works of painting and sculpture with which the restorers of art laboured to adorn these magnificent edifices during 500 years, would require more space than can be here allowed.

It is not unlikely that Buschetto, who built the cathedral of Pisa in the eleventh century, established the schools of architecture and sculpture at the same time in that city; and it is acknowledged by the Pisan writers, that there were sculptors in that city before Nicolo and Giovanni da Pisa, whose works became famous throughout Italy in the middle of the thirteenth century. They improved sculpture by the study of the antique bassi-relievi in the Campo-Santo. In their own works the compositions are simple and intelligible; the female figures are frequently elegant in their movements and their drapery. In them are occasionally seen an originality of idea, and a force of thought, seldom met with when schools of design are in the habit of copying from each other.

Andrea Ugolino Pisano, from the school of these sculptors,

designed and executed in bronze the oldest gate of the Baptistry in Florence, the compartments of which represent the life of St. John. The compositions have a Gothic and simple grandeur. He also executed some statues in marble, but they were rather inferior to the productions of Nicolo and Giovanni da Pisa.

The next distinguished restorer of sculpture was DONATELLO the Florentine. Some of his works, both in bronze and marble, might be placed beside the best productions of ancient Greece without discredit. In the Opera del Duomo of Santa Maria del Fiore, the cathedral of Florence, there is an alto-relievo of two singing boys, of extraordinary beauty in sentiment, character, drawing, and drapery. In the gallery of Florence there is a bronze statue of a lad, (perhaps a Mercury,) so delicately proportioned, and so perfectly natural, that it is excelled only by the best works of antiquity, in certain exquisite graces peculiar to the finest monuments in Greece.

The cotemporaries of this artist are not to be forgotten, although perhaps, on the whole, inferior sculptors to him. BRUMNELLESCHI executed a crucifix in wood, now in the church of Santa Maria Novella, which represents the suffering Saviour in a manner not to be looked upon with indifference. He after wards engaged in architecture, and built the much-admired church of Santa Maria del Fiore.

LORENZC GHIBERTI, the other illustrious cotemporary of Donatello, has immortalized his memory by the bronze gates of St. John's Baptistry, called the Gates of Paradise from Michael Angelo's compliment. This is a beautiful and laborious work. But the criticism of Sir Joshua Reynolds, was one indisputable proof of that great man's judgment in the sister arts. His observation amounted to this, that "Ghiberti's landscape and buildings occupied so large a portion of the compartments, that the figures remained but secondary objects, entirely contrary to the principles of the ancients."

At the close of the fourteenth century, the celebrated assemblage of artists convened at Florence to compete for the designs of the two remaining bronze gates of the Baptistry. Among this numerous assemblage, six candidates were acknowledged to surpass all the rest; and the competition was limited to them A year was assigned to them for completing their task, during which they were maintained by the state in secret, and apart from each other. They were required to produce complete panels, finished in all the details, of the same size as the originals—the subject being the sacrifice of Abraham. For the purpose of examining and deciding upon these works, a second assembly of the ablest artists was convened at Florence, where, after a long and impartial deliberation, Lorenzo Ghiberti, a youth of twenty-three years of age, was declared the successful candidate. The execution of these celebrated doors, worthy, as Michael Angelo said, of being the gates of Paradise, occupied forty years of his life. His labours were justly appreciated and nobly rewarded by his fellow-citizens, who, besides granting whatever he demanded, assigned him a portion of land, and elected him Gonfaloniere, or chief magistrate of the state. His bust was afterwards placed in the Baptistry.

Towards the middle of the fifteenth century many artists of high reputation might be enumerated. The style of this period is remarkable for simplicity, chaste fidelity to nature, and sweetness of expression, as well as an acquaintance with the antique. The object was not so much to produce ideal beauty, however, as a faithful imitation of individual nature.

The sixteenth century commenced under the most favourable auspices for art, whether we consider the moral, religious, or political state of Italy. The arts were patronized by both public and private munificence, to a degree which has never since been practised. At the beginning of this century, the versatile genius of MICHAEL ANGELO shone forth, and challenging boundless admiration, overawed criticism and rendered competition hopeless. He commenced his career by various works of sculpture, a Sleeping Cupid, a Bacchus, and a young Faun, the colossal David, and a group of Pieta, or a sitting Madonna bearing the dead Christ on her knees, which raised his fame above all his modern predecessors in the art.

The character of Michael Angelo's sculpture is lofty and original, although we must acknowledge it has been criticised with severity, because it rarely possesses the chaste simplicity of Grecian art. Yet the pensive sitting figure of Lorenzo di Medicis, in the Medici chapel, is not without this charm; and the Madonna and Child, on the north side of the same chapel is simple, and is endowed with a sentiment of maternal affection, never found in the Greek sculpture, but frequently in the works of this artist, particularly in his paintings, and that of the most tender kind.

The recumbent statues in the monument of Julian di Medicis, in the same chapel, of Daybreak or Dawn, and Night, are grand and mysterious: the characters and forms bespeak the same mighty mind and hand evident throughout the ceiling of the Sistine chapel, and the Last Judgment.

His bodily powers continued far beyond the usual date of human life, and his diligence attained to so much the greater perfection in the principles of the art. Anatomy—the motion and perspective of the figure—the complication, grandeur, and harmony of his grouping, with the advantages and facility of execution in painting and sculpture, besides his mathematical and mechanical attainments in architecture and building, which, together with the many and prodigious works he accomplished, demonstrate how greatly he contributed to the restoration of art.

After the works of the great man just mentioned, GIOVANNI DI BOLOGNA's Venus coming from the Bath, both standing and kneeling, are remarkable for delicacy and grace. His Mercury rising to Fly, is energetic and original. BENVENUTO CELLINI next deserves praise for his group of Perseus and Medusa, but the succeeding sculptors in the seventeenth century, must be looked on as having debased, rather than contributed to the restoration of art. Even BERNINI, whose reputation was so great in his time, can be praised only for his Apollo and Daphne, and for the ease and nature of his portraits. His larger works are remarkable for presuming airs, affected grace, and unmeaning flutter. He was of opinion, that to excel in the arts, one must rise above all rules, and create a manner peculiar to one's self. The influence of his style was transient.

With the exception of ALGARDI of Bologna, and FIAMMINGO —who in an age of imitation and corruption, were remarkable for their originality and natural style—the prevailing taste of this school, was to produce effect, by flying drapery, striking and affected attitudes, and strength, devoid of nature and science, till the art absolutely sank into the conventional and mechanical trade of marble-cutters, whose only occupation was restoring and patching antiques, or occasionally making a replication of some favourite statue, and whose only merit was in their bold and skilful use of the chisel. Nature was entirely overlooked. Their highest attainment was a cold and lifeless imitation of the antique.

CANOVA.

Antonio Canova, marquis of Ischia, may be considered as the restorer of the graceful and lovely style, and the founder of a new school, as far as respects softness and delicacy of execution, and excellent handling of the marble. He was born, November, 1757, at Possagno, in the Venetian territory. When a boy of twelve years, he displayed his talents by modelling a lion in butter, which was placed on the table of Signor Falieri, who was so pleased with his promising genius, that he took him under his protection, and eventually placed him with Giuseppe Bernardi, called Il Torretto, an eminent sculptor of Venice. He there gained several prizes, and excited expectations which he more than equalled in the sequel. In his twenty-third year he went to reside at Rome.

The first three years of his residence in this city was devoted to a profound and severe study of the antique, without losing sight of anatomy and living nature. He saw that by far the greatest proportion of the Grecian statuary, though preserving a generic character of classic grandeur and simplicity, was more or less destitute of a certain life, flesh, softness, and finish, only to be found in the Torso, the Dying Gladiator, the Venus di Medici, the Satyr of Praxiteles, the Mercury of the Belvidere, and others of a high class. This discrepancy he rightly ascribed to the greater number being copies, or copies of copies, or the production of second-rate artists. Convinced that the style of sculpture, as then practised, was false and corrupt, he resolved to strike out a new path of his own, founded on an assiduous study of nature and the true principles of the antique, as the only means of attaining excellence and originality.

The first group he executed in conformity with the new light he had received, was Theseus, the conqueror of the Minotaur, cut out of a mass of marble presented to him by his kind and considerate patron, the Venetian ambassador. He soon after executed the group of Cupid and Psyche, in which he first displayed his own peculiar style, of which softness and loveliness are the striking characteristics. The figures are exceedingly delicate and graceful; yet there is no point of view from which the countenances of both can be seen at the same time; besides, the wings of Cupid project disagreeably from the group, which presents too many interstices. A repentant Magdalen, of the natural size, belongs to the works in marble, in which he has carried the expression of the melting and the soft to the highest degree. The relaxing effect of repentance is expressed with great truth.

His Hebe is a delightful figure. In an easy and animated attitude, the smiling goddess of youth hovers upon a cloud, pouring nectar, with her right hand, into a bowl, which she holds with her left. Both vessels, as well as the coronet of Hebe, and the edges of her garments, are gilt. Canova is fond of a variety of material in his statues, and often attempts to give them the effect of pictures. This and the preceding statue he repeated.

Between 1792 and 1799, he amused his leisure hours in resuming painting, an art in which he had acquired considerable proficency when at Venice, under his early friend, Mingardi. Strangely enough, he was more of a colourist than of a correct designer. In 1802 he went to Paris, in consequence of an invitation from the Emperor Napoleon, to model his portrait, from which he executed statues in bronze and marble, of colossal dimensions. It is impossible to conceive of a more characteristic likeness, exhibiting at the same time the ideal character of the ancient heroic style. Among the later works of this artist, are a Washington of colossal size, in a sitting attitude, now in the State House at Raleigh, the capital of North Carolina.

He again visited Vienna, for the purpose of placing his celebrated sepulchral monument of the Duchess Maria Christina, which attracted such admiration, that he was prevailed upon, by the court, to transport his Theseus and Minotaur to Vienna, instead of Milan, its original destination. From 1800 to 1814, the following are the chief works he produced: Perseus, the size of the Apollo of the Vatican; a colossal statue of Ferdinand IV.; a monument of Alfieri; two statues of Paris; statue of Hector; model for the equestrian statue of Napoleon; model of a monument to Lord Nelson; cenotaph of count de Sousa; cenotaph of Senator Falieri; cenotaph of the prince of Orange; colossal model of a horse; dancing nymphs, with cymbals; dancing nymphs, with garlands; sitting statue of the Empress Maria Louisa, with the attribute of Concord; colossal bust of himself; statue of Peace, for Count Romanoff; busts of Murat, king of Naples, and his queen; the Graces, a group in marble, ordered by the Empress Josephine, and completed for Prince Eugene; and a replica for the duke of Bedford.

He resolved, at his own cost, to raise a colossal statue to Religion, in honour of the return of Pope Pius VI. to Rome. The model was completed, the marble laid down, and the chisel in readiness. All that was required, was that a proper site should be assigned for it. But envy, jealousy, and rival interests having intervened, it was never granted; nor was the statue ever executed. Disappointed in this object, he resolved to consecrate his whole fortune, energies, and declining years to the service of religion, by raising a temple at Possagno, that should unite the beauties of the Pantheon and the Parthenon, in which the colossal statue might be placed, besides other decorations, sculptural and pictorial. After some delay, the foundation of the building was laid, on the 8th of July, 1819. in presence of Canova, with much festivity, and amid the joyful acclamations of the inhabitants and villagers of the district. Finding, however, that the cost would be much greater than he had contemplated, and still determined to accomplish the object of his pious wishes, he again eagerly undertook new commissions. Such exertions of mind and body, at an advanced age, with a shattered frame and diminished strength, soon undermined a constitution naturally delicate, and accelerated the final catastrophe. During this resumption of his labours, some of the finest of his works were produced : the group of Mars and Venus ; the statue of Washington ; the colossal figure of Pius VI. ; the Pieta ; the St. John ; the Recumbant Magdalen ; the model of a colossal horse for an equestrian statue of Ferdinand of Naples. In August, 1821, he again resumed the brush and palette, to retouch the large altar-piece which he had painted in 1797, for the church of Possagno. He died on the 13th of October, 1822, in the sixty-fifth year of his age.

Canova made his models first of a small size, in wax ; then in clay, of the size the work was to be ; from this a cast was taken in plaster. The first shaping of the marble he left to skilful workmen.

Modest and unassuming, yet candid and independent ; affectionate, generous, religious, moral, and patriotic, Canova was beloved and respected by all. He was not only disinterested, but animated by the noblest benevolence ; he delighted in assisting young artists, and established prizes for the encouragement of the arts.

THORWALDSEN.

Albert Thorwaldsen was the son of a stone-cutter and carver. He was born at Copenhagen, in 1772. His father, observing his talents, placed him at a school of design, at Copenhagen, where he gained the first prize, which enabled him to travel for four years in Italy.

Thorwaldsen has strikingly accomplished the task of representing Christian subjects in sculpture. His professional career, which included nearly half a century, was marked by innumerable works—statues, groups, relievi, and busts—the result of his fertile genius and imagination, and his unceasing ardour and perseverance. In character he was highly estimable—modest, gentle, and unaffected. His most celebrated works are: the colossal Swiss Lion, cut out of a mass of rock near Berne, between sixty and eighty feet in height; the Poniatowski Monument, in the great square of Warsaw, consisting of an equestrian composition combined with a fountain; the Graces, models of calm, poetic beauty, with nothing of the modern and piquant, from which even Canova's Graces are not quite free. A Hebe, an Adonis, a Venus. The latter makes a near approach to the Venus de Medici. Among his relievi, the most esteemed are: the Triumph of Alexander; Priam asking back the Body of Hector; Power; Wisdom; Health; Justice; Day and Night. His last great national work was the sculptural decoration of the cathedral of Copenhagen, comprehending on the pediment, St. John preaching in the Desert; on the frieze, Christ bearing the Cross; in the vestibule, the Four Greater Prophets; around the altar, the Twelve Apostles, with the Redeemer ascending in the midst. In all his works—whether after the modern or antique—

whether the smallest medallion or the largest colossal figure—he is characterized by a wonderful creative genius; by a power, energy, and breadth, which at once fix the attention. In some of these qualities, he forms a decided contrast to the style of Canova. Thorwaldsen is, unquestionably, more masculine and powerful in conception and execution; but, perhaps, he has gone to the other extreme in coldness and harshness. Canova is the type of the effeminate and voluptuous region of Italy; the other embodies the more stern and severe character of Scandinavia. While the works of Canova are distinguished for loveliness and grace, those of Thorwaldsen exhibit a calm conception of true beauty; a simplicity and truth which seem caught from the ideals on which the works of nature are formed, and which belong only to genius of the highest order.

Whether the art will advance or retrograde at Rome under their successors, is a question of difficult solution. But as regards Rome, the state of sculpture in that city may be said to be more European than Italian; inasmuch as sculptors, from all nations, not only resort to it for study, as the emporium of ancient art, but many of them establish themselves in that capitol, or at least regard it, as their head-quarters.

French Sculpture.

Of the sepulchral and ornamental sculptures in France in the middle ages, including that of the thirteenth, fourteenth, and fifteenth centuries, France possessed many splendid and interesting specimens, a great proportion of which fell a sacrifice to the demoniacal fury of the revolution. Under the long reign of Louis XIV. the fine arts, in common with literature, received munificent encouragement. During this Augustan age of French art, including the commencement of the eighteenth century, many sculptors of eminence may be enumerated; Gerardon, Saracin Puget, Guillain le Gros, the two Coustons, &c. And it is but justice to admit, that, however corrupt when compared with purer models, they surpassed their degraded cotemporaries of Italy. Louis XVI. showed a disposition to patronize them, had he not been overwhelmed by the troubles of the revolution. The only sculptors of this period worthy of being recorded, are Bouchardon and Pigal. Napoleon, both as first consul and emperor, was a vigorous and liberal patron of the fine arts.

The reign of Louis Philippe was an era in French art. No sooner was he established on the throne, than art, in all its branches received a powerful impulse, from his munificent encouragement and enlightened taste.

If French sculpture, therefore, has not improved, it is not for want of national and extensive encouragement. That it has, however, made considerable advancement within the last ten years, cannot be denied, in spite of the severe and often unjust censure of many of their own journals.

German Sculpture.

Within the last thirty years, sculpture in Germany, under the enlightened patronage of the kings of Bavaria and Prussia, has been pursued with enthusiasm and success.

The most distinguished sculptors are Dannecker, of Stuttgart Rauch and Tieck of Berlin, Schwanthaler, Eberhardt, Bandel, Kirkmayer, Mayer of Munich, Ratchel of Dresden, and Imhoff of Cologne. Dannecker's principal works are his Ariadne and Panther, his Cupid and Psyche, his celebrated statue of Christ, and his Mausoleum of Zeppeline. He is much celebrated for his busts. Rauch was the first German sculptor, who, after a lapse of two hundred and fifty years, attempted to revive the taste of the middle ages, as manifested in the works of Albert Durer. Following neither the antique, nor the style of Canova, nor Thorwaldsen, he has revived the old German style of Fischer, improving and adapting it to the present state and intellectual progress of society. He executed a statue of the late queen of Prussia, two colossal busts of Blucher, in bronze, besides many busts and monumental statues to field-marshals, generals, &c. In all of which, he distinguished himself. Tieck's productions are very numerous, both in monumental works and busts. He has been engaged for many years on the new theatre, at Berlin; including a colossal Apollo, a Pegasus, colossal Muses, &c. The sitting statue of Iffland the great actor, is reckoned his chef-d'œuvre. Schwanthaler in some of his works, has followed in the footsteps of the great Prussian sculptor. Though influenced more or less by Thorwaldsen and the antique, he is far from being a slavish imitator. He has executed a large portion of the sculptural decorations of Munich, including those of the Walhalla. Every public edifice in the German capitals is enriched with sculpture; hence, a more extended encouragement, a more ample scope is given for its productions.

British Sculpture.

During the occupation of Britain by the Romans, their numerous temples, baths, and other public buildings, which overspread the southern part of the island, were decorated with a profusion of statues, both in marble and bronze. There is every reason to believe, that the Britons were early initiated into the practice of these arts, which they retained for nearly a century after the final departure of their Roman masters. The Saxons, like all idolatrous nations, were in the custom of carving images of their gods in wood, and probably in stone, in a rude and barbarous manner. When converted to Christianity, in the seventh century, they destroyed their idols and abandoned the art as impious. But no sooner were images of saints introduced from the continent, than the increased demand gradually brought about a revival of the art.

Sepulchral sculpture was first introduced at the Norman conquest; the figures of the deceased being generally cut in low relief, on the tombstones. The reign of Henry III. is remarkable for the improvement of architectural sculpture. One of the most interesting examples is the cathedral of Wells, rebuilt by Bishop Joceline, in the beginning of the thirteenth century, and finished in 1242. The sculpture, consisting both of statues and relievi, embraces subjects from the Holy Scriptures; the Creation; Acts of the Apostles; Life of our Saviour, &c., all executed in a style of surprising skill and truth, considering the disadvantages and the ignorance of the times. It is more than probable, that most of the artists employed on this noble building were English, because the tombs of Edward the Confessor and Henry III. executed by Italian artists, are different both in style and architecture. The reign of Edward III. introduced a new species of monument, the Norman Cross, of beautiful Gothic architecture, richly decorated with sculpture, and first raised in honour of his queen, Eleanor, who accompanied him to the Holy Land.

The reign of Henry VI. produced many monumental statues of great interest: for instance, the monument of Richard Beauchamp, earl of Warwick, in St. Mary's church, Warwick; which, in Flaxman's opinion, is excelled by nothing in Italy, of the same kind, at that period, (1439,) though Donatello and Ghiberti were then living. The Lady Chapel of Henry VII., is adorned with no less than three thousand statues.

During the long interval which succeeded the fall of the Gothic sculpture—extending nearly to the middle of the eighteenth century—sculpture in England, with the subordinate departments in wood and stone, was almost exclusively exercised by foreigners. The English native school, commencing with Grinling, Gibbons, and Wilton, has produced Banks, Newton, Bacon, Nollekens, Flaxman, Westmacott, Chantrey, Baily, Wyatt, Gibson, and other eminent artists. To the genius, fine taste, and classical conceptions of Flaxman, England chiefly owes the regeneration of sculpture.

"Within the last twenty years," says Cleghorn, "a taste for sculpture has been rapidly increasing in Scotland: several young artists of high promise having enthusiastically devoted themselves to the profession; most of whom have finished their studies at Rome—Messrs. CAMPBELL, LAWRENCE, MACDONALD, SCOWLER, STEEL, CALDER MARSHALL, SIMSON, HANDYSIDE, RITCHIE, PARK, &c. Besides busts and whole figures, they have produced monumental and poetical works of great merit.

"Scotland may now boast of having a native school of sculpture, imbued with an ardent love of the art; and a generous emulation, in spite of every discouragement, to reach excellence in the elevated branches. Sculpture, indeed, seems congenial to Scottish genius. Even the works of untutored and self-taught artists, such as THOM and FORREST, show both genius and originality. The seed is now sown. Whether the public will continue to foster the tender plant, and enable it to take root in the soil, remains to be decided. It is a bitter mockery to patronize academies and institutions for the advancement of Scottish art, if no scope or opportunity be afforded to artists for the exercise of their powers. It is not the modelling of a few busts, to be stuck up in an exhibition-room, that will enable the art to flourish. Unless encouragement be afforded, both by government and public bodies, it must again relapse into its former degradation. A taste for the fine arts is no plant of the desert, that will spring up unheeded, and spread its blossoms where there are none to enjoy its fragrance; nor a sturdy weed, that can struggle into vigour through rubbish and neglect; it is a plant whose seeds will remain inert until called into life by culture, and will spread into luxuriance exactly in proportion to the care taken of it."

NOLLEKENS.

Joseph Nollekens was born in London, in the year 1757. At the age of 23 he made his way to Italy. After ten years' profitable study at Rome, he returned to London, and resolved to commence on his own account. His long residence among the great works of art prepared many to expect much from him; the busts of Sterne and Garrick had reached his country before him; and he no sooner opened his doors than orders came in abundance. His chief strength lay in bust sculpture, and in this he was successful beyond all his predecessors. His studio became a kind of fashionable lounge for those who thought their heads of importance, either to their friends or their country.

The claims of Nollekens to distinction are three-fold: bust sculpture, monumental sculpture, and poetic sculpture. He attained to eminence in all—and to lasting fame, perhaps, only in the first. The chief attraction about his hundred busts—for that number and more he made, besides many duplicates—was ease and simplicity; the chief defect is, want of dignity and sentiment. The monumental sculptures of Nollekens are in number upwards of seventy, varying in magnificence according to the wealth or taste of the employers. There are among them single statues, such as those of Pitt and Rockingham, which merit notice, because of the persons whom they represent; and there are monuments, such as that of Mrs. Howard, which dwell in our hearts from their nature and pathos. This is a work of great beauty both in design and execution. Such a touching work in a church has the effect of a sermon. The cold serene loveliness of the mother, the natural beauty of the hapless child, and the allegorical monitress, Religion, pointing to the abode of the blessed, appeal to every heart, and touch the meanest understanding.

Nollekens produced some twenty statues and groups, five Venuses, two Junos, Cupid and Psyche, &c., &c. On these he founded his chief hopes of future fame, and he considered them with the care, and wrought upon them with the diligence, of one resolved to trust to no hasty effort in a matter concerning futurity. But his utter ignorance of classic lore could not fail to injure his works of this order. He saw, for example, but half, and less, when he saw only the Venus de Medicis—he ought to have seen the goddess breathing of Olympus, with her inspiring cestus on, soothing Helen to love, when Paris was at hand; or bearing Æneas, her beloved son, wounded and bleeding, from the tumult of battle, when assaulted by Diomed. He saw none of those glorious sights—he wanted that high genius which can render marble a diviner thing than what is present in models and fragments; he could fashion a form coldly and mechanically correct, but he was unable to make it breathe of rapture and of heaven. Of all his works, he himself preferred the Venus anointing her hair. But a beautiful form will not do alone—it must have the help of higher qualities. The Queen of Love is dropping incense upon her tresses, and looking aside; every one perceives that the action requires the assistance of the eye, and the mistake mars the beauty of the whole statue; the workmanship, however, is very fine. Nollekens reached the age of eighty-six and died in 1823.

JOHN FLAXMAN.

This excellent man, and admirable artist, was born in 1755, in the city of York, where his father at that time resided, but which he quitted while his son was yet an infant. He very soon gave indications of that observation and love for the works of art, which distinguished him in maturer life. One of the first instances was shown on the coronation day of his Majesty George the Third. His father was going to see the procession, and the child begged earnestly that he would bring him one of the medals which were thrown to the populace; he was not so fortunate as to get one; but on his way home, happening to find a plated button bearing the stamp of a horse and jockey, rather than wholly disappoint the child, who was then in a very precarious state of health, he ventured, though unwillingly, to deceive him, and gave him the button. The young virtuoso took it and was thankful, but remarked, it was a very odd device for a coronation medal. He was then five years old; at this age he was fond of examining the seals of every watch he saw, and always kept a piece of soft wax ready to take an impression of any which pleased him

While yet a child, he made a great number of small models, in plaster, wax, and clay; some of which are still preserved, and have considerable merit. At the age of eleven years and five months, he gained his first prize from the Society for the Encouragement of Arts, which was the silver palette. At thirteen he had another, and the following year was admitted a student at the Royal Academy, then newly established, and the same year received their silver medal.

One of his most admired works, previous to his going to Italy, was a beautiful group of Venus and Cupid, which was executed for Mr. Knight, of Portland-place; another was a monument in Gloucester cathedral, to the memory of Mrs. Morley, who, with her infant, died at sea; the mother and child are rising from the waves, and are received by descending angels. It is an exquisite thing, full of that more than mortal beauty so proper to the subject, and at the same time affecting, from the sentiment and expression of the composition.

In 1787, he resolved to study in Italy, and went, accompanied by his amiable and accomplished wife, intending to be absent two years. But when the time had expired, he found that a large group which he had undertaken for Lord Bristol, would require some time longer at Rome; and one engagement succeeded another, until his absence was extended to seven years.

Throughout this interesting journey, as well as during his residence in Rome, Mr. Flaxman's application was incessant. Whether he was drawing from the antique, or making studies from the living groups and figures abounding in the venerable city and its environs, each object, animate and inanimate, was to him beautiful or noble, and all inspiring. No day was lost, and, except his health and strength failed, no hour of the day was suffered to pass without some improvement.

Perhaps the most striking family monument ever executed by Mr. Flaxman, was to the family of Sir Francis Baring, in Micheldever church, Hants. It consists of three distinct parts, making an extremely beautiful whole. In the centre is a sitting figure of Resignation, inscribed, "Thy will be done" On each side is a very fine alto-relievo, also from the Lord's Prayer; the subject of one, "Thy kingdom come;" the other, "Deliver us from evil." The tranquil piety of expression in the single figure is finely contrasted with the terrific struggle on the one hand, and the extatic joyfulness of the female, who is assisted in rising by angelic beings, on the other.

Mr. Flaxman's grandest work in England, is the group of the Archangel Michael and Satan, for the earl of Egremont. This was one of the last productions of the sculptor, and is a work which in after-ages will be a glory to the nation, to the memory of the artist, and the name of the truly noble proprietor, who, besides this group, has a Pastoral Apollo, the size of life, the grace and beauty of which are admirable.

It is not possible to give a list of all the sculpture of Mr. Flaxman; those above enumerated were selected as having most interest. He died in 1826.

"Flaxman not only supported the purity of sculpture," says Westmacott, "but carried us within the dominion of poetry, and taught us its value in art. He boldly passed the barrier which had so long encircled sculpture, and walked freely into the regions of invention. His admiration of simplicity, made him regard it, in whatever age or examples he discovered it, and gave a general character of originality to his own works, but which, it must not be denied, sometimes carried him into too close a resemblance of the productions of the earlier revivers of the art.

"But the faults which may be imputed to him, are indeed no others than the excess of great and acknowledged beauties; such as a poetical imagination, a devoted admiration of purity, and a warm and enthusiastic genius inspire.

"No modern sculptor has entered so deeply into the recesses of ancient art, as Flaxman. His style was founded on their principles, combined with the simplicity of the Pisani, and others, of the fourteenth century, whilst that of Canova was a union of the ideal with nature. The one attracts us by the originality and sweetness of his invention, the other delights us with a delicacy and beauty peculiar to himself. Execution was with Flaxman subservient to invention, while Canova suffered invention to be subordinate, and seduces us by the luxuriance of execution. Each equally felt what belonged to the dignity of art; simple in their arrangements, sparing in ornament, so that the eye could not be distracted by the pomp of extraneous or unnecessary matter."

THOMAS BANKS.

Thomas Banks* was born in 1745. At the age of fifteen he was placed under Mr. Barlow, an ornament carver. Young Banks, by means of his acquaintance with the pupils of Mr. Scheemaker, the sculptor, obtained a sight of the studies, and was so struck with the collection of models and casts, that he determined to become a sculptor also, and notwithstanding that he was constantly employed from six o'clock in the morning till eight at night, for Mr. Barlow, such was his enthusiasm that, having obtained permission, he drew or modelled in Mr. Scheemaker's study every evening, from eight till ten or eleven. Having completed his time with Mr. Barlow; at the age of twenty-three he began his studies from the life, at the Academy, in St. Martin's-lane, and his determination was strengthened by the premiums offered by the Society for the Encouragement of Art. Three of these rewards he obtained—for a basso-relievo of the death of Epaminondas, in Portland stone; another of Hector's body redeemed, in marble; and a figure of Prometheus with the vulture, in clay, the size of life; as far as memory may be depended on, this figure was boldly conceived, the composition was harmonious and compact, the character was natural, and, on the whole, it was a fair earnest of his future productions.

In 1770 he received the gold medal of the Royal Academy for a basso-relievo of the flight of Proserpine, and, in consequence, was sent to Rome, at the expense of the Academy, in 1772. He

* From Flaxman's Lectures.

studied in Italy seven years, three on the Academy's account, and four years on his own.

Previous to the Reformation, although Italian artists were employed in ornamenting churches and tombs, yet in the old histories, records, and contracts of public buildings, there are abundant names of English painters and sculptors, who appear to have been considered able masters in their time, perhaps not inferior to their Italian fellow-workmen. But after Henry the Eighth's separation from the Church of Rome, Elizabeth, proceeding in the Reformation, destroyed the pictures and images in the churches; strictly forbidding any thing of the kind to be admitted in future, under the severest penalties, as being Romish and idolatrous. This entirely prevented the exercise of historical painting or sculpture in England; at the very time Raphael and Michael Angelo had brought those arts into the highest estimation on the Continent. And the rebellion in 1643 completed what the Reformation had begun.

From this time, and from these causes, we scarcely hear of any attempt at historical art by an Englishman, until it was again called forth by the benign influence of George III.

Thus, we have seen the nobler efforts of painting and sculpture driven out of England by reforming violence and fury; sculpture reduced to the narrow limits of monument-making, and by these means degraded to a sort of trade.

Such was the low state of the arts when Mr. Banks began his studies, which, though not regular under any sculptor, were attended with some peculiar advantages. He was instructed in the principles of architecture, and practised drawing under his father, who was an architect; this enabled him soon to form a correct taste in that art, and displayed itself in the beauty and propriety of his architectural forms, in the works he has left;

it besides taught him how to introduce and combine sculpture with architecture, advantageously to both. Being placed under an ornament carver, gave him a facility in his own ornamental sculpture, which may be observed in some flat foliage on Dr. Watts' monument in Westminster Abbey. Another advantage, and, perhaps, not the least, was, that having his opinions unbiased from the sculptors of that time, he escaped being tinctured with the predominant manners of their works. He studied nature diligently for himself, and copied the antique to form his taste; his constant attention to the Admiranda and Stuart's Athens, had initiated him in the Greek style and composition, to which his academic drawings and models had added an extensive knowledge of the human figure and its conformation, parts, proportions, and perspective, under the different circumstances of position, action, light, and shade. During his residence in Rome, the ancient groups and statues, the bassi-relievi, and the works of Michael Angelo in the Sistine chapel, roused every faculty of his soul, and urged him on to labour night and day, in a noble emulation of those miracles of art, and wonders of the world; what was the consequence we see in our examination of the two bassi-relievi, and the statue of Cupid, which are specimens of his employments in Italy.

The Cupid catching a butterfly on his wing, is rendered highly interesting to the mind by its philosophical allusion to the power of love, divine or natural, on the soul. Nothing can be more graceful than the attitude—the outline is finely varied in the different views; the softness of the form, the character of the face, and the adjustment of the hair, are classically beautiful. The basso-relievo of Caractacus before Claudius, is composed on the principle of those on the ancient sarcophagi, of which many are to be seen in Rome, and other parts of Europe

The subject is historical, but the characters are heroic, and a dramatical gradation of passion is expressed in a few figures. From the patriot's undaunted attitude, you perceive he is saying: "nor wouldst thou have disdained to receive me with articles of peace, because I am descended of noble progenitors, and I have ruled over many warlike nations," while the emperor listens with attentive respect.

The basso-relievo of Thetis rising to comfort Achilles, is of the epic class. The sentiment and character is beautiful and pathetic; the composition so unlike any work, ancient or modern, that the combination may be considered as the artist's own. The harmony of composition in the parts, which strengthens the unity of sentiment, is striking in these two, as well as several other works of this artist; and may be reckoned among the acquisitions which British sculpture has received from his talents and industry. Nor is this our only obligation; he laboured in every department, and the whole art of sculpture has profited by his means. Before his time, only one English sculptor (Mr. Nollekens) had formed his taste on the antique, and introduced a purer style of art. Since then, sculpture has been gradually emerging from its state of barbarity—simple emblems have supplied the place of epigrammatical conceits; and imitations of the fine heads and beautiful outlines of the antique statues, have succeeded to lifeless blocks, or caricature copies of common nature.

CHANTREY.

Francis Chantrey was born in Derbyshire, in 1781. He early evinced a predilection for art, but received no early and regular training in his chosen profession. He was, in his youth, much fascinated with the pencil and palette ; he indeed hesitated between the two arts ; but the muse of sculpture prevailed. He, however, always retained an ardent love for painting, and his criticisms on that subject were not less judicious than his observations on works in his own department of art. All his remarks bore immediately on the main purport of the work, and his first inquiry was relative to the value of the sentiment expressed, never suffering himself to be misled by finish or manner. He looked for the best and most careful execution in the heads and hands, as therein are read the emotions of the mind. To him the value of a picture existed in expression ; without the *mens divinior*, all was to him worthless. Like Canova, he was intensely alive to the beauties of colour, and the ever-varying hues and expressions of natural scenery, to him had peculiar charms.

His professional prosperity may be dated from the year 1808, when he received a commission to execute four colossal busts for Greenwich Hospital—those of Duncan, Howe, St. Vincent, and Nelson. Three years after, still young and unfriended, he sent his bust of Horne Tooke to the Academy exhibition, where its great merit caught the eye of Nollekens. He lifted it from the floor—set it before him—moved his head to and fro, and having satisfied himself of its excellence, turned round to those who were arranging the works for the exhibition, and said, "There's a fine, a very fine work ; let the man who made it be known ; remove one of my busts, and put this one in its place, for well it deserves it." Often afterwards, when desired to model a bust, he said in his most persuasive way, "Go to Chantrey—he's the man for a bust—he'll make a good bust for you—I always recommend him."

During the eight years previous to 1808, he declares that he did not make five pounds by modelling. Such a period of drudgery at the chisel had disgusted and discouraged any other than a man stimulated by the purest love of his art.

In 1816, he was elected an associate of the Royal Academy. The same year he exhibited the Sleeping Children, which won for him the warmest admiration. While the more ambitious impersonations of heathen divinities were passed coldly by, his group was constantly surrounded by sympathizing throngs; and mothers looked and wept, and returned again to gaze upon the loveliness and innocence that so appealed to their hearts.

In 1818, he was chosen a member of the Academy. The following year, he visited Italy, and was elected a member of the societies of Rome and Florence. Soon after his return, he executed four of his most admired busts—those of Lord Castlereagh, Phillips the painter, Wordsworth, and Sir Walter Scott; the last has been pronounced his best.

Sir Francis Chantrey is thought to have achieved as great a triumph, as did West, in the Death of Wolfe, in the introduction of modern costume into the higher departments of art.

In addition to his eminent talents, his heart was the seat of those virtues, which endear men to their fellows by bonds that can never be knit by the merely cold exercises of social duty. He was generous, humane, and charitable. He ever lived upon the most friendly terms with his brother academicians, and was much respected in those circles, to which by his position he was entitled to admission. "His busts," says Mr. Jones, in his "Recollections of his Life, Practice, and Opinions," "were dignified by his knowledge and admiration of the antique; and the fleshy, pulpy appearance he gave to the marble, seems almost miraculous. The heads of his busts were raised with dignity, the throats large and well turned, the shoulders ample, or made to appear so, and thus, while likeness was preserved, natural defects were obviated. George IV., the duke of Sussex, Lord Castlereagh, and others, were so struck with Chantrey's power of appreciating every advantage of form, that they bared their chests and shoulders that the sculptor might have every advantage that well-formed nature could present.

"The distinction he enjoyed in his profession, gained him the consideration of the most exalted personages in the kingdom. From three sovereigns he received great attention. George IV. evinced an affability towards him which he often mentioned with pleasure. When he modelled his bust, the king wished him to increase his price, and insisted that the bust of himself should not return to the artist a less sum than three hundred guineas."

The book above mentioned, abounds with agreeable anecdotes, in all of which the sculptor is an actor. On the varnishing days at the Royal Academy, he was very fond of joking with Turner and Constable, carrying his jokes even to an extent which might have ruffled the temper of some men. Mr. Jones relates many instances of his liberality, one of which is in reference to the monument of Northcote: "On the sculptor being asked, what it was to be, he replied, 'It is left entirely to me. I may make merely a tablet if I choose. The money is too much for a bust, and too little for a statue; but I love to be treated with confidence, and I shall make a statue, and do my best.' And probably, Chantrey never executed any thing more characteristic, or more like, than the face and figure of Northcote, for every one to whom the painter was known, started at the resemblance; and the work only wanted colour to make the spectator believe that he saw the veteran artist in his studio." Chantrey died in 1841.

Architecture.

ARCHITECTURE may be divided into civil, naval, and military Civil architecture alone, however, takes rank as a fine art; and that only, when its object is the expression of beauty or grandeur.

Protection from the weather undoubtedly led to its invention; and it was not until mankind had made considerable advance in the useful arts, that it aimed at any thing more than a shelter from the elements. But when the real necessities of man were supplied, his ever restless and aspiring mind, prompted by that innate desire for the beautiful and the true, which, though disordered and weakened, he brought with him from Paradise, sought to adorn his dwelling-places, and, above all, the temples of his religion.

"Whatever rude structure the climate and materials of any country have obliged its early inhabitants to adopt for their temporary shelter, the same structure, with all its prominent features, has been afterwards kept up by their refined and opulent posterity. Thus the Egyptian style of building has its origin in the *cavern* and *mound;* the Chinese architecture is modelled from the *tent;* the Grecian is derived from the *wooden cabin;* and the Gothic, from the *bower* of *trees.*"

The great works of many nations, whose architectural skill ranked high, are known to us only from history; time, with silent but busy finger, has scarcely left a trace to show where they stood.

The temples and palaces of the Babylonians, the Assyrians, the Phœnicians, the Israelites, and the Philistines, as predicted by the inspired prophets, have passed away, leaving but heaps of ruins to mark the situations of the cities they adorned.

Babylon, "the glory of kingdoms, the beauty of the Chaldees' excellency," presented many of the most splendid and wonderful works of ancient art. The temple of Belus was half a mile in circumference, and a furlong in height. The hanging gardens of Semiramis towered, one above another, to the height of three hundred feet. One hundred brazen gates opened through the stupendous walls of the city, which were reckoned among the wonders of the world. But according to the sure word of prophecy, "this great city hath become a heap, a dwelling-place for dragons, an astonishment, a hissing, without inhabitant."

Nineveh, the capital of Assyria, presents but a few mounds, covered over with grass, where her palaces once stood; indeed her very site was doubtful until very recently. She is "empty, void, and waste."

An interesting discovery has recently been made by M. Botta, a distinguished archæologist, French consul at Mosul—no less than the recovery of an Assyrian palace under one of the mounds of rubbish on the banks of the Tigris, marking the supposed site of Nineveh. He was unsuccessful in his first attempt; but, having continued his excavations on another mound, he was so far fortunate as to find this interesting remnant of remote antiquity. Fifteen halls of this vast edifice, with their corresponding esplanades, have been cleared. The walls are covered with sculptures and inscriptions; the former historical, and illustrative of sieges, naval battles, triumphs, single combats, &c. The characters are arrow-headed and cuneiform, and in numbers beyond all computation. On each wall are two rows of sculptures, with about twenty lines of inscriptions engraved between them. These inscriptions, including those on the garments of figures, as well as on the towers and other objects in the bas-reliefs, are most probably an historical record of the events so illustrated. This portion of the palace, it would appear, had been ravaged by fire; and to this circumstance, it is probable, it owed its preservation from total destruction, as the calcined materials would be useless for other constructions. The other, and larger part of the palace, which escaped the conflagration, must have been intentionally destroyed, by carrying off the stones for other buildings. The sculptures, though in all probability cotemporaneous with the most ancient works of the same kind in Egypt, far excel them in the spirit and beauty of the execution; and, if we are to believe the accounts, display knowledge of anatomy, perception of character, and wonderful energy. Their vases, drinking cups, and shields, adorned with lions, other animals, and flowers, as well as their ornaments, bracelets, earrings, &c., rival, it is alleged, in consummate taste, the productions of Greece. But faults are admitted in the general execution—such as frequent disregard of the relative proportions of the figures, owing, it is supposed, to different hands having been employed on the same work. The vast front entrance of the palace is now cleared; it is ornamented by six colossal bulls, with the heads of men, and two human statues, also colossal, strangling lions in their arms.

On the discovery being made known, the French government supplied the means of continuing the researches, and sent M

Flaudrin to make drawings of what could not be removed. No description has yet been given of the style of the architecture, which will no doubt be done when the whole is cleared.

Sir Stratford Canning, the British ambassador at Constantinople, has subsequently sent Mr. Henry Austin Layard to Mosul, to investigate the buried ruins of Nimrod, in the same vicinity. He has made very large excavations, and discovered the ruins of another vast palace, full of treasures of ancient art, some damaged, or in a state of dilapidation, but the greater part remaining in a good state of preservation. This edifice consists of long suites of apartments, all built of marble, and ornamented with sculptures, representing, as in that discovered by M. Botta, battles and sieges. The inscriptions are in the Babylonian character. It is conjectured that the palace was built before the Medes and Babylonians became masters of the Assyrian empire. All are said to be of the finest workmanship, and to look as fresh as if they had been newly chiselled. Several of them are described as masterpieces of art, and give a high idea of the civilization and refinement of the ancient Assyrians.

Tyre and Sidon, Jerusalem, Zabulon, Askelon, and Gaza, once filled with splendid and apparently imperishable monuments of architecture, are also in utter ruins.

In Egypt, Persia, and Hindoostan, the remains of many architectural works of great magnificence are still to be found, and from the resemblance of their leading features it is difficult to determine which country may lay claim to priority of invention. The general characteristics of these ancient works, are gigantic proportions, heavy firmness, and prodigality of ornament, striking the mind with wonder rather than delight.

In sculptural ornament, there is a marked difference between Indian and Egyptian architecture. In Egyptian, the principal forms of the structure predominate, while the ornament never interferes with the effect of the whole or its masses. In the Indian, the principal forms are lost and frittered away, in the excess of ornament and accessories. In the Egytian, the smallest edifices are grand; in the Indian, the largest have an air of littleness.

Egyptian Architecture.

The structures of ancient Egypt are of three distinct forms: caverns, grottoes, or tombs excavated in the rocks; apartments enclosed by sculptured walls, with flat roofs, supported by columns and connected by open porticoes; and the simple pyramid. We are without historic evidence with regard to the priority or succession of these several modes. Some are of opinion that caverns furnished the first dwellings and places of worship, while others contend that the colonnades were raised in imitation of groves of trees, which were the earliest places of worship.

The architecture of the Egyptians is by many thought to have been entirely original, the result of a powerful people, attaining their objects by the simplest means; others suppose their arts to have been derived from Ethiopia. Their most ancient buildings are composed merely of tapering walls, with pillars of huge dimensions placed in the intermediate spaces, to support a roof, constructed of large flat stones, always of a kind found in the immediate neighbourhood; in a few instances calcareous, but chiefly fine sandstone.

In the outlines and decorations of their columns, the changes have been very considerable. In the simplest, as those at the entrance of the tombs of Silliles, they consist of representations of bundles of reeds, bound together near the top with a cord, which is wound several times round them, having a square stone laid on their top, forming what is now known by the term abacus; and the part between this stone and the binding cord, apparently crushed down by the incumbent weight, so as to bulge out a little beyond the surface of the part which is firmly bound. The first change from this simple mode seems to have been to introduce mere bindings or belts in various parts of the shaft, and in the divisions between them, to represent alternately reeds and hieroglyphics. The bulged part near the top, was also decorated by reeds and hieroglyphics, and sometimes by triangular flutings. At a later period, this upper part was formed into elegant vase-shapes, decorated with the stalks, leaves, buds, and blossoms of the lotus, or lily of the Nile; and occasionally leaves of the palm, vine, papyrus, and date, were introduced. The capitals exhibit much variety, but may be reduced to three species—the square, vasiformed, and the swelled. When a base exists, it is plain. The part corresponding to the Greek entablature is hardly subdivided, except the upper member, or cornice, which projects considerably with a concave. The whole of this entablature is generally decorated with sculptured animals, winged globes, &c.

Little is known concerning the vast cities of this once powerful and learned people, except what may be gathered from their ruins. The origin of Thebes, which is said to have been the first city in the world, is unknown. It was the chief seat of the religion of Egypt, and abounded in gigantic temples, some of which are in a tolerable state of preservation at the present day. Their form and colossal proportions, strike the beholder with astonishment. It is a mystery how such immense masses of stone were conveyed, from great distances, and then raised to such an enormous height. A description of one of the greatest temples of Egypt, will give some idea of the magnificence and vastness of their structures. Karnac, on the eastern bank of the Nile, at Thebes, is said to have been dedicated to Priapus, god of the fields and protector of gardens, bees, goats, and sheep. The mole of this temple looks towards the Nile; it is 140 paces in length, and 25 in thickness: this leads to a court 110 paces in length, and the same in breadth. Two ranges of six columns, conduct to a portico composed of 136 columns. The two middle ranges of these are eleven feet in diameter, the others are seven feet. The length of this vestibule is 78 paces, the breadth the same as the mole. It leads into a court, where there are four obelisks and twelve colossal figures, each with a cross on the breast. Two other courts conduct to what is supposed to have been the apartments of the kings; those of the king and queen are distinguished by doors of black granite. Adjacent to the great palace, are many other buildings of great extent, connected with it by avenues of sphinxes, lions, and rams; some of the avenues extended towards Luxor, a distance of 1200 yards. The alley of lions is well preserved; they are 90 in number, and each is 15 feet long, placed couchant upon pedestals about three feet in height, and ten feet asunder. Facing the moles, which conduct to the court of obelisks of the great palace, are two, and sometimes four, colossal statues of sandstone or granite. They are either seated, or in the act of marching, the arms hanging by their sides—carrying each a crooked poignard. The pictures which decorated the exterior of these different palaces, represent military subjects, sieges of cities, combats, offers of peace and submission of barbarians, triumphs of heroes who have conquered; the hero is represented by a young man six feet high, mounted on a car precisely of the form used by the Greeks. The soldiers are scarcely one fourth of this size. The enemies put to the rout, are men with beards, wearing caps on their heads. The Egyptians are armed with arrows—the barbarians with bucklers; they have also crooked sabres, lances, javelins, and straight swords; the bridles of their horses resemble those still used in Arabia.

The celebrated Labyrinth, described by Herodotus, on the lake Mœris, is believed, by De Non, after an examination of the alleged site, to be entirely fabulous. Some have speculated on the probability of the Pyramids covering immense substructions, including numerous chambers, in which may be deposited the arcana of Egyptian lore and religion.

Indian Architecture.

THE palaces and temples of Hindoostan, owing to its inexhaustible wealth, were on a scale of great magnificence. Oude is said to have been the first imperial city of Hindoostan, and to have contained the seat of the empire fifteen hundred years, when it was removed to Canonge, thence to Delhi. It was again moved to Agra, and thence again to Lahore, and again to Delhi. The wealth and splendor of these cities was unrivalled but being only upheld by the unstable political power of the East, their glory has passed away. But from the permanence of their religion, their sacred temples have been preserved; and it is from these that we learn the character of their early architecture.

Temples of five different forms.

Of their large temples we find accounts of five different forms. First, the simple pyramid, constructed of large stones, and diminished by regular recesses or steps, as at Doegur and Tanjore; the exterior rude, and the interior having light from without only, by a small entrance door, being illuminated by a profusion of lamps, with the exception of a chamber in the middle, which has only a single lamp.

The second kind were formed by excavations in the sides of rocky mountains. At Salsette, Elephanta, and Vellore or Ellore, the excavations were not only extensive, but were divided into separate apartments, with regular ranges of sculptured pillars, and entablatures, and the walls and ceilings covered with multitudes of figures of their genii, men, women, and various animals, such as elephants, horses, lions, &c., all of excellent workmanship.

A third set were composed of square or oblong courts, of vast extent. The circumference of the outward wall, in that on the island of Seringhatu, adjacent to Trichinopoly, is said to extend nearly four miles. The whole edifice consists of seven square enclosures, the walls being three hundred and fifty feet distant from each other. In the innermost spacious square are chapels. In the midd'e of each side of the enclosure wall there is a gateway, under a lofty tower. That in the outward wall which faces the south, is ornamented with pillars of single stones, thirty-three feet long and five feet in diameter.

A fourth sort is the Benares pagoda, in the city of Casi, which, from the earliest times, was devoted to Indian religion and science. The temple is in the form of a cross, with a cupola terminated by a pyramid in the centre, and having also a tower at each extremity of the cross. From the gate of the pagoda to the Ganges there is a flight of steps.

A fifth sort are made in a circular form, as the celebrated pagoda of Juggernaut, which Hamilton compares to an immense butt, set on end.

Persian Architecture.

As the ancient Persian edifices were mostly built of brick, their remains are very scanty. The few ruins which are to be found, bear some resemblance both to Egyptian and Indian buildings, but possess features distinct from both. The ruins of a palace at Persepolis, and various tombs cut in the rock, are all that remain to guide us to the character of their architecture. No trace of Persepolis remains, except the palace, usually called the house of Darius, or Chilmenar, that is, the forty columns. Travellers, probably misled by this, have said that there were only forty columns; but Le Brun discovered the traces of two hundred and five. He found nineteen standing in 1705. He asserts that there is no appearance of any thing belonging to a temple, but that it certainly is the remains of the palace destroyed by Alexander. He traced the façade six hundred paces from north to south, and three hundred from east to west. The doorways or entrances which remain, have a perfect resemblance to those which are between the great moles at the entrance of the Egyptian temples. They have tapering outlines, and the crowning member is a large carvetto, similarly fluted. The columns are of more slender proportions than those of the Egyptians. Their capitals occupy about one-fourth of the whole height of the column, conveying the idea of rich silk and feathers having been tied around the upper part of tall wooden posts. Silks, feathers, and precious stones, have always been the gorgeous materials with which the Orientals have formed their decorations. The sculptures on the terraces and sides of the stairs are very numerous, representing triumphal processions, &c.

The principal sepulchre in Persia is that in which the body of Darius is said to have been deposited. A recess is cut in the rock for about sixty paces in depth. The front so obtained is about seventy feet in breadth at the base, forty in the decorated part, and about seventy in height. The lower columns which support the sculptured gallery have capitals composed of the heads and necks of oxen projecting from the top of the column. Upon the columns are represented four great beams as an architrave; upon this runs a cornice which has two feet nine inches projection, over which eighteen lions are sculptured, nine looking from each side towards a small vase which stands in the middle of the length. Above the lions are two ranges of human figures, fourteen in number, and nearly as large as life; they are each holding up both hands, as if to support the entablature. Above all these, there is upon three steps the figure of a king with something in his right hand, the form of which cannot be distinctly made out; but he holds a bow in his left hand. Before him is an altar with a flame rising from it, and it is said that the figure of the sun was formerly behind the king. Above the altar is a small figure too indistinct to be made out. At right angles with the line of front, in the returning face of the rock, on both sides of the front area, are niches with statues in them. Le Brun entered a tomb to the south of this; the entry had only two feet of height, and the vault was forty-six feet broad and twenty deep. Two hundred and fifteen paces south of the edifice, there is a column now standing upon its base ; and near it are the bases of eight others, at seven and eight paces distant from each other : the height of the base is three feet six inches. At the sides of the two bases towards the south, are two fragments of camels which may have been on the columns. Six hundred and fifty paces to the north is another portico, not inferior to that already described. Le Brun found about 1,300 figures of men and animals sculptured on the tombs ; the men were from 7 feet 5 inches to 10 feet 7 inchcs high ; some had parasols or umbrellas over them, and many were armed with lances, and combating lions.

Such are the splendid ruins of Persepolis—they bear incontrovertible evidence of antiquity ; and although in some things they resemble Egyptian, and in others Indian edifices, they, especially in the palace, possess leading features sufficiently distinct to entitle them to be considered as a separate school.

Hebrew Architecture.

Nothing is known of Hebrew architecture but what is recorded in Scripture, and by Josephus, with occasional allusions in classic authors.

Of all the temples of antiquity, the Temple at Jerusalem on Mount Moriah, regarded even in an architectural point of view, and waiving all consideration of its Divine origin, deep and powerful interest, and scriptural associations, must have been one of the most striking and magnificent.

We learn from Scripture and Josephus, that besides the Temple, or House, strictly so called, (comprising the Holy of Holies, the portico, and sanctuary,) the sacred edifice included numerous other spacious courts and chambers, each of which had its respective degree of holiness. The whole, including the piazzas, cloisters, towers, walls, and the palace of Herod, answered the double purpose of a sanctuary and a fortress. This superb palace became afterwards the residence of the Roman procurators. The towers and walls were half a mile in circuit, and of a stupendous height. The Temple, the magnificent portico of which rose to the height of one hundred and twenty cubits, was entered by nine gates, thickly coated with silver and gold. One of them of Corinthian brass, was of surpassing beauty, not only much larger, but more richly ornamented than the others. It is supposed to have been the "gate called the Beautiful."—Acts iii. 2. The front, or outer court of the Gentiles, was surrounded by a range of porticoes, above twenty-five cubits in height. One of these porticoes was called Solomon's porch or piazza, or the royal portico, because it was the only work of Solomon that remained in the second Temple. Magnificent as the outer and surrounding structures were, they were infinitely surpassed by the inner sanctuary. Josephus describes it as covered on all sides with plates of gold, and possessing every requisite that could strike the mind and astonish the sight; that when the sun rose upon it, the effulgence was so dazzling, that the eye could no more sustain its radiance, than the splendor of the sun itself.

Various attempts have been made to ascertain the plans and style of architecture of the temple and its courts, but they are all at variance with each other, and unsatisfactory. It seems probable, that the first and second temples were some mixture of the Egyptian and Phœnician, and that the subsequent modifications and additions by Herod and the Jews, partook of the Grecian and Roman.

It does not appear that the Jews ever had a national style of architecture. Their synagogues and prosenchæ, which were very numerous—the former in towns, the latter in rural situations—seem to have been plain, and often temporary erections of no architectural pretensions, but merely calculated for the convenience of prayer and public worship. We hear, it is true, of numerous instances of altars and images, in groves and high places, raised to Baal and other pagan deities, in defiance of the express commands of the Almighty; but there is no instance recorded of temples being constructed in imitation of those of Egypt and Phœnicia, or, in later times, of Greece and Rome.

Only three specimens of ancient Jewish art can be produced, after the most scrutinizing search: the piece of money called the shekel, bearing a cup on one side, and an almond branch on the other; the candlestick with seven branches; and the table of shewbread, on a bas-relief, under the arch of Titus.

Grecian Architecture.

It has been said that the architecture of the Greeks was formed on the model of the wooden cabin, this may have modified their style, but that they were acquainted with the works of the Egyptians, Persians, and Hindoos, is beyond doubt. And the commencement of the rapid progress of the art in Greece corresponds with the time of their connexion with Egypt, in the reign of Psammetacus. But such was their skill, and so refined their taste, that they soon surpassed every other nation then existing, nor have they since been excelled.

The most ancient specimens of architecture in Greece consist of massive walls, termed Cyclopean. These remains are generally attributed to the Pelasgi. In the earlier walls the blocks are of various sizes, having smaller stones in the interstices, those of later date are constructed more regularly.

The orders of the Greeks were the Doric, Ionic, and Corinthian. The Romans modified these, producing the Tuscan and Composite. These are called the five orders. By an order, we are to understand those forms with which the Greeks composed the façades of their temples.

The principal members of an order are, a platform, perpendicular supports, and a lintelling or covering connecting the tops of these supports and crowning the edifice. The proportioning these parts to the building and to each other, and adapting characteristic decorations, constitutes an order, canon, or rule.

DORIC ORDER.

The Doric is the most ancient of these orders, so called from Doris, where it originated. It is the most massive of the Greek orders, its proportions little differing from those of Egyptian edifices. For simplicity and majesty, its effects have not been exceeded. The temples of the Greeks, of whatever order, were of an oblong form; in some the porticoes were at the ends only in others they were on all sides. Some had a single range of columns, others more. In the infancy of the order the diameter of the column was very great in proportion to the length, being only about five diameters in height; but the proportions became afterwards more delicate.

In this order the shaft of the column is raised upon a stylobate with three steps, the shaft is fluted and without a pedestal. The upper member of the column is a square abacus, under which is a large and elegantly formed ovolo; immediately beneath which are three annulets or rings with recessed spaces between them. The architrave is plain, except that at the top is a fillet, to the under side of which, beneath regular projections in the frieze, are six small conical drops called guttæ. The frieze consists of alternate projections and recesses; two vertical channels are cut in each projection, and two half ones at the edges, from which fact these tablets are called triglyphs. The recesses between the triglyphs, called metopes, are square or nearly so, and often contain sculptures. Above the frieze comes the cornice, which in this order consists of a few large mouldings, having on their under side a series of squares, sloping projections, resembling the ends of rafters, and called mutules. These are placed over both triglyphs and metopes, and are ornamented on their under side with circular guttæ. The best specimens of the Doric order are found in the Parthenon, the Propylæa, and the temple of Theseus, at Athens. The pediment is formed by the sloping of the roof, and is surmounted by a cornice. The enclosed triangle is called the tympanum. This chaste and majestic style, was almost the only one employed in Greece, until after the Macedonian conquest.

IONIC ORDER.

The Greek colonies which settled Ionia, on the coast of Asia, reached, perhaps, a higher degree of refinement than their mother country; and, not satisfied with the simplicity and proportions of the Doric order, made such changes in it as established a new one, which is called Ionic, after the country. This order varies from the Doric in many respects; its proportions are much lighter, and its ornaments are entirely different. Its columns are from eight to nine diameters in height and are furnished with bases, which are more necessary here than in the Doric, on account of the lightness of the shaft, the pedestal giving it an appearance of stability. The capital consists of two parallel double scrolls called volutes, which support an abacus nearly square, but moulded at its edges.

Vitruvius, a celebrated architect of the time of Augustus, tells us, that as the Doric was bold and masculine, the Ionians modelled their order with female delicacy, and that the volutes of the capitals were in imitation of the curls of hair on the sides of the face. Others say that they arose from the custom of nailing ram's horns upon the top of a post. Others again, that they are imitations of the curling of the bark of a tree, crushed down by a weight; but it seems to bear a greater resemblance to a scroll, partly unrolled, than to any of these. The entablature differs from that of the Doric, in rejecting the triglyphs, guttæ, and mutules. The architrave and frieze are plain and unbroken, except that, beneath the cornice, which consists of mouldings of various curves, is a row of square teeth, called dentals. The tympanum is frequently ornamented with sculpture.

The temple of Minerva, at Athens, and of Diana, at Ephesus, are examples of the Ionic order.

CORINTHIAN ORDER.

This, which is the most delicate and elegant of the Greek orders, is said, by Vitruvius, to have been invented by Callimachus, an Athenian sculptor, who flourished 540 B. C., who is said to have had the idea suggested to him by observing acanthus leaves growing around a basket, which had been placed, with some favourite trinkets, upon the grave of a young Corinthian maiden; the stalks, which rose among the leaves, having been formed into slender volutes, by a square tile which covered the basket. It is possible that a circumstance of this nature may have caught the fancy of a sculptor who was cotemporary with Phidias; and who was, probably, in that age of competition, alive to every thing which promised distinction in his profession. But in the warmth of our devotion for the inspiration of Greek genius, we must not overlook the fact, that in the pillars of several of the temples in Upper Egypt, whose shafts represent bundles of reeds bound together in several places by fillets, the capitals are formed by several rows of delicate leaves.

If the account of Vitruvius is not true, the origin of the order is unknown. Though called Corinthian, none but Doric ruins have been found on the site of the city of Corinth.

The base of the column much resembles that of the Ionic. The shaft is generally fluted, and is often ten diameters in height. The capital is shaped like an inverted bell, covered with two rows of acanthus leaves, above which are eight pairs of slender volutes. The height of the capital is one diameter sometimes one and a sixth.

The entablature is much the same as that of the Ionic, but more highly ornamented. Beneath the cornice is a row of oblong projections, under each of which is a scroll or curled leaf, called a modillion.

The entasis, or curved line of diminution of the column—a refinement which could only have occured to a people of superior taste and perception like the Greeks—is supposed to have been of later introduction than the diminution of the column by a straight line, which was adopted in the earliest times. Mr. Cockerel was the first to discover that the entasis alluded to by Vitruvius, existed in the columns of the Parthenon, and other Doric remains By means of this curve, the column, when standing, appears of the same diameter throughout; the column at the top being actually larger than at the base, otherwise the perspective effect would have made the elevated portion seem to diminish in circumference.

Etruscan Architecture.

MASSIVE solidity of construction is the distinguishing feature of Etruscan architecture. Whether in its primitive or later style, it bears a marked affinity to the early remains of Greece. In the Etruscan parts of Italy, Mr. Hamilton alludes to various Cyclopean buildings at Noba, and other places. In the walls of Crotona, some of the stones are twenty-two Roman feet in length, and from five to six feet high, without either cramps or cement. The walls of Volterra are built in the same colossal manner. The gate of Hercules is an arch, consisting of only nineteen stones. Their temples, many of which were extant at the time of Vitruvius and Pliny, were peripteral; some constructed entirely of wood, others of wood and stone. Their pediments were decorated with statues, quadrigæ, and bassi-relievi, in terra-cotta. Their columns, entablature, and composition exhibit a general resemblance to the Grecian temples and orders. Their mythology, sculpture, and painting were characterized by the same similitude.

To the Etruscans the Romans were indebted for their knowledge of the arch, and their style of architecture, which they retained up to the Roman conquest.

Roman Architecture.

UNTIL the reign of Augustus, Rome could boast of but little architectural skill or magnificence. The buildings were chiefly of brick or wood ; but when their conquests extended into Greece and Asia, they enriched themselves with the spoils of their enemies, and learned their arts. At the triumph of Amulius, after the conquest of Macedonia, two hundred and fifty chariots were filled with images, paintings, and colossal statues. Thus a taste for the arts was implanted, and artists were invited to Rome, where the wealth and power of universal empire offered every facility to their success.

Still, their claim to originality is slight, they borrowed their architectural ideas from the Greeks, whose chaste and elegant orders they in time so loaded with ornament, that they could scarcely be distinguished. With this manifestation of a degenerated taste, commenced the decline of the art among them

The arch, though known to the Greeks, was by the Romans first applied to important purposes. It was thrown across rivers, and by its aid streams were carried for miles to supply their capital with pure water.

TUSCAN ORDER.

This order is little more than a modification of the Doric. It originated in Etruria.

Its column has a simple base, and is seven diameters in height, its capital being much like that of the Doric order. The entablature consists of plain running surfaces.

COMPOSITE ORDER.

The Composite order is a union of the Corinthian and Ionian. The upper part of the capital is of modern Ionic, which presents a similar face on each of the four sides ; beneath this are two rows of acanthus leaves. The entablature may be either Ionic or Corinthian, but the columns being bolder than those of these orders, the other members should be of corresponding magnitude.

Romanesque Style.

AFTER the dismemberment of the Roman empire, the arts degenerated so far, that a custom became prevalent of erecting new buildings with the fragments of old ones. This gave rise to an irregular style of building, which continued to be imitated, especially in Italy during the dark ages. It consisted of Grecian and Roman details, combined under new forms, and piled up into structures wholly unlike the antique originals. Hence the term Greco-Gothic, or Romanesque, architecture has been given to it. It frequently contained arches upon columns, forming successive arcades, which were accumulated above each other to a great height. The effect was, however, sometimes imposing. The cathedral and leaning tower of Pisa, and the church of St. Mark at Venice, are cited as the best specimens of this style.

Byzantine Style.

THE removal of the imperial seat of government, by Constantine, from Rome to Byzantium—the more extended demand for places of Christian worship—the absence of the models of Roman grandeur, and the rich and inexhaustible supply of materials they afforded—the schism between the Greek and Latin churches—the irruptions of the Goths—the civil wars—the separation of the eastern and western empires, forced the Byzantine architects to exercise their ingenuity and resources in devising a style of architecture better suited to their new wants and circumstances. The improved practice of vaulting, derived from the East, enabled them, with smaller and inferior materials, to throw cupolas and arcades over spaces of vast extent and span. Instead of the long aisles and colonnades of the basilica, the new Byzantine church architecture, of which St. Sophia is the most celebrated example, was thrown into the form of a Greek cross. In the centre, was raised on high a lofty dome, resting on a solid cylinder, supported by four arcades and their spandrels, converging into a circle, while semi-cupolas or conchs, closing into the arcades of the dome, surmounted the four naves or branches of the cross. The square cortile, crowned with smaller and equal cupolas, formed a graceful accessory to the new temple. Arches thus rising on arches, and cupolas over cupolas, we may say that all which in the temple of Athens had been straight, angular, and square, in the churches of Constantinople became curved and rounded—concave within and convex without ; so that after the Romans had begun by depriving the architecture of the prior Greeks of its consistency, the Christian Greeks themselves obliterated every mark of the architecture of their heathen ancestors still retained by the Romans, and made the ancient Greek architecture owe its final annihilation to the same nation which gave it birth.

The distinguishing feature of the new Byzantine church style, was the Greek cross and centre dome, to which was afterwards added the taper and lofty minaret. The columns ceased to retain any resemblance to the Greek and Roman orders ; though the shafts were round, there was no proportion observed in their diameter and height—no distinctive marks in their capitals, which exhibited a diversity of the most whimsical ornaments

Arcades, and even cupolas, began to assume fantastic forms and curves—some less than semi-circular, some greater—some curving towards each other like a horse-shoe—some like double horse-shoes, with a pillar between them; others formed of different curves, like a trefoil, or scallop; others pointed, alternating with round; others narrow and lancet; others curved inward, and then in an opposite direction; others triangular, like a pediment. Arches were likewise accompanied by sets of diminutive pillars, supporting smaller arches.

Thus arose the Byzantine style of architecture, which, besides exercising a powerful influence over Venice and other parts of Italy bordering on the Adriatic, spread its ramifications over a great part of Asia, Africa, and Europe, including the whole regions of Islamism and the Greek Church.

Gothic Architecture.

THE origin of the Gothic style cannot be traced to any one nation. It was generally practised throughout Europe until the sixteenth century, when it was supplanted by the revival of the classic style. The cognomen, Gothic, was then given, to show the contempt in which it was held by the new schools of architecture. But whatever may have been the manner in which the name was acquired, it has now become entwined with associations of grandeur and magnificence; and the attempt to change it is as uncalled for as it is vain. In the time of Theodoric, king of the Ostrogoths, architecture underwent a material change;

but the productions of this period are not what we now understand by Gothic—they are properly designated by the term Old Gothic. The modern Gothic came to maturity by a slow process. At first plain and massive, it gradually became more and more ornamented. Notwithstanding the vastness of the designs, a peculiar lightness of effect was giver to the decorations: the pointed arches, the turrets, spires, and clustered pinnacles on the exterior; and within, by groups of small columns, many often being bound into one, and by a profusion of fretted workmanship, sometimes resembling a film of lace or filagree work, and, above all, by the tendency of every part to taper upwards.

The origin of the Gothic has been the subject of much controversy and antiquarian research—of numerous learned treatises and conflicting theories. It has been succesively referred to the Druids, Saxons, Goths, Normans, Saracens, and Persians. Its invention has been claimed for Germany, France, Spain, Italy, and England. But the Lombard, Saxon, and Norman styles, from which the Gothic or pointed sprang, undoubtedly derived their origin from the gradual corruption of the Latin architecture.

The whole composition and details of a Gothic cathedral—the naves, aisles, clustered pillars, groinings, and ramifications, cross-springers of the vaults and roof, the transoms, mullions, tracery, and minute ornaments—all point to the same prototype—the interlacing of trees in the grove or forest. What is a great part of its sculpture and decorations, its trefoils, quatrefoils, cinquefoils, its finials, crockets, featherings, cusps, foliage, and fretwork, but an imitation, more or less free, of plants, flowers, fruits, and vegetable nature in general? And though certainly the essential parts—the pillars, the arches, the ribs, the groins, the cross-springers, and the ridge-plates—were not derived from the imi tation of trees planted in an avenue, it is probable that the similitude which they gradually, but incidentally acquired to trees thus disposed, gave the idea of completing the resemblance in their ornamental additions, not only by dotting every pediment and pinnacle with crotchets and finials in the shape of buds, and by filling every arch with tracery, like foliage, but by twisting the light arches and ribs themselves, so as to look like stalks of the woodbine or tendrils of the vine?

What are its stained-glass windows and oriels, but an imitation of the harmonious and chastened gleams of sunshine passing through the branches and openings of the richly-variegated foliage? The author of "The Sketch Book," in a forest scene among the prairies, remarks: "We were overshadowed by lofty trees, with straight, smooth trunks, like stately columns, and as the glancing rays of the sun shone through the transparent leaves, tinted with the many-coloured hues of autumn, I was reminded of the effect of sunshine among the stained windows and clustering columns of a Gothic cathedral." In Cowper's private correspondence, he remarks: "We also, as you know, have scenes at Weston worthy of description; but because you know them so well, I will only say that one of them has within these few days been much improved—I mean the lime walk. By the help of the axe and wood-bill, which have of late been constantly employed in cutting out all straggling branches that intercepted the arch, Mr. Throckmorton has now defined it with such exactness, that no cathedral in the world can show one of more magnificence and beauty." Bishop Warburton, in his notes on "Pope's Epistles," has the following striking passage on this subject: "No attentive observer ever viewed a regular avenue of well-growing trees intermixing their branches overhead, but he was reminded of the long vista through the Gothic cathedral-

or ever entered one of the larger or more elegant edifices of the kind, but it presented to his imagination an avenue of trees; and this alone is what can truly be called the Gothic style of building. Under this idea of so extraordinary a species of architecture, all the irregular transgressions against the art, all the monstrous offences against nature, disappear; every thing has its reason; every thing is in order; and an harmonious whole arises from the studious application of the means and proportions to the end. Nor could the arches be otherwise than pointed, when the workmen were to imitate the curve which branches of two opposite trees make by their intersection with one another; nor could the columns be otherwise than split into distinct shafts, when they were to represent the stems of clumps of trees growing together. On the same principles they formed the spreading ramifications of the stone-work of the windows, and the stained glass in the interstices, the one to represent the branches, the other the leaves of the opening grove; and both concurred to preserve that gloomy light which inspires religious reverence and dread."

The following quaint and graphic description of the ruins of Melrose Abbey will give a better idea of the early peculiarities of this style than any abstract explanation:

"This Abbey was built in 1136 by King David of Scotland. The church is built in the form of a St. John's cross. The chancel, which is a very stately fabric, is still standing; its roof is very curious, and has much of the Scripture upon it. Although much of the west part is so entirely demolished, that we cannot know how far it extended in that direction. Its length is 258 feet; breadth, 137½; circumference, about 943; height of the south window, 24; breadth, 15½; height of the steeple, 75; the spire is gone. The east window, at which was the great altar is a beautiful structure, consisting of four pillars or bars, with much curious work between them; and on each side many niches for statues. On the top an old man with a globe in his left hand resting on his knee, and a young man on his right; both in a sitting posture, with an open crown over their heads. On the north and south of this window are two others of smaller dimensions. The niches are curiously carved, bearing the figures of men and animals. On the southeast of this church are many musicians admirably carved, with much pleasantness and gayety in their countenances. Also nuns with their veils, some of whom are richly dressed. The south window is much admired for its height and curious workmanship. Niches are on each side and above it, in which have been statues of our Saviour and apostles. Besides these, there are many other figures on the east and west sides of this window: monks with their beards, cowls, and beads; a cripple on the back of a blind man; several animals carved very well, as boars, greyhounds, lions, and others. There are about 68 niches, in the whole, standing: the statues were only demolished about the year 1649.

"So much with respect to the outside of the church. Within, on the north side of the cross, are beautiful pillars, and the sculpture as fresh as if it had been newly cut. On the west side is a statue of St. Peter with a book open, his right hand on it, and two keys hanging on the left. On the south side of this statue is that of St. Paul with a sword. In the middle of the cross stood the steeple—a noble piece of architecture—a quarter of it is still standing. The roof of the south side of the cross is still standing, where is a beautiful staircase much admired, the roof of it winding like a snail cap. There were within the church a vast number of fonts curiously carved, and there were altars dedicated to various saints. The workmanship of some of the pillars resembles, in fineness, Flanders lace

"In regard to what was in part or altogether separated from the body of the church, there was a cloister on the north side, a part of the walls of which are still standing, and where may be observed pleasant walks and seats, with many flowers finely carved, as lilies, &c.; also ferns, grapes, houseleeks, escalops, fir-cones, &c. The door of the north entry of the church is curiously embossed, and the foliage, here and there, in other places, is very beautiful. There were also a vast number of fine buildings within the convent, for the residence and service of the abbot and monks, with gardens and other conveniences—all this enclosed within a high wall, about a mile in circuit. Besides the church, there has been a fine chapel, where the manse now is, and another house adjoining to it, where the foundations of the pillars are still to be seen. On the north side of this house, there has been a curious oratory or private chapel, the foundations of which have lately been discovered, and a large cistern of a single stone, with a leaden pipe conveying the water to it."

Gothic architecture has undergone many changes since the age in which this pile was erected; indeed, its peculiar genius admits of almost inexhaustible variety.

The minster of Strasburg, the cathedral of Cologne, York minster, Westminster, and Salisbury cathedral, are among the masterpieces of this style.

Arabian or Moresque Architecture.

BEFORE the appearance of Mohammed, the ancient Arabian architecture, of which very few examples now remain, was rude, compared with the neighbouring Egyptian, Chaldean, Syrian, and Persian. The Caaba of Mecca, the only temple extant of their idol worship, is a quadrangular building, lighted by one window and a door, having three octagonal pillars supporting the roof.

From the latter part of the eighth to the middle of the ninth century, the Arabians made wonderful progress in the sciences.

The finest example of the first period of Moresque architecture, is the mosque of Cordova, in Spain, commenced in 770, by Abderahman, and finished by his son Hisham. It bears, in its arrangements, a striking resemblance to the basilicæ of Rome, particularly to those of St. Agnese and St. Paola. After the conquest of Cordova, it was converted into a cathedral; and though disfigured by modern additions, it preserves much of its ancient splendor. During the second period, which includes the close of the thirteenth century, the style was greatly improved in elegance, of which the royal palace and fortress of the Alhambra of Granada is a splendid example—the most perfect specimen of pure Arabian architecture that was ever produced. In this period, no traces of the Byzantine or Romanesque are to be found. The whole of the Alhambra is one plain, so arranged as to suit the plateau of the rock. After passing the principal entrance, there are two oblong courts, one of which, celebrated in history, is called the Court of the Lions—the buildings are one hundred feet high, and fifty broad, having one hundred and twenty-eight columns of white marble. Round these courts, on the ground-floor, are the apartments of the palace—those for state looking towards the country; the others, for coolness and retirement, opening into the interior porticoes. The length of the enclosure is two thousand three hundred feet, its breadth six hundred. The walls are covered with arabesque, and ornaments of fanciful and diversified forms, and of various colours—gold, pink, blue, purple, and white—produced by painting, encrustation, mosaic, and gilding, imparting an air of refined luxury and fairy enchantment.

The third period, which extends from the close of the thirteenth century to the decline of the Saracen power, is marked by an amalgamation of the Saracen architecture with the Gothic, of which the beautiful cathedrals of Seville and Burgos are examples. Towards the latter portion of this period, the Italian orders began to be combined with the other, in detailed parts.

The Arabian and Gothic may be said to have taken their rise from the same origin—the debased Roman; the Arabian from the Byzantine, the Gothic from the Lombard; though in their progress and development they were unconnected and original.

The preceding remarks refer more especially to the architecture of the western Arabians, found in Spain; yet there is a close resemblance between it and that of the Moors of Asia and Africa.

Mexican Architecture.

The specimens of architecture found in Mexico, resemble, in many respects, those of the ancient Egyptians and Hindoos, not only in the vast magnitude of the structures, but in the general character, in the use of the pyramidal form, and in hieroglyphic inscriptions on the walls. They were not the productions of the natives found in Mexico by the Europeans, but probably of the Toltecans, a more ancient nation, who had inhabited the country.

The temple of Cholula is one of the largest structures ever erected on our globe. The base is 1440 feet in length, and the height is 177 feet. It consists of eight stories, each forming a platform, on which stands the one above it. The walls are not perpendicular, but are inclined in an angle of 70 degrees, and the terraces are very wide; the upper stories are much smaller than the base. Some of these appear to have contained sepulchral chambers for the priests, and descending galleries lead down to immense dark halls, probably used for religious mysteries.

Cholula much resembles the tower of Belus, at Babylon, as described by Herodotus.

The remains of a palace at Mitla show that it must have been an edifice of great extent and grandeur, and the walls appear to have been sculptured or tooled externally, in imitation of mat or basket work, a species of decoration characteristic of Toltecan taste, and often found in sepulchral chambers. The same building has also a portico, with plain cylindrical columns, differing from any found elsewhere.

At Teotihuacan, a few leagues to the north-east of the city

of Mexico, are an immense number of pyramids—several hundred small ones, ranged in files or lines and two larger ones, consecrated to the sun and moon. Each of the latter was divided into four platforms, the slopes between which consisted of steps, and on the summit was a colossal statue covered with plates of gold, which were stripped off by the soldiers of Cortes, who also destroyed the statue. With frantic zeal the Spaniards endeavoured to destroy every vestige of idolatry, even while they violated every precept of the Prince of peace, in whose name they committed their ravages.

Besides monuments which are chiefly works of magnificence, others exist which attest the high degree of civilization attained by the Toltecans, such as roads and bridges.

Modern Architecture.

WHILE the moderns have invented little essentially new, they have employed the principal parts of ancient architecture in new combinations. The era of modern architecture may be said to have commenced about the latter end of the 15th century. One of the best specimens of modern skill and taste is the cathedral of St. Peter, at Rome. It was begun in 1506, by Bramante of Urbino, by the direction of Pope Julius II., who resolved to construct an edifice superior to any thing then in existence. But death overtook both Pope and architect, in 1514. The work, however, was continued for 135 years, under twelve successive artists. The dome and cupola were designed by

Michael Angelo, who made a model of it in fifteen days, which cost only twenty-five crowns. It is one of the largest structures ever erected; though the ground-plan does not quite equal that of Karnac on the Nile, it reaches six times its height. The ground-plan is a Latin cross, 720 feet in length and 510 feet in breadth; the height to the top of the cross which crowns the summit is 500 feet. The western and principal façade is 400 feet in length. The columns supporting the entablature are nine feet in diameter, and one hundred in height. The dome rests upon a pedestal, which is surrounded by a colonnade fifty feet high, its base being 200 feet from the ground.

The extent of the outlines rivals the Egyptian pyramid, and the skill displayed in the construction, far exceeds any thing connected with those enormous heaps of almost rude stones.

The multiplicity of breaks in the western façade, destroys the simplicity of the horizontal lines of the entablature, which ought to represent wooden beams. The mind is perplexed in determining how timber could be worked or connected in this way, and is displeased to observe this deviation without any good cause; the same objection is more palpably evident in the colonnade which encompasses the pedestal of the dome; here the columns are placed in pairs, and there is a break over each pair, by which their connexion with each other is entirely interrupted. Instead of preserving the face of the building plain and simple, to accord with its great outlines and gigantic order, the entrance doorways are of various dimensions and shapes, and the whole building is covered with small tablets, and perforated with small windows, even the dome itself.

St. Paul's church, London, is built on the same general plan, but differs greatly in details, and is of much smaller dimensions. Its height is much greater in proportion to its base than St

Peter's. The façade consists of two orders, one above the other, which renders it greatly inferior in grandeur to that of St. Peter's. Its dome, however, is superior in point of good taste, for the entablature of its colonnade is one unbroken feature, and its columns are placed singly: the dome, also, is free from the small various-shaped windows which disfigure that of St. Peter's.

A great fault in modern architecture is caused by a desire to exhibit in the same building decorations of different ages and incongruous characters, which mar the general expression. A building should convey but one prominent idea. If it be large, majesty will be the most appropriate characteristic, but this can only be preserved by keeping all the parts on one grand scale, and by making the ornaments subordinate. If a façade, for instance, be broken by a portico in the middle, the attention must be divided three ways, and grandeur is sacrificed. In smaller fabrics, beauty, elegance, or gracefulness, may be aimed at; still the expression of a single idea should be preserved, even playfulness gentleness, contentment, may be typified by the architect.

British Architecture.

When Julius Cæsar invaded Britain, (A. D. 55,) the Britons were entirely unacquainted with the art of building in stone. The Romans not only extended their improvements over the whole province, but encouraged and instructed the Britons to follow their example. From the year A. D. 80, to the middle of the fourth century, architecture, and all the arts connected with it, made a rapid progress. The cities were surrounded with walls and adorned with temples, palaces, basilicæ, porticoes, baths, aqueducts, &c., displaying the splendor and magnificence of Roman architecture. The wall of Severus, extending from the Solway to the Tyne, with numerous towers, military stations, deep ditches, and strong outworks, was a work truly characteristic of Roman enterprise and grandeur. The native Britons had improved so much by the instructions and example of their conquerors, that in the third century they became famed as architects and artificers. About the end of the fourth century, British architecture, from various causes, began sensibly to decline, chiefly owing to the civil wars and incursions of the barbarians rendering it necessary for the Romans gradually to withdraw their troops from Britain, even at the risk of leaving the colony unprotected. Christianity had now made considerable progress in the British isles. Of the small churches in which the converts assembled for worship, few remain. One of the most remarkable is at Pieranzabuloe, in Cornwall, built by St. Pieran, about 430.*

Deserted by the Romans, the Britons became a prey to the Picts, Scots, and Saxons, and relapsed into their former barbarism.

Vestiges of Roman architecture are still numerous at York, Lincoln, and other places; but, however interesting to the archæologist, they offer little that is worthy of attention to the architect, except in the massy and substantial mode of construction. Of the monuments of remote British antiquity, Stonehenge, on Salisbury plain, is the most remarkable. The most probable opinion

* It is twenty-five feet long, and twelve and a half wi le. The walls are twelve and a half feet high. It has been imbedded in the sand for centuries, and was recently uncovered and found in a state of perfect preservation.

concerning these fragments is, that they formed a rude British temple or altar, erected by the Druids. Similar arrangements of fragments, though on a smaller scale, are found in other parts of the kingdom, particularly at Arebury, Stanton-Drew, and Lundie in Fifeshire.

Down to the Norman conquest, with the exception of some Norman edifices, built by Edward the Confessor, who was educated in Normandy, the Anglo-Saxons seem to have possessed little taste for architecture, public or private. Eddius, who wrote the life of Winfred, informs us that the church of Hexham, built in 674, was one of the most magnificent fabrics of the time, and was constructed of polished stone, with columns, subterraneous chapel, and spiral stairs. The capitals and walls of the sanctuary were decorated with histories, statues, and various figures in stone, as well as a variety of pictures. The principal architects of those days were churchmen. The Anglo-Saxon architecture was a debased Roman, differing from the Anglo-Norman in its want of harmony and purity, its semicircular apses and peculiar mouldings, without aisles or transepts.

The Norman, or new style as it was then called, was established and confirmed by William the Conqueror, who erected castles and strongholds in all the principal towns.

The Anglo-Norman castles, often of large dimensions, exhibited a certain rude grandeur, and served both for residence and defence. Though differing from each other in size and plan, the largest and most perfect were invariably distinguished by leading features. They were generally situated on an eminence near a river, or the junction of two rivers, or on a rocky precipice or promontory on the sea-shore. The whole extent of the castle was surrounded by a deep and broad ditch, sometimes filled with water, sometimes dry, called a fosse. On the inside of the ditch rose the wall of the castle eight or ten feet thick, and twenty or thirty feet high, flanked with round or square towers of three stories, for the accommodation of the principal officers. On the inside were erected lodgings for the retainers, storehouses, offices, &c. On the top of this wall, and on the roofs of the houses stood the defenders of the castle. The great gate was likewise defended by two towers, with rooms over the archway, which was closed with thick folding doors of oak plated with iron, besides an iron portcullis or grate, let down from above. Within the outer wall was a large area, called when large, a ballium or outer bayle, in which stood the chapel. On the inside of this outer bayle was another ditch or wall, flanked with towers, enclosing the inner bayle or court, in the centre of which stood the principal tower or keep of the castle, often a very large and lofty fabric of four or five stories, with gloomy apartments and small windows. It contained the great hall in which the retainers assembled to enjoy the hospitality of their chief. Under ground were the dungeons in which prisoners were confined.

In London, towards the end of the twelfth century, the houses were still of wood, while the palaces and castles of the Anglo-Norman princes, nobility, and prelates, were of stone. As building churches and monasteries was believed to be one of the most effectual means of obtaining the favour of heaven, prodigious numbers of both were erected, both in England and Scotland, in the course of the thirteenth, fourteenth, and fifteenth centuries. In the reign of Henry III. alone, one hundred and fifty-seven abbeys, priories, and other religious houses, were founded in England. Many of the cathedrals and conventual churches were large and magnificent fabrics, raised at a vast expense. In the reign of Henry VII. the purity and grandeur of the Gothic began to degenerate into an excess of minute ornament, and subdivision of compartments, known as the florid or perpendicular style, of which the superb chapel of Henry VII., at Westminster, is the most splendid example. Christ-church college, at Oxford, was built by Cardinal Wolsey in the same style and with equal magnificence.

In the reign of Henry VIII., a corrupt style was introduced by John of Treviso and John of Padua, who were brought over by Holbein. The dissolution and confiscation of the monasteries and religious houses in this reign, were the means of bringing many of them into the possession of noblemen and gentlemen, who fitted them up for their own residences. Others imitated the same style in their new buildings and additions; and thus was gradually matured the English Tudor or Elizabethan style, of which many splendid examples still remain. In the latter part of the reign of Elizabeth and beginning of that of James, the rich nobles, not content with the splendor of the Tudor style, called in the aid of Italian architecture, and produced a modification, known as the style of James I., which, in spite of its corrupt and anomalous admixture, and somewhat fantastic decorations, admitted of considerable magnificence. The distinctive features of the Tudor or Elizabethan, are the cupola with its gilded vane crowning the lofty towers and turrets, either round, square, or polygonal, connected with long, embattled galleries; the carved oriels, the deep and many-lighted bay-windows, projecting in fantastic angles and curves; the richly-embossed finials, wreathed chimney-shafts, florid pinnacles, and panelled walls; battlements and buttresses, sculptured dripstones, with all their rich mouldings and carvings.

In no country was architecture, in early times, more encouraged or better practised, according to the taste of the age, than in Scotland. The Norman and Gothic ecclesiastical edifices of Scotland, with the exception of some foreign features, exhibit the same style and characteristics, the same beauty and delicacy of taste, as those of England. They are all much dilapidated, having suffered more from the double reformation and civil wars than those of the sister kingdom.

The introduction of Italo-Roman architecture into England, was almost two centuries later than its revival in Italy. The Tudor style, as we have already seen, began, in the reign of James, to exhibit a mixture of Roman and Italian, first in porches and small parts, and afterwards in larger portions. At length, the Banqueting House at Whitehall, by Inigo Jones, Greenwich Hospital and St. Paul's cathedral, by Wren, fixed the complete introduction of the Italo-Roman style.

In proportion as the Roman and Italian styles prevailed, the Gothic began to be despised; all the architects and writers of the day, thinking it necessary to show their taste, by heaping upon it every sort of vituperation and contempt. But such is the instability of fashion, that now, while the Roman and Italian are in their turn despised and abused, the Gothic, after being consigned to oblivion and contempt for nearly a century and a half, has again come into repute. Its beauty, excellence, and science of construction, are universally recognized and appreciated

Remains of Ancient Architecture in the United States.

"THE ancient monuments of the western United States," says Mr. Squier, the author of a late work on the subject, "consist for the most part of elevations and embankments of earth and stone, erected with great labour and manifest design. They are found chiefly in the great valleys of the West, and it is a remarkable fact that they are most numerous near the positions which have been chosen for the towns which have increased the most rapidly. They are always found, when explored, to contain relics, such as personal ornaments and useful utensils, of various substances. They consist mostly of earthen vases of elegant form, sometimes with tasteful bas-reliefs on the exterior; of copper knives, bracelets, &c. The carved pipe is of constant recurrence. All of them are executed with strict fidelity to nature, and with exquisite skill. Not only are the features of the various objects represented faithfully, but their peculiarities and habits are in some degree exhibited. The otter is shown in a characteristic attitude, holding a fish in his mouth; the heron also holds a fish; and the hawk grasps a small bird in his talons, which he tears with his beak. The panther, the bear, the wolf—the heron, crow, buzzard, swallow, paroquet, toucan, and other indigenous and southern birds—together with the turtle, frog, toad, rattlesnake, &c., are recognized at a glance.

"Lines of embankments, varying in height from five to thirty feet, and enclosed areas of from one to fifty acres, are common; while enclosures of one or two hundred acres are far from infrequent. They appear to have been raised both for defensive and religious purposes. The group of works at the mouth of the Sciota has an aggregate of at least twenty miles of embankment; yet the entire amount of land embraced within its walls, does not probably much exceed two hundred acres. Perhaps the larger portion of them are regular in outline, the square and the circle predominating. The mounds are of all dimensions, from those of but a few feet in height and a few yards in diameter, to those which, like the celebrated structure at the mouth of Grave Creek, in Virginia, rise to the height of seventy feet, and measure one thousand feet in circumference at the base. The great mound at Selzerstown, Mississippi, is computed to cover six acres of ground. Mounds of these extraordinary dimensions are most common at the South, though there are some at the North of great size. The usual dimensions are, however, considerably less than the examples here given. The greater number range from six to thirty feet in perpendicular height, by forty to one hundred feet in diameter at the base.

"The embankment known as Fort Hill, in Highland county, Ohio, is one of the most interesting relics of the kind. The defences occupy the summit of a hill which is five hundred feet above the bed of Brush Creek, which flows at its base. Running along the edge of the hill, is an embankment of mingled earth and stone, interrupted at intervals by gateways. Interior to this is a ditch, from which the material composing the wall was taken. The length of the wall is eight thousand two hundred and twenty-four feet, or something over a mile and a half. In height, measuring from the bottom of the ditch, it varies from six to ten feet, though at some places it rises to the height of fifteen feet. Its average base is thirty-five or forty feet. It is thrown up somewhat below the brow of the hill, the level of the terrace being generally about even with the top of the wall—but in some places it rises considerably above. The outer slope of the wall is more abrupt than that of the hill; the earth and stones from the ditch, sliding down fifty or a hundred feet, have formed a declivity for that distance, so steep as to be difficult of ascent, even with the aid which the trees and bushes afford. The ditch has an average width of not far from fifty feet; and in many places is dug through the sandstone layer upon which the soil of the terrace rests. The inner declivity of the ditch appears to have been terraced.

"Such are the more striking features of this interesting work. Considered in a military point of view, as a work of defence, it is well chosen, well guarded, and, with an adequate force, impregnable to any mode of attack practised by a rude or semi-civilized people. As a natural stronghold, it has few equals; and the degree of skill displayed, and the amount of labour expended in constructing its artificial defences, challenge our admiration and excite our surprise. With all the facilities and numerous mechanical appliances of the present day, the construction of a work of this magnitude would be no insignificant undertaking.

"The evidence of antiquity afforded by the aspect of the forest, is worthy of more than a passing notice. Actual examination showed the existence of not far from two hundred annual rings or layers, in a large chestnut-tree now standing on the intrenchments. This would give nearly six hundred years as the age of the tree. If to this we add the probable period intervening from the time of the building of this work and its abandonment, and the subsequent period up to its invasion by the forest, we are led irresistibly to the conclusion that it has an antiquity of at least one thousand years. But when we notice, all around us, the crumbling trunks of trees, half hidden in the accumulating soil, we are induced to fix upon an antiquity still more remote." Their erection is ascribed, with most probability, to the Toltecan race, whose monuments are to be found in great numbers in Mexico

Music.

The term music is now restricted to the art, which, by the modulation, succession, and combination of sounds, seeks to imitate nature, and to affect the soul with every emotion of which it is capable. We daily perceive, in common life, the germs from which it grew up. Nature seems to have established an intimate connexion between the emotions and the sense of hearing. Of the two nobler senses, sight and hearing, the former seems to belong more particularly to the understanding. We owe to the eye, and to abstractions from the images which it presents, most of our general notions and ideas; while the ear appears to be more intimately connected with the feelings. Feeling expresses itself most readily in tones. Fear, joy, anger, have each a peculiar sound, understood by all human beings. Every musical production, to deserve the name, must be expressive of emotions, and, through them, of ideas. But though music exists wherever the human species are found, it does not follow that every good piece of music must please all men alike, or be understood by all alike, for music is an art, requiring cultivation both of the mind and heart, to appreciate it fully. Still, however, music of the most elevated kind retains so much of its character of universality, that the productions of the greatest masters delight much more generally than the best performances in other arts.

Insensibility to music may generally be referred to a defective organization in the sense of hearing; but the whole conformation of some men is probably much better fitted, than that of others, to enable them to receive pleasure from it. But in proof that a full appreciation of melody and rhythm may exist, where the faculty of comprehending and receiving pleasure from complicated harmonies is dormant, we may instance Pope, Dr. Johnson, Sir Walter Scott, and Lord Byron, none of whom could comprehend the mazy involutions of modern music, while to rhythm and simple melody, they were highly susceptible.

The effects of music are sometimes said to be merely sensual. It is addressed to the ear, indeed; but all influences from without are conveyed through the medium of the senses, and the tones of music often speak a language to the soul, richer in meaning than any words. It will hardly be pretended that feelings which cannot be expressed in words, are necessarily of a lower character than those which may be so expressed. The most elevated emotions are beyond the power of even metaphorical language. Nothing is merely sensual which makes a lasting spiritual impression upon the soul; and he who denies to music such a power, has not heard its sublimest strains, or has not the capacity to appreciate them.

Music, considered in its technical sense, rests on mathematics and acoustics. It operates in space and time, in such a way as to be susceptible of mathematical measurement. Tones, considered merely as to their duration, are magnitudes of time, which stand in a descending geometrical progression. In space, tones can be considered as magnitudes of sound, and their distances from each other in the scale, are expressed in numbers, which have reference to a mathematical division of the space between two sounds, adopted as limits—the octave, the third, seventh, &c

Similar proportions exist between the various voices—the treble, bass, &c.—and between the various keys. In instrumental music, the depth and height of the tones depend upon the proportions of the thickness, length, and lightness of the chords, in stringed instruments; the quality, diameter, and distance of the openings, in wind instruments, and the like; and all these proportions can be determined and measured according to mathematical rules. This regularity may perhaps afford the reason why the effects of music are so general, and its influence on the nerves so powerful. The same circumstance renders it incapable of expressing those fine shades of feeling which can be communicated only by the aid of reflection.

Music is based on rhythm, melody, and harmony. Rhythm is a succession of sounds in measured time—it is to the ear, what symmetrical proportions are to the eye. A faculty for rhythm may exist where there is little or no power of appreciating melody, or harmony. We find a fondness for rhythm among savage tribes, who know little else of music. With them it is generally combined with dancing, and is sometimes only signified by a regular clapping of hands. Melody is a succession of sounds in measured time, and at harmonic intervals. Harmony is the mixture of single diatonic sounds: it requires ordinarily much care and attention to comprehend its beauties, which are purely of an intellectual character. Melody alone awakens the feelings of love, joy, pity, grief, &c. Harmony or rhythm cannot express these, though they may add greatly to their effect. It was said by Dr. Burney, that, after harmony and melody had been heard together, nothing could compensate for their separation.

As precise divisions in sciences or arts, or any of the departments of human action, grow up slowly, and kindred branches are at first usually mingled, it is highly probable that dancing and music, two arts founded on measured time, were at first intimately connected, as we find still to be the case among most, perhaps all, tribes in a state of infancy. By degrees the song was separated from the dance, and instruments, which at first only served to accompany the song, became also the objects of a separate art. Tones in themselves, apart from the dance or words, were cultivated; the laws according to which they must be connected, so as best to express the language of feeling, were more and more investigated, the application of these laws further and further extended, until music was developed to that degree of perfection which we admire in the works of the greatest masters.

Perhaps the first instrument invented was the pipe of the shepherd, who, in his life of leisure, heard the wind whistle among the reeds. It seems probable that shepherds first cultivated music as an art; while warriors may have made use of the exciting war-cry and war-song before.

From the sixteenth and seventeenth centuries, there grew up at the courts of monarchs the free chamber style, and from this the theatrical style. The invention of the opera in the sixteenth century has chiefly contributed to the splendor and variety of modern vocal and instrumental music. The merit of the advancement of vocal music is claimed particularly by the Italians; the improvement of instrumental music by the Germans and French.

Ancient Music.*

Most of the ancient musical instruments were of Egyptian invention: as the triangular lyre; the monanlos, or single flute; the kettle-drum; and the sistrum, an instrument of sacrifice. The profession of music was hereditary among the Egyptians, as was the case with every other profession. This custom was imitated by the Hebrews and Dorians. And as we are told by Plato, that not only the music but the sculpture of the Egyptians was circumscribed by law and continued invariable for many ages, which accounts for the little progress they made in either, it seems that, during the time that the arts were thus rendered stationary, new music was prohibited, and that the old was sacred and so connected with religion, that it was forbidden to be used on light and common occasions.

"At the end of the passage into a sepulchre near Thebes," says James Bruce, "is the picture of a man playing upon the harp, painted in fresco, and quite entire. To guess by the detail of the figure, the painter should have had about the same degree of merit as a good sign-painter of the present day; yet he has represented the action of the musician in a manner not to be mistaken. His left hand seems employed in the upper part of the instrument among the notes in alto, as if in an arpeggio; while, stooping forwards, he seems with his right hand to be beginning with the lowest string, and promising to ascend with the most rapid execution; this action, so obviously rendered by

* The following account of the progress of music is chiefly condensed from Dr. B rney's elaborate work on the subject.

an indifferent artist, shows that it was a common one in his time, or, in other words, that great hands were then frequent, and consequently that music was well understood and diligently followed.

"If we allow the performer's stature to be about five feet ten inches, then we may compute the harp in its extreme length to be something less than six feet and a half. It seems to support itself in equilibrio on its base, and needs only the player's guidance to keep it steady. It has thirteen strings; the length of these, and the force and liberty with which they are treated, show that they are made in a very different manner from those of the lyre.

"This instrument is of a much more elegant form than the triangular Grecian harp. It wants the forepiece of the frame opposite to the longest string, which certainly must have improved its tone, but must likewise have rendered the instrument itself weaker and more liable to accidents.

"The principles upon which the harp is constructed are rational and ingenious; the ornamental parts are likewise executed in the very best manner. Besides the elegance of its form, we must observe how near it approached to a perfect instrument; for it wanted only two strings of having two complete octaves in compass. Whether these were intentionally omitted, we cannot now determine, as we have no idea of the music or taste of that time; but if the harp be painted in the proportions in which it was made, it might be demonstrated that it could not bear more than the thirteen strings with which it was furnished. Indeed, the cross-bar would break with the tension of the four longest, if they were made of the size and consistence, and tuned to the pitch that ours are at present."

This instrument is probably the Theban harp, before and at

the time of Sesostris, who adorned Thebes, and probably caused it to be painted there, as well as the other figures in the sepulchre of his father.

There is little doubt that the Egyptians had, in the most flourishing times of their empire, a music and instruments of their own, far superior to those of other countries less civilized and refined; that after their subjugation by the Persians, this music and these instruments were lost: but under the Ptolemies, music, together with the other arts of Greece, were brought into Egypt and encouraged at the court of Alexandria, more than at any other place in the known world, till the captivity of Cleopatra, an event with which both the empire and the history of the Egyptians ceased.

MUSIC OF THE HEBREWS.

Jubal is the only musician before the flood, whose name is recorded. The next mention of music in the Scriptures, is in the time of Laban the Syrian, who, reproaching his son-in-law Jacob for carrying away his daughters as captives taken with the sword, says, "Wherefore didst thou flee away secretly, and steal away from me? and didst not tell me, that I might have sent thee away with mirth and with songs, with tabret and with harp?"

The instruments of music mentioned in the Psalms, are the trumpet, harp, tabret, pipe, lute, cymbals, sackbut, shawm, cornet, and timbrel, though some of these are doubtless different translations for the same instrument.

If the least hope remain, that a true idea of Jewish instruments can ever be acquired, it must be from the arch of Titus, at

Rome, where it is supposed that the spoils brought from Jerusalem by that emperor, have been exactly represented in sculpture. Among these are several musical instruments, particularly the silver trumpets, called by the Hebrews, chatzolzeroth ; and horns, supposed to resemble the shawms, mentioned so often in the Scripture, called in Hebrew, keranim, or sacerdotal trumpets. But the arch upon which these instruments are sculptured, though, according to Venuti, of excellent workmanship, was not erected till after the death of Titus ; and, to say the truth, the instruments are of no uncommon form. The trumpets are long, straight tubes, as modern trumpets would be if not folded up for the convenience of the player ; and the horns are such as often occur in ancient sculpture.

With regard to modern Jewish music, instrumental and vocal performances have been almost banished since the destruction of Jerusalem, and the little music now used is a modern license ; for the Jews, from a passage in one of the prophets, think it unfit to sing or rejoice before the coming of the Messiah, till then, they are bound to mourn and repent in silence : the only Jews who have a regular musical establishment in their synagogues, are the Germans, who sing in parts ; and these preserve some old melodies, or species of chants, which are thought to be very ancient.

GRECIAN MUSIC.

The earlier Greek musicians, Chiron, Amphion, Orpheus, Linus, and Musæus, were also poets who sang their verses to the sound of the lyre, thus instructing mankind in the rude traditions of their times. It has been imagined, with great appearance of truth, that the occupation of the first poets and musicians of

Greece, very much resembled that of the bards among the Celts and Germans, and the scalds in Iceland and Scandinavia; chanters, who sung their works in great cities, and in the palaces of princes, where they were treated with great respect, and regarded as inspired persons.

Homer brought to perfection the strains of the historic muse, and doubtless accompanied his stirring heroics with the sound of the lyre. The mention of the practice of music in private life is frequent in Homer.

In the solemn embassy sent by Agamemnon to Achilles, during his retirement—after he had quitted the Grecian camp in disgust—it is said by Homer of the delegates, that,

> "Amused at ease, the godlike man they found
> Pleased with the solemn harp's harmonious sound:
> (The well-wrought harp from conquered Theba came,
> Of polished silver was its costly frame;)
> With this he soothes his angry soul, and sings
> The immortal deeds of heroes and of kings."

Poetry and music, in the early ages of these arts, were so much united, that all the lyric, elegiac, and even epic bards, were necessarily and professedly musicians. From the time of Homer till that of Sappho, there is almost a total blank in literature; for though several names of poets and musicians are recorded, yet of their works only a few fragments remain. Nor are any literary productions preserved entire, between the time of Sappho and Anacreon, who flourished at the distance of nearly a hundred years from each other; and between the poems of Anacreon and Pindar there is another chasm of nearly a century. After this, the works which still subsist of the three great tragic poets, Æschylus, Sophocles, and Euripides; and of the historians, Herodotus,

Thucydides, and Xenophon, together with Plato, Aristotle, Euclid, Theocritus, and many others—all produced within the space of less than three hundred years—mark this as one of those illustrious and uncommon periods, in which all the powers of human nature and genius seem to have been called forth and exerted to furnish light and instruction to mankind, in intermediate ages of darkness, indolence, calamity, and barbarism.

All ancient writers, who mention the progressive state of music in Greece, are unanimous in celebrating the talents of Terpander, who flourished about 671 B. C. Several writers tell us that he added three strings to the lyre, which, before his time, had but four. Among the many signal services which he is said to have done to music, none was of more importance than the notation, which is ascribed to him, for ascertaining and preserving melody, which before was traditional and wholly dependent on memory The invention, however, of musical characters, has been attributed by Alypius and Gandentius, two Greek writers on music, to Pythagoras, who flourished two centuries after Terpander. Plutarch, however, assures us that Terpander, the inventor of nomes for the cithara in hexameter verse, set them to music, as well as the verses of Homer, in order to sing them at the public games. And Clemens Alexandrinus, in telling us that this musician wrote the laws of Lycurgus in verse, and set them to music, makes use of the same expression as Plutarch, which seems clearly to imply a written melody. But Terpander rendered his name illustrious, no less by his performance both on the flute and cithara than by his compositions. The historian Hellanicus informs us that he obtained the first prize in the musical contests at the Carnean games; and by the testimony of Plutarch, who says that no other proof need be urged of the excellence of Terpander, in the art of playing upon the cithara than what is given by the register of the Pythic games, from which it appears that he gained four prizes, successively, at those solemnities.

It is natural to suppose that the first attempts at music in Greece, as well as in other countries, must have been rude and simple; and that rhythm, or time, was attended to before tone or melody. We accordingly find that instruments of percussion preceded all others; and that the steps in the dance, and the feet in poetry, were regulated and marked with precision long before sounds were sustained or refined. When these two circumstances first engaged attention, the flute imitated, and the lyre accompanied the voice, in its inflections of joy and sorrow.

One of the most extraordinary circumstances in the history of this art, is that the enharmonic genus, even with the diesis or quarter-tone, was almost exclusively in use before the time of Aristoxenus, the cotemporary of Alexander the Great, insomuch that it was customary, with the old masters, to give their scholars diagrams to practise of condensed scales, divided into quarter-tones, as necessary exercises for the hand or voice. Of these scales, examples are still remaining in the writings of Aristoxenus, Euclid, and Aristides Quintilianus. In the time of Aristoxenus, however, the enharmonic was upon the decline, and the chromatic daily increasing in favour. But the most important event in the history of music, was the establishment of instrumental contests at the Pythic games. From this time music became a distinct art. The choruses, which till now had governed the melody, now became subordinate. Philosophers in vain exclaimed against these innovations, which they thought would ruin the morals of the people, who (as they are never disposed to sacrifice the pleasures of the senses to those of the understanding) heard these novelties with rapture, and encouraged the authors of them. This species of music, therefore, soon passed from the games to the stage, seizing there upon the principal parts of the drama; and from being the humble companion of poetry, becoming her compeer.

It is related by several ancient writers, that Pythagoras, one day meditating on the want of some rule to guide the ear, analogous to what had been used to help the other senses, chanced to pass by a blacksmith's shop, and observing that the hammers, which were four in number, sounded very harmoniously, he had them weighed, and found them in the proportion of 6, 8, 9, and 12. Upon this, he suspended four strings, of equal length and thickness, &c., fastened weights in the above-mentioned proportions to each of them, respectively, and found that they gave the same sounds that the hammers had done, namely, the fourth, fifth, and octave, to the gravest tone, which last interval did not make part of the musical system before; for the Greeks had gone no farther than the heptachord, or seven strings, till that time.

But, though both hammers and anvil have been swallowed by ancients and moderns, and have passed through them from one to another with an ostrich-like digestion, upon examination and experiment, it appears that hammers, of different size and weight, will no more produce different tones on the same anvil, than bows or clappers, of different sizes, will from the same string or bell. But though modern incredulity and experiment have robbed Pythagoras of the glory of discovering musical ratios by accident, he has been allowed the superior merit of arriving at them by meditation and design. At least the invention of the harmonical canon, or monochord, has been ascribed to him, both by ancient and modern writers.

Pythagoras supposed the air to be the vehicle of sound; and

the agitation of that element, occasioned by a similar agitation in parts of the sounding body, to be the cause of it. The vibrations of a string, or any other sonorous body, being communicated to the air, affect the auditory nerves with the sensation of sound; and this sound, according to him, was acute or grave, in proportion as the vibrations were quick or slow. It was also known, by experiment, that of two strings, equal in every thing but length, the shorter made the quicker vibrations and gave the acuter sound. By these discoveries it was seen, that sound, considered in the vibrations that cause it, and the dimensions of the vibrating or sonorous body, was reduced to quantity, and, as such, became subject to calculation and expressible by numbers.

The monochord was an instrument of a single string, furnished with a moveable bridge, and contrived for the measuring and adjusting the ratios of musical intervals, by accurate divisions. This instrument was recommended by Pythagoras, on his death-bed, as the musical investigator, the criterion of truth. It appears to have been in constant use among the ancients, as the only means of forming the ear to the accurate perception, and the voice to the true intonation of those minute and difficult intervals which were then practised in melody.

The second musical improvement attributed to Pythagoras, was the addition of an eighth string to the lyre, which before his time had only seven, and was thence called a heptachord.

After musical ratios were discovered and reduced to numbers, they were made, by Pythagoras and his followers, the type of order and just proportion in all things; hence virtue, friendship, good government, celestial motion, the human soul, and God himself, were harmony.

This discovery gave birth to various species of music, far more strange and inconceivable than chromatic and enharmonic: such as divine music, mundane music, elementary music, and many other divisions and subdivisions, upon which the old writers never fail to expatiate with wonderful complaisance.

Pythagoras is said, by the writers of his life, to have regarded music as something divine, and to have had such an opinion of its power over the human affections that, according to the Egyptian system, he ordered his disciples to be waked every morning, and lulled to sleep every night, by sweet sounds. He likewise considered it as greatly conducive to health, and made use of it in diseases of the body as well as those of the mind. His biographers and secretaries even pretend to tell us what kind of music he applied for these purposes. Grave and solemn, we may be certain; and vocal, say they, was preferred to instrumental; and the lyre to the flute, not only for its gravity, but because instruction could be conveyed to the mind, by means of singing at the same time the ear was delighted. This was said to have been the opinion of Minerva. In very high antiquity, mankind gave human wisdom to their gods, and afterwards took it from them to bestow it upon mortals.

As Pythagoras was the discoverer of musical ratios, by the subdivision of a monochord, or single string, which before, a tradition only had preserved, Euclid was the first who wrote upon the subject, and reduced these divisions to a mathematical demonstration. Of all the writings upon ancient music that have come down to us, his seem to be the most correct and compressed.

Euclid was the first who demonstrated that an octave is somewhat less than six whole tones. What Aristoxenus called a half-tone, Euclid proved to be a smaller interval, in the proportion of 2, 5, 6, to 2, 4, 3. Didymus, cotemporary with Nero, was the first who introduced the minor tone into the scale, and, consequently, the practical major 3d 4-5th, which harmonized the whole system, and pointed out the road to counterpoint, an honour that most critics have bestowed upon Ptolemy, he seems to have a better title to the invention of modern harmony, or music in parts, than Guido.

Ptolemy having a facility, and, perhaps, a pleasure, in calculating, seems to have sported with the scale, and wantonly to have tried confusions, by dissecting and torturing it in all possible ways; and, though one of his many systems suits our present practice, it is not to be imagined that it was designedly calculated for the use of counterpoint, which was far from his thoughts. It seems, however, as if music in parts was first suggested by this arrangement of the interval; for the 3ds and 6ths, which were before so harsh and crude as to be deservedly ranked among the discords, were now softened and sweetened into that grateful coincidence with which modern ears are so much delighted. It was impossible, after hearing them, for lovers of music not to feel the charms arising from the combination and succession of these consonances; and it was from this time that the seeds of that harmony, which may be said, in a less mysterious sense than that of Pythagoras, to be implanted in our nature, began to spring up. They were certainly of slow growth, as no good fruit was produced from them for more than one thousand years after; but arts, like animals to whom great longevity is allowed, have a long infancy and childhood, before adolescence and maturity come on.

The Romans had, in very high antiquity, a rude and coarse music of their own, and had imitated the Etruscan musical establishments, both in their army and temples.

The first Roman triumph, according to Dionysius, was that of Romulus over the Cæninenses; in which, clad in a purple robe, he was drawn in a chariot by four horses; the rest of the army, horse and foot, followed, ranged in three several divisions, hymning their gods in songs of their country, and celebrating their general in extemporary verses. This account affords a very venerable origin to the improvisatori of Itaiy; as the event happened in the fourth year of Rome, 749 years before Christ, and fourth year of the seventh Olympiad.

Servius Tullius, who began his reign 578 B. C., ordained that two whole centuries should consist of trumpeters, blowers of the horn, &c., and of such as, without any instruments, sounded the charge. This shows the number and the importance of military musicians in the Roman state, nearly 600 years before Christ.

With respect to Etruscan music, whoever regards the great number of instruments represented in the fine collection of antiquities, published under the patronage of Sir William Hamilton, must be convinced that the ancient inhabitants of Etruria were extremely attached to music; for every species of musical instrument that is to be found in the remains of ancient Greek sculpture is delineated on the vases of these collections; though the antiquity of some of them is imagined to be much higher than the general use of the instruments represented upon them in Greece

Early Church Music.

With respect to the music that was first used by the Christians or established in the church by the first emperors that were converted, as no specimens remain, it is difficult to determine of what kind it was. That some part of the sacred music of the apostles, and their immediate successors, in Palestine and the adjacent countries, may have been such as was used by the Hebrews, particularly in chanting the Psalms, is probable; but it is no less probable, that the music of the hymns which were first received in the church, wherever Paganism had prevailed, resembled that which had been for many ages used in the temple worship of the Greeks and Romans. Of this, the versification of those hymns affords an indisputable proof, as it by no means resembles that of the Psalms, or of any other Hebrew poetry; and examples may be found in the breviaries, missals, and antiphonaries, ancient and modern, of every species of versification which has been practised by the Greek and Roman poets, particularly the lyric; such as the Alcmanian, Alcæic, and Sapphic. And Eusebius, in speaking of the consecration of churches throughout the Roman dominions, in the time of Constantine, says, that "there was one common consent in chanting forth the praises of God; the performance of the service was exact; the rights of the church decent and majestic; and there was a place appointed for those who sung psalms." It was during this reign that the Ambrosian chant was established in the church at Milan. St. Augustine speaks of the great delight he received on hearing the psalms and hymns sung there, at his first entrance into the church after his conversion. "The voices," says he, "flowed in at my ears, truth was distilled in my heart, and the affection of piety overflowed in sweet tears of joy." He afterwards gives an account of the origin of singing in the church service, at Milan, in the eastern manner. "The church of Milan," says he, "had not long before begun to practise this way of mutual consolation and exhortation, with a joint harmony of voices and hearts."

Music is said by some of the fathers to have frequently drawn the Gentiles into the church through mere curiosity; many of whom liked its ceremonies so well, that they were baptized before their departure.

St. Ignatius who had conversed with the apostles, is generally supposed to have been the first who proposed to the primitive Christians in the East, the method of singing psalms or hymns alternately, or in dialogue; dividing the singers in two bands or choirs, placed on different sides of the church. This is called antiphona; and the custom soon prevailed in every place where Christianity was established.

Ecclesiastical writers seem unanimous in allowing, that it was the learned and active pope, Gregory the Great, (who began his pontificate in 590,) who collected the musical fragments of such ancient hymns and psalms, as the first fathers of the church had approved, and recommended them to the primitive Christians; and, that he selected, methodized, and arranged them in the order which was long continued at Rome, and soon adopted by the chief part of the western church. It is probable, that Pope Gregory was rather a compiler than a composer of ecclesiastical chants, as music had been established in the church long before his time.

After the most diligent inquiry concerning the time when instrumental music had admission into the ecclesiastical service, there is reason to conclude, that, before the reign of Constantine, as the converts to Christianity were subject to frequent persecution and disturbance in their devotion, the use of instruments could hardly have been practicable, and by all that can be collected from the writings of the primitive Christians, they seem never to have been admitted. But after the full establishment of Christianity, as the national religion of the whole Roman empire, they were used in great festivals.

Clemens Alexandrinus says: "Though we no longer worship God with the clamour of military instruments, such as the trumpet, drum, and fife, but with peaceful words—this is our most delightful festivity: and if you are able to accompany your voices with the lyre or cithara, you will incur no censure." And afterwards he says: "Ye shall imitate the just Hebrew king, whose actions were acceptable to God." He then quotes the royal psalmist: "Rejoice ye righteous, in the Lord, praise becometh the just, praise the Lord on the cithara, and on the psaltery with ten strings."

Eusebius, in his commentary on the sixtieth psalm, mentions these instruments; and in his exposition of the ninety-second psalm, says: "When they are met, they act as the psalm prescribes; first, they confess their sins to the Lord. Secondly, they sing to his name, not only with the voice, but with the cithara, and upon an instrument of ten strings." Instruments, however, seem not to have had admission indiscriminately in the early ages of the church; the harp and psaltery only, as the most grave and majestic instruments of the time, were preferred to all others. Neither Jews nor Gentiles were imitated in the use of tabrets and cymbals in the temple service.

Bede tells us, that when Augustine the monk, and the companions of his mission, had their audience of king Ethelbert, in the isle of Thanet, they approached him in procession, singing litanies; and that, afterwards, when they entered the city of Canterbury, they sang a litany, and at the end of it, Allelujah.

But though this was the first time the Anglo-Saxons had heard the Gregorian chants, yet Bede likewise tells us that our British ancestors had been instructed in the rites and ceremonies of the Gallican church, by St. Germanus, and had heard him sing Allelujah many years before the arrival of St. Augustine. Several letters which passed between Bede and St. Augustine, are still extant.

"The principal difference," says Bishop Stillingfleet, "between the Roman and Gallic ritual, which the Britons had adopted before the arrival of St. Augustine, was in the church music, in which the Romans were thought to excel other western churches so far, that the goodness of their music was the principal incitement to the introduction of their offices."

It was then customary for the clergy to travel to Rome for improvement in music, as well as to obtain masters of that art from the Roman college. At length, the successors of St. Gregory, and of St. Augustine, his missionary, having established a school for ecclesiastical music at Canterbury, the rest of the island was furnished with masters from that seminary.

Alfred not only encouraged and countenanced the practice of music, but, in 886, founded a professorship at Oxford, for the cultivation of it as a science.

Several ecclesiastical writers mention the organ as an instrument that had very early admission into the church. To Pope Vitalian is ascribed its first introduction at Rome in the seventh century; and ancient annalists are unanimous in allowing, that the first organ that appeared in France was sent from Constantinople, as a present from the emperor Constantine Copronymus the sixth, in 757, to king Pepin; which, as well as Julian's epigram, gives the invention to Greece. The epigram runs thus: "I see reeds of a new species, the growth of another and a brazen soil; such as are not agitated by our winds, but by a blast that rushes from a leathern cavern beneath their roots; while a robust mortal, running with swift fingers over the concordant keys, makes them, as they smoothly dance, emit melodious sounds."

Organs became common in Italy and Germany, during the

tenth century, as well as in England; about which time they had admission in the convents throughout Europe.

Counterpoint was invented, or at least greatly improved, by Guido, a monk of Arezzo, in Tuscany, about the year 1022.

The ancients have left us no rules for rhythm, time, or accent, in music, but those which concerned the words or verses that were to be sung. Before the invention, therefore, of characters for time, written music in parts must have consisted of simple counterpoint, note against note, or sounds of equal length. The invention of characters for time has been given by almost all writers on music of the last and present century, to John de Muris, who flourished about the year 1330. But three centuries prior to this, Magister Franco, of Cologne, speaks, in a treatise on the subject, of earlier authorities, as well as of his own improvements in the characters used for time. John de Muris then, though not the inventor of the *cantus mensurabilis*, seems, by his numerous writings, greatly to have improved it. Indeed, every species of note to be found in his tracts, except the minim, is described by Franco, as well as used in compositions anterior to his time, and mentioned by authors who wrote upon music before him. Nor is it possible to imagine that this art was invented and received by all Europe at once; like others, it had its beginning, improvements, and perfection, in different periods of time.

Origin of the Opera.

THE opera first assumed its distinctive form in Italy. It may, however, be traced to the dramas of the ancient Greeks, which were performed with the accompaniment of musical instruments and singing. The religious dramatic representations of the middle ages, called mysteries and moralities, were performed under the sanction of the Romish church, and were the favourite entertainment of people of all conditions; from these the secular masque took its rise. Dances, songs, and choruses were introduced into these pageants, and by degrees they rose into the oratorio and opera.

The origin of the oratorio is ascribed by Italian writers to San Filippo Neri, who founded the order of the Oratory at Rome, in 1540. It was their practice to render the service of the church as agreeable as possible, in order to attract young people thither, and thus draw them away from stage-plays and other profane amusements. First, they introduced songs and choruses; and afterwards, scripture stories and incidents were formed into dramatic poems, which were recited and sung, with the accompaniment of instruments, before and after the sermon. They were founded on such narratives as the Good Samaritan, the Trials of Job, the Prodigal Son, &c. They soon acquired great popularity, and oratorios became common in the principal churches throughout Italy, where they are regularly performed to this day. These pieces are often performed in concert-rooms and theatres, but in no case is there the slightest approach to the dramatic representation of the opera.

During the sixteenth century, the Italian drama gradually

arose to a more regular form, and music seems to have been more or less employed in all entertainments of the kind. In the year 1597, the invention of recitative served to complete the union of music and the drama. This invention is claimed by Jacopo Peri of Florence, and by Emilio del Caviliere of Rome, who both speak of it as an attempt to revive the musical declamation of the Greeks and Romans. It is possible they may have equal claims to the invention, having been led to it by the same suggestive steps. It is but a narrow view of the matter to suppose that every similarity between the productions of genius is the effect of imitation.

THE OPERA IN ENGLAND.*

Down to the seventeenth century, the dramatic entertainments of England were interspersed with vocal and instrumental music. Gammer Gurton's Needle, the first regular English comedy, was so accompanied. It was written in 1551.

This admixture of music is to be found in the plays of Jonson, Beaumont and Fletcher, Shirley, Dryden, and other dramatists of the sixteenth and seventeenth centuries, and did not cease till the musical drama acquired a separate and independent existence.

Shakespeare, who was evidently a passionate lover of music, has introduced it in a number of his plays. The Tempest, even in its original form, may almost be considered a musical drama. Besides "Come unto these yellow sands," "Full fathom five thy father lies," "Where the bee sucks," and other songs, it contains a masque with music, presented by the spirits of the enchanted

* The following sketch is abridged from "The History of the Musical Drama," by George Hogarth.

island. The same is the case with As you like it, in which there are the fine sylvan glees, "Under the greenwood tree," "What shall he have, that killed the deer," and "It was a lover and his lass," the exquisite song—"Blow, blow, thou winter wind," and the music in the last scene. Many of his other plays contain beautiful lyrical pieces; and the passages descriptive of the charms of music and its effects are innumerable.

The masque held a principal place in the polite amusements of the reigns of Henry VIII. and Elizabeth. It was composed chiefly of music, dancing, and a display of grotesque characters, like a modern masquerade. Some of these masques were written by men of genius, and contain beautiful poetry. In the Inner Temple Masque, on the story of Circe and Ulysses, written by William Browne, is the following song, which Circe sings as a charm to drive away sleep from Ulysses, who is discovered sleeping under a tree:—

"Son of Erebus and Night,
Hie away, and aim thy flight,
Where consort none other fowl
Than the bat and sullen owl;
Where upon the limber grass,
Poppy and mandragoras,
With like simples not a few,
Hang for ever drops of dew;
Where flows Lethe, without coil,
Softly like a stream of oil.
Hie thee thither, gentle Sleep!
With this Greek no longer keep.
Thrice I charge thee by my wand;
Thrice with moly from my hand,
Do I touch Ulysses' eyes,
And with the iaspis. Then arise,
Sagest Greek."

The exquisite masque of Comus is probably the best known production of the kind. It was written for the earl of Bridgewater, at whose mansion it was performed. When he resided at Ludlow Castle, in Shropshire, his two sons, Lord Brackley and Mr. Egerton, and his daughter, Lady Alice Egerton, were benighted in passing through a neighbouring forest, and the young lady for some time could not be found. This adventure excited Milton's imagination, and gave rise to the masque, which was represented on Michaelmas-eve for the amusement of the family and the nobility of the neighbourhood. The two brothers were performed by the earl's sons, and his daughter was the lady. In 1637, Lawes published the poem of Comus; but the music does not appear ever to have been printed.

Thomas Augustine Arne, in 1738, established his reputation as a dramatic composer, by his music to Milton's Comus. Mr. John Dalton extended the musical portion of the piece, not only by the insertion of songs selected from Milton's other works, but by the addition of several of his own, which were very happily suited to the manner of the original author. The piece had a great run; and has since been revived, at different periods, with success.

In Comus, Arne introduced a style of melody which may be said to be peculiarly his own; being neither that of the older English masters, nor of the Italian composers of the day. It is graceful, flowing, and elegant; depending for its effect neither on the resources of harmony and uncommon modulation, nor on feats of vocal execution. It is, at the same time very expressive; and finely adapted, not only to the spirit, but to the accentuation and prosody of the poetry.

A taste for French music prevailed during the whole of the reign of Charles II., and gave way, not to the Italian music, but to the native genius of Purcell. Henry Purcell was born in 1658. While yet a singing-boy in the king's chapel, he composed several anthems, which are sung to this day. This is perhaps one of the most remarkable instances of precocity that has been recorded; for the anthem, demanding a knowledge of counterpoint, which, in general, can be obtained only by long and severe study, seems to be in an especial manner beyond the reach of a juvenile composer. His first opera, Dido and Æneas, was produced in 1677. It was followed by the Tempest of Shakespeare, adapted to musical accompaniment. It consists almost entirely of the songs and choruses of the aërial inhabitants of Prospero's enchanted island, described by the poet as being

> "full of noises,
> Sounds and sweet airs, that give delight, and hurt not."

The strange and wild character of these unearthly strains is beautifully supported, and the listener partakes of the feeling of the bewildered Ferdinand, when, amazed at the invisible chorus which reminds him of his drowned father, he exclaims,

> "This is no mortal business, nor no sound
> That the earth owes!"

The scene of the spirits deputed to bewilder the conspirators, contains the song, "Arise, ye subterranean winds!" a powerful composition, in which rolling divisions, finely adapted to a bass voice, are used with happy imitative effect. In this song, however, Purcell has fallen into the very common error of giving to particular words an expression which, though according with the words themselves, is at variance with the general tone of the poetry. The spirit is commanding the winds to

"Drive these wretches to that part o' the isle
Where nature never yet did smile;
Cause fogs and damps, whirlwinds and earthquakes there;
There let them howl, and languish in despair."

On the word "howl," the singer howls on one note for two bars. This is a piece of musical mimicry, inconsistent with the gravity of the style. In the opera of Bonduca, also, the author has been led astray by a word which has often proved an *ignis fatuus* to composers. In the passage,

"Where the shrill trumpets never sound,
But one eternal hush goes round,"

the singer breaks out into a loud and dashing passage, in imitation of the sound of a trumpet; although the whole song is an aspiration after peace, repose, and silence. Even where the trumpet is introduced, it is, negatively, in expressing a wish for some peaceful gloom, where its sound may never be heard. The "eternal hush," in the succeeding line is exquisitely expressed.

In variety of character, beauty of melody, truth and force of expression, and nice adaptation to the genius of the English language, his dramatic compositions are to this hour unparalleled. Their imperfections must be ascribed to the state of music, as a practical art, in his day; and when this is considered, it is wonderful that these imperfections are so small and so few. In regard to composition, it must be remembered that English secular melody was almost created by Purcell; the greatness of his predecessors having been derived, with slight exceptions, from their achievements in vocal harmony.

"Handel," says Dr. Burney, "who flourished in a less barbarous age for his art, has been acknowledged Purcell's superior in many particulars; yet in the accent, passion, and expression of English words, the vocal music of Purcell is, sometimes to my feelings, as superior to Handel's as an original poem to a translation. There is a latent power and force in his expression of English words, whatever be the subject, that will make an unprejudiced native feel, more than all the elegance, grace, and refinement of modern music, less happily applied, can do and this pleasure is communicated to us, not by the symmetry of the rhythm of modern melody, but by his having tuned to the true accents of our mother-tongue, those notes of passion which a native would breathe, in such situations as the words describe."

Operas, performed by complete Italian companies, were first introduced in England in 1711, when Handel arrived in that country, and such was their popularity, that the English opera was for a long time almost abandoned. The fame of Handel is spreading from day to day, and the numbers of his admirers increasing. His chief title to immortality rests upon his sublime oratorios; but a full knowledge of his genius, in all its varieties and extent, cannot be gained without exploring the treasures which lie hid in the dusty scores of his Italian operas.

As an English dramatic composer, Arne must be considered as next to Purcell, and from the popularity of his music had a still greater influence on the taste of his countrymen. His melody is more uniformly sweet, flowing, and graceful, than that of Purcell; but he was far from possessing that illustrious man's grandeur of conception, deep feeling, and impassioned energy. Arne enjoyed the advantage over his great predecessor, of writing in a more advanced age of orchestral composition. His harmonies are rich and varied, and he employed the instruments then in use, with judgment and delicacy. He was succeeded by several dramatic composers, who appeared nearly about the same time, and flourished till almost the close of the last century. Linley, Jackson, Arnold, Dibdin, and Shield, were the men of genius who threw lustre over this period.

The operas of these cotemporary composers, who were the immediate successors of Arne, are similar in form and structure. They are little dramas, generally of a comic cast, with a mixture of serious scenes, and frequently of considerable merit; their musical portion consisting of songs and duets, with occasionally a very slight introductory or concluding concerted piece or chorus.

The first decided step to the modern form of the opera was made by Stephen Storace, who, though a native of England, was of Italian parentage, and received the whole of his musical education in Italy. His first English opera was the Haunted Tower, brought out at Drury-lane in 1789. This admirable piece, which was written by James Cobb, had the utmost success. It was performed fifty times the first season; and established Storace's reputation as a composer.

In March, 1795, the Iron Chest, written by Coleman, with Storace's music, was performed at Drury-lane. His exertions in bringing out this piece, cost him his life. Though labouring under ill health at the time, having been confined to his bed for many days he insisted, notwithstanding the entreaties of his family, on being wrapped in blankets and carried to the theatre to attend the first rehearsal. The consequence was fatal, he returned to his bed, from which he never rose again, but expired a few days after the successful performance of the play, in the thirty-third year of his age.

Storace's education having been Italian, his style was formed on the works of the great masters of the Italian school: but having the advantage of a thorough acquaintance with the En glish language, his strong sense and judgment enabled him to unite pure Italian melody to the prosody and accent of English poetry, with a felicity, which has never been excelled by any other composer. His airs have the flowing smoothness and grace of Paesiello, while they are free from the slightest appearance of outlandishness, permitting the singer to deliver the words with perfect distinctness of utterance and propriety of pronunciation and emphasis. In this important particular, the music of Storace may still serve as a model to English composers: for the Italian and German phrases, of which our vocal melody is now so full, are used with such disregard of the words to which they are joined, that our own vocalists, even when singing English music, appear like foreigners singing in broken and unintelligible English.

For a number of years after the death of Storace, the stage was supplied, partly with the works of the composers who have been mentioned from Arne downwards, and partly by the ephemeral productions of Kelly, Reeve, Mazzinghi, Davy, Braham, and others; none of whom have any claim, as composers, to a place in the records of music.

When the performance of Don Giovanni, and other operas of Mozart, at the King's Theatre, made so great an impression in 1817, Mr. Bishop conceived the idea of adapting them to the English stage. By introducing these pieces to the frequenters of the English theatres, Mr. Bishop created a demand for foriegn dramatic music, and gave rise to the practice, which has prevailed ever since, of supplying the English stage, to a considerable extent, with the musical productions of Italy, Germany, and France. The taste for foreign music, especially that of the German school, was prodigiously increased by the appearance in an English dress of Der Freischutz. It was first performed in 1824, at the English Opera-house, and received with acclamations.

The immense popularity of Weber's name in England, led to his engagement to compose his opera of Oberon, for Covent-Garden. On the night of its performance, he thus describes the result: "My best beloved Caroline, through God's grace and assistance, I have this evening met with the most complete success. The brilliancy and affecting nature of the triumph are indescribable. God alone be thanked for it! When I entered the orchestra, the whole of the house, which was filled to overflowing, rose; and I was saluted by huzzas and waving of hats and handkerchiefs, which I thought would never have done. They insisted on encoring the overture. Every air was interrupted by bursts of applause." "So much for this night, dear life," he adds, in conclusion, "from your heartily tired husband, who, however, could not sleep in peace, till he had communicated to you this new blessing of Heaven. Good night!"

For several years after this time, the English musicians withdrew entirely from the field of dramatic composition; and the stage was supplied entirely by inportations from abroad. Since the year 1833, however, various operas, the production of English talent, have been well received by the public, and have, to a considerable extent, occupied the musical stage. Barnett's elegant opera, the Mountain Sylph, had an almost uninterrupted run of above a hundred nights; and is still frequently performed. Loder's Nourjahad was favourably received; and the music of Thompson's Hermann, which contains beauties of the highest order, was appreciated by the public, though the success of both these pieces was injured by their want of dramatic merit. The same cause prevented the success of several other pieces, especially that of Barnett's Fair Rosamond, a work, musically speaking, of the highest merit. It is, indeed, the *chef-d'œuvre* of this gifted composer, and contains many things worthy of the greatest masters of the German school. The principal operas of Balfe, the Siege of Rochelle, and the Maid of Artois, have gained a popularity rarely surpassed. It may be remarked in general, that, in proportion as the musical part of this entertainment has acquired an ascendency, the poetical and dramatic part has declined.

THE OPERA IN ITALY.

Venice appears to have taken the lead among the cities of Italy, in respect to the musical drama. Between 1637, when Andromeda was produced, and 1700, we are told by Riccoboni, that three hundred and fifty operas were performed there. Operas were generally represented daily, and in six different theatres, all open at once. There was no public opera-house at Rome, until 1671, nor at Bologna, until 1680. The Italian singers, from the very infancy of the musical drama, attained that superiority over those of other countries, which they have always preserved. About the end of the seventeenth century, the Italian musical drama appears, for a time, to have degenerated. Regularity of construction, consistency of character, and poetical beauty, were disregarded, provided the eye and ear were gratified with spendid sights and feats of vocal execution.

At the beginning of the last century, the Italian drama decidedly improved. "Gods and devils," says Arteaga, "were banished from the stage, as soon as poets discovered the art of making men speak with dignity." Many poets, whose names are now forgotten, even in Italy, had the merit of contributing to this reformation of the musical drama. The first musical dramatist of lasting celebrity, was Apostolo Zeno, who, for a time, was the idol of his countrymen, till he was thrown into the shade by the far greater splendor of his successor, Metastasio. At the same time that the poetry of the Italian opera was refined and exalted by the writings of Apostolo Zeno and Metastasio, its music was undergoing a similar process by the labours of Leo, Vinci, Alessandro Scarlatti, Caldara, and others. They established the distinctions between recitative and air; gave to each of these species of musical language its peculiar features, and assigned to it its proper functions.

By the middle of the last century, the Italian opera, both in its poetry and music, had been brought to a state of great polish and refinement; and had come to assume a certain form, and to be constructed according to a model from which no deviation was permitted. At that time it had established itself in Germany and England, where it had become the favourite musical entertainment of the higher classes of society. In France, however, it had then obtained no footing whatever. In the structure of an opera, the number of characters was generally limited to six, three of each sex. The piece was to be divided into three acts, and not to exceed a certain number of verses. The air was divided into several kinds. The first and highest class is the *aria cantabile*, so called by pre-eminence, while it is susceptible of great pathos, it admits of being highly ornamented; because, though the sentiments it expresses are affecting, they are such as the mind dwells on with pleasure: and, for the same reason, the subject of the *cantabile* should never border on deep distress, nor approach to violent agitation, both of which are evidently inconsistent with ornament. The motion of this air is slow, and the instrumental accompaniment is merely sufficient to support the voice. The *aria di portamento* derives its name from the term which expresses the carriage or sustaining of the voice. It is composed chiefly of long notes, such as the singer can dwell on, and have thereby an opportuuity of displaying the beauties of his voice, and calling forth its powers; for the beauty of sound itself, and of vocal sound in particular, as being the finest of all sounds, is held by the Italians to be one of the chief sources of the pleasure derived from music. The subjects proper for this class of air are sentiments of dignity, but calm and undisturbed by passion. The *aria di mezzo carattere* is a species of air, which, though expressive neither of the dignity of the *portamento*, nor the pathos of the *cantabile*, may be soothing, but not sad; pleasing, but not elevated; lively, but not gay. The movement of this air is by the Italians termed *andante*, which is the medium of musical time, between the extremes of slow and quick. In this species of air, the orchestra, though it ought never to cover the voice, is not kept in such subordination to it as in the classes already described. The *aria parlante*, or speaking air, admits neither of long notes in its composition, nor of many ornaments in its performance. The rapidity of its movement is determined by the force of the passion which it expresses. Expressions of fear, of joy, of grief, of rage, when at all impetuous, even to their most violent degrees, are all comprehended under the various subdivisions of this class. The *aria di bravura*, or *aria d'agilità*, is that which is composed chiefly—indeed too often merely—to fford the singer an opportunity of displaying extraordinary owers of voice and execution.

Imitative passages for the instruments may be employed to heighten the effect of every kind of air, even the most impassioned that can be imagined. Suppose Lear, by the cruelty of his daughters, exposed, on the barren heath to th elting of the pitiless storm," were to vent in song the passions which distract his soul—

"The tempest, in my mind,
Doth from my senses take all feeling else,
Save what beats there. Filial ingratitude!
Is it not as this mouth should tear this hand
For lifting food to it? But I will punish home.
No, I will weep no more. In such a night,
To shut me out! Pour on, I will endure!
In such a night as this! O, Regan, Goneril!
Your old, kind father, whose frank heart gave all!
O, that way madness lies—let me shun that!
No more of that!"

His accents would be the cry of suffering nature and agonized feeling; but the genius of a Beethoven would present to the imagination the horrors of the scene—the blackness of the night, and the tempest howling round the head of the desolate old man—by the gloomy harmonies and appalling sounds proceeding from the orchestra, and mingling in wild confusion with the voice of the actor. The song would express the passions of the man; the instruments would paint his situation.

The Italian opera having assumed the form which has now been described, preserved it with little alteration, for a considerable time. But the spirit of change was constantly at work. The influence of the German school, both in respect of vocal harmony and instrumental accompaniment, began to be perceptible in the style of the Italian composers; the airs were no longer composed with the same adherence to established models; and the dramatic structure of the scenes acquired a variety of new forms, by the introduction of concerted pieces and finales.

THE OPERA IN GERMANY.

We are told, that operas in the German language, and by German composers, were performed at the courts of German sovereigns, early in the seventeenth century. But they must have been very rude productions ; as all traces of them, even the names of their authors, seem to be lost. The first operas which have been commemorated, as performed in Germany, were imported from Italy. About the year 1630, Martin Opitz, who has been called the father of the German drama, translated from the Italian, the Dafne of Rinuccini ; and the music, having been adapted to German words by a composer of the name of Schutz, was performed at the court of Dresden. Soon afterwards, several other Italian operas were adapted to German words, and performed at Ratisbon, Munich, and other places. Italian operas now began to be performed in their original language. It was probably owing to the cultivation of the Italian style by the greatest German composers, who blended its grace and beauty with the strong and massive features which have always characterized their own national music, that the German opera, when once more established, has risen so rapidly to its present high and palmy state. The illustrious Gluck may be considered as the founder of the existing school of German dramatic music ; and yet it does not appear that he ever composed an opera in the German language. His musical education was, in a great measure, Italian. He studied four years under the celebrated Martini, of Milan ; but he impressed upon all his works, which were produced in the maturity of his powers, the national characteristics of his country, as well as the features of his own most original genius. For some time after his return to Germany, Gluck appears to have composed little. He was chiefly occupied in the improvement of his mind and the cultivation of his taste, in poetry as well as in music; and seems to have been gradually forming those principles with respect to the union of music and poetry, the development of which, in his subsequent works, forms an era in the art. "I wished," says he, speaking of the opera Alceste, "to confine music to its true province, that of seconding poetry, by strengthening the expression of the sentiments and the interest of the situations, without interrupting the action and weakening it by superfluous ornament. I thought that music ought to give that aid to poetry, which the liveliness of colouring and the happy combination of light and shade afford to a correct and well-designed picture—animating the figures without injuring their contour. I have, therefore, carefully avoided interrupting a singer in the warmth of dialogue, in order to wait for a tedious ritornel; or stopping him in the midst of a speech, in order to display the agility of his voice in a long passage. Fortunately the poem of Calzabigi has wonderfully favoured my views. The celebrated author, having conceived his own plan of the lyric drama, in place of flowery descriptions, useless compositions, cold and sententious morality, has substituted strong passions, interesting situations, the language of the heart, and variety of action. The success of the piece has justified my ideas; and the universal approbation of so enlightened a city has proved to me, that simplicity and truth are the greatest principles of the beautiful in the productions of the fine arts."

Haydn composed many Italian operas, but they seem never to have travelled beyond the private theatre of his patron, Prince Esterhazy; and the scores of them were destroyed by an accidental fire in the palace of that prince.

Gluck's successor, as a German dramatic musician, was the unrivalled Mozart. The greatest part of his theatrical works were Italian operas.

In the year 1768, when he was twelve years old, Mozart, by order of the Emperor Joseph the Second, composed an Italian comic opera, called La Finta Semplice. It received the approbation of Hasse and Metastasio, who were then at Vienna; but in consequence, it is said, of a cabal among the singers, it was not performed. In the following year he went to Italy, where he was received with enthusiasm, and composed several Italian operas, which were performed at Milan and other places with the greatest success. Of these early operas, the names are all that survive. The first opera on which Mozart's celebrity is founded, is Idomeneo. The scene is laid in the island of Crete. Idomeneus, returning from the Trojan war, is shipwrecked, and his fleet dispersed, by a tempest raised by the anger of Neptune. His son, Idamante, with Ilia, the daughter of Priam, (whose life he had saved in the storm,) and a number of Trojan captives, arrive in safety at home; but it is believed that Idomeneus has perished. A passion has sprung up between the Trojan princess and her deliverer; and at the beginning of the piece, Idamante declares his love, and, in token of it, gives the Trojan prisoners their freedom. Idomeneus, with his ships, is driven upon the shore of Crete, having made a vow, as a propitiation, to sacrifice to Neptune the first person he should meet upon his landing. Idamante hastens to the port to greet his father, who perceives, with horror, that his son is the destined victim. Unable to consummate the shocking sacrifice, he resolves to send his son to some distant land, hoping to find some other way of appeasing the offended deity. He therefore orders his son to convey Electra, the daughter of Agamemnon, (who had been residing at his court,) to Argos, her native country. Electra, who nourishes an unrequited passion for the prince, mingled with jealousy and hatred for her rival, is full of joy at the prospect of departing with him, while the lovers are in despair at the separation. All is prepared for the departure of Idamante and Electra; but a storm arises, and a dreadful monster issues from the angry waves, spreading dismay and death among the people. The king and his family have retired into the interior of the palace, when a great body of people enter, with a priest of Neptune at their head, who calls on the king to appease the monster, by offering up the victim whom he demands. Idomeneus, thus admonished, proclaims his fatal vow, and declares Idamante to be the victim. While the people are expressing, in smothered accents, their grief and astonishment, joyful cries are suddenly heard without. The prince has attacked and slain the monster, and now rushes in to offer himself a willing sacrifice for his country. Idomeneus is about to strike the blow, when the Trojan princess interposes and wishes to sacrifice herself for her lover. While this contest is going on, a subterraneous noise is heard; the statue of Neptune moves; and an awful voice from heaven declares that love has conquered—that Idomeneus is pardoned, but that he shall cease to be king; and that Idamante, with Ilia as his queen, shall reign in his stead. This denouement produces the effects which may be expected, on the different personages; and the piece ends with a choral strain of general joy. This story has given room for many tragic and impassioned scenes, which are beautifully treated by the composer.

Passing over Mozart's intermediate productions, the Zauberflöte and La Clemenza di Tito were produced in 1791, the last year of his life. Dramatic music, for the most part, owes its popularity to the piece to which it belongs being attractive in the theatre;

but to this the music of the Zauberflöte is a remarkable exception; for, though the opera is almost unknown, yet its airs are generally familiar—some of them as much so as the most popular English ballads. And not only its airs, but its concerted pieces and choruses are the delight of every one who derives any enjoyment from music. The Zauberflöte illustrates the close alliance between the utmost simplicity and the highest beauties of the art. When this opera was first produced, its melodies were instantly heard in every dwelling, from the palace to the cottage—they resounded in the streets, the highways, and the fields—and it was truly said that Mozart had enchanted all Germany with his "Enchanted Flute." Their beauties are not of that recondite kind, which are perceptible only to the practised ear and refined taste; "the spinners and knitters in the sun" listen to them with the same heartfelt pleasure. They reach the heart at once, and the impression remains for ever.

THE OPERA IN FRANCE.

It is now admitted by French writers, that they owe the establishment of the opera to the Italians. Rinuccini, who went to France in the suite of Mary of Medicis, on her marriage with Henry IV., first introduced Italian music into that country. The first Italian company of performers appeared in Paris, in 1577. "They attracted such multitudes," says an old writer, "that the four best preachers in Paris had not such numerous assemblies when they preached." Another Italian company was brought to Paris by Cardinal Mazarin, in 1645. But the Italian opera seems to have been little encouraged at that time. French pieces, called ballets, though they appear to have had words as well as dancing and music, were the favourite amusement of the court; and it was in composing the music of these pieces, that Lulli first brought his talents into notice. He was the only French dramatic composer of any reputation, prior to the end of the seventeenth century. Lulli contributed greatly to the improvement of instrumental music. He appears to have been the inventor of the overture to dramatic pieces; and was so successful in this species of composition, that even Handel, in his opera-overtures, took him for his model.

Addison gives a lively description of the French opera at the beginning of the eighteenth century. "The music of the French," he says, "is indeed very properly adapted to their pronunciation and accent, as their whole opera wonderfully favours the genius of such a gay, airy people. The chorus, in which that opera abounds, gives the parterre frequent opportunities of joining in concert with the stage. This inclination of the audience to sing along with the actors, so prevails with them, that I have sometimes known the performer on the stage to do no more, in a celebrated song, than the clerk of a parish church, who serves only to raise the psalm, and is afterwards drowned in the music of the congregation. Every actor that comes on the stage is a beau. The queens and heroines are so painted, that they appear as ruddy and cherry-cheeked as milkmaids. The shepherds are all embroidered, and acquit themselves in a ball better than our English dancing-masters."

The French musical drama continued in the state which has now been described, till nearly the middle of the last century. The stage was supplied with the productions of Lulli and his imitators, till a new era was created by the appearance of the operas of Rameau. This celebrated musician was born in 1683, and spent the earlier part of his life at Clermont, in Auvergne, where he was organist of the cathedral. In this retirement, he pursued those scientific researches, which gave birth to that famous system of harmony which made him so long regarded in France as the Newton of the musical world. He reached the age of fifty without being known as a dramatic composer.

Though Rameau reigned in undisputed supremacy over the serious opera, a great impression was made upon the Parisian public by the arrival of an Italian company, who, in 1752, obtained permission to perform Italian burlettas and *intermezzi* For nearly two years, the Italian company (or Bouffons, as they were called) went on very successfully, performing a number of the best burlettas of their own country. But the public, when it ceased to dispute about them, began to grow weary of them. Thus neglected, the Italians took their departure in the beginning of the year 1754; and their disappearance was celebrated in the journals of the day as a national triumph, which was solemnized by a splendid performance of Rameau's *chef-d'œuvre*, Castor et Pollux.

Gretry's operas appeared, in regular succession, from the year 1767 to 1791; and a few were produced, at long intervals, down to the year 1797. His last opera was Anacreon, a work which had considerable success. He died in 1813.

The principal composers who have since devoted their talents to the French stage, are Auber, Meyerbeer, and Halevy. Auber was first brought into notice in 1823, by his opera, La Neige, which became very popular not only in France but in Germany, and is frequently performed in that country. His Fra Diavolo, and his celebrated piece, La Muette de Portici, (or Masaniello,) are well known all over Europe.

AN ALPHABETICAL LIST

OF

PAINTERS, ENGRAVERS, SCULPTORS, ETC.

THE MOST EMINENT IN THEIR DEPARTMENTS.

NATION.	NAME AND PROFESSION.		BORN.	DIED.
Gr.	Agatharcus, the inventor of perspective scenery in theatres	*Painter*		B. C. 480
Gr.	Ageldas	*Sculptor*	f. B. C. 5th cent.	
Gr.	Agesander (sculptor of "Laocoon and his Children")	*Sculptor*	B. C. 5th cent.	
Ital.	Albano, Francis ("the painter of the Graces")	*Painter*	1578	1660
Ital.	Alberti, Leo Baptist, a Florentine	*Pa. Sc. & Archit.*	1400	1490
Ital.	Albertinelli, Mariotto	*Painter*		1520
Gr.	Alcamenes (pupil of Phidias)	*Sculptor*	f. B. C. 450	
Scotch.	Allan, Sir William	*Painter*		
Amer.	Allston, Washington	*Poet & Histor. Painter*	1779	1843
Ital.	Angelo, Michael (Buonarotti), a pre-eminent	*Pa. Sc. & Architect*	1474	1563
Ital.	Angelo, Michael (Caravaggio)	*Painter*	1569	1609
Gr.	Apelles, the most celebrated of ancient painters	*Painter*	f. B. C. 330	
Gr.	Apollodorus, an Athenian	*Painter*	f. B. C. 408	
Ital.	Appiani, of Milan	*Painter*	1754	1817
Gr.	Aristides, of Thebes	*Painter*	f. B. C. 240	
Fr.	Audran, Gerard, a celebrated	*Histor. Engraver*	1640	1703
Ital.	Baccio, Della Porta (known as San Marco)	*Painter*	1469	1517
Eng.	Bacon, John	*Sculptor*	1740	1799
Flem.	Balen, Henry Van	*Painter*	1560	1632
Ital.	Bandinelli, Baccio	*Sculptor*	1487	1559
Eng.	Banks, Thomas	*Sculptor*	1745	1805
Irish.	Barry, James	*Painter*	1741	1805
Ital.	Bartolini	*Engraver*		
Ital.	Bartolomeo, Fra, di St. Marco	*Painter*	1469	1517
Ital.	Batoni, Pompey	*Painter*	1708	1787
Eng.	Beechy, Sir Wm.	*Landscape Painter*	1753	1893
Ital.	Bella, Stephano Della, a Florentine	*Engraver*	1610	1684
Flem.	Berchem, Nicolas	*Engraver*	1624	1689
Do.	Bird, Edward	*Painter*	1772	1819
Eng.	Blake, William,	*Painter & Engraver*	1757	1826
Dutch.	Both, John and Andrew	*Painters*	1610	1650 & 56
Fr.	Bourdon, Sebastian	*Painter & Engraver*	1616	1671
Swiss.	Bourgeoise, Sir Francis (born in London)	*Painter*	1756	1811
Eng.	Boydell, John (a printseller, and lord mayor of London)	*Engraver*	1719	1804
Ital.	Bramante D'Urbino, Francis L. (1st of St. Peter's Church)	*Architect*	1444	1514
Dutch.	Brentel, Francis	*Painter*	f. 1635	
Dutch.	Brill, Matthew	*Painter*	1550	1584
Flem.	Bruges, John of, or John Van Eyck	*Painter*	1370	1441
Ital.	Buonarotti, see Angelo.			
Eng.	Burnett, James	*Landscape Painter*	1788	1816
Ital.	Cagliari, Paul (known as Paul Veronese), a celebrated	*Painter*	1532	1588
Ital.	Cagliari, Benedict, Carletto, and Gabriel, brothers and sons of Paul.			
Eng.	Calcott, Sir A. W.	*Landscape Painter*		
Gr.	Callimachus	*Sculptor & Architect*	f. B. C 540	
Ital.	Cambiaso, Lucus, a Genoese	*Painter*	1527	1585

NATION.	NAME AND PROFESSION.		BORN.	DIED.
Ital.	Canaletto, Anthony, a Venetian	*Landscape Painter*	1697	1718
Ital.	Canova, Antonio,	*Sculptor*	1757	1822
Ital.	Caravaggio, see Angelo.			
Ital.	Caracci Lodovico	*Painter*	1555	1619
Ital.	——— Agostino	*Painter*	1588	1601
Ital.	——— Annibale	*Painter*	1560	1609
Ital.	Carpi, Ugo da, discoverer of the art of printing in Chiaro-oscuro—with three plates—to imitate drawings	*About*	1700 1846	
Fr.	Casas, Louis Francis	*Painter & Architect*	1756	1827
Span.	Castilio Y Saavedra, Anthony	*Painter*	1603	1667
Ital.	Cavendone, James	*Fresco Painter*	1577	1606
Ital.	Cellini, Benvenuto, a Florentine	*Engraver & Sculptor*	1500	1570
Flem.	Champagne, Philip de	*Painter*	1604	1674
Gr.	Chares	*Painter* f. B.C.	300	
Eng.	Cosway, Richard	*Painter*	1740	1826
Eng.	Chantry, sir Francis	*Sculptor*	1781	1841
Fr.	Chaudet, Anthony Denis	*Painter*	1763	1810
Ital.	Cimabue, Giovanni, a Florentine	*Painter*	1240	1300
Ital.	Claude Gelé—called Claude Lorraine	*Painter*	1600	1682
Gr.	Cleomenes, an Athenian (The Medicean Venus)	*Sculptor* f. B. C.	180	
Amer.	Clevenger	*Sculptor*		1844
Amer.	Cole, Thomas	*Land. & Hist. Painter*	1802	1848
Eng.	Collins, William	*Land. & Fam. Life Pa.*	1788	
Eng.	Constable, John	*Painter*	1776	1837
Eng.	Cooper, Samuel	*Miniature Painter*	1689	1776
Amer.	Copley, John Singleton (born in Boston)	*Painter*	1737	1815
Ital.	Corregio, Ant. (founder of the Lombard school)	*Painter*	1493	1534
Ital.	Cortona, Pietro da, a Tuscan	*Painter*	1596	1669
Fr.	Courtois, James (known as Il Borgognone)	*Painter*	1621	1673
Fr.	Couston Nicholas (also his brother William)	*Sculptor*	1658	1731
Dutch.	Cuyp, Jacob G.,	*Landscape & Cattle Pa.*	1568	1649
Dutch.	Cuyp, Albert (son of above)	*Landscape & Cattle Pa.*	1606	1667
Dutch.	Cuyp, Benjamin	*Historical Painter*	1650	
Eng.	Daniel, Thomas	*Landscape Painter*		1840
Ger.	Dannecker, John Henry—(Adriadne, &c.)	*Sculptor*	1758	1841
Fr.	David, James Louis, a celebrated	*Painter*	1750	1825
Fr.	David (Founder of recent French school)	*Sculptor*	1780	
Fr.	Delaroche, Paul	*Historical Painter*		
Ger.	Denner, Balthaser	*Portrait Painter*	1685	1747
Gr.	Dinocrates, a Macedonian (builder of Alexandria, &c.)	*Architect* f. B. C.	330	
Ital.	Dolci, Carlo	*Scripture Painter*	1616	1686
Ital.	Domenichino (excelled in expression)	*Painter*	1581	1641
Ital.	Donatello, or Donato, a Florentine	*Sculptor*	1383	1466
Dutch.	Douw, Gerard	*Familiar Life Painter*	1613	1674
Fr.	Dubuffe	*Historical Painter*		
Fr.	Dufresnoy, Charles Alphonso	*Painter*		
Amer.	Dunlap, William	*Historical Painter*	1766	
Ger.	Durer, Albert (and author)	*Pa. Eng. Sc. & Arch.*	1471	1528
Ger.	Eberhardt	*Sculptor*		
Eng.	Eginton, Francis (restorer of the art of painting on *glass*)	*Painter*	1737	1805
Eng.	Etty, William	*Historical Painter*	1789	1849
Gr.	Eupompus (founder of school at Sicyon)	*Painter*		
Dutch.	Eyck, John Van (said to have invented painting in *oil*)	*Painter*	1370	1441
Eng.	Flaxman, John	*Sculptor*	1755	1826
Swiss.	Fuseli, Henry (resided in England)	*Painter*	1741	1825
Eng.	Gainsborough, Thomas	*Landscape Painter*	1727	1788
Ital.	Ghiberti, Laurence, a Florentine	*Sculptor*	1378	1456
Eng.	Gibson	*Sculptor*		
Ital	Giordani, Luke (The Proteus of painting)	*Painter*	1629	1704
Ital.	Giorgione, Barbarelli	*Painter*	1477	1511
Ital.	Giotto (one of the earliest modern)	*Painter, Sculp. & Arch.*	1276	1336
Fr.	Giraldon, Francis	*Sculptor*	1630	1715
Fr.	Girodet—Trioson, Aime Louis	*Painter*	1767	1824
Fr.	Gougon, John ("The French Phidias")	*Sculptor*		1572
Ital.	Guercino (real name Francis Barbieri)	*Painter*	1590	1666
Ital.	Guido Reni (excelled in beauty of expression and grace)	*Painter*	1574	1642

NATION.	NAME AND PROFESSION.		BORN.	DIED.
Eng.	Harlow, George Henry	*Painter*	1787	1819
Eng.	Haydon, R. B.	*Historical Painter*	1786	1846
Eng.	Heath, Charles	*Engraver*		1849
Eng.	Hilton, William	*Historical Painter*	1786	1839
Flem.	Hobbema, Mynderhout	*Landscape Painter*	1611	1699
Eng.	Hogarth, William	*Painter*	1697	1764
Swiss.	Holbein, Hans	*Portrait & Historical Pa.*	1498	1554
Ger.	Hollar, Wenceslaus (executed 2400 plates)	*Engraver*	1607	1677
Flem.	Honthorst, Gerard (called Gherarda dal Notte)	*Painter*	1592	1660
Dutch.	Houbraken, Jacob (600 portraits)	*Engraver*	1698	1780
Fr.	Houdon (executed statue of Franklin)	*Sculptor*	1746	1828
Fr.	Houel, John (Picturesque Travels, &c.)	*Painter & Engraver*	1736	1813
Amer.	Inman, Henry	*Portrait & Landsc. Pa.*	1801	1846
Dutch.	Huysum, John Van (flowers and fruit)	*Painter*	1682	1749
Eng.	Jones, Inigo	*Architect*	1572	1652
Flem.	Jordaens, Jacob	*Painter*	1595	1670
Ital.	Julio, Romano	*Painter & Architect*	1492	1546
Swiss.	Kauffman, M. A. Angelica C. (in England)	*Poetical Painter*	1747	1807
Ger.	Kneller, Sir Godfrey (resided in England)	*Painter*	1648	1723
Eng.	Landseer, Edwin	*Animal & Historical Pa.*		
Dutch.	Lairesse, Gerard (excelled in expedition)	*Painter & Engraver*	1640	1711
Fr.	Landon, C. P. (more eminent as an author of works on the fine arts)	*Painter*		1826
Eng	Lawrence, sir Thomas	*Portrait & Hist. Painter*	1769	1830
Fr	Lebrun, Charles (painter to Louis XIV)	*Painter*	1619	1690
Ger.	Lely, sir Peter (painter to Charles II. of England)	*Painter*	1618	1680
Fr.	Le Sieur, Eustace (the French Raphael)	*Painter*	1617	1655
Fr	Leyden, Lucas, Dammesz	*Painter & Engraver*	1494	1533
Eng.	Liverseege, Henry	*Painter*	1803	1832
Gr.	Lysippus (made 600 statues)	*Sculptor*	f. B. C. 324	
Amer.	Malbone, Edward G.	*Miniature Painter*	1777	1807
Flem.	Matsys, Quintin	*Painter*	1460	1529
Ital.	Masaccio	*Painter*	1402	1427
Ger	Mayer	*Sculptor*		
Ital.	Mazzuolo, Francis (inventor of *etching*)	*Painter*	1503	1540
Ger.	Mengs, Anthony R. (the Raphael of Germany)	*Painter*	1729	1779
Fr.	Mignard, Peter	*Painter*	1610	1695
Swiss.	Mind, Gottfried	*Painter*	1768	1814
Eng.	Moreland, George	*Painter*	1764	1804
Span.	Murillo, Bartholomew S.	*Painter*	1613	1682
Eng.	Newton, Gilbert Stuart	*Historical Painter*	1785	1835
Eng.	Nollekins, Joseph	*Sculptor*	1737	1823
Eng.	Northcote, James	*Painter*	1746	1831
Eng.	Opie, John	*Painter*	1761	1807
Dutch.	Ostade, Adrian Van (interiors)	*Familiar Life Painter*	1610	1685
Dutch.	Ostade, Isaac (winter scenes)	*Painter*	1617	1671
Eng.	Owen, William	*Painter*	1769	1825
Fr.	Pajou, Augustin	*Sculptor*	1730	1809
Ital.	Palladio, Andrew	*Architect*	1518	1580
Span.	Palomino de Castro Y Velasco, A. A.	*Painter*	1653	1726
Gr.	Parrhasius, of Ephesus	*Painter*	f. B. C. 420	
Amer.	Peale, Charles W.	*Histor. & Portrait Pa.*	1741	1827
Fr.	Perrault, Claudius (designed the Front of the Louvre)	*Architect*	1613	1688
Ital.	Perugino, Peter (the master of Raphael)	*Painter*	1446	1524
Swiss.	Petitot, John (excelled in enamel)	*Painter*	1607	1691
Gr.	Phidias (the most famous of ancient sculptors)	*Sculptor*	B. C. 498	B. C. 431
Fr.	Picart, Bernard	*Engraver*	1663	1733
Fr.	Pigalle, John Baptiste	*Sculptor*	1714	1785
Fr.	Piles, Roger de (an author and painter)	*Painter*	1635	1709
Ital.	Piranesi, John Baptiste (16 vols. folio)	*Engraver*	1707	1778
Gr.	Polycletus (statue of Juno at Argos)	*Sculptor*	B. C. 430	
Ital.	Pordenone, Regillo da	*Painter*	1584	
Dutch.	Potter, Paul (unequalled in *animal* painting)	*Painter*	1625	1654
Fr.	Poussin, Nicholas (excelled in landsc. painting)	*Painter*	1594	1665
Ital.	Poussin, Gaspar (Dughet) landscape	*Painter*	1613	1675
Gr.	Praxiteles	*Sculptor*	f. B. C. 350	
Amer.	Pratt, Matthew	*Painter*	1734	1805
Fr.	Prudhon, of Cluny	*Painter*	1760	1823
Fr.	Puget, Peter	*Sculp. Pa. & Arch*	1622	1694
Gr.	Pythagoras	*Sculptor*		

NATION.	NAME AND PROFESSION.		BORN	DIED.
Ital.	Raphael (real name Sanzio) a pre-eminent	*Painter*	1483	1520
Ital.	Rembrandt, Paul	*Painter*	1606	1647
Eng.	Reynolds, sir Joshua	*Painter*	1723	1792
Fr.	Roland, Philip L. (Homer in the Louvre)	*Sculptor*	1746	1816
Eng.	Romney, George	*Painter*	1734	1804
Ital.	Rosa, Salvator (scenes of gloom)	*Painter*	1614	1673
Eng.	Rowlandson, Th. (caricature—Dr Syntax, &c.)	*Painter & Engraver*	1756	1827
Flem.	Rubens, Peter Paul, a celebrated	*Painter*	1577	1640
Scotch.	Runciman, Alexander	*Painter*	1736	1785
Dutch.	Ruysdael, Jacob	*Landscape Painter*	1636	1684
Dutch.	Ruysdael, Solomon	*Painter*	1616	1670
Eng.	Rysbrach, John Michael (works in Westminster Abbey)	*Sculptor*	1694	1770
Ital.	Sanmicheli, Michael	*Architect*	1484	1559
Ital.	Sarto, Andrea del—see *Vanucchi*			
Ital.	Scamozzi, Vincent	*Architect*	1550	1616
Ger.	Schadow Rudolf	*Sculptor*	1786	1822
Dutch.	Schalken, Godfrey (candlelight scenes)	*Painter*	1643	1706
Gr.	Scopas	*Sculptor*	B. C. 460	B. C. 353
Eng.	Sharp, William	*Engraver*	1740	1824
Eng.	Sherwin, John Keyse	*Engraver*		1790
Amer.	Smybert, John	*Painter*	1728	1751
Flem.	Snyders, Francis (landscape and animal)	*Painter*	1579	1657
Fr.	Soufflot, J. G. (church of St. Genevieve at Paris)	*Architect*	1714	1781
Dutch.	Spaendonck, Gerradvan (flower)	*Painter*	1746	1822
Scotch.	Strange, Robert	*Engraver*	1721	1722
Eng.	Strutt, Joseph (an author and painter)	*Painter*	1749	1802
Eng.	Stuart, James (author of the "Antiquities of Athens")	*Architect*	1713	1788
Amer.	Stuart, Gilbert (pupil of Benjamin West)	*Portrait Painter*	1756	1828
Flem.	Teniers, David, the elder (pupil of Rubens)	*Painter*	1582	1649
Flem.	Teniers, David, the younger (pupil of Rubens)	*Painter*	1610	1694
Dan.	Thorwaldsen	*Sculptor*	1772	1844
Gr.	Timanthes (contemporary with Parrhasius)	*Painter*	f. B. C. 420	
Ital.	Tintoretto (a Venetian—pupil of Titian)	*Painter*	1512	1594
Ital.	Titian (the greatest painter of Venetian school)	*Painter*	1480	1579
Amer.	Trumbull, John	*Historical Painter*	1756	184
Eng.	Vanbrugh, sir Jn. (Blenheim and Castle Howard)	*Architect*	1672	1726
Dutch.	Vandervelde, William (marine and battle)	*Painter*	1610	1693
Dutch.	Vandervelde, the younger	*Painter*	1633	1707
Dutch.	Vandervelde, Adrian	*Landscape Painter*	1639	1672
Dutch.	Vanderwerf, Adrian	*Historical Painter*	1654	1718
Flem.	Vandyke, sir Anthony (the greatest of portrait painters)	*Portrait Painter*	1598	1641
Ital.	Vannucchi, or Andrea del Sarto	*Painter*	1488	1530
Ital.	Van Vitelli, Louis, a Neapolitan	*Architect*	1700	1773
Ital.	Vasari, George (a biographer of artists)	*Architect & Painter*	1512	1574
Sic.	Vasi, Joseph, a designer and	*Engraver*	1710	1782
Span.	Velasquez, James R. de Sylvia Y	*Painter*	1599	1660
Fr.	Vernet, Joseph	*Painter*	1714	1789
Fr.	Vernet, Horace	*Historical Painter*		
Am.	Ver Bryck C.	*Landscape Painter*	1813	1844
Ital.	Verrochio, Andrew (inventor of the method of taking the features in a plaster mould)	*Sculptor*	1422	1488
Ital.	Veronese, Paul (see Cagliari)			
Eng.	Vertue, George (500 plates)	*Engraver*	1684	1756
Ital.	Vignola, James (Caprarola palace and St. Peter's)	*Architect*	1507	1573
Ital.	Vinci, Leonardo da	*Painter*	1452	1519
Gr.	Vitruvius (temp. Augustus)	*Architect*	f. B. C. 30	
Ital.	Volpato, John	*Engraver*	1733	1802
Fr.	Vouet, Simon, founder of Fr. sch. (temp. Chas. I.)	*Painter*	1582	1649
Fr.	Wailly, Charles de	*Architect*	1729	179
Eng.	Warren, Charles (perfecter of engraving on *steel*)	*Engraver*		1823
Amer.	West, Benjamin	*Painter*	1738	1820
Scotch	Wilkie, David	*Familiar Life Painter*	1785	1841
Eng.	Wilson, Richard	*Landscape Painter*	1713	1782
Eng.	Woodlet, William	*Engraver*	1735	1785
Dutch.	Wouvermans, Philip	*Painter*	1620	1668
Eng.	Wren, Sir Christopher (St. Paul's, &c.)	*Architect*	1632	1723
Eng.	Wyatt, James (Panthaon, Kew Palace, &c.)	*Architect*	1743	1813
Ital.	Zablia, Nicholas	*Architect*	1674	1750
Gr.	Zeuxis, a celebrated ancient	*Painter*	B. C. 490	B. C. 400
Ger.	Zincke	*Enamel Portrait Pa.*	1684	1767
Ital.	Zuccaro, or Zucehero, Taddeo	*Painter*	1529	1566
Ital.	Zuccaro, or Zucchèro, Frederigo	*Painter*	1539	1619
Ital.	Zuccarelli	*Painter*	1710	[illegible]

www.ingramcontent.com/pod-product-compliance
Lightning Source LLC
LaVergne TN
LVHW020923110826
845150LV00004B/752

* 9 7 8 1 4 2 5 5 5 4 0 2 6 *